RACE IN THE CRUCIBLE OF WAR

A VOLUME IN THE SERIES
Culture and Politics in the Cold War and Beyond
EDITED BY
Edwin A. Martini and Scott Laderman

RACE IN THE CRUCIBLE OF WAR

African American Servicemen
and the War in Vietnam

GERALD F. GOODWIN

University of Massachusetts Press
Amherst and Boston

Copyright © 2023 by University of Massachusetts Press
All rights reserved
Printed in the United States of America

ISBN 978-1-62534-683-4 (paper); 684-1 (hardcover)

Designed by Sally Nichols
Set in Minion Pro
Printed and bound by Books International, Inc.

Cover design by Frank Gutbrod
Cover photo by unknown photographer, *African American Veterans*, c. 1967, Vietnam. Courtesy African American Registry.

Library of Congress Cataloging-in-Publication Data
Names: Goodwin, Gerald F., author.
Title: Race in the crucible of war : African American servicemen and the war in Vietnam / Gerald F. Goodwin.
Other titles: African American servicemen and the war in Vietnam
Description: Amherst : University of Massachusetts Press, [2023] | Series: Culture and politics in the Cold War and beyond | Includes bibliographical references and index.
Identifiers: LCCN 2022022441 (print) | LCCN 2022022442 (ebook) | ISBN 9781625346834 (paper) | ISBN 9781625346841 (hardcover) | ISBN 9781613769638 (ebook) | ISBN 9781613769645 (ebook)
Subjects: LCSH: Vietnam War, 1961–1975—Participation, African American. | United States—Armed Forces—African Americans. | African Americans—Civil rights—History—20th century. | Race discrimination—United States—History—20th century. | United States—Race relations—History—20th century.
Classification: LCC DDS559.8.B55 G66 2023 (print) | LCC DDS559.8.B55 (ebook) | DDC 959.704/337308996073—dc23/eng/20220726
LC record available at https://lccn.loc.gov/2022022441
LC ebook record available at https://lccn.loc.gov/2022022442

British Library Cataloguing-in-Publication Data
A catalog record for this book is available from the British Library.

Parts of chapters 1, 2, and 3 were previously published in "Black and White in Vietnam," *New York Times*, July 18, 2017. An earlier version of chapter 5 appeared as "'You and me-same same' and 'They called me "monkey"': Conflicting African American Views of Vietnamese Civilians," *World History Connected* (June 2017), https://worldhistoryconnected.press.uillinois.edu/14.2/goodwin.html (July 20, 2022), used with permission.

"Only you saw what took many time to see, I dedicate this to you for believing me."
—CL Smooth and Pete Rock

Mom, Dad, Maria, and Gabrijela

Contents

Acknowledgments ix

Author's Note xiii

Introduction
1

CHAPTER 1
"We Was Just Us"
De-Racialization on the Front Lines
of the Vietnam War
11

CHAPTER 2
**"Brothers as Many Brothers
as They Can Find"**
Prejudice, Discrimination, and
Death in Vietnam
44

CHAPTER 3
"Tearing the Services Apart"
Racial Violence and the
Other War in Vietnam
81

CHAPTER 4
"I Thought of My Own People Back Home"
African American Servicemen and Vietnamese Civilians

124

CHAPTER 5
"'You and Me—Same Same" and "They Called Me 'Monkey'"
Conflicting African American Views of Vietnamese Civilians

152

CHAPTER 6
"We Won't Shoot You, but We'll Shoot the White Guy"
African American Views of Vietnamese Communist Forces

174

CHAPTER 7
"I Had Left One War and Come Back to Another"
African Americans Return Home

202

Conclusion
222

Notes 229

Index 269

Acknowledgments

While researching, writing, and revising my book I have received significant advice and support from many people. Let me begin by thanking the staff at the University of Massachusetts Press especially Matt Becker, Brian Halley, Sally Nichols, and Rachael DeShano. Matt is owed a particular debt of thanks for his continued support from my initial proposal to publication. Rachael was also a great source of encouragement and patience during the editing process. I would also like to thank Margaret Hogan for serving as copy editor. Additional thanks are owed to the reviewers of my original manuscript, Robert F. Jefferson, Geoffrey W. Jensen, and the anonymous reviewer. Without question their comments helped me improve the final product.

My interest in the experiences of African American servicemen during the Vietnam War began when I was an MA student at the University of Kentucky and continued when I was a PhD student at Ohio University. Many professors have helped me along the way. Thank you to Professors Chester Pach, Ron Eller, Joanne Pope Melish, Ingo Trauschweizer, Katherine Jellison, Patrick Barr-Melej, William Frederick, David Olster, Lien-Hang Nguyen, and Robin Muhammad.

I would like to extend my heartfelt appreciation and thanks to every veteran and nonveteran who shared their experiences with me. I could not have written this book without their participation. Thank you Melvin Adams, David Addlestone, David B. Almond, Arthur C. Barham, Theodore Belcher, Walt Boomer, Ron Bradley, Thomas Brannon, Lorenzo Clark, Ben Cloud, Ron Copes, Bruce Crawford, Howard J. De Nike, Lewis Downey, Constance Edwards, Freddie Edwards, Kent Garrett, Wes Geary, Eddie Greene, Mike Hagee, George Hicks, Jim Houston, Clyde Jackson, Richard Jacobs, Reuben "Sugar Bear" Johnson, Billy Jones, Jack Keane, James Lewis,

Frank Libutti, Robert Louis Jr., Karl Marlantes, Anthony Martin, Bernard McClusky, Patrick McLaughlin, Nate Mondy, Ron Osgood, Susan Osnos, Lawrence Parsons, Louis Perkins, Cephus "Dusty" Rhodes, Stanley Ricketts, Scott Riley, Thomas Rogan, Brian Settles, Jake Shaky, Lap Siu, Gary Skogen, Bob Steck, Lamont B. Steptoe, Sinclair Swan, Willie J. Thomas Jr., Lawrence Van Kuran, Robert Vonner, Jack Whitted, and Anthony Zinni.

I would like to take special notice of a few veterans who went above and beyond in their support. In 2008 I met James Gillam at a conference in Texas. He was the first Black Vietnam veteran I ever interviewed, and his interest and support over the years helped convince me that my research was on the right track. I met Ron Armstead at this same conference, and he has been supportive of my work ever since. He is owed particular thanks for suggesting I contact UMass Press. Wayne Smith is owed a debt of gratitude for not only passing my name on to other veterans but also for always being there with a friendly and supportive word. I am also incredibly appreciative of George Brummel and his wife, Maria, for their longtime support and friendship. When I met George in 2011, he not only welcomed me into his home but he began calling every veteran he knew to arrange interviews with me. His interest in my research sometimes made me wonder if he was under the impression that he was receiving a finder's fee for each referral. Thank you, George. Horace Coleman and Wes Geary were both very supportive of my research. Horace frequently mailed and emailed any information he thought would be of interest. Wes routinely contacted other veterans encouraging them to speak with me about their experiences. Unfortunately, both men passed away before my book was published. Rest in peace.

I would also like to thank the following veteran's organizations: Vietnam Veterans Against the War, Vietnam Veterans of America, Blind Veterans Association, Veterans for Peace, the National Association for Black Veterans, National Women Veterans United, and the National Association of Buffalo Soldiers and Troopers Motorcycle Club.

Additional thanks are owed to others who have supported my work, including Sylvester Bracey Jr. and family, Marc Jason Gilbert, Lee Hancock, Sarah Kramer, Marc Leepson, Mel McMurty, Lynn Novick, Jenna Ridgeway Corliss, Hasha Riley, Libra Riley, Clay Risen, Nina Tamrowski, and Janice Terry, the widow of Wallace Terry.

I have been blessed with a wonderful group of friends and family, who have been there for me in a myriad of different ways. Thank you Alice Angelique, Mark Baldwin, Alice Baraka, Amina Byishimo, Elisa Byishimo, Sara Charest, Mahoro Cloudine, Jordana Cox, Zachary Cox, Rafi Hasan III, Sebastian Hurtado-Torres, Samuel Irankunda, Thomas

ACKNOWLEDGMENTS xi

Jolicoeur, Dr. Rebekah Kaufman and the medical staff at St. Joseph's Hospital (Labor-Delivery and Mother-Baby Units, Primary Care West), Jeff Keith, Gabrielle Lazarovitz, Pollyanna Ling, Patrick Lumumba, Sylvia Maombi, Christina Matzen, Patrick McGuire, Nancy McKean, Carly Muetterties, Huong Diu Nguyen, Baraka Nyiramugisha, Heather Petsche, Kerry Rennie, Sabrina Sahle, Angel Sandrine, Dave Sarizin, Annet Sifa, Ed Sloane, Rose Tantine, Richard Twardowski, Solange Uwineza, Joe Venosa, Francesca Williamson, Steven Williamson, and Justine Zawadi. Each of you has helped in your own way, and I am forever appreciative. Patrick M. and Thomas are owed particular thanks. They are not only great friends but Patrick served as my research assistant on a trip to Pennsylvania and Washington, DC, and Thomas helped with transcriptions.

I would like to thank the Goodwin, Johnson, Zoretic, and Jadi families, especially my siblings, Gillian, Graham, and Gibson; mother-in-law, Zlata; and father-in-law, Ivan. My grandfathers, George F. Goodwin and Francis Meridith Johnson, served in World War II, and their military service served as an inspiration.

Three people have gone above and beyond in their support of my dissertation: my mother, Adrienne Johnson Goodwin; my father, Fred Goodwin; and my wife, Maria Zoretic-Goodwin. I could write another book detailing the level of love and support each of you has given me over the years. My parents have been a constant source of love and encouragement throughout my life. I never needed to look for heroes in movies, music, or sports, as my heroes ate at the dinner table with me every night. My father deserves special recognition for all his help with the editing process (sorry for the late nights).

My wife, Maria, has served as a source of encouragement and inspiration throughout the writing process. I could not ask for a better partner or a more supportive best friend. The last two and a half years have required courage since a global pandemic separated us from our friends and family, but with her by my side I knew I was never alone. As luck would have it, while my book progressed through the various stages of editing, we learned we would not be alone for long. Even while she was pregnant and working full-time at a stressful job in uncertain times, Maria made sure that I had the time to write and edit. Even when our daughter Gabrijela was born a week and half before the final editing was due, Maria, with some emergency babysitting support from my parents, ensured that I was able to finish my book. Thank you, Maria, and thanks to Gabrijela for being a (somewhat) agreeable late-night assistant.

Author's Note

Please note that racial slurs are used within this book when directly quoting interviewees or other source material. While it is now unusual to see this sort of offensive language in formal writing, where it is generally considered inappropriate, and its presence may understandably be upsetting to some readers, I believe it is important to retain this language in the quotations here to accurately reflect what people said, especially given the subject matter of the book.

RACE IN THE CRUCIBLE OF WAR

INTRODUCTION

On March 30, 1970, *Black Journal*, a public affairs show on National Education Television, broadcast an hour-long examination of the experiences of African Americans in the Vietnam War. Filmed on location in various regions of Vietnam, as well as Okinawa, which was under the authority of the U.S. Military, the episode featured interviews with a cross-section of Black servicemen—low-ranking draftees; enlisted men; officers; Brigadier General Frederick E. Davison, the first Black combat general in the history of the U.S. Army; as well as L. Howard Bennett, deputy assistant secretary for civil rights. William Greaves, host, producer, and director of *Black Journal*, argued this focus was necessary because of "the distorted picture usually seen in the press and on our home television screens." He argued that the media often provided an overly optimistic, as well as simplistic, account of the Black experience in Vietnam, cautioning, "When we look at television and newspapers, we are led to believe that only an occasional Black man serves in the military and then in perfect harmony with the white GI."[1] The reality was much different.

Black participation in the military was not new, but Vietnam was the first major conflict in which the armed forces were fully racially integrated. Executive Order 9981 officially desegregated the armed forces in 1948, but many units remained segregated until late 1954.[2]

African American participation in Vietnam was also not new when the crew of *Black Journal* arrived in late 1969. When the first two American marine battalions waded ashore at Red Beach Two in Da Nang on March 8, 1965, African Americans were among them.[3] Raymond Leon Horn was a Black corporal from Chicago, who had been drafted the previous year and was among the marines stationed in Quan Nam province. His time in Vietnam was short as he was killed by an explosive device on May 1, making him the first African American to die in Vietnam.[4] He would not be the last.

As the military commitment increased, so too did the involvement of African Americans. Their contributions were considerable. Of the roughly 2.5 million Americans who served, 300,000 were African American, approximately 12 percent. African Americans represented 12.6 percent of the 58,022 Americans who died in the war.[5] Both percentages were slightly higher than their percentage of the civilian population, which was between 10.5 and 11.1 percent at the time.[6]

When correspondent Kent Garrett and *Black Journal* traveled to Vietnam and Okinawa, they were concerned with more than the contributions and sacrifices of African Americans. Garrett's interviews sought to investigate and bring attention to race relations and discrimination in the military. The focus was understandable given that the start of the Vietnam War coincided with successes in the civil rights movement such as the Civil Rights Act of 1964 and the Voting Rights Act of 1965.

However, racial tension, continued discrimination, and even violence also characterized domestic race relations between 1965 and 1970. Post-1965, southern whites continued to resist integration. Rioting in Chicago, Detroit, Newark, and dozens of other American cities in the aftermath of Martin Luther King Jr.'s assassination in April 1968 made it difficult to argue that racial equality had been achieved or racial relations were improving.

Black Journal knew well the realities of race relations. The show was created as a response to the Kerner Commission's conclusion that the lack of Black perspectives in the media had contributed to the 1967 Detroit and Newark Riots.[7] Fully funded by the federal government and premiering in June 1968, *Black Journal* was created to help prevent future rioting.[8] Ironically, the first show was broadcast only a few months after the rioting in dozens of American cities following King's assassination.

King's assassination also impacted race relations in the American military in Vietnam. By the time of *Black Journal*'s report in 1970, race tensions, discrimination, and violence were widespread. African Americans were clearly not living in "perfect harmony with the white GI."

Black Journal understood that relations were poor, discrimination was common, and similarities existed between the Black experience with racism in the United States and in Vietnam. Historically, many African Americans viewed military service as an escape from the racism inherent in American civilian life, but *Black Journal* found little difference between levels of discrimination in the United States and in the military. Greaves noted, "Blacks in the service recognize familiar patterns of discrimination common to civilian life."[9]

Garrett similarly observed, "Carrying a rifle in the infantry is just like pushing a broom in civilian life. The Black man doesn't escape it in the infantry for the same reasons he doesn't escape it on the outside—inferior education and opportunities in a racist society." This experience led Black servicemen to question "whether the real war is in Vietnam or America. In Saigon or Harlem."[10]

As *Black Journal*'s reporting suggests, Black experiences with race and issues related to race in Vietnam were inextricably linked to their experiences with these same issues back home. *Race in the Crucible of War* argues that African Americans experienced and interpreted racial issues—race relations, prejudice, and discrimination—in Vietnam through a lens heavily influenced by their personal experiences with these same issues in the United States, as well as the larger historical experiences of African Americans. Current and historical American racism and race relations loomed large in Vietnam. Fighting a war in a faraway country did not allow African Americans to escape the longstanding racial environment they grew up in nor did it enable them to forget their personal encounters with racism back home. These experiences continued to influence them. War is often viewed as a crucible, but American racism, race relations, and racial perspectives proved remarkably resilient and durable despite the potentially corrosive effects of war.

As the first conflict in which Blacks and whites served in desegregated units from the beginning, race relations were a significant aspect of the Black experience. It was difficult to predict what relations would be given the armed forces' limited experience dealing with race relations, especially during wartime. This "new" environment provided an opportunity for a changed experience for African Americans serving their country in war.

This integrated environment provides us with an opportunity to ask new questions: Would Black and white servicemen view and treat one another as equals? Would Black servicemen encounter the same levels of racial prejudice and discrimination faced by African Americans back home? Would Black experiences change over the course of the war? How would events back home influence relations between Black and white servicemen? Would racial tensions rise and fall?

As we will see, there was little stability or consistency regarding race relations in Vietnam. Race relations could be typified by friendship and cooperation in one time period, warzone, or unit, while discrimination, tension, and even violence were the norm in the next. Sometimes these realities overlapped. Even when African Americans appeared to be living in "perfect harmony with the white GI," this was only part of the story. Vietnam provided no escape from the racism and discrimination commonplace back home. African Americans routinely and justifiably complained of racial discrimination including allegations that they were disproportionately assigned menial duties, not promoted to the ranks they deserved, and unfairly targeted for punishment.

The impact of racial discrimination in Vietnam was eerily familiar. Greaves noted that "Blacks above the grade of junior officer are just as rare as Black civilians with positions of power." A Black serviceman interviewed by *Black Journal* argued that military service was a dead end for African Americans looking for meaningful career advancement. He noted, "I was in Viet Nam for 26 months. I was still a fucking private after 26 months and I am still a fucking private now."[11]

African Americans found themselves targeted in other ways as well, especially in the first few years of the conflict. Garrett commented, "The Black man in the army is more likely than his white counterpart to be sent to Vietnam in the first place. Once there more likely to wind up in the frontline combat units, and thus, within the combat unit is more likely than the white to be killed or wounded."[12] There was considerable merit to his analysis.

Black servicemen could not escape the knowledge of escalating tensions back home. In the first years of increased military intervention, racial violence was generally confined to the southern states, where white racists attacked Black demonstrators and their supporters. However, race-related riots in Watts (in Los Angeles) in 1965, Detroit and Newark in 1967, and particularly in numerous American cities after Martin Luther King Jr.'s assassination in 1968 revealed racial disharmony on the home front.

To paraphrase Malcolm X, the "chickens came home to roost in Vietnam." American racial discord traveled readily to Vietnam, and incidents of racial tension and violence were commonplace in the years following King's assassination. Relations deteriorated to such an extent that *Time* journalist Wallace Terry reported in September 1969 that there was "another war being fought in Vietnam—between Black and white Americans."[13]

Black Journal arrived in Vietnam in late 1969, and nearly every African American they interviewed acknowledged that incidents of racial conflict were widespread and routine. These men directly linked increased tensions and incidents of violence to the unwillingness of Black servicemen to accept racial discrimination. Asked for his perspective, a Black naval patrolman named Hayes responded, "The common Black man. He has been pushed, pushed, pushed, and pushed all his life. He reached the point now where he wants to push back, you know. I am not going to go out there and be no Tom or anything to nobody and I feel like you pushed me too far, I am going to definitely strike back at you."[14]

The "other war" in Vietnam damaged the cohesion and morale of the American fighting forces, as well as distracted them from their stated purpose—the defense of the Republic of Vietnam (RVN) and its citizens from the forces of the National Liberation Front (NLF) and the People's Army of Vietnam (PAVN), which sought to overthrow the government. The American military effort undoubtedly suffered as a result.

Race relations were complicated by the presence of the Vietnamese. African Americans encountered many different groups in Vietnam: civilians, members of the RVN armed forces, and supporters or even members of the NLF or PAVN. These interactions were an important element of African Americans' experiences during the war.

Black interactions with and impressions of the civilian population were complex. Their perceptions reflected and raised questions about race, identity, discrimination, and the solidarity of oppressed groups. How did African Americans view the civilians they were tasked with protecting? How did African Americans believe the Vietnamese viewed them? How did the racial views African Americans brought with them impact these perceptions? How did racial developments in the United States influence their views?

American servicemen's perceptions of civilians were influenced by the difficulty they had in identifying Vietnamese affiliations or loyalties. African American poet and Vietnam veteran Lamont B. Steptoe identified this problem in his poem "Uncle's South Sea China Blue Nightmare." Steptoe writes,

> In country
> Vietnamese shine boots wash laundry
> make love to you
> some even try to end your
> life with a bang.[15]

As his poem suggests, the average American serviceman—Black or white—had varied and contrasting images of Vietnamese civilians. They could be a servant, a sexual partner, a co-combatant, or a killer.

Even Black servicemen whose interactions with civilians were limited often developed strong impressions of the local population. Knowing very little about Vietnam or its people, African Americans interpreted what they observed from a perspective shaped almost entirely by their own experiences back home. They saw a parallel between the poverty and discrimination experienced by African Americans and the poverty and mistreatment experienced by Vietnamese civilians. African American soldier Thomas Brannon quickly recognized that Vietnamese people were "struggling like hell," which he could understand as being mistreated was "part of our history." He further elaborated, "A lot of us who are Black Americans, if not having lived it ourselves, can tell you about the times in our collective history where our families have struggled with the boot on the neck."[16]

African Americans believed that Vietnamese civilians empathized in turn with them as victims of racial discrimination. This perception suggested that the Vietnamese were not only aware of American racism and racial politics more generally but also that this knowledge led them to empathize with African Americans. Yet Black-Vietnamese relations were complicated by the behavior and actions of racist whites who brought racist views to Vietnam and broadcast them. *Black Journal* interviewed Bobby Jenkins, a Black sailor who described meeting a seven- or eight-year-old Vietnamese shoeshine girl who told him, "the Black man is ugly, he a monkey, got a tail." Certain of where the young girl had gotten these opinions, Jenkins recalled, "she never knew what Black was before, before the white man come on. He bring us way over here to teach people something like that." Jenkins concluded that Vietnam was "just like the world in Georgia, Alabama, wherever you are, even in the north."[17]

Civilians were not the only Vietnamese African Americans encountered. Like all servicemen, African Americans were tasked with fighting NLF and PAVN forces. What did African Americans think about these groups? What did African Americans think communist forces thought about them and their participation in the war? What role did race play in forming these perceptions? How did developments back home sway these impressions?

While the circumstances of these two interactions were quite different, African Americans nonetheless developed strong opinions of Vietnamese communist forces. Their views were not entirely dissimilar to their impressions of the civilian population. This sympathetic depiction might seem surprising. However, Black views were influenced by communist propaganda circulated in leaflets and radio broadcasts that expressed sympathy for African Americans and support for the civil rights movement. This propaganda also linked the Black experience in Vietnam to the Black experience with discrimination in the United States. African Americans were not the only ones for whom the American racial situation loomed large.

Despite the significance of the Black experience in the Vietnam War, and the central role played by race and racism on that experience, there is relatively little written about the topic. The limited historiography includes two books by historian James E. Westheider: *Fighting on Two Fronts: African Americans and the Vietnam War* (1997) and *The African American Experience in Vietnam: Brothers in Arms* (2007).[18] Herman Graham III's *The Brothers' Vietnam War: Black Power, Manhood, and the Military Experience* (2003) is another useful source. While these books expand our understanding, they are fairly limited in their scope. Westheider focuses on how the war and experiences of Black servicemen changed African Americans' image of military service as a means of advancement. Graham's book is a gendered analysis of how the armed services used images of masculinity to attract African Americans to military service.[19]

Other works touch on issues related to the Black experience. Lawrence Allen Eldridge's *Chronicles of a Two-Front War* is first and foremost an examination of ways in which the Black press covered the war.[20] Jeremey Maxwell's *Brotherhood in Combat: How African Americans Found Equality in Korea and Vietnam* tries to compare the Black experience during the Korean and Vietnam Wars.[21] Kyle Longley's *Grunts: The American Combat Soldier in Vietnam* provides a limited discussion of Black-white relations and Black complaints of discrimination.[22] Christian G. Appy's *Working Class War* briefly considers Black servicemen and racial issues in general. Richard Moser's *The New Winter Soldiers* and David Cortright's *Soldiers in Revolt* discuss the experiences of African American servicemen who opposed the war while also investigating incidents of social unrest and complaints of racial discrimination.[23]

Isaac Hampton II's *The Black Officer Corps* examines the experiences of Black officers in Vietnam.[24] George Lepre's *Fragging: Why U.S. Soldiers Assaulted Their Officers in Vietnam* is a useful discussion of attacks on officers by enlisted men. Lepre analyzes incidents that appear to be connected to racial issues.[25] Kimberly L. Phillips's *War! What Is It Good For?* provides an interesting window into the rise of Black protest within the military during the period.[26] Gary D. Solis's *Marines and Military Law in Vietnam* and William Thomas Allison's *Military Justice in Vietnam* provide limited discussions of incidents of racial violence.[27]

Collectively, these sources describe aspects of the Black experience in Vietnam. However, they do not analyze fully how that experience was influenced by race and racism. They also do not examine sufficiently the relationship between domestic racial developments and racial relations in the military. Some of these works recognize the existence of racial tensions and violence during the conflict, but they understate the prevalence and significance of such issues. They also underplay the level of discrimination African Americans faced. They provide no significant discussion of African Americans' perceptions of and interactions with Vietnamese civilians and combatants.

One must be cautious generalizing about the Black experience given the large number of African Americans who served and the diversity of experiences they could and did have. The use of limited sources could result in a biased or inaccurate account. To reduce the possibility of bias or inaccuracy, I have used a wide variety of sources, many of them previously unexamined by historians.

African American Vietnam veterans have published numerous memoirs.[28] There are also published collections of oral histories that include the testimonies of African Americans. The most valuable is African American journalist Wallace Terry's *Bloods: An Oral History of the Vietnam War by Black Veterans* (1984). A journalist for *Time* magazine, Terry spent years interviewing servicemen in Vietnam, and *Bloods* includes twenty interviews with Black veterans about their wartime experiences.[29] Eddie Wright's *Thoughts about the Vietnam War: Based on My Personal Experiences, Books I Have Read and Conversations with Other Veterans*, which includes interviews with six Black veterans, as well as the author's own remembrances as a Black veteran, provides some useful insights.[30]

I have also used less traditional sources such as documentaries and poetry. *Same Mud, Same Blood* (1967), *No Vietnamese Ever Called Me Nigger* (1968), "The Black G.I." (1970), and "The Bloods of 'Nam" (1986) are documentaries that provide valuable information concerning the experiences of Black servicemen in Vietnam.[31] I have likewise employed poems written by veterans including Lamont B. Steptoe's *Mad Minute* (1993), *Dusty Road* (1995), and *Uncle's South China Sea Blue Nightmare* (1995), and Horace Coleman's *In the Grass* (1995).[32]

I have utilized articles published in contemporary newspapers and magazines including the *Baltimore Sun, Boston Globe, Chicago Daily Defender,*

Chicago Tribune, Christian Science Monitor, Cleveland Call and Post, Ebony, Hartford Courant, Jet, Los Angeles Sentinel, Los Angeles Times, Newsday (New York), *New York Amsterdam News, New York Times, Norfolk [VA] Journal and Guide, Philadelphia Tribune, Pittsburgh Courier, Globe and Mail* (Toronto), and the *Washington Post*. These articles, which number in the hundreds, provide valuable information about a host of issues relevant to the Black experience. Many of these articles directly quote African Americans serving in Vietnam, which provides a vivid and immediate expression of how individuals felt about numerous issues of importance. Articles written by such African American journalists as Wallace Terry, Ethel L. Payne of the *Chicago Daily Defender*, Thomas A. Johnson of the *New York Times*, and Donald Mosby of the *Chicago Daily Defender* are especially valuable as these journalists spent significant time interviewing Black servicemen about their experiences.

In addition to information found in memoirs, films, and contemporary news sources, I have conducted extensive archival research. I have used materials found at the U.S. Army Heritage and Education Center (USAHEC) at Carlisle Barracks, Pennsylvania, and particularly the Deputy Chief of Staff for Personnel (DCSPER) Policy Files on Discrimination in the Army collection. Included in this collection are official military reports of racial tension and violence on American military bases in the United States, Europe, Asia, and of course Vietnam. Of particular interest are hundreds of military criminal incident reports, which contain information on racially motived crimes including assault and murder.

I have also relied heavily on research conducted at the National Archives at College Park, Maryland (NACP). The U.S. Forces in Southeast Asia, 1950–75, collection (USFSEA) includes hundreds of reports about incidents of racial violence. These reports, most of which concern incidents occurring between 1969 and 1971, depict racial friction and even violence as commonplace in the cities of Vietnam and on military bases.

Collectively these materials provide a more complete picture of race relations in the military during the Vietnam War. These sources reveal that incidents of tension and even violence were far more common and pronounced than previously thought. They provide convincing evidence that African American complaints of discrimination were widespread throughout the conflict. Lastly, they reveal that the armed forces were aware of tensions in the military and of Black complaints of racial discrimination.

To augment the information garnered from memoirs, news sources, archives, and other media, I have interviewed dozens of Black veterans who served at various times and in different zones of the war. I have also interviewed white veterans, lawyers, and a Black army psychiatrist. These interviews have provided me with the opportunity to compare and even verify information found in other sources as well as to ask more detailed questions about issues addressed and not addressed in other sources. These interviews were particularly helpful in gaining additional knowledge about the complexities of race relations in Vietnam, especially regarding African American interactions with and perceptions of the Vietnamese, a topic all but ignored by previous historical works. I am the only historian to have conducted detailed interviews with such a large cross-section of African American Vietnam veterans. My book will, I hope, properly place Black voices in the forefront of the discussion.

Collectively, these sources provide great insight into the experiences of African American service members in the Vietnam War. Race—race relations, prejudice, and discrimination—was central, as was the strong link between race and racism in the United States and the wartime experience of African Americans. African Americans understandably interpreted what they experienced in Vietnam from the vantage point of their own racial histories and personal experiences. They left the United States temporarily, but they could not leave its racial heritage behind.

CHAPTER 1

"WE WAS JUST US"

De-Racialization on the Front Lines
of the Vietnam War

In 1967 NBC journalist Frank McGee spent nearly a month living with soldiers of the 101st Airborne Division as they fought Viet Cong forces for control of the region west of Phu Lai. On the surface, McGee's assignment, which resulted in the NBC documentary *Same Mud, Same Blood*, was not unique. Hundreds of journalists were in Vietnam, and McGee was hardly the first to try to cover the conflict from the perspective of servicemen. However, McGee's approach was distinct because he was not particularly interested in portraying combat, war strategy, or really the war effort at all. *Same Mud, Same Blood* shows little actual fighting. Instead, McGee focused his attention on race relations among the forty Black and white soldiers who served under Platoon Sergeant Lewis B. Larry, an African American from Mississippi.[1]

McGee's interest in the Black experience in Vietnam and his focus on race relations reflected several changes in both military and civilian life. For one thing, the Vietnam War was the first conflict in which the armed forces were fully integrated.[2] Given these circumstances, McGee asked, "Our history books have taken little notice of the Negro soldier. How do the troops of this war, Black and white, want its history written?"[3]

McGee's time in Vietnam occurred just a few years after the passage of the Civil Rights Act of 1964 and the Voting Rights Act of 1965. McGee correctly recognized that the Vietnam War, the dominant foreign policy issue of the 1960s, was interlocked in many respects with civil rights, the most important domestic issue of the era. Civil rights laws contributed to a growing political and social equality for African Americans, but full equality and significant racial integration remained elusive on the home front as whites, particularly in the South, continued to resist efforts to achieve these goals. Additionally, urban rioting in Detroit and Newark had led many to question to what extent race relations had really improved.

Paradoxically, considerable achievements in the efforts to achieve political and educational equality existed contemporaneously with racial segregation, increased tension, and even violence. The deterioration of domestic race relations provided the background for *Same Mud, Same Blood*. McGee noted more than once that racial tensions, including riots, were common back in the United States.[4]

In the jungles of Vietnam McGee found a much different situation. He saw no evidence of racial tension among the men of the 101st Airborne. They shared food and drink, told stories and jokes, and empathized with each other without regard to racial background. When asked about race relations, Sergeant Larry stated firmly, "There's no racial barrier of any sort here," an assessment echoed by the men in his command. Wilkenson, a Black lieutenant, agreed, asserting that Blacks and whites were viewed as human beings and not as people of different races. Asked about the significance of racial difference, Anthony Mavroudis, a white captain, replied, "That feeling doesn't exist in the Army, we're all soldiers. And the only color we know is the khaki and the green. The color of the mud and the color of the blood is all the same."[5]

McGee noted that "for this report the fact that Larry is a Negro is of paramount importance; to the officers and men he serves with it's a matter of total irrelevance." Race was simply not something of great significance for the men serving under Larry. As McGee spent more time with them, he noticed that he too began looking at individual soldiers without noticing their color.[6]

Collectively, these experiences led McGee to reach strong conclusions. He noted, "Nowhere in America have I seen Negroes and whites as free, open and uninhibited with their associations. I saw no eyes clouded with resentment." He further concluded, "What the Army has achieved is what America, despite bigots Negro and white, hopes someday to achieve, the elimination of race as a factor in human existence."[7]

While *Same Mud, Same Blood* does not reveal the full story of the African American experience in Vietnam or of race relations during the war, it accurately depicts the nature and level of cooperation and friendship shared by many Black and white servicemen in combat. They experienced a level of racial harmony largely unknown in other sectors of American life.

Many African Americans agreed with McGee's assessment of racial relations in combat. Speaking of his military service, Robert Sanders concluded that "the only thing that was good about Vietnam" was the "unity and harmony" witnessed and experienced by Blacks and whites in combat units.[8] This lack of antagonism was more than simple toleration; rather, prejudices broke down and strong bonds of camaraderie formed.[9] An anonymous Black marine stationed outside of Da Nang accurately described the shared Black-white experience: "Racial segregation is for the birds. When you're in combat, you're equal in everything. You live together. You sleep together. You eat the same things. You fight the same way. You stink the same way."[10]

The testimonies of African Americans also reveal that socially constructed and enforced ideas of race and notions of proper behaviors between Blacks and whites had begun to break down. Many came to view the front lines as a de-racialized space. In the words of an unnamed African American sailor in Saigon, "The question of race is always there for the Negro. He would either be blind or insane if it were not. But Vietnam is a buffer or isolation ward to the whole question of race as we know it."[11] As this sailor suggested, existing conceptions of "race" were not nearly as controlling in Vietnam as they were at home. McGee reached a similar conclusion, finding that race was so unimportant "that the men I was with, had difficulty reorganizing their thoughts to match mine and answer questions on a subject [race] they've stopped thinking of."[12]

"No Such Thing as Black, White, or Brown"

In June 1966 *Jet* magazine reported that Black and white servicemen shared the same tents, socialized, and worked together free of racial animus or incident. They concluded that in Vietnam "an American is an American and no one stops to judge color."[13] In April 1967 journalist Leon Daniel, who had long covered the American civil rights movement, provided a similar account of race relations. He noted that in Vietnam the hostility that often typified race relations in the United States was all but absent. Blacks and whites were dependent on one another, sharing the same "risks as well as their canteens." He concluded, "Deep in the jungles, where bullets are color blind and living seems more important than pigmentation, racial tensions ease."[14]

A May 26, 1967, *Time* article, "Armed Forces: Democracy in the Foxhole," compared race relations in the 173rd Airborne Division to those in the United States, concluding that "black-white relations in a slit trench or a combat-bound Huey are years ahead of Denver and Darien, decades ahead of Birmingham and Biloxi."[15] A few months later the *Christian Science Monitor* declared, "To a marked extent, race is forgotten on the battlefield."[16] In the spring of 1968 Donald Mosby traveled to Vietnam where he found that "the men in the line companies who are fighting and dying in the war have pushed through the barriers of race and ethnic prejudice."[17] Mosby maintained race had become a nonissue for Blacks and whites.

Thomas A. Johnson spent fourteen weeks in the spring of 1968 interviewing Blacks and whites in Vietnam about race relations. He concluded that "Vietnam is like a speed-up film of recent racial progress at home." Analyzing the Black perspective, Johnson asserted, "Negroes in Vietnam say that the closest to real integration that America has produced exists here."[18] In May 1968 the *New Pittsburgh Courier* similarly contrasted the racial situation in Vietnam with the United States proclaiming, "The Negro in Vietnam has achieved the most genuine integration and fullest participation in policies that America has yet granted."[19]

In August 1968 *Ebony* dedicated an entire issue to discussing the experiences of African Americans. Thomas A. Johnson maintained that "racial differences between Blacks and whites have disappeared on the fighting fronts." He reported that African Americans much preferred the racial situation in Vietnam to that of the United States. A Black officer told Johnson that "the brother does all right here. . . . You see it's just about the first time in his life that he finds he can really compete with whites on an equal—or very close to equal basis." This officer claimed that many Blacks enjoyed their equal status to such an extent that they chose to extend their tours.[20]

Many African Americans reached similar conclusions about race relations, believing Vietnam provided them with their first opportunities to interact with whites as equals and potentially befriend them. As an anonymous Black soldier explained, "The Negro sees the white boy—really sees him—for the first time. . . . He's just another dude."[21] Jim Houston of Cleveland served with the 25th Infantry Division in 1966, and he described Black-white relations in Vietnam as "a brotherhood thing for us. . . . We was like brothers, you know like your real brother, like you might love your real brother. You know you love your family, that's the way we were."[22]

Houston was not the only one to claim that the men he served with were like family. Robert Sanders of San Francisco served with the 173rd Airborne in 1968–69, and he recalled feeling closer to the men he served with "than I do my own blood sisters and brothers." Furthermore, he asserted that "we was so close it was unreal. That was the first time in my life I saw that type of unity, and I haven't seen it since. And that was ten years ago. It was beautiful. It sort of chills you, brings goose bumps just to see it, just to feel it."[23]

Don L. Jernigan, who served with the 198th Infantry Brigade in 1967-68, recalled, "The brothers were just family. And the white guys that were crew were family."[24] Wayne Smith spoke of the Black and white men he served with in the 9th Infantry Division in 1968-69 in familial terms stating, "We truly were brothers and in some cases far closer to each other than anyone before or since in our lives."[25]

African Americans reported experiencing prejudice when they first arrived but that these feelings quickly dissipated. Robert M. Watters of Louisville, Kentucky, concluded that at "the beginning of the Nam there was racism, there was racism going over on the plane, okay, there was racism in the field, but there, it wasn't all of a sudden." He further stated that "while I went to the Nam [in 1965] with some real bigots, and some real racists, okay. I saw a whole new change."[26]

Racism was not unknown in basic training. When Bob Steck, a white Texan who served with the 17th Air Cavalry, was in basic training in Fort Lewis, Washington, a Black member of his platoon misplaced a firing pin and the southern supply sergeant wouldn't let him leave until he found it. Steck believed, "I am sure racism was a not unsubstantial part of his reaction to this guy losing his M-16 firing pin." Steck was so upset by the incident, he briefly went absent without leave (AWOL) and was demoted.[27]

David Parks of New York City reported that the whites he met in basic training "don't let you forget you're colored and that they're white for one minute." Parks believed that many whites arrived feeling that socially accepted definitions of "Black" and "white" were desirable and permanent. However, these beliefs were challenged in Vietnam. Parks remembered that "the most positive thing that came out of the war was the comradeship that developed between black and white combat soldiers."[28]

Anthony Martin served in 1966-67 with the 3rd Marine Division, and he reported a similar transformation. As the only African American in his graduating class at the Marine Corps Tracked Vehicle School in Twentynine Palms, California, Martin faced harassment from other trainees and was a target for undue criticism from his superiors. He understandably believed this poor treatment was racially motivated. Things were different in Vietnam. He theorized that "people began to realize you needed each other to get through this . . . and they know that the guy to the left and the right of him, regardless of what color he is, that person's going to help you be able to put that next mark on your countdown calendar."[29]

Robert Sanders experienced prejudice when he first arrived, but it was soon replaced by "total unity and total harmony. It was really great, man. It was beautiful. That was the only thing that really turned me on in Vietnam. That was the only thing in Vietnam that had any meaning."[30]

Keith Freeman met a white soldier from Colorado who confessed to his previous prejudices and asked for forgiveness. Acknowledging that his parents had taught him to be prejudiced against Blacks, the man apologized, stating, "I'm sorry I ever learned like that because now I'm here and we're out here fighting together watching guard for each other, when you're asleep I'm on guard, when I'm asleep you're on guard and my life is in your hands."[31]

Many African Americans understood they were serving alongside whites who were taught that Blacks were inherently inferior, with the corollary that they should be treated with disrespect and discrimination. Both groups learned that these prejudices could recede. Combat enabled whites and Blacks to move beyond their previous social conditioning and form positive relationships. George Brummell, who served with the 25th Infantry Division in 1966, spoke for many African Americans when he stated that Vietnam taught him "that we can get along together regardless of race."[32]

When these prejudices receded, friendships were able to form. Daniel Burress, a Black marine from Chicago who served in 1965-66, developed a close friendship with Clark, a white corporal. On Burress's last day with his unit, he was promoted to lance corporal and invited to the noncommissioned officers' (NCO) tent, which was considered a major privilege. Instead of going to the tent he spent the night celebrating with Clark, who had bought an expensive bottle of wine to celebrate the promotion. Burress felt conflicted over having to leave his friend, stating, "I was upset because I knew I was leaving the next day and I knew he would be there. . . . We cried that night. We cried for different reasons. We cried for numerous reasons."[33] Burress's promotion and removal from combat were not enough to lessen his concern for Clark, who would remain.

Dave Dubose of New Haven, Connecticut, became close friends with Condon, a white soldier, while serving with the 199th Infantry Brigade in 1966-67. Dubose remembered that he and Condon were as close as brothers, and that their friendship revealed to him that the "barrier of color is false."[34] Lee Ewing of Jeffersonville, Indiana, served in 1967-68 with the 3rd Bridge Company of the 1st Marine Division, becoming good friends with Charles Sheehan, a white marine from Connecticut. They shared numerous "firsts" together including trying drugs and alcohol for the first time. Ewing recalled, "He's really significant in my mind. . . . We was together all through those firsts, and he kind of looked up to me as the big brother."[35]

Stanley Goff of Tyler, Texas, served in 1968–69 with the 196th Light Infantry Brigade and became close with two white soldiers, Emory and Doc. After their unit became embroiled in a firefight with the People's Army of Vietnam (PAVN), Doc recommended Goff for the Distinguished Service Cross. Goff was shocked that a white man would recommend a Black man for such a distinguished award. Doc's support did not end there. When the brigade needed a bugler, Doc recommended Goff, which effectively ended Goff's time in combat. Doc instructed Goff not to tell anyone else about the recommendation, but he found himself unable to do so. The first soldier he told was Emory. He recalled, "I wasn't thinking white or black; I had to tell the men that allied themselves with me, like Emory."[36] Goff eventually told his Black friends as well, but he told his white friend first, which is important because it provides further evidence that the existing boundaries shaping Black-white relationships were being blurred, if not erased.

"The First White Friend I Had, I Had in Vietnam"

African American servicemen had a wide range of experiences with whites before entering the military. Scott Riley was born in Rye, New York, later moving with his family to nearby Mamaroneck where he attended high school. He recalled that he was "usually the only black kid in my classes. . . . Actually my high school graduating class, jumped to about three or four people." There were so few African Americans in these communities that whites rarely saw them as any sort of threat. Riley was aware that race relations were far worse in other parts of the country, especially because his "dad's family had been chased out of South Carolina by the Ku Klux Klan, because the Klan had murdered his cousin."[37]

Bernard McClusky grew up in a predominantly Italian neighborhood in Springfield, Massachusetts, where race relations were mostly positive. He went to integrated schools and had white friends. At the same time, he, like Riley, was aware that this was not the case everywhere. He noted, "My family was from the South.... I knew about racial tensions, but I sort of lived in a glass bubble. It wasn't until I left my native land, until I left my community, that it was real for me."[38]

Growing up in Providence, Rhode Island, Wayne Smith experienced discrimination but he also had white friends.[39] Horace Coleman grew up in an integrated neighborhood and attended integrated schools in Dayton, Ohio. Raised in this environment he didn't have a negative view of whites before entering the military.[40] As a young man in the Bronx, New York, Ron Bradley delivered newspapers for a white grocer to mostly white customers and never had any trouble. He even had a white girlfriend when he began high school.[41]

Others described relations between whites and Blacks as complex and multifaceted. Raised in Summit County, Ohio, James Gillam and his brother were the only African Americans at their school. Through playing football he made white friends, but there was always an undercurrent of racism in town. He recalled, "I never got to swim at the local swimming pool."[42] For Lamont B. Steptoe race relations were similarly complex in his hometown of Pittsburgh. He attended integrated schools where relations were decent, but Blacks were barred from some swimming pools. He also experienced occasional incidents of racial harassment.[43]

In many areas of the country Blacks and whites had limited interactions with one another. Growing up in Washington, DC, Stephen A. Howard recalled that "the first white friend I had, I had in Vietnam."[44] Raised in Baltimore, Sinclair Swan had few meaningful interactions with whites because he attended segregated schools.[45] Nate Mondy was raised exclusively around African Americans in New Orleans and had few interactions with whites before joining the military.[46] Clyde Jackson grew up in Richmond, Virginia, where legally sanctioned segregation meant he rarely engaged with whites.[47] George Brummell grew up in Federalsburg, Maryland, and had few interactions with whites outside of his job picking cucumbers. He was bused to an all-Black school sixteen miles out of town, and Blacks were not allowed in local stores or restaurants.[48]

Race relations were tense in many areas of the country. Anthony Martin grew up in Chicago where neighborhoods were heavily segregated and race relations were poor. Fighting between Black and white youths was common, and it was dangerous to travel outside of one's own neighborhood alone.[49] Raised in an all-Black neighborhood in Muncie, Indiana, Brian Settles remembered, "Race relations were not good in Muncie.... I played basketball outside of the colored YMCA, we couldn't even use the white YMCA downtown."[50]

Blacks from the segregated South had particularly poor experiences with whites. Many likely would have agreed with Reginald Edwards of Phoenix, Louisiana, who recalled, "In them days we never hang with white people. You didn't have white friends. White people was the aliens to me. This is '63. . . . You expected them to treat you bad."[51]

In Roosevelt Gore's hometown of Mullins, South Carolina, racial segregation prevailed and whites routinely mistreated Blacks. Gore's father worked as a sharecropper for a tenant farmer who cheated Black workers. Gore remembered, "The white man could get away with cheating because he wouldn't let my father or any of his other tenant farmers keep records." Gore grew up feeling "like an outcast. . . . I was actually glad to get drafted in 1966. I wanted to get away from the environment I was living in."[52]

Robert Louis Jr. was raised in rural Louisiana where most African Americans worked as sharecroppers in servitude to whites. Louis described this work environment as "as close to slavery as possible," but there were variations in the ways whites treated Blacks. Louis claimed wealthy whites tended to be racist and abusive while poorer whites were respectful.[53]

In James Lewis's hometown, Lake Charles, Louisiana, race relations were limited and involved Blacks working in subordinate positions to whites. His father, who worked at a lumber company, always called the eleven-year-old son of his boss "Mr." Discrimination was so severe that Lewis joined the military largely because he realized his only other option was to "stand on the corner and eventually be arrested for something I did not do," a circumstance that young Blacks in his hometown routinely faced.[54]

Eddie Greene grew up outside of Marion, Alabama, where segregation was total and oppressive. The threat of violence was very real. In 1956 Greene's father was murdered by a group of whites. Greene also attended school with the sister of Jimmie Lee Jackson, an unarmed protestor who was shot and killed by an Alabama state trooper in 1965 and whose death inspired the Selma to Montgomery march.[55]

Growing up in Pampa, Texas, Wes Geary was very aware of the dangers inherent in being Black in the South. He recalled, "They had lynched a Black kid one time and burned down the courthouse in town. . . . That whole region, almost every town had been the scene of a lynching, at least one lynching. And so Black people knew their place. . . . You didn't even think about crossing that line."[56]

African Americans who traveled to the South were often exposed to racism and prejudice. While waiting in army fatigues at a bus terminal in Columbus, Georgia, in 1959, Sinclair Swan was accosted by a white man who instructed him to stay in the colored area of the terminal.[57] In 1966 Bernard McClusky was told "we don't serve your kind here" when he asked for change while on his way to Fort Jackson, South Carolina, for basic training.[58] Horace Coleman's grandfather was lynched in Mississippi but it wasn't until he arrived in Panama, Florida, for basic training in 1966 that he experienced southern racism firsthand. After entering a restaurant, he was told by one of the workers, who was a Scottish immigrant, "I am sorry I can't serve you." Coleman recalled, "This woman isn't even a citizen, and she's telling me I can't eat here. . . . This is the South alright."[59] In 1967 Arthur Barham attended Advanced Infantry Training at Fort Jackson in South Carolina where the Ku Klux Klan (KKK) routinely assaulted African Americans who wandered off-base, forcing them to travel in groups.[60]

"He Was a Southerner That I Thought I Was Not Going to Like"

African Americans sometimes found friendship in unexpected places. While serving with the 4th Cavalry Regiment of the 1st Division in 1966–67, Thomas Brannon of Sewickley, Pennsylvania, learned that his company commander was a southerner. His initial reaction was, "Oh God, stereotypical southern guy, I am going to catch hell now." Brannon's initial skepticism of Harold Wilkins, which was based primarily on Brannon's father's and grandfather's experiences with white southerners, proved incorrect. Wilkins ended up promoting Brannon to executive officer, and the two developed a close bond. Thinking back, Brannon concluded, "Harold Wilkins, who I thought was probably going to be the most racist son of a bitch I ever knew just based on my own prejudice and stereotypical way of looking at things, turned out to be first a great soldier and a great and good person. . . . He was a southerner that I thought I was not going to like, but he was a southerner that I revered."[61]

Black servicemen were aware that these "new" relationships formed in a "new" environment contrasted with prevailing racial mores back home. Ron Bradley remembered that "a lot of reality got served from soldiers from the South and North when we got together. Because normally, obviously, before you went in the service, you weren't around [each other]. You were only around people pretty much like yourself." As a squad leader who served in an aviation company with the 9th Infantry Division in 1967–68 near Can Tho, Bradley was given the difficult responsibility of leading a squad of mostly white southerners, one of whom claimed to be the son of a Ku Klux Klan Grand Dragon. Many were initially resentful about having to follow Bradley's orders, but over time these resentments subsided as they started to realize they were more alike than dissimilar. He recalled, "Especially with the guy whose father was a Grand Dragon, he came around and started denouncing his father and what his father stood for. . . . He said, 'I didn't realize that blacks were like this . . . he lied to me.'"[62]

Ed Emanuel of Los Angeles served as a long-range reconnaissance patrolman (LRRP) with the 51st Infantry Regiment Airborne in 1968–69, becoming close friends with Barney, a white soldier whom Emanuel described as a "brother straight from the hills of Kentucky. I knew in my heart that this buck sergeant was totally blind to color."[63] While serving with the 23rd Division in 1969–70, Charles Strong of Pompano Beach, Florida, befriended Joe, a white soldier from Georgia. Strong acknowledged that the initial impression many Blacks formed of Joe was that he was a "redneck, ridge running cracker," but in reality he was "the nicest guy in the world." The two men spent their leisure time listening to music and talking about their family and friends. They became so close that they pitched their tents together and Strong "would give him food and he would share his water. And food and water was more valuable than paper money."[64] Strong and Joe shared water, food, and sleeping accommodations in Vietnam, which is significant given that back home white southerners were resisting the integration of lunch counters, the end of segregated drinking fountains, and above all residential and school desegregation.

Stephen A. Howard developed a particularly strong bond with Rosey, a white soldier from Georgia, while serving in the 145th Aviation Company. They "ended up in each other's room every night" discussing "a lot about our personal lives. Having a girlfriend that you really were serious about marrying. Wanting to have a son one day. What our families was all about." Howard and Rosey, whom Howard described as a "redneck," spent time discussing their different cultures.[65]

Their close relationship spread to Blacks and whites in their unit. Howard stated that "when the rednecks got together and started to stomp and holler, you either had to go over there and pour beer on the floor and do your little jumpin' up and down, or you stay out of it. That was their thing, and we had our thing. It was good to do it together, 'cause we were all in the war together."[66]

This account is revealing. Howard was in Vietnam from January 1968 to August 1969, a period when race relations back home were particularly tense.[67] Nonetheless, he developed a close friendship with Rosey, a white southerner. Rosey showed an interest in Howard's culture, a level of respect rarely seen in the United States, especially in the South. Considering the prevalence of social segregation in the South, it is unlikely that Howard and Rosey would have even had the opportunity or inclination to discuss their dreams, families, and cultures with a person of another race back home.

Their conversations revealed that Rosey was the son of a poor sharecropper, making his family much poorer than Howard's. For what was likely the first time in his life, Howard met a white person who was poorer than he was. He even felt guilty when Rosey discussed going without food and "not having some of the basic things I knew deep down inside I had."[68]

While the men who served with Howard and Rosey accepted their friendship, this was not always the case. Lamont B. Steptoe befriended a white southerner from Alabama while serving in Cu Chi with the 25th Infantry Division in 1969–70. As a scout dog handler, Steptoe was only allowed to be in the field for a maximum of seven days at a time, with the rest of the time spent on base. He believed that race relations were fine in the field and Black-white friendships were accepted, but this was not always the case outside of combat. Sensing these frictions, he informed his friend, "You know some of your fellow compatriots from down south are going to call you aside one day and ask you why you're a nigger lover." Unmoved, the man informed Steptoe that he would beat up anyone who questioned their friendship. When Steptoe went on rest and recuperation (R&R) he returned to find that "those soldiers in our unit from the South had in fact done exactly what I said they were going to do and he did exactly what he said he was going to do, he beat the shit out of them."[69] Steptoe's friend's actions are all the more remarkable when contrasted with the reactions of most Alabama whites to the civil rights movement and subsequent civil rights legislation.

Archie Biggers was a marine officer from Colorado City, Texas, who served with the 9th Marine Regiment in 1968–69. One of the few Black officers in Vietnam, Biggers had the unique task of commanding white troops, many of them from the South. Many of these marines were initially reluctant to take orders from a Black officer, but Biggers eventually developed a close relationship with them, becoming their confidant. They trusted him and felt comfortable coming to him with professional and personal problems. One white marine offered to give Biggers a picture of his sister, stating, "she's white, but you'd still like her. Look her up when you get back to the States."[70]

This remark is significant because most white southerners and even northerners would have opposed such a relationship. In *Race and Mixed Race*, Naomi Zack argues that the belief that Black men lusted after white women "was the ultimate justification for the disenfranchisement of southern blacks, for segregation, and for the lynching of blacks." Black-white sexual relations were viewed as so offensive and contrary to nature that they were described by a separate word: miscegenation. This repulsion led to the passage of anti-miscegenation laws in thirty-eight states, which made it illegal for Blacks and whites to have sexual relations, marry, or have children. Until the 1967 U.S. Supreme Court decision of *Loving v. Virginia* thirteen states still had anti-miscegenation laws, including Biggers's home state of Texas.[71] He arrived in Vietnam only a year after anti-miscegenation laws were overturned in Texas, which makes the white marine's comments even more remarkable.

Equally meaningful are the words the white marine chose to use. By stating that "she's white, but you'd still like her," he made it clear that he held no biases against Blacks, nor did he imply that dating a white woman was a privilege he was conferring on Biggers. He recognized that Biggers might not be interested in dating his sister.[72] The white marine's offer demonstrates that socially constructed boundaries involving race were breaking down.

"It Hurt Me Bad When They Got Joe"

Black and whites risked and sacrificed their lives for one another in Vietnam without any concern for race. Wayne Smith remembered, "I met some white people that I am very glad to call my brother. . . . Some of the best people (Black and white) I ever met, were those men, who were in combat, who were willing to risk their lives for me, and I them."[73]

Harold Bryant of East St. Louis, Illinois, served with the 1st Cavalry Division around An Khe in 1966–67, and he related an incident in which a fellow Black soldier saved the life of a white soldier who was a member of the KKK. The men in Bryant's unit were close, but the presence of a KKK member fueled quite a bit of anger among African Americans. During a firefight with the NLF, the Klan member froze and refused to move, forcing a Black soldier to drag him back to safety. Bryant claimed the incident "changed his perception of what black people were about."[74] Scott Riley, who served with the 1st Cavalry Airmobile in 1967–68, had a similar experience with a white soldier from Georgia named Sykes. He described Sykes as a "rampant racist" who made it clear he wanted nothing to do with African Americans. However, after Riley saved Sykes from an enemy soldier, the two became friends. Sykes later admitted to Riley that his father was a Grand Dragon in the KKK who had taught him to hate African Americans. Their friendship taught Sykes "a different side of Black people," and he promised to "kick his father's ass" when he returned to the United States.[75] It is hard to imagine these two scenarios ever occurring in the United States. However, Vietnam provided the opportunity for even the most extreme transformations in racial thinking.

Memphis native Terry Whitmore, who served with the 1st Marine Division in 1967–68, was wounded in a firefight. A badly injured white marine stayed by his side rather than seek safety. Whitmore explained, "He was wounded. He couldn't stand or even kneel.... He just dragged me through the dirt, back about five or six yards." After dragging Whitmore to safety, the man shielded him with his body as American planes dropped napalm overhead. The white marine encouraged him to hold on, telling him, "Hold on babe. You gonna be all right." Whitmore believed he would not have survived had it not been for the protection and encouragement given by the unnamed white marine.[76] The willingness of a white marine to risk his life for a Black marine he did not even know further illustrates the lessening of racial consciousness on the battlefield.

During a PAVN ambush in 1968, Bob "Pee Wee" Jefferson, a sergeant and squad leader from Chicago, came upon a badly injured white soldier. Despite having been shot twice in the leg, Jefferson hoisted the man over his shoulder and carried him to safety. Years later the *Chicago Tribune* noted that Jefferson had saved the young soldier even "though he never knew the white kid's name. He had never seen him before and would never see him again." Speaking of the incident, which earned him a Bronze Star for bravery, Jefferson recalled, "Over there we did that for each other. We all did. Didn't matter where you came from or who you were, rich or poor. You did for a man what you hoped they'd do for you."[77]

Edgar A. Huff of Gadsen, Alabama, served in 1967–68 and again in 1970–71, and he recalled an incident in which he risked his own life to save a white marine. Huff was the first Black sergeant major in the Marine Corps and one of the highest-ranking Black NCOs. He was the superior to nearly all enlisted men, Black or white, he encountered. During a firefight outside of Da Nang, NLF soldiers pinned down a young white radio operator. Over the objections of his colonel, Huff saved the marine. He reasoned, "I knew I might get killed saving a white boy. But he was my man. That's all that mattered."[78] Huff was willing to risk his own life to save the marine, regardless of race, because he was "his man."

African American servicemen occasionally found that race had little impact on who was reliable or not. James Gillam served with the 4th Infantry Division from late 1968 until early 1970, and he remembered that "the ironic thing about this race thing is on one of the worst days of the worst week I spent in Vietnam I got in a firefight and all the Black men I was with ran away and left me and the only two guys that stayed with me were two white guys." While understandably angry at the soldiers who had abandoned him, Gillam felt this incident demonstrated that race was not a determinant of reliability.[79]

Others made the ultimate sacrifice. During an intense firefight in October 1965, Milton Lee Olive, an African American soldier from Chicago, jumped on a grenade, saving the lives of four soldiers. The *Los Angeles Sentinel* reported that "race was obviously no factor in the mind of the young Chicagoan when he saw the grenade coming over the thicket. . . . Olive without hesitation grasped the grenade in his hand and flung his body atop it," sacrificing his own life and saving the lives of four soldiers. Olive was posthumously awarded the Congressional Medal of Honor.[80]

In 1966 *Jet* described a battle involving the 101st Airborne where Harry Goodman, a white soldier, was shot and badly wounded. With little regard for his own life, Harry Garnett, a Black soldier, crawled out to save Goodman. Unfortunately, Garnett was killed in the process.[81]

Black servicemen reacted to the deaths of their friends, whether Black or white, with grief and anger. In *Same Mud, Same Blood* Wilkenson described a recent battle that had resulted in casualties. He recalled, "We had so many casualties and nobody said we had one colored and five whites. I mean they were all casualties."[82]

After Hosea Dyson's squad was ambushed along the demilitarized zone, he and his fellow marines crawled through the jungle to retrieve the bodies of their deceased squad members. Dyson recalled, "We didn't care whether they were black or white.... We just wanted to get them back so they could have a decent burial.... I know one thing. I've got friends here, black and white, who would find my body and bring it back."[83] Wilkenson and Dyson were not alone in viewing the deaths of Black and white servicemen as equally important. Many African Americans shared Don L. Jernigan's sentiments: "I remember most profoundly some of the white guys too, my grief, believe it or not is for as many of them as it is for my black brothers."[84]

Jernigan's view was not atypical. While serving with the 101st Airborne in 1966–67, Moses L. Best Sr. of Fayetteville, North Carolina, initially avoided making friends because he did not want a relationship with anyone at such a high risk of being killed. He eventually became close friends with Chitwood, a white soldier. Against Best's advice, Chitwood volunteered for a particularly dangerous position and was killed. Best described Chitwood "as a real nice guy, Chitwood. I often think about him. He was probably the closest friend I ever had over there."[85]

Charles Strong's white friend Joe was killed when he stepped on a booby trap. Strong was only a short distance away, and he was forced to watch his friend suffer and eventually die. He explained that "it hurt me real bad when they got Joe." While guarding the Medevac that came to pick up Joe, Strong, looking for revenge, prayed "to the Lord to let me see some VC [Viet Cong], anybody jump out on the trail."[86]

On January 27, 1983, the *Chicago Tribune* published letters written in 1967–68 by Freddie King, a white soldier from Hammond, Indiana, to his family. These letters demonstrate the close bond that many Blacks and whites formed with one another and the grief they felt when one of their "brothers" was killed. In one of the letters, King mentioned his close friend Willie Ellison, an African American from Texas. He even sent pictures of the two men together to his parents and siblings. Unfortunately, on November 25, 1968, both men were killed when the vehicle they were in ran over a mine.[87]

The *Tribune* included letters that Freddie's family received after his death. One of these was from Clarice Ellison, Willie's mother. Clarice was aware of her son's close friendship with King, and her comments reveal numerous details about their relationship. She stated, "Your son was a dear friend of my son because your son wanted to come home with him.

What I love about your son. My son couldn't write, your son taught him how to write letters to me." She was also sent pictures of her son and King together.[88]

Jim Jones, an African American soldier, wrote a letter to King's family which explained that he was a "Negro, but I just wanted to let you'll know that we aren't like animals and not care what happens to each other (over here) like most people think we do in the states." Jones elaborated on their friendship: "I knew your son, Freddie, and me and him were real good friends . . . and it really hurt me when he met his death." King's death so affected Jones that he "offered to bring his body home but they wouldn't let me so I thought I would write you'll a letter and try to express my sorrow."[89]

"No Room for Rednecks"

African Americans were not the only ones to experience a breaking down of racial barriers. In *Same Mud, Same Blood* a white soldier nicknamed "Arkansas" described the African Americans he served with: "You look at them and they're just another guy out there. A guy that you can bum a cigarette off of if you're out. Or get a drink of water off if you're out or a can of food. Everything is share and share alike." Arkansas grew up in a state where Blacks and whites were legally required to drink from separate water fountains, but his time in Vietnam led him to reject the attitudes and customs he was taught as a boy. He recognized that many whites in Arkansas would not approve of his fraternization with Black troops but dismissed any criticism noting, "If they came over here and spent a couple months they'd learn it too, the hard way." When pressed whether this new commitment would remain when he returned home, Arkansas replied, "After I've gone through what I have over here, if a white man tried to get me riled up against the negro, maybe go through a riot demonstration or something, I think I'd just get mad enough to shoot him period and be done with it."[90]

Hawkins, a white Chicagoan, came to a similar conclusion. He maintained that in Vietnam "you're not looking at a man's color" but rather his character and his ability to get the job done properly. Speaking of the soldiers in his platoon, Anthony Mavroudis added that "you can't divide them as a group, it's the man it's not the color and as far as I am concerned, the credit for anything that happens in this war, no matter what the outcome is, belongs to both, the white, and negro."[91]

Testimonies from white veterans also provide evidence of Black and white friendship. As Richard Traegerman, a white soldier from Philadelphia, saw it, Vietnam taught whites to view "Negroes as intelligent and brave as anybody else."[92] Growing up in New Mexico and Mississippi, Lewis Downey had limited interactions with African Americans, but this changed in Vietnam. He expected to be assigned to a shortwave radio station in Long Binh, but his orders were lost, and he feared being sent to an artillery unit. He sought help from an African American sergeant who allowed him to use a telephone to straighten the matter out. Downey recalled, "I have good feelings about Black people. . . . He helped me, and that simple twist of fate meant the difference between doing something for people instead of dropping high explosives on people." One of the people Downey was able to help was a Black cook named Pie. After Downey managed to connect a phone call for Pie to his mother, "he came out of the phone booth with the biggest grin on his face . . . and he said, 'I just talked to my mother.'" This moment continued to have great significance for Downey more than forty years later.[93]

Growing up in Boone County, West Virginia, Theodore Belcher had few meaningful interactions with African Americans. In Vietnam he became close friends with several African Americans, including George Brummell. When Belcher served with the 25th Infantry Division in 1966–67 Black-white friendship was not unusual. He remembered, "I know for a fact that every one of them . . . the Blacks and the whites, met someone of the opposite race that they were tight with, they were close to."[94]

Belcher argued that there was "no room for rednecks" in Vietnam, and those displaying prejudice were quickly isolated. He remembered an incident in which Manning, a white soldier, called a Black soldier a "nigger" and suggested that if they were back in Arkansas, he would hurt him. Belcher angrily and publicly confronted the soldier, screaming, "Manning you're not fucking in Arkansas alright, and you will not refer to this man as a nigger and you will not come up with your little bullshit. . . . Cut yourself on the frigging arm, this man cuts himself on the arm, you'll see red blood coming out of your fucking veins. Alright, so just consider yourself, we're all in it together." After Belcher confronted him, Manning's perspective on African Americans and race relations seemed to change, and he became friends with a few Black soldiers. When Manning was later killed in combat, Belcher took solace knowing Manning was "integrated" before being killed.[95]

Thomas Rogan, a white soldier from Springfield, Massachusetts, became close friends with Thomas Brannon, a Black soldier, when they served as platoon leaders in the 1st Squadron of the 4th Cavalry Regiment of the 1st Division in 1966–67. Rogan believed that their friendship developed more out of shared interests than their shared rank. The other platoon leader in the squad was a Mormon and their forward observer was a Christian Scientist, which meant they abstained from drinking alcohol. Rogan found himself relating better to Brannon, who, like him, enjoyed drinking beer. Their already strong friendship was cemented when Rogan saved Brannon's life during an ambush.[96]

In 1966–67 Jack Whitted, a white soldier from Wheatley, Arkansas, commanded the 1st Battalion of the 28th Infantry Regiment of the 1st Infantry Division, which placed him in charge of around eight hundred to a thousand troops. He recalled there being no racial tension in his battalion and that Black-white friendships were common. After a white chaplain was dismissed for incompetence, Whitted befriended his replacement, Wes Geary, the only Black chaplain in the division. The two even traveled together to Thailand on R&R. Whitted also became close friends with Sinclair Swan, a Black company commander in the 1st Infantry Division. Late at night, when everyone else was asleep, Whitted and Swan would sing "My Darling Clementine" and other songs to each other over the radio.[97]

Whitted's friendships with Geary and Swan are particularly noteworthy considering Whitted was born in the 1920s in rural Arkansas. Whitted recalled of his upbringing, "My father was probably the most anti-Black fellow that ever lived."[98] In 1919 his father was an active participant in putting down the "Elaine Race Riot," which resulted from an attempt by Black sharecroppers to unionize. In the aftermath, a white mob, including Whitted's father, killed more than a hundred African Americans.[99] Despite his upbringing and ancestry, Whitted was able to develop close friendships with African Americans in Vietnam.

Thomas Titus, a white LRRP, became close friends with Willie, a Black LRRP. Titus recalled, "I found my other family in Vietnam. My friend Willie was just like another brother to me, no matter whether I had skin practically snow white and he had skin practically Black as night." During an enemy ambush, Willie tripped over a detonator wire causing an explosion. Titus tried to save Willie's life, but his injuries proved fatal. The death of his best friend haunted Titus. He recalled, "Thirty-one years later I am still carrying around a hell of a lot of guilt" over Willie's death.[100]

In December 1965 Milton Sands, a white soldier from Doylestown, Pennsylvania, wrote a letter from Vietnam to the *Philadelphia Tribune* praising the contributions and sacrifices of African Americans. After witnessing the death of a young Black soldier, Sands "felt the need to tell someone of his death in the hope that the value of his sacrifice, of a life just barely lived, will not be lost.... This colored boy died for America." Sands made a larger point about the continued mistreatment of African Americans. He reminded those "who might have denied him the right to food, lodging or a job" that this Black man and many like him did not shirk their duties. Sands concluded, "May God grant all Americans the vision... to become more 'democratic' Americans whether at work, at the lunch counter, or on the battlefield."[101]

Hosea Dyson remembered a white marine who upon leaving their squad told him that "he'd been proud to be in the same foxhole with me.... It made me feel good, so good. I would have felt good if a Negro had said it, but it struck me that someone white should do it." When asked if white perceptions of African Americans had changed, Dyson replied, "I think the war changes men.... It will make a difference when we get back. Out here, they see us as people. Before, you were just a shadow or something. Now they know."[102]

Dyson's experiences raise an interesting question about the permanency of the friendships Black and whites formed in Vietnam. Did these friendships continue once servicemen returned to the United States? Herman Graham III acknowledged that friendships between Blacks and whites developed, but he argued these relationships were situational. Once they left Vietnam, old racial prejudices resurfaced.[103] To an extent these relationships were temporary. Many veterans did lose contact as was the case in previous wars. However, there is no evidence that this happened more with Vietnam veterans than veterans of previous wars, or that race had anything to do with it.

Occasionally, these interracial friendships continued. Ed Emanuel maintained that "Vietnam exposed a biracial brotherhood that proved to be the beginning of lasting friendship."[104] Roosevelt Gore, who served with the 1st Infantry Division in Di An in 1967–68, remained close friends with two white soldiers, David Simpson and Ted A. Burton, fellow South Carolinians, nearly twenty-five years after they served together.[105] Thomas Brannon remained friends with Harold Wilkins and Thomas Rogan for more than forty years after their service in Vietnam.[106] Theodore Belcher and George Brummell remained friends for more than forty-five years after their initial time together.[107] Speaking of his more than forty-five-year-long friendship with Wes Geary, Whitted commented, "My daughter has his address and phone number and I have told her that I want Wes to preach at my funeral when I die and that will probably raise a lot of hackles in Bay County to have a Black chaplain come in here and preach a funeral."[108]

Even for those servicemen who permanently parted company after Vietnam, these friendships remained an important part of their memories of the war. Dave Dubose did not remain in close contact with Condon after he was shot and evacuated from Vietnam, but their friendship still left an indelible imprint on Dubose. By chance, years later, he met a member of Condon's family. He recalled, "I got excited and told this family member how Condon and I loved each other. It must've appeared funny to this person for a black man to tell a white man that he loved him. I knew him in a different time then they did. Condon and I were very close."[109]

These interracial friendships often had an impact on their post-Vietnam lives. Reflecting on his experiences as an air traffic and intercept controller with the air force in 1967–68, Horace Coleman remembered that "one of the things that the war did in a positive sense was it forced Blacks and whites in Vietnam to work together." Coleman believed Vietnam provided an opportunity for Blacks and whites, many of whom had grown up in segregated environments, to develop friendships but also to learn about people with whom they had few previous interactions.[110] Akmed Lorence became close friends with a white soldier from a prominent Washington, DC, family while in Vietnam. During a discussion on race relations, Lorence told his friend that America was a corrupt and racist society. When his friend denied that this was true, Lorence challenged him to observe whites in his own community. After doing so, the friend told Lorence, "You were right. . . . I watched them and most of them don't care for anyone who's not white. . . . I am a man without a country."[111]

Eighteen years after Thomas Brannon's time in Vietnam ended, he received a phone call from Bobby Metter, a white soldier he had served with. Brannon was understandably surprised to hear from Metter, but his sense of shock was only heightened when he learned that Metter was calling to thank him for educating him about racial equality. Metter's interactions with Brannon convinced him that Blacks and whites were equal and deserved equal treatment. While this view was not shared by most whites in Metter's hometown of Salem, Virginia, he continued to express support for racial equality in his community. He also passed these values on to his children. Reminiscing on his time in Vietnam and his conversation with Metter, Brannon affirmed, "Maybe I made an impact on Bobby Metter's life that will affect whites in his community that look at people like me and can accept me as an American even though I'm darker than them."[112]

As prejudices broke down and friendships developed, the rigidity and importance of racial categorizations weakened to the extent that many African Americans believed their race and skin color were no longer definitive. The positive race relations Robert Sanders experienced led him to conclude, "For the first time in my life, I saw people as people. We was just us, you know man, it was US."[113] Sanders believed combat service provided him with the opportunity to see his fellow servicemen not as Black or white but just as people.

Sanders was not the only African American to express this new perspective. Sinclair Swan, a captain with the 1st Infantry Division in 1966–67 and again with the U.S. Army Republic of Vietnam (USARV) in 1968–69, recalled, "When we were beating the bush it didn't matter what color you were and like the old song says 'Everybody's Green.'"[114] Ed Emanuel believed that "there was no such thing as black, white, or brown Lurp [LRRP] in the jungles of Vietnam. We were all camouflage green. Somehow, that way of thinking seemed to weave its way into the fabric of our every day."[115] David Parks agreed: "Olive green was the only color that mattered."[116]

Cephus "Dusty" Rhodes of Apalachicola, Florida, served with the 1st Infantry Division in 1966–67, and he believed that there was no recognition of color among the men in his unit. He remembered, "If the guy next to you is good you don't know what color he is. If he's not good you don't know what color he is.... He could be purple if he was doing the job. He could look like your mother if he's not doing the job."[117] As far as Rhodes was concerned, reliability was more important than skin color.

When Stanley Goff left his combat unit, his friends, Black and white, saw him off. Seeing the unity in his company, he reasoned that maybe this "could mean that black didn't matter." Instead of seeing him as a Black man leaving the war, the men saw "just a man that was going out of the war."[118] Goff, like many other African Americans, perceived the front lines as a deracialized space in which Blacks and whites could enjoy real friendships "free" from socially constructed racism.[119]

Death and Dependence

Several factors explain why race relations were largely positive in combat. The military encouraged unity and discipline among its troops, especially those engaged directly in combat. This was, of course, nothing new. Samuel Stouffer's extensive study, *The American Soldier: Combat and Its Aftermath,* shows that during World War II servicemen were taught to sacrifice their own interests in deference to the interests of the armed forces. Stouffer argued that "the soldier was not an individual atom in the tide of warfare; he was an integral part of a vast system of discipline and coordination . . . who was simultaneously guided, supported, and coerced by a framework of organization." This framework encouraged loyalty to the military, the unit, and one's fellow servicemen.[120]

While we might question the strength of this indoctrination or whether it was anything more than rhetorical, many servicemen reiterated the idea that army or marine green was the only color of importance. Robert Sanders stated that his captain instilled in the men "that there wasn't no black and white in Nam."[121] While the military encouraged unity, this was more a reflection of sound strategy than any deep commitment to remaking relations between Blacks and whites.

The very real possibility of being killed explains in great part why there was so little racial tension in combat and why so many men formed such close ties with one another. The American strategy of search and destroy, and the fact that the NLF and PAVN initiated most engagements, meant that each man's life was continually under threat.[122]

As was the case in past conflicts, combat tended to have a unifying effect. Few had the inclination or willingness to live by their learned racial prejudices with bullets flying past their heads. It made sense to try to work together as this increased one's chance of survival. A 1975 *Journal of Social Issues* article, "Black-White and American-Vietnamese Relations among Soldiers in Vietnam," closely addressed the topic of race relations. M. Duncan Stanton, a psychologist from the University of Pennsylvania, argued that "race and racial differences seemed to lose their importance" in combat because Blacks and whites were heavily dependent on one another for survival and racial prejudice was viewed as disruptive. Jonathan F. Borus, a physician at Harvard University, also concluded that because servicemen were continually confronted with the possibility of being killed, they depended on one another and rejected race as a factor of importance.[123]

Many African Americans agreed with these interpretations. Gerald Lynch, a Black marine from Boston, participated in the Battle of Khe Sanh in 1968. He argued that in times of intense combat, "everybody thinks along one common line and that is survival."[124] Scott Riley agreed that survival took precedence over all else. He noted, "Even if somebody doesn't like you, or you don't like them, you very quickly find out that you are inexorably tied or your fates are tied."[125] James Lewis served with the 589th Engineer Battalion Combat in 1968–69, and he believed "there was no racism in the combat zone" because African Americans and whites alike "were all like rats pressed in a can and having to fight together to stay alive and so nobody gave race much thought."[126] Eddie Greene believed that race was not an issue in Vietnam when he served there in 1970 because "it was a life or death situation and no one had time for any racism."[127]

St. Louis native Willie Thomas, who served with the 1st Battalion of the 525th Intelligence in 1969–70, explained that most servicemen had the perspective of, "I don't have time to hate you. My life might depend on you in the next five minutes."[128] Hosea Dyson maintained, "In war there isn't any color line" because "you have to work together. You depend on each other to survive out there."[129] Similarly, Freddie Edwards, who served with the 1st Marine Airwing in 1970–71, believed that the intimacy of combat provided a sort of protective shield from racial distinctions.[130]

Others agreed that the shared experience of combat and the very real possibility of being killed contributed to the bonding of Black and white servicemen. Anthony Martin distinguished between the way marines acted before their first firefight and how they acted afterward. Initially, "the whites hung with whites and Blacks hung with Blacks," but after his unit's first taste of combat, "the bodies were brought back to the ships, there was silence, and a lot of the nonsense was kind of put aside."[131] Wayne Smith noted that the immediacy of death and the possibility that "the last person you're talking to on this earth could be fucking Vietnamese or could be no one" created a sense of brotherhood.[132] Clyde Jackson, who served in 1966–67 and again in 1971–72, also believed that the existence of a common enemy explained why African Americans and whites got along so well with one another.[133]

Survival became the paramount goal for all servicemen in Vietnam, and this reality united Black and white troops. This perspective became more pronounced as the war dragged on and large numbers of servicemen became skeptical that the stated goals of the conflict could or would be met.[134]

The fact that Blacks and whites were reliant on one another for survival does not fully explain why they formed such close bonds. Combat troops did not spend all their time fighting. Frank McGee noted that there was always the chance that "buried racial antagonisms might surface" after the shooting stopped if someone was viewed as acting inappropriately, cowardly, or dangerously in combat.[135]

That this rarely happened suggests that the de-racialized environment was more permanent than the aftermath of a single firefight. In many respects troops were just as dependent on one another when they weren't facing enemy fire. Thus, bonds of friendship were formed out of an overall shared experience of sacrifice and hardship. Psychologist Jonathan Shay correctly notes that "extreme dependency on others is fundamental to modern combat," but this dependency was not limited just to the periods where servicemen were actively fighting. Shay reminds us that combat forces in Vietnam often experienced "shortages of all sorts—food, water, ammunition, clothing, shelter from the elements, medical care," and even of effective and sensible leadership.[136] Black and white servicemen faced these challenges together, which helped in the bonding process.

African Americans recognized this overall shared dependency. George Hicks, who served with the Army Security Agency in 1969–70, agreed that Blacks and whites got along primarily because they "endured the same thing.... You are over there suffering the same pain I am.... I am eating the same C-Rations you are eating."[137] Speaking of the men he served with, Cephus Rhodes remembered, "We share the same hardships, we share the same aspirations, get through tonight, win this battle, take this hill, cross this river, be here when the sun comes up in the morning and we're together in that."[138] Jim Houston believed that a "brotherhood" developed between Blacks and whites because "that's the only way you're going to make it back." He maintained that relationships formed "because you had to depend on each other. We ate out of the same dish, drink out of the same bottle."[139]

Ron Bradley remembered, "We all realized we were dependent on each other to stay alive." This shared dependency was not restricted just to combat. Bradley recalled, "You were spending all your time together 24/7 so obviously you would talk.... You would be drinking beer, or you know sitting there smoking cigarettes, or passing stories back and forth about, you know, where you lived and how you grew up. So, a lot of ideals were altered by being together in such close proximity."[140]

Horace Coleman recalled, "Everybody there knew that you had to depend on other GIs. They were going to be cooking your food, transporting your food and drink to you, or your ammunition. You had to depend on the person next to you, in front of you, in back of you, to do their job so you could do yours. To make a combined effort to stay alive."[141] Ron Copes of Hartford, Connecticut, believed that positive race relations reflected this shared dependency. Speaking of his experiences serving with the 1st Infantry Division in 1966–67 and again with Military Assistance Command Vietnam (MACV) in 1969–70, he recalled, "Everybody had a job to do, there was a need to depend upon the guy on your left and right. When you're out there engaged you want to know that somebody's gonna have your back or get you what you need."[142]

"Race Was Like, That's Bullshit That Happens Back in the World"

This shared dependency no doubt united African Americans and whites, but it was not the only reason that race relations in combat were so harmonious. Combat service placed African American lives at risk, but it also physically separated them from the racism and prejudice that often defined race relations in the United States.

The Civil Rights Act of 1964 and the Voting Rights Act of 1965 provided greater political and social rights for African Americans, but full equality and complete racial integration proved elusive. Most whites did not support civil and voting rights for African Americans. In May 1965 a major polling firm found that 42 percent of whites supported civil rights demonstrators, an all-time high for the period. By June 1967 support had dropped dramatically as 82 percent of whites reported having an unfavorable opinion of the civil rights movement.[143] These statistics demonstrate that the civil rights movement never had majority white support, and by 1967, incidentally before the Newark and Detroit Riots, whites by a wide majority were unsupportive if not outright hostile toward groups seeking legal and civil rights for Blacks.

Numerous incidents took place in the United States during the Vietnam War era that confirmed how easily racial tensions could erupt. On August 11, 1965, the arrest of a Black motorist by white police officers in Los Angeles triggered six days of violence, known as the Watts Riot, in which between seven and ten thousand people rampaged through the area looting and burning buildings, attacking firefighters, and confronting police. It took ten thousand National Guardsmen to end the rioting but not before thirty-four people were dead, more than a thousand were injured, and four thousand arrests were made.[144]

On July 12, 1967, in Newark, New Jersey, the arrest of a Black taxi driver by white police sparked the Newark Riots. Over five days, 26 people were killed, 1,100 were injured, 1,400 were arrested, and there were more than 350 incidents of arson. While the prevailing image from the Newark Riots was that of a Black sniper shooting at police, law enforcement fired 13,325 rounds of ammunition.[145]

On July 23, 1967, police officers raided an illegal, after-hours bar in one of Detroit's largest Black neighborhoods. Like events in Watts two years before and in Newark two weeks earlier, the situation escalated into violence. Over the next five days, 43 people died—30 of them killed by police officers—7,231 people were arrested, and 2,509 buildings were looted and burned.[146]

Race relations continued to fracture the following year. After Martin Luther King Jr.'s assassination on April 4, 1968, riots broke out in several cities, most notably Washington, DC, Baltimore, Chicago, Kansas City, and Pittsburgh.[147]

The Vietnam War removed servicemen, even if only temporarily, from this toxic racial environment back home. This distance created a space where they could escape their social conditioning and form new relationships that contradicted existing racial norms.

To an extent, antagonistic race relations in the United States explain why it took time for Black and white servicemen to establish new relationships. When Stanley Goff first arrived in 1968, race relations were tense, which he found unsurprising given that many whites, especially white southerners, came from a culture that taught them African Americans were inferior and only useful as servants. In Goff's words, many white soldiers came from families and communities which had taught them that Blacks were inferior:

> You can see it in their eyes. They look at you as though you're supposed to ask them, "What can I do for you?" You know? It's as if they're saying, "This is what I want you to do, boy." You just see it in their eyes and their actions. They sit back and have an offhanded look at you: "I am going to be better than you, and I can think and I'm smarter than you." Being from the South, I'd seen that look all my life.[148]

Despite these prejudices, Goff credited white soldiers for recognizing that they were "stuck out here in the boonies, and the white guy from the South is stuck out here, and it's life and death, we'd better begin to erase all this coloration immediately." As a Black southerner, Goff had experienced racism firsthand, and he understood that white southerners had to fight strongly against their own upbringing. They needed to learn to respect African Americans and treat them as human beings.[149] Goff believed these sorts of transformations were common in Vietnam. However, it is difficult to imagine these same transformations occurring in the United States given that their racist ideas about African Americans originated there.

In *Same Mud, Same Blood* Mavroudis talked about whites who arrived in Vietnam believing in the inferiority of African Americans. He claimed that combat allowed whites to "really see that the Negro is not everything that their social group said they were, and they'll know that they're not because they fought alongside them. . . . They'll be able to go back and tell them, 'you can feed your lies and bias from now till doomsday, but I'll know better.'"[150]

Many African Americans recognized the importance of place in determining racial attitudes and behavior. James Lewis found no racism in combat, but occasionally when whites returned from R&R, their old racial views remerged, and "if there was any racism shown it would be shown then." He believed that this behavioral change happened because "they were back in the world without the pressures that were necessitating them being cohesive and being as one. The band of brothers thing broke down the minute they would go out the door." Once they returned, they were forced to readopt a nonprejudicial outlook.[151]

Lewis was not alone in his assessment of race relations outside of combat. Many African Americans recognized that relations on rear-line military bases or in Vietnamese cities could be problematic. Ron Copes recalled, "When you were in the field it was great" but in rear-line areas, relations between Blacks and whites were noticeably colder and at times filled with tension.[152]

Vietnam veteran and author Karl Marlantes pays particular attention to racial issues in his novel *Matterhorn*, which is based heavily on his own experiences serving with the 3rd Marine Division in 1969. He believed that relations were generally good in combat but the exact opposite outside of it. He recalled, "It fascinated me how it could be so different coming out of the bush and going to the rear."[153]

Freddie Edwards recalled, "I wasn't in Da Nang three weeks when I am in a fight with a white guy. . . . He was racist. . . . He just didn't like Black folks." In contrast, when Edwards was stationed in a remote area outside of Da Nang, he no longer encountered any racial problems.[154]

Wayne Smith similarly believed that race relations were excellent in combat but problematic elsewhere. Smith claimed, "The further you got from combat the more bullshit there was."[155] Comparing relations at Camp Tien Sha to those in combat, G. L. Stanley, a Black sailor from Milwaukee, declared, "Tien Sha is definitely not the bush. . . . It's more like the real world."[156]

When African Americans proclaimed that relations in the rear were reminiscent of race relations in the "real world," that is, the United States, they did not mean it as a compliment. It was widely understood among African Americans that race relations in the "real world" were poor. A 1975 study conducted by the *Journal of Social Issues* concluded that African American Vietnam veterans believed overwhelmingly that race relations were better in Vietnam than back home.[157]

In *Same Mud, Same Blood* Frank McGee asked soldiers how they felt about the recent racial disturbances in the United States. Each man was perplexed by the racial situation, especially as it contrasted sharply with his own experiences in Vietnam. When asked about the rioting, Lewis B. Larry responded, "I see all the stuff on television, I say, 'What the devil is this? . . . I am confused and I am sure a lot of other people are confused because I refuse to believe that people just can't just live together.'" When asked about the possibility of Black veterans participating as snipers in urban riots, Larry answered confidently, "If he was standing in that mob or firing at somebody, and he had to face one of the people he faced while he was in the army, he'd probably throw his weapon down and run and hide his face." Hawkins, a white soldier, became upset when McGee asked him to imagine a race riot in which he faced off against Larry. Hawkins answered, "I'd probably cry. I would expect him to draw back and hit me as hard as he could. I would get up and walk away. That's how much I feel for the man, and I say man, not colored man. I would feel like a dog. I pray this never happens."[158]

Domestic race relations were so poor that some African Americans openly wondered if they were better off staying in Vietnam. In a September 1, 1966, letter to *Jet* magazine, Robert L. Jackson, a Black marine, referenced the recent riots in his hometown of Chicago: "It appears to me that racial injustice is about to take over the U.S; it's spreading like malignant disease." Racial problems back home were enough to cause Jackson "to wonder if it is safer to stay here and fight or return home and fight a never-ending battle between the races."[159]

In December 1966 John Davidson, a Black infantryman serving with the 173rd Airborne Division, wrote a letter to his mother explaining his decision to extend his tour for an additional six months rather than face reassignment in Augusta, Georgia. He preferred "the crawling terrors of the Bien Hoa jungles" to the prejudice and discrimination he believed he would face in Georgia. He concluded, "I'd like to come home if things were different . . . but in Vietnam, I get along with some of the white guys as well as I do with Negroes. This place means something special to me."[160]

Wayne Smith claimed that Blacks and whites were able to form friendships with one other in large part because they were separated from the toxic racial environment of the United States. He noted that most servicemen had an attitude of "race was like, that's bullshit that happens back in the world." He further elaborated that when "you take people away from their kind of culture . . . and you no longer look at what are the differences between us, but rather you emphasize what we have in common and we've always had far more in common than different," more positive relations naturally develop.[161]

Smith was not alone in arguing that physical distance from the United States contributed to more positive relations. Lamont B. Steptoe discusses the distance African Americans felt from America in his poem "Uncle's South Sea China Blue Nightmare." Steptoe writes,

> In country,
> Afro-Irish-Italian-Jewish-Latino-
> Hispanic-Angelo-Saxon-Asian-Native
> American sing
> in one beer hall voice . . .
> In country
> America is forgotten
> even in the midst of its
> own war
> life is finally understood.[162]

Clearly, Steptoe believes that Vietnam provided the opportunity for comradeship among various racial and ethnic groups, and for the racial animosities that existed in the United States to be forgotten.

Ron Bradley also believed that distance from the racial environment in the United States allowed Black-white friendships to flourish. He recalled, "We became a cohesive group and the prejudices, and the past ideologies were thrown out the window because most of them were proven to be false and they had been perpetrated on a lot of people especially from the South." He credited this shift in outlook to the fact that Vietnam was an environment far removed from the United States, stating, "You know it's like you learn the truth. You learn the reality. You learn that we're all the same. You know that instead of being divided by environment or what state or by ideology." As Bradley saw it, once Blacks and whites left their previous environments, their commitment to past indoctrinations dissolved and they realized that much of what they had been taught to believe about each other was false. He recalled, "For those in the South it was like 'well yes we've been led to believe this about the North and we've been led to believe this about Blacks and we've been led to believe that about whites.' All that went to the wayside."[163]

Clyde Jackson felt that Vietnam provided Blacks and whites with an opportunity to interact with one another that otherwise wouldn't have existed back home. He remembered, "Whether Black or white, I think it was a bridge for a whole lot of them, a bridge as far as communicating with each other and the closeness that they had . . . because there wasn't a lot of communication between Blacks and whites at the time."[164]

Ed Emanuel argued that the "time and place allowed the bond between LURPS and fellow soldiers to transcend the not-so-important barriers like 'race.' The time and Place also gave us a chance to see the true color; green. . . . Vietnam probably helped bridge the gap between the races in the late sixties and early seventies."[165] Samuel Vance recalled a conversation he had with a fellow Black soldier named Gibbs. When Gibbs's mother passed away, he was given a brief leave to travel back to the United States for her funeral. Upon returning, Gibbs told Vance that Vietnam was different because "the black man looks upon that white man as a man, as a friend, as a soldier, but most of all as an American. . . . If only the people back home could feel that way about us, without looking at the color of our skin." To Gibbs the racial situation in America was so bad that upon arriving there, he "wanted to get back to Vietnam."[166] When David Parks was flying home on the plane he wrote, "I'm a Negro and I'm back home where color makes a difference."[167] For these African Americans the fraternal bond they shared with whites in Vietnam was not possible back home.

Conclusion

The friendships Blacks and whites formed with one another in Vietnam were genuine and significant. Socially constructed categories of "Black" and "white" and conceptions of "normal" relations between the two groups became blurred and changed. This shift occurred because African Americans and whites were heavily dependent on one another and because service in Vietnam separated them from the toxic racial environment of the United States. African Americans learned that friendship with whites was possible but also that white racial prejudice could be penetrated, and that socially constructed categories of race were not impervious to change.

Contrary to the opinions expressed by Frank McGee, service in Vietnam did not "eliminate race as a factor in human existence." This was far too rosy a conclusion. Friendships between Blacks and whites were common, but as we will see, so too were incidents of racial prejudice and discrimination. Race remained central to the Black experience.

Race relations were not always amicable. Relations on rear-line military bases were always noticeably frostier than in combat units. By the summer of 1968 these bubbling tensions frequently exploded into violence. In September 1969 L. Howard Bennett observed that there were no "reports of racial conflicts among the combat troops who are under fire in South Vietnam," but violent racial incidents occurred often "among noncombat troops and those in the rear echelon."[168] In October 1969 Commandant of the Marine Corps General Leonard F. Chapman Jr. acknowledged "instances among marines of violence and other unacceptable actions which apparently stem from racial differences." Chapman claimed these incidents were "almost unheard of among marines in combat" but relatively common outside of it.[169] In January 1971 Brigadier General James J. Ursano, deputy chief of staff personnel and administration, reported that "relations between races in the command are generally good. When engaged in performances of duties or in tactical situations, there is little or no tension." However, "in the rear areas, there have been incidents of racial unrest."[170]

Despite these growing tensions, Blacks and whites continued to form close friendships with one another, especially in combat. In late 1969 Wallace Terry reported that there was a significant rise in racial tensions on military bases in Vietnam. However, he also acknowledged that "the black soldier in the bush still helps his comrade and wants his help as well." He mentioned an incident in which a Black medic jumped on a grenade, sacrificing himself to save a white marine. In another incident, eleven white marines held a wounded Black lieutenant above their heads to protect him from napalm smoke until a rescue helicopter could arrive.[171]

Years later, Terry elaborated even further, noting that "part of Martin Luther King's dream came true in Vietnam. In his famous 1963 speech at the Lincoln Memorial he said he had a dream that one day the sons of former slaves and the sons of slave owners would sit at the same table. That dream came true in only one place, the front lines of Vietnam." Terry believed that thousands of Blacks and whites "found their common humanity on the front, where they shared the last drop of water, where they gave their lives for each other."[172]

These friendships sometimes meant new allies in the African American struggle against prejudice and discrimination. In April 1968 Thomas A. Johnson was invited to a "soul session" in Vietnam. When he asked what whites were "doing attending a soul session," others explained to him they were "honorary souls," and the criticisms of racist whites proceeded.[173]

CHAPTER 2

"Brothers as Many Brothers as They Can Find"

Prejudice, Discrimination, and Death in Vietnam

In the 1986 *Frontline* documentary "The Bloods of 'Nam," Wallace Terry acknowledged the importance of Black-white friendships, noting that many servicemen "became brothers against a common enemy. If Vietnam had any redeeming value it was this friendship." However, Terry recognized that these friendships were only part of the racial story. He also characterized Vietnam as "a place of discrimination."[1]

Terry's observation was accurate as African Americans consistently complained of racial discrimination in the armed forces. Black complaints were often eerily similar to complaints of racial discrimination in the United States. Servicemen argued that they were disproportionately assigned menial duties, mirroring frustrations about the lack of economic opportunities available to them back home. They complained that they were not promoted to the levels they deserved—a conclusion supported by the scarcity of Black officers. These grievances suggested that the armed forces did not offer African Americans equality or even fair opportunity for advancement. African Americans also criticized the military justice system, asserting that they were unfairly and disproportionately punished with nonjudicial punishments known as article 15s and more serious punishments that resulted from courts-martial.

Black complaints were justified. There is considerable evidence that African Americans were disproportionately assigned menial duties, denied promotions, and punished more harshly and more frequently than whites. Vietnam was no escape from the racial discrimination prevalent in the United States. Instead, military service paralleled the Black historical experience in civilian life—discrimination and inequality. African Americans increasingly felt mistreated and ignored, evidenced by an anonymous

Black soldier's assertion, "The regular chain of command and the normal grievance system won't work for the Black man in the Army. We fear it and will never trust it."[2]

African Americans complained that they were disproportionately sent to combat units. Dalton James, a Black veteran from Harlem who appeared in the 1968 documentary *No Vietnamese Ever Called Me Nigger*, initially trained to become an air traffic controller—a position he hoped would translate to a civilian job. Despite his training he was given an assignment chauffeuring officers. When he complained, he was sent "to the jungles in Phuoc Binh with the 1st Infantry Division 5th Artillery Group."[3] James's experiences suggested that African Americans had only two options in the armed forces—menial work or dangerous combat duty.

In the early years of the conflict, African Americans were disproportionately drafted and assigned to combat units, leading to a higher number of them being killed. On March 5, 1967, the *Washington Post* cited a recent study by the National Advisory Commission on Selective Service, which found that "under the current military service system, the qualified negro is more apt to be drafted, to be placed in a combat unit, and to meet death in Vietnam than the white man." Furthermore, the commission found that Black participation in the draft was in "several ways inequitable."[4]

As the war continued, Black draft rates increased; however, the percentage of African Americans serving in combat units and who died decreased. Unfortunately, the damage was done and rumors continued to circulate that the military viewed African Americans as expendable fodder for an unpopular war. Some African Americans even believed that the military was purposely sending them to their deaths in Vietnam to achieve the ultimate goal—the reduction and eventual extermination of Blacks in American society.

While there is no evidence that the government or military had a secret plot to exterminate anyone, these rumors demonstrated the level of distrust many African Americans felt toward the armed forces. They came to see military service not as an escape from the racism of American civilian life but as an extension of it. African Americans had physically left the United States, but prejudice and discrimination followed them to Vietnam.

"The Hardest, Dirtiest, and Most Unpleasant Chores"

From the American Revolutionary War until the Korean War, the experiences of African Americans servicemen followed a common pattern. They were excluded from combat by white officers who doubted their competency or feared that arming them would have disastrous domestic repercussions. As a result, African Americans served primarily in menial positions in support of white troops. Blacks were eventually permitted to serve in combat but only in response to protests.[5]

By the time of the Vietnam War African Americans were no longer prohibited from combat, but many felt that whites continued to see them as suitable only for menial work. Company-level officers and noncommissioned officers (NCOs) had wide latitude in determining who was assigned such mundane tasks as digging ditches, filling sandbags, disposing of human waste, and low-level food preparation.[6] African Americans believed they were targeted for these duties and similar ones more frequently than whites.

In February 1966 the *Philadelphia Tribune* reported on the experiences of Georgie Woods, a popular Black Philadelphia disc jockey, who spent two weeks traveling through Vietnam entertaining troops. Woods remarked, "I talked to hundreds of Negroes in Vietnam and some of them bluntly told me they are constantly given the hardest, dirtiest, and most unpleasant chores."[7] In December 1968 State Senator Charles Chew, a Democrat from Illinois, described letters he received "from our black fighting men who have made some terrible charges of racism in Vietnam," including "that menial tasks are assigned only to black soldiers."[8]

Complaints of this sort continued for the duration of the conflict. In June 1970 L. Howard Bennett noted that Blacks often protested the lack of "fairness in selection for duty detail."[9] In December 1971 *Jet* discussed the findings of Bennett's successor Frank W. Render II, who revealed that one of the primary complaints voiced by Black troops was that they were always "given the menial tasks."[10]

David Parks, who served with the 9th Infantry Division in 1966–67, consistently complained in his diary that African Americans were unfairly targeted for the least desirable jobs.[11] On January 13, 1967, Parks wrote, "One Sergeant, Paulson was his name, had me put on the shit detail (latrine duty) . . . no FDCs [Fire Direction Control] are supposed to pull that detail, but I got it nevertheless." On February 2, 1967, Parks wrote, "Paulson is a real ass. He's always telling me that Negroes are lazy and won't help themselves.... I tell him he's full of shit and end up filling sandbags." Parks was not the only one targeted by Paulson. Parks lamented, "Pratt and Gurney are pretty bright souls. But every time you see them they are pulling a shit detail while the white cats lie in their bunks enjoying life."[12]

As a member of a fleet marine force, Anthony Martin spent a lot of time on ships along the Cua Viet River. He recalled, "Aboard the ship, African Americans did more KP [Kitchen Patrol]. I peeled more potatoes than any white boy on that ship. And you know my floors and, particularly on the USS *Ogden* they used to have me a cleaner on the ship.... I learned how to iron clothes very well."[13]

Clyde Jackson agreed with Martin's assessment, remembering, "As far as KP and stuff like that a lot of Blacks had those jobs.... Most of the time Blacks were doing KP."[14] Ron Sawyer, of Mount Vernon, New York, served from January 1968 to February 1969 with the 380th Strategic Air Command. He recalled, "I was constantly ordered to do menial details even though there were men of lesser rate standing about."[15]

James Gillam noted that whenever it was time to burn feces, "they come to get the brothers because the brothers have no rank. They do a lot of the dirty jobs."[16] Gillam's explanation was perceptive and accurate. Most African Americans were draftees or volunteers of low rank, which increased their chances of being assigned "dirty jobs." However, Parks's and Sawyer's experiences suggest that white officers targeted Blacks for duties even when their rank was supposed to exempt them.

Many African Americans took for granted that they would be forced to do the worst jobs. As one unnamed African American stated, "What do they do when I come out of the field? They say shine your shoes and burn the shit."[17] David Addlestone, an attorney with the Lawyers Military Defense Committee (LMDC), remembered that Blacks frequently complained of being placed on "shit burning detail" once they returned from the field.[18]

In 1969–70 Vietnam experienced a steep increase in incidents of racial violence, a topic addressed in the next chapter. In October 1969 Infantry Commander Major General Orwin C. Talbott initiated the creation of a five-man Race Relations Coordinating Group in response to increases in racial tension in the 197th Infantry Brigade. The group's primary task was to organize and monitor race relations seminars where soldiers could express their concerns. The seminars occurred stateside, but the brigade was made up of six thousand soldiers who had served in Vietnam, two thousand of whom were Black. One of the most frequently voiced complaints from African Americans was that "white NCOs always put black soldiers on the dirtiest details."[19]

In September 1971 military officials in Da Nang interviewed African Americans who complained "that they were being discriminated against when extra duty was assigned." Upon investigating, they discovered that a company commander, when asked to choose fourteen men for additional duties, chose ten African Americans. Officials did not say whether they believed the commander was prejudiced, but they were critical of his decision-making, noting, "This was not a very good procedure and could lead to misunderstandings." They recommended that the company commander choose men randomly from duty rosters when determining assignments.[20]

In 1970 Major General Michael P. Ryan ordered battalion commanders in the 2nd Marine Division at Camp Lejeune in North Carolina to conduct "leadership discussions" where Black marines, most of them Vietnam veterans, were encouraged to express complaints or concerns involving racial matters. The sessions, which probably involved hundreds if not thousands of African American marines, found that "the Black marine is especially sensitive to any indications that menial tasks are given mostly to him while most whites are spared the 'dirty' tasks."[21]

In June 1970 *Armed Forces Management*, a military journal, found that Black servicemen overwhelmingly believed that they were "singled out for hard labor details while whites get the 'soft' ones." One anonymous African American alleged that "the best assignments go to whites because they control the personnel system." There was truth to this allegation as a marine general had recently found an all-Black detail working outside of his headquarters. To the general's credit, "the white NCO-in-charge was quickly informed that the appearance of discrimination is just as bad as evidence of it and some whites were immediately exchanged for blacks to achieve a balanced scene."[22] While the general's intervention demonstrates that some commanders were concerned about accusations of discrimination, it is worth remembering that he was responding to another commander's decision to assign only Blacks to a work detail. Other units were likely not led by generals with the same commitment to fairness and equality.

The disproportionate assigning of menial duties resonated strongly with many African Americans because it coincided with their historical experiences in the armed forces and back home. African Americans had fewer opportunities and historically were restricted to unskilled jobs. They were also less likely to "control the personnel system," resulting in less influence over who received what assignment. African Americans understandably felt as though they were placed in an inferior position and were meant to stay there.

"When Promotions Come Along Whites Get Promoted"

There were very few Black commissioned officers in Vietnam. African Americans represented only 2 percent of the officer corps, and the low percentage was not lost on the media or servicemen themselves.[23] In 1966 Georgie Woods reported seeing "less than five Negro officers all the time I was there . . . and most of them seemed to be highly specialized, either doctors or chaplains. I don't recall meeting any Negro officers who actually were involved in setting policy or making assignments."[24] In May 1967 *Time* magazine reported that of the 380 combat-battalion commands in Vietnam, only 2 were headed by Black officers. In one case a Black colonel was promoted to a desk job that had not existed previously "simply to keep him from being assigned to a line command."[25] African Americans had plenty of evidence that whites continued to view them as unsuitable for leadership positions in combat.

In August 1968 *Ebony* complained that of the "400,000 officers in the military, only 8,325 are Negro," representing about 2 percent of all officers. Most of these officers, 5,471, were in the army, but even there they represented only 3.4 percent. In the air force there were 2,417 Black officers out of a total of 77,997, or 3.1 percent. The percentage was even lower in the Marine Corps where there were only 167 Black officers out of a total of 27,000, a mere 0.6 percent. In the navy there were only 330 Black officers out of 52,300, representing roughly 0.6 percent.[26] Not much had changed by 1971, as *Jet* reported that Blacks made up only 3.4 percent of officers in the army, 1.8 percent in the air force, 0.7 percent in the marines, and 0.3 percent in the navy.[27]

The scarcity of Black officers was only part of the story. Black officers often were not encouraged or promoted to the degree they deserved. Sinclair Swan believed there was blatant prejudice in the ways promotions were awarded. There was no effort to encourage Black officers or to create equal opportunities for them. He believed this disinterest or even opposition to seeing African Americans advance explained why he was not given a company command with the 101st Airborne.[28]

Louis Perkins, who served with the 5th Infantry Division in 1966–67 and again as an advisor to the Army of the Republic of Vietnam (ARVN) in 1968–69, asserted that Black officers definitely "didn't get the command spots" they deserved. He pointed out that when African Americans were promoted, they received command spots in service headquarters rather than in combat.[29]

One of the reasons so few African Americans were promoted was that they were more likely to receive poor evaluations from their superiors, who were almost universally white. A 1972 report presented to the Department of Defense (DOD) revealed that between 1956 and 1972 African Americans were consistently rated ten points lower on their Officer Efficiency Reports (OER) than whites. Remarkably, African Americans received on average the same OER ratings in the late 1950s that they did in the early 1970s.[30] This report demonstrates that there was validity to Swan's and Perkins's claims.

Ron Copes felt that "an African American had to do more than a white officer to get the same amount of credit."[31] Willie Thomas saw the scarcity of Black officers as the result of Blacks not having full access to places like West Point.[32] In 1968 there were only 17 Black cadets at West Point. Combined there were only 98 African Americans at Annapolis Naval Academy, West Point, and the Air Force Academy. Between 1969 and 1972 only 105 Black cadets out of a total of 18,887 graduated from these three institutions.[33]

If Black officers were unlikely to be promoted or receive command positions, enlisted men had similar complaints. Robert Louis Jr., who served in 1966–67 with the 25th Infantry Division, believed that Blacks were always assessed with the expectation that they would not or could not succeed. As a result, there was little interest in promoting them.[34]

In February 1969 Roman Metcalf, a Chicagoan serving with the 3rd Marine Division, complained that even after he was appointed squad leader, he was not promoted. This lack of promotion was all the more alarming as he had the "duties of a higher ranking officer."[35] Richard Devore, a Black airman at Bien Hoa Air Base in 1969, claimed that he knew Black NCOs who were in the service for "14–16 years and have not been promoted from grade E5 to E6."[36]

The *Black Journal* television program interviewed Dave, a high-ranking Black enlisted man, who spoke in detail about the lack of promotions afforded to African Americans. He lamented, "I've been in the service 22 years and I feel that if I were a Caucasian, that I would be a Sergeant-Major right now.... I definitely feel that I have been held back because of the fact that I'm Black." Over the course of his career, Dave received everchanging explanations for why he was not promoted. He was told he was not promoted because his white peer was a little bit older than he was even though Dave felt like "he couldn't do the job as well as I could do the job." Other times, he was told he did not have the rank or seniority for a position, but once he did qualify, they would transfer him and give the promotion to a white candidate. A friend of Dave's who was in the military for the same length of time observed, "Everybody else is advancing.... The white GIs were just getting promoted with less qualification than I had."[37]

Part of the problem was that it was easy for those in charge to come up with reasons not to promote African Americans that were not explicitly racial. Dave noted, "Sometimes they hide things in your records when you go before a promotion board... little things that you can never prove that's really prejudicial." It was not always clear who was responsible for African Americans missing out on promotions. Dave believed that "it's not the big brass that's holding you back, it's the little subtle things that are done in a command that you're assigned to that the big brass is not even aware of."[38]

Remarkably, while *Black Journal* was given permission to travel throughout Vietnam and interview essentially anyone willing to talk to them, the Pentagon set up a few interviews for them with Black servicemen, including those with Dave and his friend. Kent Garrett, who conducted all the interviews for *Black Journal* in Vietnam and Okinawa, understood that the Pentagon was arranging these interviews to influence how racial issues would be depicted. In most cases, this strategy worked, as the interviewees chosen by the Pentagon provided a vague or uncontroversial depiction of race relations in the armed forces.[39] In contrast, Dave and his friend spoke candidly about the challenges they faced as Black officers who were consistently denied promotions. Their willingness to speak critically not only showed considerable bravery on their part but also suggested that these types of complaints were common and widespread. If even the career military officers handpicked by the Pentagon to speak favorably of the military had these complaints, how could anyone truthfully deny they existed?

Official military records reveal that those in command positions were aware of Black complaints regarding this issue. Seminars organized by Major General Orwin C. Talbott in October 1969 revealed that African

Americans often questioned, "When are whites going to give the blacks equality on the duty roster and in promotions?"[40]

During L. Howard Bennett's trip to Vietnam in November 1969, investigators routinely encountered African Americans dissatisfied with their lack of advancement. African Americans in the 145th Aviation Battalion complained about the "difficulty in attaining lower enlisted-grade promotions."[41] African Americans in the USARV in Long Binh "perceived that Caucasians were moved up faster, and that black troops spent a longer than average time in grade." An investigation into the 12th Tactical Fighter Wing stationed at Cam Ranh Bay revealed that "promotional opportunities were believed to be slower for blacks," and that "black personnel train Caucasians on how to perform a job correctly; when promotions come along whites get promoted, but black trainers left back." A Black E-4 was given tasks appropriate for an E-6 but "was told when promotions come up that he is not eligible for promotion to E-5." Others complained that they were "assigned the worst jobs (e.g., walking the flight line in sand and dust when jets are operating)."[42]

Bennett's investigation discovered that African Americans with the MACV in Saigon "are losing confidence in the system—-they believe complaint and grievance systems are brought with subtle and overt, real and imagined threats of retribution; promotions are slow, assignments are inferior." Black members of the Navy Support Activity in Saigon also complained that there is "perceived to be an intangible core of prejudice in promotions and assignments."[43]

On December 6, 1969, Bennett wrote to Commander in Chief, Pacific Command Admiral John S. McCain informing him that African Americans "complained that they are discriminated against in promotions . . . that they will stay in grade too long, that they will train and teach whites who come in and pretty soon their trainees pass them by and get the promotion." Others complained that "they will work in grades higher than that which they occupy," and that even when they do an excellent job they aren't promoted. Unfortunately, there is no record of McCain's response to Bennett's letter.[44]

Black complaints regarding promotions continued. In September 1970 army surveillance revealed that African Americans at Camp McDermott in Nha Trang felt that "promotion opportunities" were unavailable to them.[45] During a November 1970 Race Relations Conference at Fort Monroe, Virginia, attendees learned that African Americans overwhelmingly believed "whites are promoted faster than Negroes."[46]

In late 1969 the armed forces under Bennett's guidance began to experiment with Human Relations Councils, which were designed to determine the root causes of racial tension in the military. Bennett hoped that these councils would provide African American servicemen with the opportunity to express their complaints and have them addressed in an open forum. Official documents concerning these councils provide a window into the issues about which African American servicemen were concerned. On September 3, 1971, a Human Relations Council report revealed that African Americans at Camp Baxter in Da Nang "continue to believe that they are treated unfairly in matters of promotions."[47]

During a November 1971 hearing organized by the Congressional Black Caucus (CBC) witnesses testified that African Americans repeatedly failed to "win key command positions over less qualified whites."[48] After traveling to Vietnam in December 1971, Frank W. Render II stated that one of the most often heard complaints from African Americans was that the "system of promotions is discriminatory."[49] A 1972 Human Relations Council study found that African Americans overwhelmingly believed "whites are promoted faster than blacks."[50]

The situation was no better outside of Vietnam. According to Lorenzo Clark, a Black paratrooper, race relations at Fort Bragg were quite poor when he was stationed there with the 82nd Airborne Division in 1970–71. One of the major points of tension was that African American soldiers, many who had served in Vietnam, were not promoted to the extent they deserved. He recalled a specific incident in which a company clerk position became open, "but rather than the company commanders and those folks interviewing and selecting someone, man, they just grabbed the white guy and gave him a job." When Clark and other African Americans questioned why other, more qualified Black candidates were not interviewed, officials claimed it was because the white soldier had taken some college courses. This wasn't exactly a convincing explanation, as Clark and other Black soldiers had even more college experience than the white soldier. He complained, "When they do stupid, arrogant things like that, I mean that generates animosity within the ranks."[51]

Bennett's investigations determined that African Americans serving with the 7th and 13th Air Force in Udorn Rtafe, Thailand, "alleged that there were two promotion lists on base, one for blacks and one for whites," and that whites were always given preference.[52]

"A Total Lack of Confidence in the System of Military Justice"

Complaints about the disproportionate assignment of menial work and the lack of promotions suggested that the armed forces had a narrow view of Black capabilities. African Americans could complete basic tasks but they were not meant to lead or be rewarded for their service. Black complaints regarding the justice system in Vietnam hinted at other potential roles for African Americans—that of a criminal or prisoner. Throughout the war, African Americans complained with considerable justification that they were disproportionately targeted for punishment or punished more severely for the same infractions. Ron Copes recalled, "One of the things that I did see happen with African American soldiers when it came to discipline . . . they were prone to get the harshest punishment for the same thing whereas a white soldier might get a more lenient punishment for the same crime. . . . It wasn't equal."[53] Wayne Smith also believed that African Americans were more likely to receive tougher punishments for violations than whites.[54]

Ron Sawyer felt that "sentences meted out to blacks" were rarely deserved and that discrimination was common. Sawyer was targeted by a racist white southerner, who accused him of leaving his job ten minutes early, but when "three white airmen signed a statement which said that not only was Sawyer there but that on that particular night had worked overtime," he was released. He understood the situation could have turned out differently: a conviction would have meant a reduction in rank from sergeant to airman basic, the lowest rank; a fine of two hundred dollars; and a thirty-day jail sentence.[55]

L. Howard Bennett's investigations in Vietnam revealed that many African Americans displayed "a total lack of confidence in the system of military justice," viewing anyone connected with the system, including staff judge advocates, company commanders, and reviewing authorities, with suspicion and distrust. Accordingly, "Sentences are viewed in comparison to what 'whitey' got for the same offense, and Blacks perceive that they are getting more and harsher punishments."[56]

Investigators noted that Black members of the 3rd Marine Expeditionary Force in Da Nang had complained that when marines with previously clean records were charged with the same offense, Blacks always received harsher punishments. The Judge Advocate General (JAG) Corps warned that in the 12th Tactical Fighter Wing there was a "growing feeling among the young troops that the system of military justice is not equitable." African Americans with MACV in Saigon believed the justice system "punishes blacks harder and more often than whites." In Long Binh, African Americans in the USARV complained that they were "'busted' for offenses where whites were reprimanded," leading to the belief that "the minute you make rank the (white) Man is looking for a way to take it away."[57] These complaints indicated that even when Blacks were promoted, they faced the prospect of having their rank reduced by a racist justice system.

Complaints regarding inequalities in the justice system continued for the duration of the war. A December 1970 report on race relations revealed that African Americans believed they "are more likely to be charged or to receive stiffer punishment for similar offenses than whites."[58] A September 1971 Human Relations Council report concerning race relations at Camp Baxter revealed that African Americans felt the justice system was unfair and discriminatory toward them.[59] A 1972 Human Relations Council study found African Americans believed they were far "more likely to be charged or to receive stiffer punishment for a similar offense than whites."[60]

Not all punishments came from a quasi-judicial inquiry. Article 15s were nonjudicial, informal punishments assigned at the discretion of unit commanders, who had the authority to assign article 15s for minor violations like having a dirty uniform, but also more serious ones. In July 1972, six or seven commanders in the 23rd Infantry Division reportedly offered "article 15s for possession of heroin" in lieu of a court-martial.[61]

The nature of article 15s meant they could be handed out with little evidence of guilt. The LMDC provided legal advice and representation for hundreds of servicemen in Vietnam between 1970 and 1972. Attorney David Addlestone estimated that "most of the people that sought out our services were African American, probably about 80 percent, everything from the full range of marijuana possession, of being one day late, of murder."[62] The LMDC found that article 15s were used by "commands as a means of punishing men for conduct that did not happen and cannot be proven." Servicemen had the right to decline article 15s, but if they did, they opened themselves up to being court-martialed for the same charge. Fearing even greater punishment in the form of a "court-martial, jail, and a permanent federal criminal record," many servicemen accepted article 15s without complaint.[63]

This did not mean that recipients of such charges were guilty, or that there was enough evidence to convict them. Around one hundred service members sought the legal advice of the LMDC on whether they should accept article 15s. The LMDC advised approximately forty of them to refuse the charges as they were "totally unfounded or could not be proven." In each case, commanders refused to go any further with their investigation once the charge was refused.[64]

Frequently, African Americans were the recipients of article 15 violations. L. Howard Bennett's investigations concluded, "Article 15 . . . continues to be an object of constant complaint. Blacks characterize sentences as highly arbitrary and subjective, often bearing little discernible relationship to the offense committed or the sentences received by others for the same offenses." Recipients were often given only a minute or two to explain themselves, and appeals were seen as a formality, not a legal challenge to be taken seriously. Investigators reported that African Americans felt so alienated by the justice system that they refused to fill out appeals or speak to Staff Judge Advocates about their concerns, deeming these actions a waste of time. Officials believed that some barracks lawyers purposely misled Blacks about their right to file appeals.[65]

Other evidence supported the conclusions reached by Bennett's investigation. In September 1970 Army Counterintelligence observed meetings involving seventy-five to one hundred, mostly Black, soldiers at Camp McDermott in Nha Trang. During these meetings, the men complained of being discriminated against through the assignment of article 15s.[66] A December 1970 report on race relations in the military concurred with this assessment, noting, "Military justice is a source of friction. Article 15 is greatest area of concern, especially when the commander administers this punishment in writing and not orally."[67] This report demonstrates that there were officers dispensing punishments without first discussing the facts with the individuals being punished, contrary to military policy.

Frank W. Render II reported that "an overwhelming number of Blacks were being processed through the system of military justice through the use of Article 15."[68] In April 1972, Human Relations Council officer Lieutenant Roland Day received a complaint about Michael Hayes, a Black soldier with the 56th Transportation Company in Long Thanh. Hayes accused his former commander Major Robert E. Short of giving him six article 15 punishments in a three-week period to damage his military record just as his tour of duty ended.[69]

Hayes's complaints were valid. The LMDC reported that African Americans regularly "found themselves confronted with charges consisting of numerous petty specifications (often saved up by a commander for the right time)." Blacks were more likely to receive article 15s for things like uniform violations than whites. Receiving an article 15 was not insignificant as violations had the potential of adding up to more serious charges. The LMDC highlighted the case of one Black GI who was charged with seventeen petty offenses and placed in pretrial confinement. He was later convicted on a single charge of having a dirty rifle.[70]

A November 1972 Defense Department study found that African Americans received 25.5 percent of nonjudicial punishments, far higher than their percentage of the military population. They were twice as likely as whites to be punished for such "confrontation or status-type offenses" as disrespect or inappropriate gestures.[71] Blacks stationed outside of Vietnam also complained that they were unfairly targeted with article 15s.[72]

African Americans argued they were more likely to be punished through courts-martial. Seminars organized by Major General Orwin C. Talbott in October 1969 revealed that African Americans frequently questioned "why more blacks than whites get court-martialed?"[73] In September 1970 Black soldiers at Camp McDermott in Nha Trang protested the unfair use of courts-martial against them.[74] In December 1970 State Senator Charles Chew received numerous letters from African Americans in Vietnam who "have been court-martialed for fighting while white soldiers were freed."[75] The perception that African Americans were more likely to receive courts-martial is backed up by available statistics. A 1972 study by the DOD found that of the 1,471 servicemen who received courts-martial, 34.3 percent were African American, a number more than three times their percentage of the military population.[76]

Frank W. Render II acknowledged that African Americans were targeted for "special and general courts-martial which, in many cases, lead to less than honorable discharges."[77] Statistics support his observations. In 1970 African Americans received 18.4 percent of less-than-honorable discharges in the army.[78] A 1970 investigation conducted by the CBC found that while African Americans made up only 11.7 percent of air force membership, they received 28.9 percent of less-than-honorable discharges.[79] In October 1971 *Jet* revealed that of the 105,888 servicemen who received less-than-honorable discharges between May 1970 and May 1971, 40 percent were African American.[80]

In 1971 a DOD taskforce found that "less than fully honorable discharges were disproportionately given to Blacks when compared to whites of similar educational levels and aptitude."[81] David Addlestone observed that African Americans "received less than honorable discharges for every reason disproportionately to their numbers in the military."[82]

Less-than-honorable discharges could potentially disqualify the recipient from receiving veteran benefits, unemployment insurance, and welfare. In addition, a negative discharge made it difficult for returning veterans to find employment, pushing them even further toward the fringes of civilian society.[83] African Americans were aware of the consequences of receiving these discharges. Bobby Jenkins accurately described the dilemma faced by African Americans, noting that while the treatment they received made them want to rebel, "you can't cause every brother knows the BCD [bad-conduct discharge], dishonorable discharge right, they give it to you in a minute. If you get it, you know it's going to be hard when you get back." Jenkins understood that white officers were aware of the damage these discharges could cause and held the threat of a negative discharge over the heads of African Americans to keep them in line.[84]

Undesirable, bad-conduct, and dishonorable discharges were the three forms of less-than-honorable discharge. Undesirable discharges were used to remove drug addicts, homosexuals, radicals, militants, and those assessed as disruptive. Servicemen typically requested undesirable discharges, but Bennett's investigations revealed that commanders sometimes forced them to accept these discharges against their will.[85] The LMDC pointed out that many African Americans "having little faith in what appeared to be a lily-white system of justice would accept an undesirable discharge" if it meant getting out of jail and avoiding more serious charges that could come from a court-martial. Overworked JAG lawyers sometimes advised clients to request undesirable discharges.[86] This largely explains why in 1970, African Americans represented 18.6 percent of undesirable discharges in the army and the marines.[87]

Bad-conduct discharges were reserved for servicemen who had committed multiple minor infractions, a felony, or a serious breach of the military code of conduct. In 1970 African Americans received 15.5 percent of bad-conduct discharges in the army and 19.2 percent in the marines. Dishonorable discharges were much rarer as they were reserved for those who had committed serious crimes including murder. Like bad-conduct discharges, dishonorable discharges could only be given after courts-martial. In 1970 African Americans received 24 percent of dishonorable discharges in the army and 28.8 percent in the Marine Corps. They received 16.7 percent of dishonorable discharges in the navy while making up only 8.1 percent of all personnel.[88]

David Addlestone found that there were discrepancies even in the way serious crimes were prosecuted in Vietnam. At Camp Eagle near Hue, a white NCO in the 101st Airborne Unit discovered "a bunch of draftees... sitting in a bunker on guard duty and smoking marijuana." The NCO threw a claymore mine into the bunker killing the men. He was acquitted of murder, leading JAG lawyers to conclude that there was a "mere pothead rule"—the lives of servicemen who used drugs were of little worth.[89] While this case did not involve race, it did demonstrate that the justice system did not value the lives of every service member equally.

There was often great hypocrisy in the way the justice system treated whites and African Americans accused of committing serious crimes. David Addlestone remembered a case from 1971 in which a white soldier shot and killed a Black soldier who was a member of a group attacking him. The white soldier was acquitted of all charges.[90]

In contrast the LMDC defended Gerald McLemore, a Black soldier accused of killing a white soldier. The details of the case reveal a clear double standard. On September 25, 1970, after weeks of racial tension in Chu Lai, there was a fight at an enlisted men's club. McLemore, who was not involved in the fight and was the only African American in his hooch, noticed white soldiers gathering outside his window. He heard the men state, "there's a nigger in there," as well as the sound of a grenade pin scratching at the window. McLemore grabbed his gun and exited his hooch, immediately encountering a white soldier holding what looked like a grenade under his window. When the white soldier moved close enough to touch McLemore, the gun went off, killing the white soldier instantly and setting off what turned out to be a smoke grenade.[91]

McLemore was convicted of voluntary manslaughter. The white soldiers were acquitted of all charges.[92] Addlestone felt strongly that McLemore was defending himself and not guilty of any crime. He was deeply dismayed by the verdict, but when he visited McLemore in the stockade, he "took it in stride and said, 'What do you expect I'm Black?'"[93] As McLemore's words make clear, African Americans were hardly surprised when the justice system discriminated against them.

Accusations that the justice system was discriminatory were made by African Americans stationed outside of Vietnam as well. In September 1969 John Barnes, a Black soldier at Oakdale Army Camp near Pittsburgh, complained that authorities used "double standards" when punishing soldiers. Accused of missing work, Barnes was given the choice of accepting a demotion or facing court-martial. He claimed he was on sick leave during the day in question and that the military was trying to get rid of him. Robert Curry, a Black Vietnam veteran, echoed Barnes's complaints:

"There was definitely a 'double standard in existence at the camp as far as the black and white men were concerned.'"[94]

In November 1970 Thomas A. Johnson revealed that Black servicemen in Germany frequently complained about "the dispensation of military justice." A Pentagon investigation found that African Americans received 25 percent of all battalion punishments. Equally troubling, they were more likely to "receive special discharges allowing them to leave the service under other than honorable conditions and without normal veterans benefits." Johnson interviewed a white company commander at Fulda who admitted "he got rid of problem soldiers by convincing them to leave under provisions of the Army regulation providing for such special discharges." A white senior officer confirmed, "You're goddamn right they get them out! We're running an Army, not a permissive society high school."[95] In 1971 the National Association for the Advancement of Colored People (NAACP) found that African Americans in Europe received 45 percent of less-than-honorable discharges.[96] When Thaddeus Garrett, legal assistant to New York Democratic representative Shirley Chisolm, traveled to Greece and Turkey in December 1971, he found that "about 83 percent of courts-martial were slapped on blacks."[97]

Prisons

More likely to be punished, African Americans were consequently more likely to end up in military stockades. For example, on August 28, 1968, Long Binh Jail, the most infamous stockade in Vietnam, included 343 Black and 338 white prisoners.[98] By December 1969, 58 percent of Long Binh prisoners were African American.[99] Greg Payton, a Black prisoner in 1968–69, described the prison population as "ninety percent black, maybe more.... Conditions were horrible.... There were a lot of sadistic kinds of guards there."[100] While Payton was incorrect about the percentage of Black prisoners at Long Binh, they did represent a clear majority.

The situation was similar at other military prisons. In December 1969, 42.4 percent of prisoners at the III Marine Amphibious Force Brig in Da Nang were Black.[101] The LMDC, which worked predominately with soldiers imprisoned at Long Binh and marines imprisoned at Da Nang from 1970 to 1972, found that "stockade populations were consistently 60 percent black with disproportionate numbers of black men in maximum security."[102]

African Americans were overrepresented in military prisons outside of Vietnam as well. In 1971 Thaddeus Garrett traveled to Germany, Greece, and Turkey where he found that "blacks often make up as much as 65 percent of the total prison population." At Manheim Stockade in Germany, 55 percent of prisoners were African American.[103]

Most prisoners in Vietnam were not violent criminals. Many had yet to be tried, let alone convicted, of anything. Instead, they were imprisoned before their cases had reached trial, a process known as pretrial confinement. While one might think that pretrial confinement was reserved for those accused of committing violent crimes, this was not the case. The decision was made entirely at the discretion of the service member's commander. It occurred without a hearing and could only be challenged at trial. Quite often there was no trial, as the accused would resign from the service to get out of jail and avoid court-martial. Thus, commanders were never forced to explain why they sent servicemen to pretrial confinement.[104] USARV regulation 633–1 dictated that servicemen could only be placed in pretrial confinement for a maximum of fifteen days, but this regulation was routinely ignored.[105]

A Department of the Army report from June 24, 1968, revealed that most prisoners at Long Binh Jail were accused of committing nonviolent crimes, which for the most part reflected their dwindling support for the war. The most common crime by far was going AWOL, which four hundred prisoners were accused of committing. An additional ninety-seven were accused of assault or willingly disobeying an officer, ninety-four with failure to obey an order or regulation, eighty-eight with a general article infraction (generally drug possession), and sixty-two with insubordinate conduct toward an NCO. It is difficult to know how many were charged with assault as authorities placed it in the same category as disobeying an officer. Even by the most conservative estimate, 87 percent of prisoners were there on nonviolent charges or had been convicted of nonviolent crimes.[106]

The (mis)use of pretrial confinement largely explains why prison populations grew exponentially from 1966 to 1968. The jail was built to house 400 prisoners, but by August 1968 the number had ballooned to 719. In one month alone, from late May to the end of June 1968, the population grew from 500 to 704. Military authorities were aware that the overreliance on pretrial confinement contributed to the growth of the prison population, and they knew that regulation 633–1 was regularly ignored, and prisoners awaiting trial frequently spent more than fifteen days in jail.[107]

This was especially problematic as servicemen were not given credit on their sentences for the time they spent in pretrial confinement.[108]

A December 1967 USARV review of the prison population revealed major problems with the use of pretrial confinement. Too many prisoners were being held and for far too long. Authorities reported, "There are prisoners in pretrial confinement status who were confined in July 1967," a period of more than six months. In response, the USARV recommended that 145 prisoners be granted clemency immediately, and 84 were released.[109]

On July 8, 1968, the provost marshal sent a note to commanders reminding them that it was against military policy to hold prisoners in pretrial confinement for more than fifteen days. This note was especially relevant as 227 prisoners at Long Binh Jail had been held for more than thirty days. Commanders were encouraged to consider granting clemency to prisoners who had received or faced sentences of six months or less, which would have covered nearly every prisoner. The provost marshal directed Long Binh officials to release 147 prisoners immediately "because further confinement will serve no useful purpose."[110]

Lastly, commanders were told about regulation 27-1, a new directive which established that "only in exceptional cases involving serious offenses should sentences to confinement of first offenders be ordered." The regulation stated that "prisoners serving sentences should be released as soon as it appears that confinement has accomplished the desired corrective and deterrent effect."[111]

A later official army investigation found that most prisoners at Long Binh were good candidates for either a suspended sentence or outright clemency. They were not violent or incapable of reform and should not have been there in the first place. The investigation admitted that the "large percentage of Negroes in confinement in relation to their distribution within society and more particularly the U.S. Army" contributed to racial tensions.[112]

Billy Jones, a Black army psychiatrist attached to the 93rd Evacuation Hospital in Long Binh in 1969–70, observed that most of the prisoners he treated were neither violent nor dangerous. Instead, "The soldiers were there for these minor kinds of things" like drug possession. Jones acknowledged that "the use of drugs was rampant," but the military's strategy of placing suspected drug users in pretrial confinement demonstrated that they "didn't really have a plan of how to deal with it."[113]

Drug use became particularly pronounced in the post-1968 period. A 1969 study revealed that at least 50 percent of servicemen had used marijuana in Vietnam, with roughly 30 percent admitting to "heavy usage." In response, the armed forces cracked down on its usage. But there would soon be greater problems afoot. By 1970 heroin imported from neighboring Burma, Thailand, and Laos became readily available. Sold at two dollars per vial, the drug was inexpensive, odorless, and easy to conceal from authorities.[114] As one of David Addlestone's clients told him, he and his friends preferred heroin because it didn't smell, which meant "you can be at work and smoke heroin as opposed to marijuana."[115]

Addlestone witnessed just how pervasive drug use was in Vietnam firsthand. While riding on a military bus, he witnessed a serviceman lace a cigarette with a substance from a vial. After taking a few puffs from the cigarette, the man "passed it around the bus and almost everybody took a puff of it. I was quite stunned."[116]

Another time, Addlestone's friend who worked in the JAG office decided to collect any empty heroin vials he came across while traveling from his home to the office. Without much effort the man collected over a hundred vials.[117] Susan Osnos, LMDC office manager, recalled that her husband, *Washington Post* correspondent Peter Osnos, once decided to see "how far he had to go from the USO before someone offered to sell him this stuff, and it was nine feet."[118]

By 1971 the American government had taken clear notice of the heroin problem in Vietnam. On May 27, 1971, Congressmen Morgan F. Murphy (D-IL) and Robert H. Steele (R-CT) released a report titled "The World Heroin Problem" to the House of Representatives Committee on Foreign Affairs. The report claimed that "as many as 10 to 15 percent of our servicemen are addicted to heroin."[119] A DOD survey revealed that 10 percent of servicemen used heroin daily, while another 28.5 percent admitted to casual use. Given that many servicemen were likely hesitant to admit to illegal drug use, even in anonymous surveys, the percentage of heroin users was probably even higher than these numbers suggest. Another report from 1971 revealed that among the 450 returning GIs interviewed, 35 percent admitted to using heroin in Vietnam.[120]

High rates of drug use in Vietnam prompted the Nixon administration to launch the "War on Drugs." Beginning in June 1971 the military started requiring servicemen to pass a urinalysis test before being allowed to leave Vietnam. The fact that only 3.6 percent of servicemen tested positive for heroin has led some historians to conclude the drug problem has been overstated.[121] However, servicemen knew exactly when they were going to be tested, they only needed to pass a drug test at the end of their service, and the tests only revealed very recent drug use. Even in 2022 urinalysis testing is only able to detect heroin reliably within forty-eight hours of last use.[122]

Significantly, a 1974 report on drug use from the *American Journal of Public Health* revealed little correlation between servicemen who tested positive for heroin and those who admitted to using it. The report, which focused on veterans who had left Vietnam in 1971, found that of the 470 men interviewed, 23 percent tested positive for narcotics on departure while 43 percent openly admitted to using them.[123] This suggests that many servicemen who would have otherwise tested positive found ways to pass the test.

Commanders increasingly used pretrial confinement as a way of removing suspected drug users from their units. In 1972 alone, hundreds of servicemen suspected of possessing or selling heroin were placed in pretrial confinement. The evidence used to justify sending these servicemen to jail frequently came from illegal searches. Dede Donovan, a lawyer with the LMDC, came into possession of a letter written in 1972 by a battalion commander that declared "war on drug abuse in this Battalion. In the last five days, in a series of seizures I've confiscated 112 vials of heroin. . . . There will be more shakedowns and inspections. . . . Officers and senior NCO's are now authorized to conduct unannounced searches of any man on this compound."[124]

African Americans were the primary victims of these sorts of crackdowns. In general, studies reveal that Blacks were disproportionately placed in pretrial confinement. One study found that 40 percent of African Americans accused of going AWOL were placed in pretrial confinement, while only 15 percent of whites received the same punishment.[125] A 1971 study conducted by the CBC discovered that African Americans represented 50 percent of airmen held in pretrial confinement. A DOD taskforce found that Black detainees were placed in pretrial confinement an average of five days longer than whites. Whites were also twice as likely to be released without any additional disciplinary action.[126]

Billy Jones recalled, "There was that many Blacks in the stockade percentage wise to whites" because authority figures "were more likely to let white soldiers slide then the Black soldiers." When Blacks committed minor infractions, "they got dinged for it. While that would not be the case with the white person. Okay. Now, the truth of the matter is that probably neither one of them should have been dinged for it."[127]

African Americans were targeted in other ways as well. Jones encountered numerous African Americans who were placed in pretrial confinement for wearing Black power paraphernalia, "slave bracelets," or having an Afro.[128] David Addlestone agreed. He observed, "My impression was they [African Americans] were more likely to get pretrial confinement than not. A lot easier in those days to put people in pretrial confinement with no remedy."[129]

The LMDC concluded that commanders were eager to remove anyone they saw as potential troublemakers, and "too often this would mean that a black would be placed in pretrial confinement at the discretion of his commander for the slightest offense—for example the refusal to take a poster off his wall." They noted that while "firm policy was issued by the Defense Department" discouraging the use of pretrial confinement, it was "lost somewhere along the chain of command. Racism manifested itself with discouraging regularity in almost every phase of military life . . . arbitrariness, unfairness, and latent discriminatory practices render the stated policy almost meaningless."[130]

That African Americans were disproportionately placed in pretrial confinement was not lost on Black servicemen. T. Joseph Remcho, a lawyer with the LMDC, remembered a protest in Chu Lai in 1971 involving "seventy to eighty blacks demonstrating before the commanding general's house against what they felt was racial discrimination and improper pretrial confinement of blacks."[131]

"Brothers as Many Brothers as They Can Find"

Many Blacks believed that the military viewed them as servants not meant to advance beyond menial servitude. Yet this perception conflicted with the disproportionate assignment of African Americans to combat divisions and often dangerous field assignments. In earlier wars Blacks had demanded the opportunity to engage in combat against the enemy; now they feared that white officers were purposely increasing their chances of injury or death.

These fears were articulated even in the first years of the war. On March 26, 1966, the *Philadelphia Tribune* revealed that unidentified congressmen had "filed inquiries for their constituents based on rumors that Negroes were being given a disproportionate share of dangerous assignments."[132]

On May 28, 1966, the *Pittsburgh Courier* reported that the Joint Chiefs of Staff had received numerous complaints that Blacks were assigned "in disproportionate numbers to the most dangerous areas in Vietnam."[133]

In a letter to his mother, Roman Metcalf stated that Blacks were placed "in the field at all times.... We're always the first through to get the dangerous assignments." Equally troubling, his superiors seemed committed to ensuring that he stayed in combat. Metcalf alleged that he was denied R&R in favor of whites even though he "outranked them and have been over here longer."[134]

Metcalf was not the only one to voice these types of complaints. In November 1970, fifty to sixty Black soldiers in the 23rd Infantry Division protested on the Chu Lai Base. Among their complaints was the allegation that "blacks with noncombat MOS's [military occupational specialty] are put in the field where whites with combat MOS's are placed in noncombat MOS's."[135]

In November 1970 the Department of the Army Race Relations Conference was held at the Continental Army Command, Fort Monroe, Virginia. Members from all major army commands as well as representatives from other services were in attendance. Lieutenant Joseph Anderson, who had recently returned from a fact-finding trip to Vietnam, revealed that African Americans frequently claimed they were "harassed, placed on details, and given undesirable guard posts more frequently than whites."[136] A 1971 CBC hearing revealed that Blacks regularly complained that they "get the most dangerous combat jobs in Viet Nam if they show signs of black militancy."[137]

African Americans were very specific about the jobs they believed whites were assigning to them. David Parks claimed that Blacks were disproportionately given the job of forward observer (FO), which he jokingly claimed stood for "Fucked Over." FOs carried a visible phone with an antenna, making them an easy target. With only three FOs to cover sixteen squads they were constantly on duty, which increased their chances of being injured or killed. Parks suspected that his selection as FO was no accident. On January 31, 1967, his diary read, "Sgt. Paulson hand-picks the men for this job. So far he's fingered only Negroes and Puerto Ricans. I think he's trying to tell us something." Parks's suspicions were predictive. On February 9, 1967, he wrote, "Just got kicked out of my beautiful . . . job. The good Sgt. Paulson strikes again. He gave me the news with a smile, I am now Forward Observer Parks. . . . It's a Sergeant's job, but Paulson's not going to promote me."[138]

Lamont B. Steptoe dropped out of Officer Candidate School (OCS) two weeks before being commissioned, and his company commander responded by demoting him to E-2 and making him a scout dog handler, an extremely dangerous position. He recalled, "Now the mission of the scout dog is to walk point element for combat patrols in Vietnam. So I felt like they were trying to kill me." Steptoe's commander might have given this assignment as punishment for dropping out of OCS, but Steptoe believed his race played a role in the decision.[139]

African Americans frequently alleged they were disproportionately assigned as point man, a particularly dangerous job because it was at the head of the platoon and usually the first to be shot at during an attack. Ron Copes believed that "a lot of African Americans were on point, on night patrols, and things of that nature."[140] Roosevelt Gore recalled, "I was always the point man, maybe because I was black."[141] Arthur Barham, who served with the 173rd Airborne Division in 1967–68, noted, "Chances were whoever was going to be on point was going to be Black, whoever was on the flank was going to be Black."[142]

In August 1967 the *Christian Science Monitor* reported that African Americans disproportionately found themselves in a "position of consummate danger—point man on the leading patrol creeping warily into enemy ground."[143] In May 1968 *Newsday* quoted James Barnes, a Black marine, who observed, "When you're on patrol and moving into an area, it's always the Negro who's walking point. That means he's the first to get it if a mine explodes. . . . That's the kind of assignment we get from the whites. . . . Look at the guys who go out on sweeps, who protect hills. Brothers, as many brothers as they can find."[144]

Robert Louis Jr. believed that African Americans were picked for dangerous duties like machine gunner or point man because they were considered strong and capable.[145] However, most agreed with Barnes that they were chosen for these positions because they were viewed as expendable.

African Americans in other branches of the armed forces likewise believed Blacks were disproportionately assigned to point man. Brian Settles, who served in 1968–69 as a navigator pilot with the 390th Fighter Squadron, recalled that even among Black pilots and grounds crews, "it was widely felt that a lot of times the Black GIs were being sent to point or . . . more dangerous positions than their white counterparts."[146]

In a November 19, 1971, *Time* magazine article, Wallace Terry reported that "the cost of being too militant was to be sent to serve as a point man on the Demilitarized Zone." Terry believed that there were officers who intentionally assigned African Americans whom they deemed troublemakers or militants to serve as point men as a means of punishing them.[147]

The belief that African Americans were targeted for dangerous duties extended beyond traditional infantry units in the army or marines. Kent Garrett interviewed Black navy patrolmen whose job included frequent patrol runs along the upper Saigon River. These men claimed that African Americans were disproportionately assigned to night patrols, which were far more dangerous than daytime patrols as they were required to set up ambushes for enemy boats. Garrett recalled that "the guys felt that they had been unfairly assigned too many of those. It hadn't been distributed equally among the various boats and troops."[148]

Complaints over the disproportionate assignment of dangerous jobs to African Americans suggested there was another place for them in the military outside of menial work or prison—the front lines—where they could serve and possibly die for a country that did not value them as equal citizens or provide them with equal rights. There is insufficient statistical evidence, however, to substantiate that Blacks were more likely to be assigned these positions. Historian James E. Westheider has noted that it wouldn't have made any "sense to let someone lead who was not good at it, or did not want to be there, because it would endanger the individual and the entire unit."[149]

Westheider's point is valid in theory, but Vietnam was not a perfectly executed war, and servicemen were routinely asked to do things they had no interest in doing or were not particularly good at doing. After all, the war relied on draftees, many of whom did not want to be there at all. Stanley Goff recalled that his friend Carl, who was Black, was ordered to carry an M-60 gun that weighed 25 pounds, even though he himself only weighed 130 pounds. Carl was not given this job because he was competent—he struggled to carry it and was a lousy shot—but because of shortages in the company.[150]

It is possible that incompetent or irresponsible officers targeted Blacks for more dangerous duties. Edward Gillam was put on point duty with the 3rd Marine Division while suffering from malaria and dysentery. A river current swept him away, and he was found a week later in the jungle delirious and unarmed. Designating him point man was a poor decision lacking in sound strategy or common sense, but his superiors did it anyway.[151] Some officers acted inconsistently, irresponsibly, and dangerously, but that does not prove they were racially motivated. However, even if only capable and willing African Americans were targeted, if officers chose them over equally qualified whites because they were viewed as more expendable, such actions would be prejudicial.

African Americans and the Draft

Allegations that Blacks were unfairly assigned dangerous duties related to larger complaints that they were disproportionately drafted. The percentage of Black draftees increased over time. In 1966 African Americans represented 13.4 percent of all draftees.[152] In 1967 they represented 16.3 percent.[153] By 1970 the percentage of African American draftees had risen to 17.3 percent.[154] Between 1965 and 1970, which was the height of American military involvement in Vietnam, Blacks represented 14.3 percent of draftees.[155]

Significantly, a 1967 study conducted by Congressman Robert Kastenmeier, a Democrat from Wisconsin, found that while only 29 percent of African American candidates for the draft were deemed acceptable, 64 percent of this number were drafted. By contrast, 63 percent of white candidates were deemed acceptable but only 31 percent were drafted. Eligible African Americans were drafted at twice the rate of eligible whites.[156] This imbalance was more apparent in certain localities. In New Haven, Connecticut, African Americans made up 4.2 percent of the population but 9 percent of all draftees. In Shreveport, Louisiana, a city with a much larger Black population, they comprised 32.7 percent of the population but 41.3 percent of all draftees.[157]

There were fewer avenues of escape for African Americans who wanted to avoid the draft. Freddie Edwards noted that Blacks "didn't have an excuse" to get out of the war like many whites did.[158] They were less likely to receive academic and medical deferments. Many African Americans attended poorly funded segregated high schools, which limited their opportunities to attend college. Many colleges had few, if any, Black students and did not encourage African Americans to attend. Lastly, most Black families could not afford college. Collectively, this helps explain why only 5 percent of African Americans attended college during the war.[159]

In 1966, the only year in which this data was recorded, white inductees were 50 percent more likely to fail their preinduction physicals than Blacks.[160] Even obvious health problems did not necessarily earn African Americans medical deferments. Susan Osnos recalled a particularly troubling incident in which a young African American serviceman of "cannon fodder rank" came into the LMDC office looking for legal advice. While filling out forms, the man fell to the ground and had a grand mal seizure. When he came to, Osnos "asked him whether that had ever happened to him before. I thought maybe it was the first time." She was shocked to learn that he had been having seizures since he was a child. When Osnos asked him if he had told the military about his condition when he was drafted, the man responded, "Yeah, but they didn't care."[161]

Local draft boards granted conscientious objector (CO) status or hardship deferments, and they further contributed to the disproportionate drafting of African Americans. The more than four thousand local draft boards were in no way representative of the communities they served. In 1966 there was not a single Black draft board member in Alabama, Arkansas, Georgia, Louisiana, Mississippi, or South Carolina, despite each state having a large Black population.[162] In Maryland and Virginia African Americans represented only 2.7 and 2.2 percent of draft board members.[163]

Draft boards also showed a willingness to target individual African Americans. A Mississippi draft board rejected the CO application of Bennie Tucker, a Black civil rights worker, because he "caused nothing but trouble." When Tucker was later elected to city council, he immediately received four induction orders. Robert James was initially granted CO status but his exemption was revoked when the Mississippi draft board became aware of his civil rights work. After Jeanette Crawford, a civil rights leader from New Orleans, refused to testify before the Louisiana House Committee on Un-American Activities, her three sons received draft notices the following week. The draft board claimed that her oldest son had not registered for the draft even though he had been in the army for thirteen years and was stationed in Germany.[164] In 1966 civil rights leader and Georgia state representative Julian Bond's antiwar position gained the attention of the chairman of the Atlanta draft board, who referred to Bond as "this nigger" and expressed regret that the board was unable to draft him.[165]

Even African Americans who failed to meet the physical or intelligence standards did not necessarily avoid military service. Project 100,000, a program conceived and implemented by the DOD from 1966 to 1972, was intended as a means by which poor and uneducated Americans could gain marketable skills from military service, which they could later use in civilian life. More than 300,000 males initially deemed unfit were drafted through this program.[166] Of these recruits, 45 percent were African American.[167]

"Brothers as Many Brothers as They Can Find" 71

Historian Geoffrey W. Jensen has challenged the notion that Project 100,000 was a complete failure. He argues it was designed with the altruistic goal of providing job opportunities to men of lower socioeconomic status, including many African Americans, and was not dissimilar to other efforts connected to the War on Poverty.[168]

Jensen is aware that Project 100,000 was never popular. Many in the military viewed it as a "waste of time, resources, and objected to its use of substandard manpower." Others blamed those who entered the military under the program for rising discipline and drug problems. Jensen perceptively argues that men who entered the military through Project 100,000 servicemen were often unfairly maligned and scapegoated.[169]

Prominent African American leaders were even harsher in their criticisms. Congressman Adam Clayton Powell of New York proclaimed that the program was "nothing more than killing off human beings that are not members of the elite." William Booth, chair of the New York City Human Rights Commission, asserted that Project 100,000 was "another attempt to get more negroes into conflict."[170]

Jensen's criticisms of these interpretations are misplaced. Project 100,000 may have been motivated by a paternalistic desire to help disadvantaged African Americans, but this did not happen. It may not have been designed to send disproportionate numbers of African Americans into combat but that was the result.

Despite or because of their lack of qualifications, many of the men who entered the armed forces through Project 100,000 were assigned to combat infantry. In the army 44.5 percent of African Americans who entered the military through this route were sent into combat. In the Marine Corps 58.3 percent were sent into combat.[171] Equally disturbing, 80,000—roughly 20 percent of the men who entered the military through Project 100,000—received undesirable, bad-conduct, or dishonorable discharges.[172] Many were African American.

Black leaders were correct to criticize the project even if their objections as to its intent weren't always fair or factual. That so many saw the program in negative terms should have given Lyndon Johnson's administration pause. Programs designed to help specific communities or demographic groups must be supported by them to be effective. Project 100,000 was initiated not in response to demands coming from the Black community but from a false belief among white members of the Johnson administration that military service would benefit African Americans. In many cases, African Americans had no choice in the matter as they were drafted. Even if the Johnson administration thought the program would help African Americans, it was "help" they neither asked for nor wanted.

"We Didn't Understand Why We Were Getting More Black Soldiers"

In the early years of the war, African Americans were disproportionately assigned to combat infantry units. In 1965 African Americans made up a shocking 31 percent of all U.S. combat troops, and in certain units the percentage was as high as 70 percent.[173]

On May 26, 1967, *Time* magazine reported that African Americans represented 23 percent of combat troops.[174] In April 1968 Thomas A. Johnson reported that African Americans made up 20 percent of all combat troops. Equally significant, African Americans represented as much as 45 percent of airborne units and as high as 60 percent for airborne rifle platoons.[175]

As Johnson's reporting suggests, individual units often had an even higher percentage of African Americans. In April 1967 *Washington Post* journalist Jesse M. Lewis, upon returning from Vietnam, observed, "There appears to be a higher concentration of Negroes in airborne, infantry, and cavalry units than in artillery. In many of the smaller combat units in Vietnam, like platoons and squads, Negroes seem to make up 60 to 70 percent of the strength."[176] On May 14, 1968, Senator Robert F. Kennedy, a Democrat from New York, told college students in Omaha, Nebraska, "If you look at any regiment or division of paratroopers in Vietnam, 45 percent of them are black."[177] Senator Kennedy was sometimes not far off.

The large number of African Americans in combat did not go unnoticed. In December 1967 the *Cleveland Call and Post* interviewed Black Vietnam veteran David Tuck, who claimed that of the "117 men in his unit 106 were Negro."[178] Ron Bradley observed, "We were disproportionately, number wise, out there in the field as compared to whites."[179] Robert Louis Jr. claimed that his company was 40 percent Black when he first arrived in Vietnam. As replacements entered his company, the percentage only grew. He recalled, "We didn't understand why we were getting more Black soldiers."[180] As Louis's account suggests, it was often painfully obvious that Blacks were overrepresented in combat units. When Scott Riley first arrived in Vietnam, he was placed on a chopper flight to meet with his company in the Central Highlands. During the flight, he recalled, "I looked down and I see what appears to me to be black ants and as we land,

I see that it's all these black guys.... And then I came to realize who was actually fighting this war. Poor people of America."[181]

In early 1968 Thomas A. Johnson spent fourteen weeks interviewing African Americans in Vietnam. One anonymous Black soldier told him, "You take a good look at an airborne rifle company it'll look like there ain't no foreign [white troops] there." Another African American soldier in the 4th Battalion of the 173rd Airborne Brigade stated that when he joined the platoon in the summer of 1967, "there were 20 brothers and 8 foreign troops."[182]

Even African Americans not in traditional marine and army combat units seemed aware of these discrepancies. The *Black Journal* interviewed Hayes, a Black naval patrolman, who commented, "I've seen a bunch of Black guys out there. I mean a whole bunch of them out there. I don't know why they are out there. I can go up there and see about, out of 40 men, half of them are Black. I don't know why the army does that. I don't think it's right. You know. I don't think it's right at all."[183]

The reasons why African Americans were disproportionately assigned to combat units are complex. Assignments were determined through standardized testing in the form of Armed Forces Qualification Tests. Cultural biases exist in any standardized test, but given that as many as 90 percent of African Americans who served in Vietnam came from working-class or poor backgrounds, and that many were educated in segregated schools with fewer resources, most were ill-prepared to take the test and succeed. In 1965, 41 percent of African Americans scored at the lowest levels of the test, while only 10 percent of whites scored as low.[184] In August 1967 the *Christian Science Monitor* reported that the national failure rate for qualifying tests was 67 percent for African Americans and 19 percent for whites. Only 4 percent of Blacks tested in the top two classifications in comparison to 40 percent of whites. When examining the top three classifications, the statistics remained as divergent with only 22 percent of Blacks qualifying in comparison to 74 percent of whites.[185]

In March 1967 the *Washington Post* perceptively observed that the "same educational and social handicaps that bring proportionately more Negroes than whites into service also channel Negroes into combat."[186] Cephus Rhodes similarly noted that the social and political status of African Americans all but guaranteed they would end up as infantrymen.[187] Racial inequality ensured that most African Americans would score worse on the tests than whites, have fewer opportunities, and likely end up in an infantry unit.

A November 1969 report on race relations in the Navy Support Activity in Saigon revealed that many African Americans understood that the methods of testing and training for job assignments purposely excluded them. Blacks were pushed into "unskilled categories like supply, infantry," which were positions with "little opportunity to acquire a marketable skill" but which "increased [the] likelihood of being killed."[188] Scholars have supported this contemporary assessment. Historian Christian Appy notes, "Blacks might have taken advantage of opportunities to fill higher-paying, noncombat positions, had they been offered." In the early years of the war, "even those blacks who scored in the highest test category were placed in combat units at a level 75 percent higher than that of whites in the same category."[189]

Many elite combat units were made up entirely of volunteers. Two of the first combat units sent to Vietnam, the 101st Airborne Division and the 173rd Airborne Brigade, which were 21 and 24 percent African American respectively, were all volunteers.[190] Money was often the primary motivation for joining these elite units. On average volunteers with paratroop units received $55 extra a month, as much as 50 percent more than in regular infantry units.[191]

In May 1968 the *Christian Science Monitor* noted that "many Negroes appear to favor combat arms, particularly such elite units as airborne, Special Forces, and Rangers," because of the "extra pay each month."[192] While serving with the 173rd Airborne Division in Pleiku, Lawrence Harkless explained that African Americans volunteered for elite units like airborne "because of pride and the $55 extra a month."[193] Victor Hall claimed African Americans volunteered for more elite units "for the same reason I did it and for the same reasons most of the Negroes here (Fort Bragg, N.C.) did it. They did it because you get incentive pay in the airborne." Charles Donald, a Black paratrooper, agreed, explaining that he volunteered for jump duty "because of the $55 extra."[194] Lamont B. Steptoe likewise believed that many African Americans volunteered for dangerous assignments or missions for monetary reasons.[195]

Just because many African Americans volunteered to serve in elite units to secure better pay does not mean racial inequality was an insignificant factor in their decision. Because of their race, African Americans had fewer opportunities available to them in the domestic economy and in the military. Had their opportunities been greater, they might have made different decisions. They didn't have these options because they were Black.

The lack of economic opportunities available to African Americans influenced many to join the military. Anthony Martin, who enlisted in the Marine Corps in 1965, spoke for many when he stated, "For a young African American growing up . . . there wasn't a very bright outlook so the military became a venue of escape if you will." He believed that his job options were limited to working with his father at the post office or as a streets and sanitation worker.[196]

Cephus Rhodes joined the military in 1953 largely because he perceived "that the military was better than life in north Florida . . . and the pay was better than school teaching pay," which he believed was his only other potential job prospect.[197] Robert Louis Jr. joined the army after graduating from high school in Petersburg, Virginia, because job opportunities for African Americans were extremely limited in his hometown.[198] James Lewis actually joined the military twice, in 1959 and 1963, each time out of economic necessity. He recalled, "I only had one reasoning to join the military and that was I was dirt poor."[199]

In the early 1960s Horace Coleman attended Bowling Green State University where he was required to join the Reserve Officers' Training Corps (ROTC) for two years. When his two years were finished, he accepted a commission, which sent him to Vietnam. His motivations for doing so were largely economic.[200] Ron Copes was required to complete two years of ROTC training at Lincoln University, but he signed up for four because he wanted the money.[201]

Money also motivated African Americans to reenlist, thus increasing their chances for combat duty and possible death. Those who reenlisted received bonuses of between $900 and $1,400, which in the mid-1960s was approximately one-third of the median family income for Black families.[202] In 1965 the reenlistment rate for African Americans in the army was 49.3 percent, compared to 13.7 percent for whites. In 1966 the rate for African Americans rose to 66.5 percent, while it was 20 percent for whites.[203]

In August 1968 *Ebony* remarked that "in virtually every case, reenlistment is, on the conscious level, a matter of dollars and cents." One anonymous air force reenlistee observed, "That's an awful lot of money to a young black cat who's never had more than $150 at one time in his life." The armed forces recognized the economic motivations behind reenlisting as "the pitch a young man receives upon walking into an Armed Forces recruiting office has nothing to do with patriotism or loyalty. It is, plainly and simply, an economic pitch."[204] Many African Americans were susceptible to this economic pitch because they were poor, and racism limited their opportunities for economic advancement in the United States.

"I Think We're Being Killed Off"

Considering the disproportionate number of African Americans in combat during the early years of the war, it was not surprising that a similarly disproportionate number of Blacks were killed during the same period. By late 1965 nearly 25 percent of all combat deaths were African American.[205] In 1966 African Americans accounted for 16.3 percent of those killed in action.[206] Death rates were even higher in certain divisions. In 1966 African Americans accounted for 26 percent of all combat deaths in the 1st Cavalry Division and 27.8 percent in the 173rd Airborne Brigade.[207]

The significance of these high death rates was not lost on the Black press, the public, or Black service members themselves. On March 19, 1966, the *New York Amsterdam News* reported, "Negroes Dying Faster Than Whites in Vietnam."[208] That same month, the *Philadelphia Tribune* noted the "High Vietnam Negro GI Death Rate."[209] On May 28, 1966, the *Pittsburgh Courier* announced, "Negro Deaths Exceed Whites' in Viet Nam."[210] On March 2, 1967, the *Los Angeles Sentinel* stated that recent DOD statistics had shown conclusively that "the death rate in Vietnam was proportionately higher for Negro than for white U.S. servicemen."[211]

The Pentagon was aware that African Americans were being killed in disproportionate numbers. Their initial official reaction was to praise African Americans for their service. In May 1966 the *Pittsburgh Courier* quoted a Pentagon official who claimed that high death rates were a "measure of Negro valor in combat."[212] Privately, military officials were concerned that high Black death rates sent a message that Black lives were expendable. In response, the Pentagon ordered the armed forces to reduce the assignment of African Americans to combat positions.[213] The results were striking. By 1967 the death rate for African Americans had fallen considerably to 12.7 percent and for 1968 it remained at a similar level of 12.9 percent. By 1970 the death rate had fallen even lower to 8.8 percent.[214] By 1972, the final year of active American participation, only 7.6 percent of deaths were Black. In total, African Americans represented 12.6 percent of those killed in Vietnam.[215]

The overall percentage of African Americans killed during the entire Vietnam War was only slightly disproportional to their percentage of the American population, but this does not make the disproportionate death rates during the first two years of the war insignificant. By 1967 Black death rates had decreased, but it is doubtful this gave much solace to the families of Black servicemen who had already been killed in 1965–66 in widely unequal numbers.

On August 25, 1966, the widow of Lorenzo Maulden, a Black soldier recently killed, wrote a letter to President Lyndon Johnson asserting, "Everyone knows that the majority of the boys that are getting killed in Vietnam are negro boys . . . hardly no white."[216] This claim was incorrect, but her concern that African Americans were dying in disproportionate numbers was valid.

Mrs. Maulden's letter received an official response from the Director of Military Personnel Policy Major General F. W. Norris. In addition to sharing his condolences, he claimed that "casualties among the units in Vietnam are generally proportionate to the number of Negroes." He further stated that the "belief that any one race suffers a disproportionately large percentage of the combat deaths" was not "borne out by the facts."[217] It is hard to know what "facts" Norris was alluding to, but African Americans were being killed in disproportionate numbers when Maulden was killed in July 1966.[218]

Concern that a greater number of African Americans were dying continued even as Black death rates decreased. Many African Americans remained convinced that something sinister was afoot. In the spring of 1968 *Newsday* journalist Paul Hathaway spent more than a month interviewing hundreds of Black servicemen in Vietnam. Hathaway discovered that one of their major concerns was whether "he is being used as cannon fodder."[219]

Throughout the conflict, African Americans believed that they were dying in much greater numbers than whites. James Gillam recalled that he and other Blacks "always would have conversations, you know, damn, all of us were getting killed and none of them."[220] The high number of African Americans being killed in combat made Clyde Jackson question whether they were purposely being used as cannon fodder.[221] Louis Perkins believed that the high percentage of African Americans in combat suggested at the very least that Black lives were seen as disposable.[222] White servicemen also questioned whether military officials valued their lives. Patrick McLaughlin, a white soldier from Cleveland, Ohio, believed that some officers used ordinary soldiers, Black and white, as cannon fodder.[223] However, it is hard to imagine any white serviceman believing that his race made him more likely to be killed in the Vietnam War.

Rumors spread among African Americans that the military or government was using the Vietnam War as an opportunity to get rid of them. These rumors were vague as to who was behind the plot, but they almost always suggested that Black people's removal from the United States was intended to weaken the civil rights movement specifically and to reduce the size of the Black population more generally. Even as African American death rates plunged, the accusation remained pervasive, and many Blacks continued to believe that they were disproportionately being used, sacrificed, or purposely "killed off."

On May 1, 1967, Cleveland Sellers, a prominent member of the Student Non-Violent Coordinating Committee, refused induction into the army under the justification that the military was "trying to draft black people to commit genocide."[224] On October 22, 1967, the New York State NAACP voted to condemn American involvement in the war on the basis that the war "had, at a disproportionate rate, killed off 'black youth' who are potential leaders."[225]

Sellers and the NAACP were hardly the only ones to suggest racist whites were using the war as an opportunity to get rid of African Americans and "solve" domestic pressures. On November 30, 1968, the *Chicago Daily Defender* noted that military elites were well aware that "the phenomenally high death rate of blacks in combat areas means fewer blacks coming back to the ghettos to be dealt with," suggesting at the very least that the military knew of and viewed positively high Black death rates.[226] At worst, the *Defender* suggested that the military was part of a conspiracy to get rid of troublesome Blacks by sending them to Vietnam. In September 1972 *Jet* pointed out that the high percentage of Black casualties in the early years of the war led many African Americans to believe that the "Pentagon and the Defense Dept. were guilty of genocide."[227] The LMDC reported that many "blacks maintained they had been sent as cannon fodder. The more militant charged the United States with deliberate genocide."[228]

In May 1968 *Newsday* interviewed an unnamed Black soldier in Cam Tho who recalled a recent incident in which only Black soldiers were chosen for a night patrol, while the white soldiers were placed on guard. He wondered, "What if this was an ambush? We'd be wiped out and the whites would be safe." *Newsday* interviewed a Black marine in Dong Ha who theorized, "I think we're being killed off."[229]

When speaking of Black death rates, Richard Devore maintained, "I earnestly felt they were trying to exterminate us."[230] Lamont B. Steptoe pointed to the high percentage of African Americans in combat as proof that the military didn't value Black lives as much as whites. He reflected,

"Statistically they were putting us in harm's way as a means of ethnic cleaning. I understood that."[231]

Rumors of this sort were not restricted just to draftees. George Brummell, who entered the army in 1962 and was a sergeant in Vietnam, remembered conversations with other Black soldiers about whether they were purposely being targeted as a means of removing them from the United States. He recalled, "There was always discussion that they put us in the combat arms so that the chances were much greater to be killed or we would be more expendable." Brummell did not believe that it was official armed forces policy to disproportionately send Blacks into combat, but he did feel individuals may have targeted them for combat on their own.[232] Cephus Rhodes likewise did not think the government was seeking to get rid of Blacks by sending them to Vietnam, but even as a major, he was aware of the rumor, suggesting it was widespread among African Americans regardless of rank. The rumor was not restricted to draftees.[233]

Others pointed out that that while the rumors may not have been technically true, the result was the same. The high percentage of African Americans killed during the first years of the war had a destabilizing effect on the Black community. Willie Thomas recalled, "I heard it and I thought it myself.... Look at all these Blacks you got over here dying, it cuts down on the problems back home." Thomas did not believe that the government was actively trying to kill African Americans, but he did think that this was the result.[234] When speaking of these rumors, Nate Mondy, petty officer first class on the USS *Kitty Hawk*, lamented, "I think that they didn't do it by knowing that they were doing it, but if you look at the number of Blacks being incarcerated and the number of Blacks who were killed and the number of children without fathers today, they are directly related to what happened in Vietnam."[235]

Conclusion

African Americans traveled halfway around the world in service to their country, but in some respects it was as if they had never left the United States. American racism followed them to Vietnam, which was clearly "a place of discrimination." Throughout the conflict, African Americans complained that they were disproportionately assigned menial duties and denied deserved promotions. These complaints suggested there was little place for them in the military, outside of lower-echelon positions with little to no chance of advancement. The potential for advancement in the armed forces was not any better for African Americans than it was in the civilian world.

African Americans also charged that the military justice system was rife with prejudice and discrimination. Complaints about the justice system suggested there was another place for African Americans in the military outside of menial jobs—as prisoners in military stockades. There is substantial evidence to confirm that African Americans were assigned to menial jobs, denied promotions, and given harsher punishments in disproportionate numbers. American racism remained alive and well in Vietnam.

Others complained that Blacks were disproportionately given dangerous duties and jobs which proved that the armed forces believed Black lives were expendable. These charges reflected the reality that in the early years of the war African Americans were disproportionately drafted, placed in combat units, and killed. High draft and fatality rates suggested that there was another place for Blacks in the military—in combat, where their chances of being killed were dramatically increased.

African Americans took notice, charging that the government or military was trying to get rid of them to achieve domestic goals. Ron Bradley believed that the government wanted to "minimize the number of Blacks who were educated coming back and becoming a force to be reckoned with ... so they thought they could kill most of us who were high school and college educated, that would slow down if not eliminate the movement."[236] Bradley, and others who agreed with him, believed that the government was using the Vietnam War, the dominant foreign policy issue of the era, as an opportunity to eliminate the civil rights movement, the dominant domestic crusade of the period.

Domestic events loomed large in other ways as well. During the 1965–67 period there were numerous race riots in cities across the United States. American race relations were fractured and quickly deteriorating. In contrast, during this same period there were almost no reported incidents of racial violence in Vietnam, which could suggest there were not any racial issues there. Black complaints of discrimination reveal this was never the case. The image of a military free of racial problems was at best a veneer, and this would soon become obvious. Between the last six months of 1968 and the end of 1971 the American military in Vietnam experienced thousands of incidents of racial violence. The racial rioting and violence that had previously been contained to the streets of major American cities had arrived in Vietnam.

CHAPTER 3

"Tearing the Services Apart"

Racial Violence and the
Other War in Vietnam

At approximately 11:45 pm on August 29, 1968, prisoners in the "A" and "B" sections of the Long Binh Jail, a military stockade in the southeastern RVN, overwhelmed guards and escaped into the exercise yard. Several of these prisoners entered the "disciplinary segregation area" where they freed selected prisoners. Simultaneously, prisoners in minimum security forced open their gate and joined the other newly freed prisoners. The Long Binh Riot had officially begun.[1]

Utilizing bunk adapters and knives stolen from the mess hall, rioting prisoners, 90 percent of whom were Black, focused their frustrations and anger on any guard who remained in the area. When the jail's commander, Lieutenant Colonel Vernon D. Johnson, confronted the rioters, he was beaten badly. Some Black prisoners attacked white prisoners. Using handmade torches made of rolled newspaper soaked in gasoline, others lit buildings and tents on fire. For a few hours violence and chaos reigned supreme.[2]

Authorities regained a level of control the following morning, but roughly fifteen Black prisoners continued to control sections of the stockade for nearly a month.[3] When the riot ended, one white prisoner was dead and eight stockade staff, including Lieutenant Colonel Johnson, and twenty-six prisoners were hospitalized. Seven buildings, including the mail room, and nineteen tents were burned to the ground or otherwise destroyed, resulting in more than $100,000 worth of damage.[4] The rioting that had engulfed Newark and Detroit in the summer of 1967 and dozens of American cities after Martin Luther King Jr.'s assassination in the spring of 1968 had officially arrived in Vietnam.

Race relations in the United States and Vietnam were in many ways interconnected. King's assassination was the catalyst for rioting in over sixty American cities, but it also increased tensions in Vietnam. Black anger was compounded by the response of military officers who appeared unsympathetic and white servicemen who celebrated the news that King had been killed. When discussing the reasons behind the riot, Charles W. Griswold, a clinical psychologist in the jail, theorized, "It is deeper than the stockade. It has to do with what is going on at home. It goes to Martin Luther King, who had an intense effect on these people."[5]

The Long Binh Riot was not an aberration. Over the next few years, thousands of violent racial incidents were reported in different military units in all four tactical zones of the RVN. In 1970 alone, the Marine Corps reported a shocking 1,060 violent racial incidents.[6] Official armed forces incident reports from 1970–71, most of which deal with army units, reveal hundreds of incidents. This situation led journalist and retired Colonel Robert D. Heinl Jr. in 1971 to conclude that racial conflicts were "erupting murderously" and "tearing the services apart."[7]

To a considerable extent the armed forces' own behavior contributed to these outbreaks of violence. As discussed in the previous chapter, African Americans had long complained of discrimination, and these complaints were often justified. However, between 1965 and 1968 their complaints were largely ignored. This unwillingness to address Black grievances alienated many African Americans, led to mistrust and suspicion, and had a negative effect on Black-white relations. An October 1971 report on race relations in the 84th Engineer Battalion in Da Nang noted that "the belief among Black soldiers that authority figures . . . were hostile toward them" impacted the way they viewed the military and interacted with their white peers.[8]

When racial conflicts began "erupting murderously," the military's first reaction was to blame African Americans. They failed to differentiate between those who peacefully protested racial discrimination and those involved in violent incidents. These same officials minimized or disregarded the roles whites played in provoking violence. They also failed to recognize that these incidents reflected their own failures to address adequately Black complaints of racial discrimination. In Vietnam racial discrimination and racial violence were inextricably linked.

"Some Redneck Cracker Would Crack His Mouth Off about MLK and the Fight Would Be On"

The state of race relations often depended on location. As discussed in chapter 1, combat service tended to challenge prejudices. Race relations were noticeably more strained on military bases or in cities. However, even in these areas there were only a few incidents of racial violence reported in the first years of the war. On September 22, 1966, *Jet* reported a "riot" that occurred on a naval installation in Vietnam involving two hundred white and Black sailors after "a white sailor called a Negro fireman 'Nigger.'"[9] On August 19, 1967, Frank Frazier, a Black marine at Camp McCarly in Phu Bai, revealed in a letter to his mother that "a fight broke out or should I say a race riot.... One of them (whites) got his rifle and fired two rounds—meaning to kill someone."[10]

In March 1967 Edith Payne described race relations in Cam Ranh Bay as "marred by near riots" after several incidents in which Black servicemen allegedly assaulted white servicemen. In response, officials posted a one-hundred-dollar reward for any information regarding these assaults. One anonymous African American charged, "They don't put up any such notice when we're attacked.... They put lynch ropes on our bunks and write warnings in the latrines, but if we even look like we want to go after them, the company commander threatens us."[11]

These incidents should not be dismissed, but racial violence was not widespread during 1965–67. These events appear to have been isolated. Contemporary accounts, including those from *Jet* and Payne, depict race relations as generally positive.[12] However, these few outbreaks of racial violence should not be seen as evidence that African Americans were satisfied with their experiences. Complaints of discrimination were widespread throughout the war. The rise in tensions was a "slow burn" that developed over time and was influenced by several factors. First and foremost, racial discrimination led many African Americans to conclude that the military had no intention of treating them fairly. Racism was a major obstacle in the United States, and it remained a major obstacle in the armed forces. Little had changed.

Events back home intensified the feeling that despite the successes of the civil rights movement, discrimination and prejudice remained pervasive. Martin Luther King Jr.'s assassination on April 4, 1968, angered African Americans, but it also served as confirmation that Black rights and lives were not respected or valued in American society.

Most African Americans viewed King as a hero who advocated nonviolent tactics to solve the racial problem in the United States. Because he was an outspoken critic of the war, many saw him as *the* Black representative of the antiwar movement. King's assassination challenged the notion that racism, prejudice, and war could be ended through peaceful protest. It also provided further evidence of just how endemic racism was. An unnamed African American working for the DOD in Da Nang spoke for many when he opined, "Now take Dr. King's assassination. I've been here in Vietnam for two years. All that time, I've been told the Viet Cong are my enemy. Now I think otherwise."[13]

Not everyone agreed with King that nonviolent protests were the best method of battling racism and ending the war. The civil rights movement began to split in 1966 between those who agreed with King and others like SNCC and the newly formed Black Panther Party (BPP). These groups and others rejected King's nonviolent approach as ineffective, promoted Black pride, largely excluded whites from their ranks, and created self-defense groups to defend Black neighborhoods from police harassment. For many, King's assassination seemed to confirm what Black activists like Stokely Carmichael of SNCC and Eldridge Cleaver of the BPP had argued for some time: nonviolent protests were ineffective and would only get Blacks killed. Violent protests or the threatened use of violence needed to be an option.[14]

Black servicemen were not immune to this line of thinking. Don F. Browne, who was stationed in Saigon, recalled, "When I heard that Martin Luther King was assassinated, my first inclination was to run out and punch the first white guy I saw. I was very hurt."[15] Allen Thomas Jr. was serving with the 4th Infantry Division in Kontum when King was assassinated, and he quickly realized "the young guys wanted to hurt somebody." He and other Black NCOs gathered hundreds of Black servicemen in a field where they stayed for several days. Thomas remembered, "We (the black NCOs) went to the officers, asked them to back off. The last thing you wanted to do was set them off.... Let them get over their anger and hurt."[16]

In May 1968, Donald Mosby spoke to African American servicemen in Vietnam about the significance of King's assassination. Mosby recognized "that these young men were deeply distressed by Dr. King's slaying" but also that "they had no intention of allowing things to stay the way they were when Dr. King was murdered."[17]

In reaction to King's murder many African Americans in the United States began to support the burgeoning Black power movement. SNCC was the first organization to articulate Black power policies, beginning in 1966, but by the spring of 1968 it had all but collapsed. In its aftermath, the BPP, initially a small organization in Oakland with little national profile, rose to prominence. After King's assassination hundreds of African Americans rushed to became members. By the end of 1968 there were chapters in twenty-eight cities. By 1970 sixty-eight cities had chapters.[18]

The Black power movement gained influence in Vietnam as well. African Americans decorated their "hooches" with Black power symbols, wore slave bracelets, and developed complicated handshakes called "dapping" as a representation of Black unity.[19] The depth of influence of Black power organizations is harder to gauge. In late 1969 *Black Journal* journalist Kent Garrett saw plenty of slave bracelets, dashikis, and dapping in Vietnam, but he saw no evidence of an organized BPP presence.[20] That same year Wallace Terry conducted a survey of 392 Black servicemen in Vietnam, which revealed significant sympathy for the Black power movement. When asked whether they planned to join a militant group like the BPP or Students for a Democratic Society when they returned to the United States, 31 percent of Black enlisted men said that they would, while another 17 percent said they might. However, these statistics speak more to a general antipathy toward the war and the military than an outright endorsement of BPP ideology. Additionally, the wording of the question suggests that there was little to no official BPP presence in Vietnam as it asked whether they would join in the future when they returned home.[21]

The BPP frequently criticized the war and its impact on African Americans in speeches and in the pages of its newspaper, *The Black Panther*, but it is not clear the party's message reached many Black servicemen. Most were at best vaguely aware of BPP messaging. Certainly, some of the BPP's opinions on racism resonated with servicemen, but this does not mean these ideas came directly from the party. African American opinions on race and the war came primarily from their own experiences with these issues in the United States and Vietnam.

Black power advocates also expressed views that would likely have alienated Black servicemen had they been aware of them. In an October 1966 speech, Stokely Carmichael depicted any African American who fought in Vietnam as a "black mercenary."[22]

Others went much further, criticizing any African American who willingly served in the military and encouraging communist forces in their efforts to defeat American forces. In August 1968 George Murray, BPP minister of education, gave a speech in Cuba in which he proclaimed,

"Every time a Vietnamese guerilla knocks out a U.S. soldier, that means one less aggressor against those who fight for freedom in the U.S." During a subsequent speech at Fresno State College in October, Murray argued that "every time an American mercenary is shot, that's one less cat that's going to be killing us in the United States." He further elaborated that when the 101st and 82nd Airborne were sent to Newark and Detroit, they had already been "depleted by the victorious fighters of the National Liberation Front." Murray acknowledged that this was unfortunate "because a lot of those soldiers were brothers," but it only occurred "because they were criminals fighting against another people of color." In an interview with *Rolling Stone* magazine the next month, Murray challenged the idea that Black servicemen could be "Black" and "proud" while fighting in Vietnam, which he labeled a "crime against all of us descendants of slaves in the U.S."[23]

In a March 22, 1970, *Black Panther* article, Eldridge Cleaver directly addressed African American servicemen in Vietnam, arguing that they were "flunkies for the white organization—the U.S.A.—for whom you have picked up the gun." He further expressed the position that any African American who did not immediately quit the military or start "destroying it from the inside" was committing a "form of treason against your own people."[24]

As the preceding comments demonstrate, prominent Black power leaders struggled to empathize with African American servicemen in Vietnam. They failed to differentiate between those who had joined the military and those who were drafted. Likewise, they did not directly address the social and economic conditions that might lead African Americans into the armed forces. Groups like the BPP argued that Blacks should avoid military service even if it meant jail or leaving the country. There was no acceptable excuse for Black military service.

These positions, depending on how widely they were circulated, would likely have frustrated any effort by the BPP to attract direct support from Black servicemen. There were oft-repeated rumors that Black servicemen were members of the BPP, but given the party's insistence on draft avoidance and public statements about military service, this seems highly unlikely. The BPP included veterans like Geronimo Pratt, Bobby White, Bobby Harding, and Mike Tagowa, but they joined after serving in Vietnam.[25]

Black servicemen formed their own organizations to represent their collective interests and to protect themselves. In 1969 Wallace Terry noted several Black "self-defense" organizations like the Blackstone Rangers, De Mau Mau, and Ju Ju, all of which had allegedly formed to protect Blacks from racist whites.[26] Other organizations included the American Minority Servicemen's Association, the Concerned Veterans Association, Black Brothers United (BBU), the Zulu 1200s, the Black Liberation Front of the Armed Forces, and the Black Brothers Union.[27] Information about these groups is limited, but some were undoubtedly influenced by aspects of Black power ideology. However, it would be erroneous to assume their political perspectives were identical to domestic Black power groups or that they advocated for or engaged in violent activities.

Freddie Smith, a Black marine who served with the 7th Marine Division in 1970–71, claimed, "Just about every black veteran of the Marine Corps was . . . associated with the De Mau Mau at one time or another." Smith claimed De Mau Mau's primary concern was educating "blacks that didn't know the UCMJ [Uniform Code of Military Justice] or laws of the Marines. . . . A lot of times they used to protest and maybe go on some type of semi-strike." Smith's assertion that every Black marine was a member of the De Mau Mau is certainly an exaggeration, but it is difficult to know how large these organizations were. The BBU had hundreds of members spread throughout Vietnam, while smaller organizations had as few as twenty members.[28]

Many of these groups formed in the aftermath of King's assassination, a period that saw a dramatic increase in racial incidents. Jim Heiden, a white soldier, recognized the significant effect of Martin Luther King Jr.'s death on race relations. He observed, "Reactions to Tet and things like that, they were minimal. . . . But when Martin Luther King was assassinated . . . people fought. People had fist fights."[29]

Journalist Zalin Grant reported that after King's assassination incidents of racial violence became so frequent at Camp Tien Sha in Da Nang that "the camp's biggest threat is race riots, not the Vietcong."[30] Incidents were also reported outside of Vietnam. A few weeks after King was killed, Blacks and whites fought one another in Yokosuka, Japan, with *Jet* concluding that the fight "broke out over Negro resentment over the murder of Dr. Martin Luther King Jr."[31]

Black anger over King's assassination was compounded by the way some whites reacted to his death. President Lyndon Johnson designated Sunday, April 7, 1968, as a day of national mourning, but not everyone used the time to grieve. Grant reported seeing a Confederate flag hanging in front of the navy headquarters at Cam Ranh Bay immediately following the assassination.³² On April 16 the DOD received a complaint from the American Veterans Committee that "Confederate flags were being flown in Vietnam" to the great consternation of African Americans serving there.³³

Confederate flags were always a source of contention. In 1966 the NAACP petitioned Secretary of Defense Robert McNamara to ban the flag after white GIs waved one during Bob Hope's Christmas Day performance. An anonymous Black soldier complained, "No one in authority stopped to think what effect this had on the morale of the [black] GIs. No one there knew that perhaps the very next day or the next week, many of those same guys would give their lives for America."³⁴

After King's assassination, Blacks viewed the flag with particular disdain. Don L. Jernigan believed whites flew Confederate flags "to intimidate and to antagonize and to let you know in a quiet kinda way that they were in support of what went down" when King was killed.³⁵ So many complained about the flag that the army and marines briefly banned its usage. When southern congressmen complained, officials reversed course, assuring them that the "ban had been only temporary, confined to Confederate flags, and aimed at easing racial tensions during the days following Dr. King's death."³⁶

The display of Confederate flags was hardly the only offensive action taken after King's assassination. Zalin Grant reported that a month later two whites burned a twelve-foot-high cross near a barracks occupied by African Americans.³⁷ Wallace Terry noted that white servicemen in Da Nang and Cam Ranh Bay burned crosses to celebrate King's murder.³⁸ Brian Settles overheard a white major and pilot instructor react to news of King's death with, "Well, he finally got what he was asking for."³⁹ Gerald Lynch recalled a drunken white marine stating, "It should have happened a lot sooner."⁴⁰

Don F. Browne remembered, "A few days after the assassination, some of the white guys got a little sick and tired of seeing Dr. King's picture on the TV screen. Like a memorial." One soldier commented, "I wish they'd take that nigger's picture off." Browne and three other African Americans gave the man "a lesson in when to use that word and when you should not use that word. A physical lesson."⁴¹ As Browne's account suggests, many African Americans were not willing to let insults of King and his memory go unchallenged. Gary Skogen, a white soldier stationed in Lahnstuhl, Germany, recalled that violence was "really commonplace in the first couple of months after MLK died.... Some redneck cracker would crack his mouth off about MLK and the fight would be on."⁴²

The armed forces could have been more sensitive to the feelings of African Americans. On April 17 the *Chicago Daily News* published a letter written by James Woods, a Black soldier stationed in Da Nang. Woods alleged that "when Martin Luther King was killed, a group of about 150 Negro soldiers went to the chapel, which always has been open 24 hours a day, to say a prayer for him." They were refused entry. Woods and eleven others went to the enlisted men's club, where "a white sergeant told us to move aside and we promptly obeyed. We began talking again and he ordered armed guards in as though we were rioting." Woods theorized, "We are supposed to be American soldiers fighting a war in Vietnam. But it seems as though the white man thinks we're still at home."[43]

An army investigation conducted in response to Woods's letter essentially confirmed his account. The investigation further revealed that the soldiers were also trying to meet with the chaplain on the night in question to ensure he would eulogize King the following day. Investigators admitted that the soldiers were refused access to the chapel but justified this decision on the basis that the chapel was being cleaned at the time. While admitting that the soldiers had been denied access, investigators also accepted the contradictory claim made by officials on the ground that "the chapel was opened 24 hours a day for anyone." Additionally, they seemed more concerned with identifying the Black soldiers involved than addressing their concerns. They confronted Woods, whose accusations they dismissed in large part because he "had only been in Vietnam for a period of six days at the time of the incident." Investigators concluded that "the allegation of racial prejudice being practiced could not be substantiated."[44]

On April 19, 1968, Herbert Turner, a Black chaplain with the 52nd Artillery Group in Pleiku, requested permission to conduct a memorial service for King at the chapel. Turner's commander rejected the request, claiming that "it was better not to make a big thing out of it," and "that it was not in the best interest of the group to conduct a special service."[45]

Long Binh

In the months following King's assassination racial incidents occurred with increasing frequency. On August 16, a couple of weeks of before the Long Binh Riot, a confrontation erupted between prisoners and guards at the III Marine Amphibious Force Brig in Da Nang after a white guard allegedly made a racist remark to a Black prisoner. Prisoners, most of whom were Black, broke out of their cells, set cellblocks on fire, and assaulted prisoners who they believed were informants.[46] The event gained little media attention.

The Long Binh Riot was the first incident to receive significant attention from the press and from military officials. Historian Cecil Barr Currey's *Long Binh Jail: An Oral History of Vietnam's Notorious U.S. Military Prison* is the only monograph to examine the riot. In a transparent effort to elicit hostility toward the prisoners, Currey claims that of those he interviewed, most are "damaged goods" incapable of having normal relationships with women or acting as supportive fathers to their children. He further argues that had they committed similar crimes in civilian society, they would have also ended up in jail.[47]

In contrast, Currey depicts the guards as upstanding citizens who strictly upheld military law. This is a particularly bizarre assertion as many guards admitted to prisoner abuse, a direct violation of military law. Currey dismisses these admissions as unimportant. Other servicemen were being killed in combat; therefore, prisoners had no right to complain about their treatment. He similarly rejects JAG Herbert Green's assertion that the widespread use of pretrial confinement meant "the presumption of innocence was systematically ignored. Also ignored was Article 13 of Uniform Code of Military Justice, which prohibits pretrial restraint any more rigorous than that necessary to insure the presence of the accused for trial."[48] Currey appears to believe that those in positions of power and authority are exempt from military law. Because a war was being fought, human rights and military law should be ignored.

Many of Currey's claims are demonstrably false. As previously shown, most prisoners had not even been accused of committing a violent crime, let alone been convicted of one. They were jailed for military violations that would not have warranted any form of prosecution in the civilian world, let alone criminal prosecution. Leaving work early, having a dirty uniform, or refusing to follow directions at work are not crimes in the United States. Prisoners accused of violent crimes like murder were transferred out of Vietnam as quickly as possible. Billy Jones, a psychiatrist, treated a white Marine who killed two of his coworkers at the U.S. embassy, and he was transferred to Japan almost immediately.[49]

Currey's claim that most prisoners were hardened criminals is weakened by the fact that there were only a few violent incidents reported in the months before the riot. Between January and August 1968 there were thirty-nine escape attempts, thirty-five cases of marijuana possession, six assaults, and two suicide attempts.[50] Prisoners seemed desperate to escape Long Binh more than anything else.

The army investigation conducted after the riot provides a more nuanced account of its causes. Investigators interviewed thirty-seven people including prisoners, medical officials, and military police. Investigators admitted that "the single event which sparked the disorder was not discernable," but they listed numerous factors they believed contributed to the riot. On August 18 Confinement Officer Vernon Johnson imposed a new policy, in response to the widespread smuggling of marijuana, requiring all prisoners returning from appointments or work assignments to be strip-searched. This policy change angered prisoners because they felt the searches were inhumane and it deprived them of access to marijuana.[51]

Overcrowding contributed greatly to the riot. The prison was built to hold 400 prisoners, but there were 719 prisoners living there at the time, limiting each prisoner to 36.5 square feet of living space. As the population increased, the number of correctional officers and custodial workers did not. The prison required a force of "282 mature, trained, and experienced personnel," but there were only 90 direct personnel and 64 support personnel working on the day of the riot. Not helping matters, guards received no formal specialized training, which led them to "either overreact to prisoner infractions or to underreact—even to the extent of turning their backs."[52]

Drugs, overcrowding, and a lack of personnel were not the only factors increasing tensions. Investigators recognized an obvious racial factor as "the large percentage of Negroes in confinement in relation to their distribution within society and more particularly the U.S. Army focused Negro prisoner attention on their individual plight." They also acknowledged "that racial conditions in the United States" influenced how Black prisoners viewed their imprisonment. African Americans faced discrimination at home, and their preponderance in the prison population supported the belief that they also faced discrimination in Vietnam. Investigators believed that rioters hoped their actions would help "achieve partial redress for real or imagined maltreatment suffered at some point in their lifetime."[53]

Investigators emphasized the role played by two Black leaders. In the preceding weeks, Charles C. Planter, a respected Black leader, had been placed in disciplinary segregation, a decision that angered many prisoners. Planter's absence allowed David E. Coppage, another Black prisoner, to gain greater influence. Coppage would play a pivotal role in instigating and leading the riot.[54]

Investigators were hardly complimentary about how Long Binh was run. However, a more thorough examination of the interviews they conducted reveals even greater reason for criticism. Marijuana usage was common, but more dangerous drugs were also readily available. Joshua Williams, a Black guard, confiscated "pills, Bensedrine [sic], liquid opium" on numerous occasions. Robert Henderson, a white prisoner, claimed that Darvon, an opioid, was regularly smuggled into the jail, where prisoners would boil it down and inject it. He claimed that "a lot of prisoners" were using Darvon the night of the riot. Coppage believed that some Black prisoners were using Binoctal, a barbiturate. Another white prisoner reported seeing seven Black prisoners injecting a drug, likely Darvon or Binoctal.[55]

Coppage alleged the source of the drugs was not a fellow prisoner but two guards. His claims were corroborated by a white prisoner who witnessed "the tower guard throw two packets of cigarettes, one syringe and needle, and a package of Binoctal tablets" over the fence to Black prisoners the day before. Another white prisoner also claimed that it was a guard who supplied prisoners with drugs.[56] Coppage's claims might be suspect on their own as he was accused of having an active role in the riot and had reason to shift blame onto others, but the two white prisoners were not involved and had no reason to lie.

Investigators acknowledged overcrowding in the jail, but they said almost nothing about the conditions in maximum security, where "troublesome" prisoners were housed in Container Express (CONEX) shipping boxes, six feet high, nine feet wide, and six feet long. It was oppressively hot inside with temperatures regularly above a hundred degrees.[57] Making matters worse, guards kept the lights on, which increased the temperature and made it difficult to sleep.[58] Scott Riley, a prisoner in maximum security at the time of the riot, recalled, "You're basically sitting in this, I don't know what the dimensions were, but a very small space, naked. . . . They would put you on a regimen of basically, you know, bread, water, a couple of vegetables." When prisoners became "weaker and weaker from being on this restrictive diet, they would take you out, and, you know, put you through a medical check to make sure you're not going to die or something like that, and throw you back in the box." Riley concluded, "They basically tried to make it as miserable for us as possible."[59]

It was not just misbehaving prisoners who faced the prospect of being placed in the "box." JAG Herbert Green recalled that new prisoners, including those being held pretrial, were routinely put inside to "get the prisoners' attention."[60] Prisoners complained of being put in the box for minor violations or for no clear reason. James Hutchinson, a white prisoner, told investigators he was put in the box for nine days after he argued with a guard. Jack Adams, a Black prisoner, claimed that he was put inside after going through the chow line twice. Antonio Aguinaldo Gibel argued that there was a clear racial component to the way the box was utilized. He complained, "Sending all the Negroes to the box—to them it is a racial matter.... A lot more were put in the box ... only on suspicion of a crime." Corrections officer Thomas Kenney admitted that "prisoners get put in the box for small things.... I think they should have something besides the box."[61]

Investigators acknowledged complaints of abuse, but they claimed that the inspector general and USARV had determined they were unfounded. However, many interviewees provided evidence of abuse. Dr. Robert Blackmon recalled treating "two or three" prisoners who claimed they were assaulted by guards, but medical officials admitted they did not "attempt to record the causes of injuries to prisoners whom they treat." Earl Redman, a counselor at Long Binh, heard multiple complaints of abuse. He also witnessed four guards "beating some of the prisoners" in maximum security. They were allegedly relieved of their duties after he complained.[62]

Charles Griswold, a psychologist, witnessed a guard named Stewart beat a prisoner for asking to use the bathroom. Joseph Bullard, a white prisoner, claimed that he was beaten severely in the box by two guards. He recalled, "They hit me in the jaw, beat me, and kicked me. I know other people they have beaten." His request to see a doctor was denied. Bullard's experiences highlight one of the problems in trying to determine how common abuse was—assaults were most likely to occur in the box, to which doctors and counselors had limited access.[63]

Confinement Officer Eugene Murdock, who took over for Vernon Johnson shortly after the riot, admitted that despite his best efforts at reform, "some of my people in the hole were still mistreating prisoners." A few days after the riot, he "relieved one of the NCO's just to get him out of here" as he was abusing prisoners.[64]

Witness interviews clarify Planter's and Coppage's roles in the riot. According to William James Davidson, a Black corrections officer, Johnson believed that Planter had participated in several assaults on white prisoners over the last few months. Planter insisted that "if he saw any negroes beating up white prisoners, he would try to stop it," but Johnson put him in the box anyway on a charge of "investigation." Planter understood that this decision would not be greeted lightly by other prisoners, warning Johnson that if Black prisoners saw him being sent to the box for no reason, they would "burn the place down."[65] Two weeks later, they did just that.

Johnson believed that separating Planter from other prisoners would alleviate tensions, but it had the opposite effect. Ernest Talps, a Black guard, reported that Black prisoners resented "Planter being held for no apparent reason" and petitioned for his release. Talps also reported that "there were many Caucasian prisoners who approached me about the same thing." These white prisoners "wanted Planter out of segregation because he gave them protection" from some of the other Black prisoners. Talps agreed that there was no justification for putting Planter in the box, and he urged Johnson to release Planter. However, Planter remained in the box until he was freed during the riot.[66]

Johnson viewed Planter as a dangerous agitator, but he did not support the riot and did everything in his power to prevent other prisoners from hurting anyone once it began. According to an unnamed guard, when Black prisoners freed Planter, he instructed them, "Don't touch those guards." Davidson reported that "the night of the riot Planter brought two guards out alive and they thanked him for saving their lives." After exiting the area, Planter turned his attention toward Johnson yelling, "I told you it was going to happen. I told you they were going to do it." Murdock agreed that putting Planter in the box was not the best idea, as "we could have used him later to calm his people."[67]

While 90 percent of the rioters were Black, most African Americans did not participate. Scott Riley was freed from maximum security during the riot, but he was not an active participant. Initially, he wasn't even sure what was happening. He remembered, "The night of August 29, I was in the box. . . . We were hearing this noise and all this yelling and screaming . . . and next thing I remember was, my door got broken open." He used his newfound freedom to eat a sheet cake taken from the kitchen.[68]

Like Planter, many African Americans tried to protect guards and prisoners once the riot began. When Robert Henderson was taken hostage along with other whites, a Black prisoner interceded and brought them to a secure area where they were released. Henderson recalled, "He said he had to get some more men out. He came back with several more Caucasians." Joseph Bullard, a white prisoner, witnessed John Bullock, a Black prisoner, trying to protect another white prisoner. Bullock cried at the sight of the violence because "he did not want to fight. He did not want to participate in the fighting in Vietnam" and only ended up at Long Binh because "he refused to go to the field."[69] Bullock didn't exactly fit the stereotype of a violent criminal destined for prison.

When a Black prisoner with a torch approached a white prisoner's tent, another Black prisoner "told that man not to set our tent on fire." Simultaneously, a different Black prisoner paced outside the tent repeating, "You stupid fucking fools, you're doing it all wrong." This man then told the white prisoner that he should leave immediately for his own protection.[70] The chapel orderly credited three Black prisoners with protecting him from a small group of rioters. A white prisoner in the minimum custody section reported that African Americans in his tent prevented rioters from entering and assaulting him and other whites. A white guard recalled that Black prisoners were among those who brought injured white prisoners to safety.[71]

Some Black prisoners, including Coppage, assaulted guards and prisoners. Six weeks before the riot, Coppage had been confined to the medium section of the jail, separating him from the general population. On August 27 he asked Davidson to be moved back, but his request was rejected as he had previously received eighteen disciplinary violations in general population. Davidson warned his superiors that "if Coppage is turned loose he would cause trouble and I would not be surprised if there would be a riot in the stockade." However, Coppage was transferred when Davidson took the afternoon off for his birthday. Fearing that "something was going to happen," Davidson asked for an explanation but got no answer. Later that night the riot began with Coppage as an active participant.[72]

Investigators said little about Colonel Johnson's role in the riot even though his decisions increased tensions. He was entirely responsible for Planter being in the box and for Coppage's transfer to general population. These decisions increased the chances of a violent confrontation. Johnson also ignored the advice of experienced Black guards. Two of the guards had apparently offended him shortly before the riot. After Davidson transported a prisoner to the United States, Johnson relieved him of his position as provost sergeant. Davidson, who had been in the military for twenty-six years, learned of the demotion not from Johnson but from a soldier of lower rank. He was not even sure what his assignment was as his "position and title now have not really been explained to me." Johnson had recently ordered Ernest Talps's transfer too. A rumor circulated widely that Johnson had fired him, which further aggravated Black prisoners. Davidson and Talps were not the only ones in authority to criticize Johnson's leadership or suggest dysfunction. Charles Griswold described a "building resentment" between Johnson and his staff in the weeks before the riot. Increasingly, he witnessed guards "yelling screeming (?) calling the prisoners names," and even assaulting them.[73]

Much to the dismay of the investigator, Griswold criticized the way Blacks were treated, and while not condoning the violence that took place, insisted their anger was justified. He argued that "racial hatred" was the primary reason for the riot, and that "this hatred stems from civilian life, from military life which is more limited and from stockade life which is more limited than that." Griswold asserted that many of "the men come to the stockade disgusted with their units. They say that they have no one to listen to their problems."[74]

Alphonso Frost, a Black guard, believed that the causes of the riot lay not only in how African Americans were treated in the jail but more generally in the military. He told investigators that Black prisoners were bitter and angry over being imprisoned for minor crimes, and they saw "their confinement as a symbol of persecution."[75]

Race War in Vietnam

Long Binh is the best-known incident of racial violence in the Vietnam War, but the nature and level of violence that occurred there would soon become commonplace. In September 1968 Black soldiers in the 9th Division Base Camp in Dong Tam cut a white soldier's throat, an injury that resulted in fifty-two stiches. There were six other violent racial incidents at Dong Tam around the same time, involving guns, knives, and brass knuckles.[76]

On November 2, 1968, the *Pittsburgh Courier* noted an increase in racial incidents on naval bases. One event involved a Black sailor who, after being thrown out of a club at Camp Tien Sha, pulled a .45-caliber pistol and fired inside. Shortly after this, a Black sailor was found dead under mysterious circumstances.[77] On November 23, 1968, the *Philadelphia Tribune* reported large-scale fighting between Blacks and whites in service clubs in Da Nang and Long Binh, leading them to conclude that servicemen were "Fighting Each Other 'Harder' Than [the] Vietcong."[78] Zalin Grant alleged that in late 1968, "racial incidents occurred at the nearby China Beach recreation area and in Danang clubs and dining halls" on an almost daily basis. In the most serious incident, a Black security guard was shot and killed.[79]

The United States Army Pacific reported one hundred "disorders" from January to September 1969, most of which had racial overtones. Among them was a March 8, 1969, fight between Blacks and whites at an NCO club at Camp Hochmuth in Phu Bai during which an unknown person fired an M-16 into the club. On May 22, 1969, a white soldier was beaten to death by two Black soldiers at the Long Binh Post barracks.[80]

In September 1969 Wallace Terry reported on "another war being fought in Viet Nam—between black and white Americans." Terry described Blacks and whites regularly fighting one another on military installations in Da Nang, Cam Ranh Bay, Dong Tam, Saigon, and Bien Hoa.[81]

Official armed forces reports from 1969 to 1971 reveal hundreds of incidents of racial violence. In October 1970 Deputy Chief of Staff for Personnel (DCSPER) Lieutenant General Walter T. Kerwin reported, "In the past year racial discord has surfaced as one of the most serious problems facing Army leadership."[82] A provost marshal report on "Crimes of Violence with Racial Overtones" revealed that from July 1970 to April 1971 there were 269 incidents of racial violence including 9 murders, 10 attempted murders, and 186 aggravated assaults.[83]

Racial violence surged out of control in many areas. For example, in the I Corps region where the III Marine Amphibious Force at Camp Horn in Da Nang was located, racial violence exploded. On the same base, in the same military unit, and within twenty-four hours of one another—December 7–8, 1969—there were a half-dozen assaults. During one incident, five Black marines assaulted a white marine outside of the enlisted men's club. Elsewhere, two African Americans assaulted a white sergeant "possibly in retaliation for being too strict in his attitude toward other Negroes." Another time a white private threatened a white sergeant, insisting that his "black brothers" would be willing to help him, demonstrating that Black-white cooperation was not unknown in the rear. A white corporal, who lived in the same hut as this sergeant, was later assaulted by four or five African Americans, suggesting the white private made good on his threat. Another incident began when a white marine expressed a desire to "kick some black ass tonight." Confronted by a Black marine, the white marine and his friend assaulted the Black man. Another time, a Black and white marine reportedly fought over a cot, the confrontation ending only when the white marine fired his rifle into the ceiling. In total, between December 1969 and January 1970 there were at least thirty-three incidents of racial violence at Camp Horn. The violence occurred almost daily.[84]

Camp Horn was not the only military installation in Da Nang to experience severe racial problems. During a February 5, 1970, concert at Camp Brooks Marine Base, a Black marine lobbed two fragmentation grenades, killing one marine and injuring sixty-two others. An investigation found that the attack was a "deliberate, carefully thought out attempt to kill a hell of a lot of people strictly because of racial problems."[85]

When attorney David Addlestone arrived in November 1970, "there was like an open war going on in Da Nang between whites and Blacks."[86] Sixteen incidents of racial violence were reported at Camp Baxter between December 1970 and October 1971. On December 17 a fight occurred involving dozens of African Americans and whites brandishing "clubs, knives, and hand grenades." Afterward, fifteen to twenty Blacks stole a M-79 grenade launcher, a M-14 rifle, and two M-16 rifles from the company command post.[87] On January 18, 1971, a white MP was shot and killed by a Black soldier at the base camp of the 101st Airborne Division.[88] On March 25 a white soldier shot and killed a Black soldier leading investigators to write the word "racial" on the report. On September 8 a Black soldier was assaulted, leading to a fight involving approximately three hundred Black and white soldiers in the 84th Engineer Battalion. During the fight someone "threw a concussion grenade in the area of the white soldiers," injuring two.[89] An October 1971 report on race relations in the same battalion noted a recent "racial confrontation" involving sixty-five whites and sixty-five Blacks.[90]

Race relations were equally fractured in Chu Lai where there were at least twenty-three racial incidents between July 1970 and March 1971. Racial violence was common enough that Michael Harger, a white soldier, was stabbed on two separate occasions.[91] On September 25, 1970, in the aftermath of a brawl at the enlisted men's club, Gerald McLemore, a Black soldier, killed a white soldier after a group of armed whites surrounded his hooch.[92]

Racial incidents were reported in Phu Bai, Duc Pho, and Quang Tri. In Phu Bai racial violence was frequent enough that Harry Avant, another white soldier, was also stabbed on two different occasions in September.[93] On January 8, 1971, two white soldiers in the 1st Battalion 77th Armor Regiment at Quang Tri became embroiled in a confrontation with Black soldiers over a cassette tape.[94] That same month in Quang Tri, B. W. Flint, a Black radar technician with the 5th Mechanized Infantry Division, shot two white soldiers, injuring one and killing the other.[95]

The II Corps experienced significant racial tension. There were thirteen incidents reported in Cam Ranh Bay between August 1970 and March

1971.⁹⁶ An incident that began on March 16, 1971, outside of the 191st Ordinance Battalion Motor Pool reveals how racial tensions escalated to the level of violence. Jeffrey Cole, a white soldier, called Oswald Pendleton, an African American soldier, a "nigger," and a fight broke out. Cole and fifteen other whites later assaulted Robert Driver, a Black soldier. Cole and two other whites were subsequently assaulted by forty to fifty African Americans.⁹⁷ Two days later, eighteen to twenty African Americans entered a billet and attacked four whites with chains and hoses.⁹⁸

An Khe also experienced racial violence. On September 20, 1970, Willie Clayborne, a Black soldier at Camp Radcliff, threatened "to kill every officer and NCO in the Unit." He made good on his threat a few hours later, firing his M-16 at several white soldiers, killing two and injuring another.⁹⁹

In January 1971 several racially motivated incidents in An Khe climaxed with the killing of a troop commander, Captain William F. Recihert. At the time, David Addlestone noted that race relations in An Khe were "denigrating steadily, in large part because of a racist first sergeant and a racist first lieutenant. A confederate flag flew over the encampment; blacks were referred to as 'nigras' 'colored' or just 'you people.'"¹⁰⁰ On January 10 "two blacks were gassed with riot CS [tear gas]," and a few days later an M-16 was fired into a room occupied by African Americans. On January 26, after someone "tried to gas some blacks with riot CS," a group of African Americans warned the squadron commander "that if something were not done about the matter that night and changes made around the troop, someone would get hurt very soon." Although a white lieutenant admitted to knowing who was responsible, "nothing was done about the matter." The next day two African Americans confronted Recihert over what they believed were unfair field assignments. When he randomly assigned a different African American to the position, one of the men pointed his finger at the commander and shouted, "I am tired of getting f—ked with." When Recihert reached for his pistol, one of the African Americans "fired an automatic burst into the Troop Commander's head," killing him instantly.¹⁰¹

There were additional incidents in Tuy Hoa, Nha Trang, Phu Tai, Cha Rang Valley, Phan Thiet, Cai Nhon, Phu Hiep Village, Phan Rang, Qui Nhon, An Son, and Pleiku.¹⁰² On January 9, 1971, MPs were called to "stop a racial fight involving 200 personnel" at an enlisted men's club in Tuy Hoa.¹⁰³ Shortly afterward, an unidentified person threw a fragmentation grenade outside the club injuring twenty-nine people.¹⁰⁴ After a Black servicemen was arrested for his involvement in an assault on February 20, "incidents of Molotov cocktails and CS throwing" occurred frequently over the following week.[105] In Nha Trang nine incidents of African Americans robbing and/or assaulting whites were reported in September and October 1970 alone.[106]

The III Corps also experienced numerous instances of racial violence. Long Binh was "the enclave with the largest troop concentrations," so it is not surprising that there were twenty-seven incidents of racial violence reported between July 1970 and March 1971. On August 21, 1970, six African Americans and one white attacked a white serviceman. The participation of a white servicemen could mean there was no racial motivation behind the attack, but investigators insisted that "there were racial overtones involved in this incident."[107] On October 24 a confrontation between a white soldier on guard duty and two Black soldiers stationed with the 79th Maintenance Battalion ended when one of the Black soldiers, "fired approx 15 rounds from his M-16" into the white soldier's body killing him. It isn't clear what precipitated the dispute, but all three men were on perimeter guard duty.[108] On December 31 several African Americans exchanged gunfire with two white Criminal Investigation Command agents: one agent and one Black serviceman were killed, while two unidentified African Americans were badly injured.[109] Similar incidents were reported in Di An, Saigon, Tan Song Nhut, and Bien Hoa.[110]

On September 15, 1971, an incident erupted on Whiskey Mountain in Phan Thiet after Black soldiers organized a memorial for a two-year-old Black girl killed by police in Los Angeles. The morning after the service, some refused to report for work, and an explosive device was thrown into their tent. When they exited, the men were confronted by military police, arrested, and charged with mutiny.[111]

There were numerous racial incidents in the IV Corps, most notably in Vinh Long. During a February 14, 1970, fight among members of the 611th Transportation Company, Ulysses Wright, a Black soldier, had his jaw broken by several whites. When Wright arrived at the hospital, he was not treated immediately, leading Blacks to complain that doctors were treating whites first. Numerous fights broke out, which caused medical officials to barricade themselves inside. When MPs arrived, they used tear gas on African Americans who had gathered, creating greater chaos. The crowd was eventually dispersed at gunpoint.[112]

In a complaint to Republican senator Hugh Scott of Pennsylvania, Larry Delorne, a Black soldier, elaborated on the night's events. He claimed that tensions arose after a white soldier pinched a Vietnamese woman who was engaged to a Black soldier. Delorne described the fight as "GI's having a normal Saturday night brawl," suggesting that these incidents were weekly occurrences. After the fight was broken up, Wright was "pelted in the cranial area viciously by the white soldiers with large stones.... He was kicked, stomped, slugged, and beaten into a near state of unconsciousness." Particularly troubling, a white senior commissioned officer walked by the "gruesome beating" but "did not intervene nor mutter one word of protest." When Wright and other African Americans arrived at the hospital, they were confronted by whites who threatened to "kill every one of you nigger bastards." Making matters worse, doctors seemed more interested in treating whites with minor injuries than Wright, who was severely injured, an attitude that Delorne described as "to the rear of the line, nigger."[113]

Delorne described MPs as needlessly aggressive outside of the hospital. Several African Americans "were jabbed with clubs for no perceptible reason." Later that night, armed whites, some of whom were not MPs, confronted and threatened Delorne and other African Americans. Had a colonel not intervened, Delorne believed they would have been "slaughtered in cold-blood." He further warned that "this base has become a tinderbox, ready to explode under any spark."[114] While Wright's depiction of events differs from the official version, both accounts describe a base rife with racial tension and violence. There were additional incidents of racial violence reported in Vung Tau, Binh Thuy, and Can Tho. On April 11, 1970, a Black private beat a white sergeant in his company to death with a baseball bat in Vung Tau.[115]

Violent racial incidents were frequent, but there were also acts of violence that were not necessarily racial. "Fragging," derived from fragmentation grenades, refers to servicemen attempting to murder their commanding officers. Historian George Lepre provides the most thorough account of fragging, and he notes that in most cases where "the races of the perpetrators and their intended victims were known," there is little "indication of whether the assaults were racially motivated."[116] A provost marshal report revealed that in 1969 there were 96 fraggings, 12 of which were believed to be linked to race. In 1970, of the 209 fraggings reported, 16 had a racial motivation behind them. During the first three months of 1971 there were 68 fraggings, 7 of which were motivated by race. In each year the motivation behind the great majority of fraggings remained unknown.[117]

Colin Powell, a Black executive officer in 1968–69 with the 23rd Infantry Division, believed that tensions were so high in Duc Pho that he moved his cot every night in large part because he "did not rule out attacks on authority from within the battalion itself."[118] Bruce Crawford, a white first lieutenant with the 101st Airborne, remembered that soldiers routinely fought each other and that there were several attempted fraggings in Phu Bai in 1971. Some of the incidents he knew about had a clear racial component, while others did not. Crawford recalled, "All the time I was executive officer I was afraid for my life. I slept with a .45 under my pillow and an M-16 locked and loaded by my bed. I got more sleep and rest in the jungle than when I was an executive officer."[119] Crawford was not alone. By 1970 several commanders had become frightened enough of the men under their command that they restricted who had access to explosives and firearms.[120] In 1971 Major General James Baldwin, commander of the 23rd Infantry Division, admitted that fraggings were "a very significant problem" and that fragmentation grenades were "no longer issued to G.I.s going on bunker guard duty" in Chu Lai.[121]

The U.S. Navy was not free of racial violence either. One of the most publicized incidents of violence occurred on October 12, 1972, aboard the USS *Kitty Hawk*. The ship had been at sea for eight months, and there had long been signs of racial tension. When Black Executive Officer Ben Cloud arrived aboard on August 12, it was obvious "there were problems, you know Blacks chose to live in one area of the ship and the whites in another... which was not good."[122] Magnifying these problems, Petty Officer Nate Mondy, who was also the human resources manager of minority affairs, recalled that many Black sailors had come into the military through Project 100,000 and were less than thrilled about being there.[123]

In the days leading up to the *Kitty Hawk* Riot, several fights involving Black and white sailors were reported at bars in the area around Subic Bay, Philippines, where the ship was docked.[124] On October 12 a dispute erupted between Blacks and whites in the mess hall.[125] Cloud noted, "Tempers were very high all over the ship before the riots started. Everybody was on a tinder edge. All you needed was just a little spark to get it started and that's what happened."[126]

According to Mondy, African Americans were mistakenly blamed for the incidents in Subic Bay. Angered by what they felt was a biased investigation, around thirty African Americans protested on the mess decks. Cloud and Mondy managed to convince them to leave the area peacefully, but as they left, they were confronted by marines who had received conflicting orders.[127] The confrontation escalated, and before long small groups of Black sailors were rampaging through the ship attacking white sailors.[128] Rumors spread that Captain Marland Townsend Jr. was killed, and this led Cloud to take control of the ship. He confronted a large group of Black sailors telling them that, as a Black man, he identified with their concerns but that they needed to trust him as a Black leader to represent them in a nonviolent way. To prove that he was credible, Cloud gave the Black power salute. He recalled, "I felt that because I was who I am and that I was dealing with at that time, a whole bunch of Black sailors, that there had to be some credibility associated with that."[129] His efforts proved effective, and the sailors dispersed. The threat of violence wasn't entirely over though as Cloud then had to calm down white sailors who were threatening to retaliate against the Black sailors.[130]

The *Kitty Hawk* Riot resulted in forty-six injuries.[131] If Cloud had not been willing to put aside navy protocol and appeal to the rioters along racial lines, however, the violence likely would have been worse. He recalled, "Many people have told me since that they felt that gesture was something that defused the situation. . . . Many people who felt that by doing that I saved not only the ship but a number of lives."[132]

Four days after the *Kitty Hawk* Riot, another incident occurred on the USS *Hassayampa* while it was docked at Subic Bay. An argument erupted after ten African Americans realized that money had been stolen from their wallets. They blamed white sailors and a fight erupted, resulting in four injuries.[133] On November 3 eighty African Americans staged a sit-in on the USS *Constellation*, alleging that they were unfairly denied promotions and targeted for general discharges. Ten hours into the sit-in, Captain John Ward ordered five hundred white sailors to surround the protestors. Armed marines also arrived. It was only through the intervention of two officers, one Black and one white, that a violent incident was averted.[134]

As these accounts suggest, violent confrontations were not restricted to Vietnam. Relations were particularly poor in Okinawa. In a December 26, 1969, letter to Congressman Bob Mathias, a Republican from California, Dalinda Johnson claimed that her son Rockland Gaxiola feared for his safety in Okinawa because "white and collored [sic] service men are having their own civil war in and among our own U.S. Army installation."[135] Anthony Zinni, who served with the 3rd Marine Division in 1970–71, depicted Okinawa as a bleak place, characterized by segregation, drug use, and racial hostility. As guard officer, he spent most of his time trying to prevent violent racial incidents from occurring or investigating them when they did. Black militant groups like the "Mau Mau" and the "Bushmasters" operated on base and in the surrounding town of Koza, and he responded to numerous reports of members attacking white marines. In one particularly noteworthy incident an officer of the day was disarmed and assaulted after he confronted a group of Black marines. Racially motivated actions were not one-sided as the KKK had a chapter on base, and Zinni investigated at least one confirmed cross burning.[136]

Michael Hagee, a white platoon commander in 1970, provided a similar account of life in Okinawa. He received a telephone call from a major who asked, "Hey Mike, would you come up and meet me and escort me down to your company?" Hagee was shocked that "in broad daylight in the middle of a marine camp, he called me and wanted me to escort him down." The major's fears proved not to be unfounded as a white marine in Hagee's company was later killed.[137]

Race relations were also poor in Europe. On July 4, 1968, a group of white servicemen stabbed and killed three African Americans during a brawl in Karlaruhe, Germany.[138] In August 1970 a race riot occurred at McNair Barracks in Berlin following a fight between Black and white troops. The fight began after two whites were overheard referring to Black soldiers as "niggers."[139] Racial incidents occurred on military bases in Ulm, Frankfort, Hohenfels, and Crailsheim.[140] A white NCO in Frankfort revealed the severity of racial problems in a news story, remarking, "Race is my problem . . . not the Russians, not Vietnamese. . . . I just worry about keeping my troops—Black and white—from getting at one another." Similarly, a Black sergeant claimed that they "no longer functioned like an Army platoon but like two street gangs. . . . Racial problems take all my time."[141] Servicemen in Vietnam were aware of how bad race relations were in Germany. Bob Steck recalled that when he was in Vietnam in 1970–71, Black and white soldiers alike would state, "I'd rather be in Vietnam than Germany" because relations were so poor there.[142]

Relations were not any better stateside. Race relations at Camp Lejeune in North Carolina were particularly tense with officials reporting 190 racial assaults in the first half of 1969. The most significant clash occurred on July 20 when a minor disagreement escalated into violence, resulting in dozens of injuries and the death of a white marine.[143] This was not the first death at Camp Lejeune: the previous summer a Black marine had been beaten to death by two white marines.[144]

"Discrimination Was the Spark"

As these accounts make clear, racial violence was a serious problem. However, many commanders remained in a state of denial. A provost marshal report covering racial incidents between July 1970 and April 1971 reveals that many commanders provided optimistic assessments of race relations while contrastingly noting numerous racial incidents. A commander of a medical support unit in III Corps reported that relations were "considered good," even though they reported twenty racial incidents. There were twenty-two racial incidents in the 1st Signal Brigade, but its commander noted, "Relations appear fair, but uneasiness exists." The commander of the 18th Military Police Brigade claimed that "units were free of racial tension" despite documenting thirteen racial incidents. Twenty-five racial incidents were reported in the 1st Aviation Brigade, which had units all around the country, but their commander claimed that relations were "excellent."[145] It is hard to tell whether these commanders were ignorant or just in denial. They may have feared displeasing or alarming superiors. Whatever the case, they failed to acknowledge reality. They weren't alone.

The day after the "mutiny" on the USS *Constellation*, 122 Black and 8 white sailors staged another sit-in protest. Despite two protests involving hundreds of sailors in less than twenty-four hours, Captain John Ward remained resolute: "I don't believe we have a racial problem. I believe what we have had is an uprising that was aided, abetted, encouraged and promoted by a few individuals possibly using racism as their vehicle."[146]

Ben Cloud acknowledged that officers were often ignorant about the levels of racial discord in the armed forces. He recalled, "We thought that things like that, racial problems, could not exist in the U.S. Navy and yet they did." Leaders often ignored the warning signs. Officers "tolerated segregation, primarily because we weren't educated enough to know that those kinds of situations were very incendiary" and had the potential for violence.[147]

Officials who acknowledged and tried to address racial issues were not necessarily rewarded; such actions could damage their careers. Cloud was the person most responsible for ending the *Kitty Hawk* Riot and saving lives in the process, but he was not rewarded for his efforts. He was likely informally punished for using the Black power salute and for his connection to the riot. Cloud observed, "I was promoted to captain, given further opportunities, but the Kitty Hawk situation has dogged me ever since." He believed he was never promoted to admiral because of his connection to the riot.[148] Townsend was also never promoted to admiral, one of only two commanders of aircraft carriers during the Vietnam War never to achieve this rank.[149]

If some commanders failed to acknowledge openly the existence of racial violence, others refused to admit the existence of racial discrimination and its role as a catalyst. While Martin Luther King Jr.'s assassination and the contrasting reactions of Blacks and whites provided a significant catalyst for the breakdown in relations, the long-term existence of racial discrimination created fertile ground for the escalation of tensions. King's assassination did not create racial discord; it simply intensified it. As the *Pittsburgh Courier* noted in a November 2, 1968, article concerning an armed standoff between Blacks and whites at China Beach, "discrimination was the spark."[150]

The armed forces didn't take complaints of racial discrimination seriously. In 1968 the Office of the Inspector General (OTIG) of the U.S. Army received 208 complaints of racial prejudice or discrimination but determined that only 4, or 1.92 percent, were justified. OTIG found that there was not a single instance of racial discrimination relating to assignment, promotion, demotion, or duty. In 1969 OTIG received 326 allegations of racial prejudice but found only 6 justified, a miniscule 1.84 percent. It did not accept a single complaint of prejudice in assignment, demotion, or promotion. African Americans complained again and again that they were given menial, difficult, or dangerous assignments and that they were not promoted to the rank they deserved, but for two years OTIG believed there was not a single justified complaint in these areas. The office stated without a hint of irony that "the small number of justified discrimination cases received in OTIG during FY 68 and FY 69 provides no basis for determining a trend."[151]

It is difficult to believe that in the 1960s nearly 99 percent of all allegations of racial discrimination in the armed forces were unfounded. Certainly, OTIG's conclusions did not encourage Blacks to voice their complaints through official channels. While the armed forces took racial violence seriously, they did not take charges of racial discrimination seriously, never acknowledging that the two issues were closely connected.

Equally troubling, in 1969 an army-commissioned study revealed that between November 1966 and October 31, 1969, commanders failed to report 423 accusations of racial discrimination to the DCSPER.[152] One of the major impediments to ending discrimination was that officials often refused to acknowledge that complaints of racial discrimination existed and were legitimate. To quote an anonymous white officer, "When my battalion commander tells me there is no discrimination in this outfit . . . I say there is no discrimination in this outfit whether there is discrimination or not."[153] In 1970 even Brigadier General Daniel "Chappie" James Jr. and Brigadier General Frederic E. Davison, the only two Black generals, claimed, "There is no such thing as inequality of opportunity in the armed forces today."[154]

In 1969–70 Billy Jones, a Black army psychologist, was involved in a Pentagon study examining racial tension among medical units in Vietnam. Jones's research revealed that tensions were high between NCOs, most of whom were white, and Black enlisted men. Blacks routinely complained they were punished harshly for minor violations while whites were not punished at all. Jones found many of these complaints credible, especially as they helped explain "why a lot of them [African Americans] ended up in the stockade for petty kinds of things," and why the prison populations were disproportionately Black. He reported his findings but had little confidence that anyone took them seriously. He recalled, "I had the distinct feeling that while the Pentagon asked that we do this study, that I did the focus groups for, that it went somewhere and sat on somebody's shelf and it never went anywhere else."[155]

The experiences of African Americans support the conclusion that Black complaints were not taken seriously. In January 1968 Ray Morrissette, a Black soldier in Baumholder, Germany, complained that someone set his door on fire and left a burning cross and a racist sign in front. The following day another sign reading "niggers don't have the balls to come out and fight and they know it" appeared. Morrissette complained, but his troop commander accused him of orchestrating the incident.[156] Investigators were equally unsympathetic. They acknowledged that "there were two signs posted in the troop area that were of a derogatory nature regarding the Negro race; a door in the troop was singed in connection with one of the before mentioned signs and a cross was burned outside the troop billets," but the authorities made no effort to catch the perpetrators. Investigators did, however, devote part of their report to criticizing Morrissette, noting that he was known for defying authority and avoiding work.[157]

In the months preceding the Camp Lejeune Riot in 1969, a biracial group of officers warned their superiors that most white commissioned and noncommissioned officers "were prejudiced and that Black marines were subject to discriminatory action by the military police." They charged that the "lack of informed courageous leadership in dealing with racial matters is widening the gulf of misunderstanding between the races," and if not fixed, violence was imminent.[158] No action was taken, but the group's statements confirm that discrimination was common and that some high-ranking officers were aware of it but unwilling to do anything.

Officials were likewise aware that racial discrimination was damaging the armed forces' reputation and contributing to a rise in racial tension and violence. Two days after the riot at Camp Lejeune, Colonel Louis S. Hollier, chair of an ad-hoc Committee on Equal Treatment, issued a report on recent racial problems to the commanding general of the 2nd Marine Division. Hollier placed considerable blame on "white officers and non-commissioned officers [who] retain prejudices and deliberately practice them.... The major offenders in this regard are among the relatively senior officers and enlisted marines." These officers were such an impediment that they "blocked and frustrated" all attempts to encourage better relations.[159]

Most commanders struggled to acknowledge that racial discrimination was a major problem. After the riot at Camp Lejeune, Commandant General Leonard F. Chapman Jr. admitted that racial discrimination existed but was unsure of how big of a problem it was. He noted, "Some of the complaints about discrimination I have heard appear to be valid, but many are based on rumor and misapprehension."[160] Brigadier General James J. Ursano, deputy chief of staff personnel and administration, was only willing to admit that the Black *perception* of "discrimination in promotions, punishment and assignments" contributed to incidents of racial violence.[161]

L. Howard Bennett, deputy assistant secretary of defense for civil rights, was one of the few to acknowledge the seriousness of the problem. Following his trip to Vietnam in December 1969, a report was released which recommended that the military track promotions to ascertain whether Blacks were overlooked. It also recommended that policies be changed to ensure greater transparency and universality in the justice system. A serviceman needed to receive a list of "all charges and specifications," "a printed outline of his rights, and the procedures he should follow to exercise and protect them," and "an outline of the manner in which regulations prescribe that the case shall proceed including timetables and formats for motions, evidence, witnesses, and appeals."[162]

Responding to Black complaints regarding the assignment of article 15s, the report recommended that "every company commander maintain, on a standard Departmental form, a log of non-judicial punishments administered by case number, rank, race, offense, prior offenses, other mitigating or negative considerations and punishment awarded." These changes would create a universal standard for punishments and a paper trail as to who received what punishment and from whom. This policy would also discourage officers from unfairly targeting African Americans for punishment and educate Blacks about their rights. Lastly, the report suggested the creation of a race relations council to oversee racial matters, a recommendation Bennett had voiced previously.[163] Unfortunately, military officials largely ignored his recommendations until 1972, when the armed forces finally adopted some of his suggested reforms in military justice.[164]

In 1971 Frank W. Render II, Bennett's successor, also investigated allegations of discrimination. He determined that African Americans were disproportionately punished through article 15s and courts-martial. He pointed out that discrimination in promotions and in the delegation of duties damaged morale. Render's findings were also ignored, and he was fired after fourteen months by Assistant Secretary of Defense Roger T. Kelley allegedly "because the rate of complaints about the maladministration of military justice had not decreased." However, Kelley admitted that Render "had no authority to order changes or enforce regulations already in effect." Render described feeling "like a second lieutenant or a staff sergeant" rather than the highest-ranking African American in the Pentagon, whose "rank was the equivalent of two and a half star general."[165] Between July 1963, when the position was created, and 1972 nine different men held the position. The turnover suggests disorder and dissatisfaction for all those involved.[166]

"Especially Vigilant When They Encounter Incidents or Activities Involving Black Troops"

The reaction of officials to racial violence often aggravated tensions and further alienated Black servicemen. Official military reports reveal more incidents of Blacks assaulting whites than whites assaulting Blacks, but one should be careful when interpreting these reports. Collectively, they show that racial violence was widespread and severe but provide little context or detail. The perpetrators, as well as factors that might have caused an incident, were often unknown, and the only information available came from those who remained at the scene. Investigations were often perfunctory.

There is a noticeable difference in how these reports depict Blacks and whites, however. In many instances whites who brandished weapons are described as doing so for their own protection or to calm tensions. Whites are sometimes depicted as justified in using weapons, but this is not the case for African Americans.

The reports discounted the possibility that whites might bear a degree of responsibility for racial violence. The possibility that African Americans might be responding to acts of discrimination or violence was similarly given little consideration. Part of the problem was that many officials were not sympathetic to Black concerns. Karl Marlantes recalled that many of the white NCOs and officers he interacted with were unlikely to care about discrimination, especially as they routinely referred to Blacks as "niggers."[167] Bob Steck trained with white U.S. Navy Seal sergeants who were openly hostile to the sole Black lieutenant. They claimed he had only become an officer through racial favoritism and that they would not follow his lead in battle. When Steck later served with the 17th Air Cavalry, white pilots said the same thing about the lone Black pilot.[168]

As a first lieutenant and then captain, Constance Edwards was one of the few Black female officers in Vietnam. She experienced both sexism and racism while serving in 1967–68 as a nurse attached to the 24th Evacuation Hospital in Long Binh. While one might think the injured men she was treating would be appreciative, this was not always the case. She recalled, "I had white patients tell me, 'well, I ain't having no nigger take care of me.'" These incidents occurred even when Edwards was the only nurse on staff. She also experienced hostility from some of the white corpsman who reported to her. She continued, "One of my subordinates that worked with me, he told me he was not going to obey what I had to say. . . . He called me the 'N word' and told me he was not taking orders from me." Edwards reported him to the disciplinary board, and while he was punished, these incidents demonstrate that racism was widespread among some troops.[169]

White racism was generally tolerated or excused. The Confederate flag flew on bases throughout Vietnam, Asia, Europe, and the United States, but the military tolerated other extreme expressions of racism as well. In April 1965 eleven white officers attended a party on a military base in Germany dressed as KKK members, even placing a burning cross at the head of their table. A senior officer eventually ordered them to remove their costumes and extinguish the cross, but the men were not punished because their actions were not thought to be "indicative of harmful intent." Instead, an internal investigation concluded that their costume choice was influenced by the "accessibility of costume materials," not racist ideals.[170]

In 1968 Bobbie Lee Pace, a white soldier in Augsburg, Germany, was promoted even after it was revealed that he was a high-ranking member of the American Nazi Party. His commanding officer explained that "he was a 'good soldier' who kept his racial theories separate from his duties." African Americans justifiably wondered whether military officials would have been as lenient had Pace been Black and a member of a militant organization.[171]

In September 1970 Congressman Louis Stokes, a Democrat from Ohio, received a letter from Jerry Boyd, a Black soldier in Babenhausen, Germany. Boyd claimed that KKK-like groups operated on base with impunity, leaving many to conclude that the "army has a laissez-faire attitude toward the racial situation in Europe." Boyd believed the army's failure to act against these groups had a disastrous effect on troop morale as it embittered African Americans and empowered white racists.[172]

In September 1969 the deputy commanding general on Okinawa produced a memorandum on racial disturbances based in part on statements made by local commanders. While there were cross burnings at Okinawa and incidents of whites attacking Blacks, nearly the entire report focused on the role African Americans played in these incidents. Their recommendations for improving race relations demonstrated they had no idea how to deal with racial problems. The memorandum included such absurd suggestions as the organization of bridge, charade, and debate clubs; the acquisition of more shuffle boards; and the purchase of new mattresses. There was little discussion of the issues African Americans routinely complained about. Even more bizarrely, it was suggested that "a full-time white junior officer" be appointed "racial relations officer" to address racial matters. Some commanders recognized this appointment was discriminatory, but its inclusion reveals a severe disconnect. This memorandum reveals that many military officials were completely out to sea when confronting racial problems.[173]

Anthony Zinni arrived in Okinawa a year later, and he concluded that poor leadership was a major factor contributing to racial violence. He found a split among officers between those who favored strong actions like wholesale arrests and others who wanted to ignore the situation. He felt strongly that these positions made things worse and contributed to further violence. Zinni believed that the military needed to be sympathetic to Black complaints of discrimination and address them openly and honestly, as "the previous philosophy of there are no Black marines or white marines, all marines are green" was insufficient since it allowed "no appreciation for what minorities might be going through or how they feel, either real or perceived."[174]

Zinni recruited African Americans to serve in the guard, but battalion commanders "complained to the regimental commander, 'he's not going to be able to recruit any Black guys, they're not going to want to be a part of the guard,' and of course that wasn't true. But see there was an assumption there." Zinni felt many white officers looked at every African American and saw a "Mau Mau" or "Bushmaster" rather than a marine.[175]

The general response of military officials was to regulate the behavior of Black servicemen. African Americans complained that white officers banned dapping, Afros, slave bracelets, and any other clothing associated with the Black power movement.[176] On December 12, 1968, *Jet* published a letter by Black airmen stationed at Pleiku Air Base. They complained that whites were permitted to wear their hair in various lengths and styles, but Blacks with anything but short hair were labeled troublemakers deserving of punishment. Equally troubling, whites were allowed to fly Confederate flags in commemoration of those who "rebelled against democracy and freedom," while the military banned Black professions of pride. The letter included a picture of Craig Gibson, a Black airman, standing in front of a poster stating, "PROUD TO BE BLACK," which was banned on base.[177]

In September 1969 General Leonard F. Chapman acknowledged that some officers had banned Afros. He clarified that the haircut was in accordance with marine regulations. He further stipulated that while "dapping" and the "black power salute" were not permitted during ceremonies, they were not otherwise expressly prohibited. Chapman's phrasing suggests that commanders were incorrectly punishing Black marines for dapping.[178]

Dapping remained a point of contention. David Addlestone recalled that it was not uncommon for white NCOs to try to prevent African Americans from dapping. He remembered, "We had one case where five Black soldiers were talking, greeting each other with an elaborate handshake and a southern NCO came and told them to move on and they didn't: a fistfight broke out."[179] A November 1972 investigation concerning race relations in the 39th Signal Battalion in Long Binh revealed that the battalion commander had banned dapping and slave bracelets. Furthermore, he refused to reverse these bans even when informed they were counter to official military policy.[180]

In general, the armed forces were hostile toward Black forms of cultural expression. A common point of contention was the style of music played in service clubs. Typically, whites preferred country or rock music while African Americans preferred soul or rhythm and blues. African Americans rarely got their way, and clubs routinely refused to play their choice of music. In 1969 *Black Journal* interviewed Black sailors stationed at Nha Be who described their experiences. Bobby Jenkins recalled, "We was listening to soul music and the guy said, 'We don't like that shit. Turn it off. We don't dig your dancing at all.'" Ironically, Jenkins had served on shore patrol duty at this same club where he was forced to listen to country music. As he pointed out, "We have to listen to it. We never complain or anything." Jenkins and his friends did not receive the same courtesy, and when a white soldier tried to rip the radio off the wall, a fight broke out. Jenkins was convicted at court-martial of assault and refusing to obey an officer who had allegedly told him to stop dancing.[181]

L. Howard Bennett readily admitted that Black complaints about music reflected larger issues related to representation, respect, and equality. He observed, "I think that when you begin to talk with so many of these young men about soul music, they're really talking about a lot of other things. Soul is just a convenient handle ... but behind it are ... not very good conditions existing between Blacks and whites in the armed forces." Bennett insisted that the military was making a "real effort" to ensure "that the people who are selecting the music and selecting the entertainment incorporate soul music and Black entertainers."[182]

Even when clubs agreed to play soul music, tensions didn't necessarily end. A Black marine named Sylvester Bracey recounted an incident that occurred on July 4, 1969, in Dong Ha, which suggests that resistance to providing entertainment enjoyed by Blacks was about more than different musical tastes. He was attending "a soul show, people might say, because most of the songs were Black." After the show ended, he and his friends were confronted by "all these beasts with M-16 rifles and what-not pointing at us, threatening to kill us." The men reported the incident to authorities, but they refused to punish the men responsible. Bracey did not specify if the "beasts" were military police or random marines but insinuated that any gathering of African Americans was regarded as a threat and needed to be dealt with violently.[183]

There is substantial evidence that many military officials viewed any gathering of African Americans as threatening. Black sailors at Nha Be in 1970 described a particularly tense racial environment where shore patrol would routinely harass African Americans. An unnamed Black sailor recalled, "If they see two to four brothers together in Vietnam, the first thing they say is 'what are they up to? They getting ready to plot something.'" According to the sailor, this was the case wherever they went. He clarified, "If we go outside right now and all of us be together you watch the eyes beam down on us. . . . If you go over to the club and we be in the club, you'll notice how many SPs [shore patrols] they have in there on duty in the club because we are in there."[184]

Black Journal interviewed Black marines on Okinawa who made similar claims that the marine corps was surveilling them and placing heavy restrictions on Black behavior. One marine complained, "We've been stripped of all culture and heritage. . . . What really belongs to us? Our cultures, our heritage. They don't want us to regain it." Accordingly, once Black marines started wearing dashikis, the marine corps banned them. One marine noted, "They saw so many brothers styling in their dashikis they decided well, boom, we ought to put a stop to this."[185]

Black soldiers at the Army Medical Center in Okinawa provided similar complaints. One soldier opined, "A guy can wear a cowboy getup into all the clubs. He can get his tall hat on, the fringes and the boots and everything and walk in the club and there's not one word said. But you let a man put on a dashiki and the whole club and General Lampert and everybody else will hear about it."[186] Kent Garrett confirmed that military restrictions on Afros and clothing caused considerable tension in Okinawa. He explained, "Black guys wanted to wear things that reflected their culture . . . and this was not against military rules. Whereas they felt that the white guys who were into the western garb and boots and that sort of thing, they got to wear theirs and the blacks couldn't have their Afro." Additionally, while military officials viewed these complaints as relatively minor, they were "really very significant" because African Americans saw them as an attack on Black culture and "were very angry about that."[187]

Authorities also placed restrictions on bracelets and dapping. Sylvester Bracey recalled, "They don't want us to give a power hand, it's nothing but a greeting, that's all. We can't wear our bracelets in the movie, how come? It's illegal they say, it's against regulations. They come down hard." He similarly complained that while the marine corps allowed Afros, Black marines were pressured to cut their hair.[188]

Military clubs in Okinawa were also unwilling to play requests for Black music. One Black soldier wondered, "I think it was a mutual feeling among all Black people in the United States army in the medical center that why the fuck should we have to put up with a country and western night without having any soul at all?" When the soldier and his friends went to a club anyway, they were confronted by military police who questioned why they were there.[189]

As in Vietnam, authorities in Okinawa viewed any gathering of African Americans as a threat. Sylvester Bracey noted that the marine corps had a policy in which there "can't be no more than five brothers on the streets at one time, you know, can't sit nowhere, no more than five, you know, or else the riot squad is going to come."[190] Robert Vonner, a Black marine who was stationed in Okinawa, similarly complained that officials "told Blacks that they couldn't congregate together. Couldn't have more than two. . . . Fifty whites can get together, but no more than two Blacks can get together."[191]

Officials were aware that commanders were implementing restrictive policies on African Americans. In 1971 Major Richard F. Ward, the Human Relations Council officer for the USARV, noted that when "black GI's are together it is viewed as a threat to all. While Caucasian soldiers cause no concern when they group together."[192]

In 1970–71 Army Counterintelligence routinely surveilled African Americans under the pretext of preventing racial discord. One counterintelligence report noted, "During the past four and a half months a concentrated effort has been made by army counterintelligence to detect and neutralize any organized effort to create a racial unrest within the US Army Vietnam."[193] At face value these goals appear commendable, but the "real" aim was to "neutralize" any effort by African Americans to organize. There is no evidence they surveilled whites.

The report advised, "Commanders at all levels must be especially vigilant when they encounter incidents or activities involving Black troops." Investigators claimed "that most incidents have evolved from so-called Black grievance committee or group meetings, which were formed by Blacks to discuss what they believed were injustices being experienced by all Blacks in the military as well as in the civilian communities." The authors admitted there were "black organizations striving to improve social conditions of Black troops," but "it is this type of group, which under the guise of a legitimate activity such as grievance committees," would eventually be subverted by extremist Black groups.[194] In other words, no gathering of Blacks could be permitted as participants would eventually fall under the influence of violent extremists.

The military was concerned about the rise in Black power–affiliated organizations but they did not differentiate between nonviolent groups which complained of racial discrimination and more militant groups. In

1963 Secretary of Defense Robert S. McNamara announced that members of the military were allowed to participate in civil rights demonstrations provided they were not in uniform or on duty. In response, civil rights organizations began welcoming service members into their ranks. However, not everyone was happy with military members being affiliated with civil rights. In January 1968 a base commander banned African Americans from joining the NAACP under the pretense that it was a subversive and violent organization equal to the KKK and the Communist Party.[195]

In June 1970 African American soldiers led by Sergeant Eddie Scott requested permission to form a NAACP chapter at Fort Leonard Wood in Missouri. Quizzically, the DCSPER office seemed to believe Scott's efforts might be a larger part of attempt to organize NAACP chapters across military bases in "Korea, Germany, Fort Rucker, Fort Bragg, etc." Brigadier General Winant Sidle, chief of information for the army, ultimately rejected Scott's request, but his reasoning for doing so demonstrated that the army had little interest in combating racial discrimination. He acknowledged that the NACCP was a nonviolent organization dedicated to attaining "its goals thru negotiations, political action, peaceful protests, demonstrations, and public information program," but the problem with them was that they used these tactics in benefit of issues like "school desegregation," which were by nature "political issues." Accordingly, the military had a responsibility to not show "active support for or against these issues," especially given "their political impact on soldiers and civilian communities, particularly in the southern states." In other words, the NAACP held political positions on issues like school desegregation that were anathema to the local white southern population. It was obvious whose opinions the army valued more.[196]

Sidle added that the NAACP could not be allowed on base because the name implied that it would only promote "one race of people" and its membership "would obviously be oriented toward black people." While presumably many organizations on base were more likely to attract one group of people or another, and the NAACP has never rejected white members, Sidle seemed convinced that the NACCP was a problematic organization. His criticisms were not that far removed from the commander who compared them to white supremacist organizations. Sidle even warned that if the NAACP were allowed on base, "Organizations promoting the advancement of other groups or colors would have to be extended the same cooperation, further compounding the racial problems in the army."[197] By this logic, if the NAACP were allowed on Fort Leonard

Wood, the army would have to allow the KKK and the American Nazi Party to form chapters as well. There was no difference in Sidle's mind.

Counterintelligence reports provide further evidence that the army did not differentiate when it came to African Americans organizing. Often the only thing counterintelligence uncovered were African Americans meeting peacefully to discuss the pervasiveness of racial discrimination in the military. On September 11–13, 1970, seventy-five to one hundred servicemen, most of whom were Black, met at Camp McDermott in Nha Trang to discuss a racist broadsheet found on base. Counterintelligence believed that the meeting could lead to violence, but instead participants discussed inequalities in promotions and the targeting of African Americans with article 15s and courts-martial. Counterintelligence was not sympathetic, labeling these criticisms as "ridiculous" and the soldiers who made them as having "low IQ's."[198]

On November 22 sixty African Americans with the 855th General Support Company met at Camp Carter in Da Nang to discuss the overrepresentation of African Americans in military jails. On November 29 fifty African Americans from the same battalion met and formed a "solidarity group" to discuss and articulate Black grievances. Large groups of African Americans met four more times in December to discuss similar complaints of discrimination.[199]

On November 23 roughly forty to fifty Black soldiers "gathered at the USO club" and marched toward the 23th Infantry Division headquarters in Chu Lai where they "requested permission to present a list of grievances to a General Officer." The march was organized because "the Negro soldiers apparently felt that their grievances were not being communicated to the CC (Company Commander) through the chain of command."[200]

The armed forces seemed particularly concerned with the BBU. Led by activists like Sergeant Andrew Love and Mildred Majette, assistant director of the United Service Organizations (USO) in Cam Ranh Bay, the BBU held "regular meetings of several dozen members and investigated allegations of discrimination regarding promotion, punishment, and command." Its leaders were primarily interested in teaching Blacks about military law, regulations, and proper use of chain of command. They formulated petitions, wrote letters, and organized demonstrations while also taking strong antiviolence and antidrug positions.[201]

Despite these commendable efforts Army Counterintelligence viewed the BBU as a militant and dangerous organization that warranted constant surveillance. Curiously, their own surveillance revealed that "discussions at BBU meetings are often centered around personal problems encountered by members," and that meetings in Long Binh "are mostly for listing grievances to be presented to the military authorities." They further noted that the BBU "never made any statements advocating violence or hostile acts toward Caucasians."[202]

Counterintelligence reports reveal that African Americans who viewed violence as an option often saw it as a last resort. On September 14, 1970, one hundred Blacks and ten whites in Saigon presented "five senior camp commanders a list of grievances which the Blacks related, if not corrected would result in violence of an unspecified nature." During a December 1 meeting in Long Binh involving 130 African Americans, the participants formed a council "to take black grievances to the appropriate commanders. If the commanders took no action on the grievances Blacks would then themselves 'rectify' the situation."[203] They did not immediately turn to violence but considered it in frustration when they felt their legitimate complaints of discrimination were ignored.

When Blacks felt they were being listened to, tensions eased. On May 14, 1971, roughly fifty African Americans approached the USA Support Command headquarters in Cam Ranh Bay requesting to speak with the company commander and deputy commander regarding the confinement of two Black soldiers. The deputy commander met with the group, and while the two men were not released and the group left unsatisfied, his willingness to speak with them alleviated some of the tension.[204]

On November 23, 1970, roughly one hundred African Americans with the 23rd Infantry Division at Chu Lai met with the inspector general and voiced complaints regarding "racial injustices and discrimination in the award of medical profiles, medical treatment, job assignments in rear areas, promotions, and disciplinary action." The group "indicated that commanding officers and first sergeants either would not listen to their problems or did not understand them," demonstrating that these complaints were hardly new. The inspector general responded that "appropriate corrective action would be taken" and "the group then dispersed and returned to their units."[205]

On December 17 African Americans in Da Nang met after a fight between Black and white soldiers. They elected four representatives and demanded a meeting with a Colonel Meerbot. During the meeting representatives complained that Billy Lee, a Black soldier from the 870th Transportation Company, was unfairly placed in pretrial confinement. After reviewing the case, Meerbot agreed that "an injustice had been done to Lee" and ordered his immediate release. Accordingly, "tensions eased after Lee's release."[206]

"Compulsory Education Program in Race Relations"

Most commanders were not particularly interested in or sympathetic to Black complaints of discrimination. Billy Jones's investigation of racial tensions in medical facilities included the organization of focus groups composed of servicemen of various ranks at four major hospitals across Vietnam. When Jones met the commander of one of the hospitals, the commander asked, "Why do they have to do this? They should let sleeping dogs lie. . . . Leave this alone." Jones took this reaction as a clear sign he was "going to find shit" but also that the commander had ignored previous racial problems.[207] It was hard to accomplish much when commanders were either disinterested or opposed.

L. Howard Bennett promoted Human Relations Councils as "a forum which enabled the concerned, the aggrieved, and the complaining to come to a group, which was representative of the total composition of a given unit, and have that Human Relations Council or committee directly communicate this concern to the commander." Bennett acknowledged that military officials had failed to deal with complaints of discrimination, but he was hopeful that these councils would "effectively communicate upwards the grievances and complaints of the men so that it gets up to the highest command position."[208] Bennett understood that complaints of racial discrimination often went unaddressed in part because the command was not informed there was a problem.

Bennett genuinely hoped that his efforts would improve race relations and effectively address Black complaints of racial discrimination. Kent Garrett thought that some of the officers he interviewed for *Black Journal*, like Brigadier General Frederick E. Davison, were not very forthcoming when discussing racial discrimination in the military, but Bennett was different. According to Garrett, Bennett "seemed to understand that there was a systemic problem in the institution, and that they were going to try and deal with it."[209] Garrett also interviewed Black sailors at Nha Be Naval Base who were involved in some of the first Human Relations Councils. One unnamed sailor traveled to Saigon where he met with Bennett, who was sympathetic and supportive, and they discussed incidents of racial discrimination. The sailor recalled, "He said he is going to look into it.

Okay, well as far as what he's been doing, he is looking through everything. I can see some changes in the base right now. One or two."[210]

Many commanders were not interested in creating or sustaining these councils. Olivier, another Black sailor, was asked to join an effort to "help the brothers and the white man get along." He was told he and a white counterpart would design a plan to improve race relations and address racial problems. However, it soon became clear that whoever organized the council had no intention of addressing anything. Olivier was shocked to find that "every time I go up there to discuss a problem with the man, the white man ain't ever there. They ain't got no white man." He believed there were ulterior and more sinister motives at play. He concluded, "They just want a Black man in there so they can find out everything a Black man is doing."[211] Given that the military routinely spied on peaceful meetings of African Americans, it is possible certain commanders hoped to use these councils as another opportunity to keep tabs on Black service members.

In March 1971 the DOD announced that there would be a "compulsory education program in race relations for the entire American military."[212] Human Relations Councils and other groups were established to provide these educational programs, but they had a mixed record. They often provided African Americans with a needed venue to express grievances, and some of the people involved were well-intentioned. In December 1971 Richard F. Ward acknowledged that racial discrimination provided the "root causes of racial tensions," specifically "complaints of discrimination in promotions, military justice and assignments." He concluded that "there is evidence that real racial discrimination does exist" in the form of "everyday selections, preferences, and actions."[213] Unfortunately, the efforts of Ward and others were hindered by commanders who refused to cooperate with council initiatives, preferring instead to "use special discharges, pretrial confinement in the stockade and transfers to other units" as a means of easing racial problems.[214]

In 1972 Chief of Naval Operations Admiral Elmo Zumwalt "introduced 200 human relations programs to relieve racial tension and accommodate Navy institutions to black lifestyles." Minority assistance officers were appointed to all commands.[215] However, a minority affairs committee set up by Zumwalt after the *Kitty Hawk* Riot found that "too many Navy leaders are paying lip-service to Zumwalt's liberalizing directives rather than making sure they are implemented." The committee asserted that "if the navy was serious in its efforts to eradicate racial discrimination," it needed to do more than just blame and punish African Americans for every violent incident as this created "an ever widening credibility gap in the minds of the minority populace, and in fact appear to put the Navy stamp of approval on racism." The group concluded that the navy recruiting slogan of "you can be black and Navy too, is false advertising."[216]

The Congressional House Armed Services Committee undercut Zumwalt's efforts when it ruled that the problems on the *Kitty Hawk* and *Constellation* were caused not by racism but by African Americans of "below average mental capacity" who needed to be removed from the military. Shortly thereafter, Zumwalt issued a directive discharging thousands of sailors thought to be agitators or malcontents.[217]

Events on the USS *Constellation* confirmed that many African Americans were unhappy with their treatment, but they also revealed that some commanders were opposed to reform efforts. Captain John Ward was neither sympathetic nor supportive of Zumwalt's efforts. Between April and October 1972 the Human Relations Council on board met once and the minority affairs committee never met.[218]

Human Relations Council investigations from November 1972 revealed that the commander of the 39th Signal Battalion in Long Binh had prohibited dapping, intending "to eliminate it altogether if possible." He also banned slave bracelets, refusing to reverse course even when told they were not in violation of armed forces policy. Investigators concluded that they "found little understanding for and empathy with minority groups" among leadership.[219] Even late in the war when Human Relation Councils' initiatives were supposedly fully implemented, many commanders refused to implement their recommendations.

Even supportive commanders struggled to implement properly council initiatives. Responding to previous racial problems at Fort Carson in Colorado, a Racial Harmony Council was created in 1970–71 with the support of the base commander, Major General John C. Bennett. The council sought to "solve race-related problems before they erupted into violence." The council opened a clothing store and restaurant designed to appeal to African Americans and other minorities. It established college classes on African American and Hispanic history and invited prominent activists like Julian Bond and Dick Gregory to speak.[220] Nonetheless, Bennett's leadership on racial issues was far from perfect. He alone appointed the council members. He also regularly disregarded the advice of Black officers believing he knew better. Wes Geary, a chaplain on base, recalled that Bennett "had a philosophy that every Black Officer above the rank of captain was an Uncle Tom and he would tell people this. And he said that we didn't have any credibility with the young soldiers."[221] In 1972 Bennett readily admitted, "We don't put Uncle Toms on the Council."[222]

The problematic nature of Bennett selecting council members became obvious when he fired a Sergeant Baile, the chair, without warning. Outraged, Black soldiers threatened various forms of protest and asked Geary to intervene on their behalf. Their meeting began poorly when Bennett referred to Geary as "Les." Geary bluntly told Bennett, "You insult a lot of people. . . . When you fired Sergeant Baile you insulted this guy. You insulted the whole Black [race] 'cause he's one of them." Refusing to serve as a go-between, Geary asserted, "These Black soldiers want to talk about stuff. They want to talk about how they feel, and you need to let 'em, and you need to listen to 'em." To Bennett's credit, he met with the soldiers and announced he was reinstating Baile as chair. After the announcement, a Black soldier demanded Bennett apologize to Baile, his family, and all Black soldiers. Bennett agreed, apologized, and the crowd erupted in cheers.[223]

Bennett was not perfect, but he was more sensitive to the needs of African Americans than most military commanders. He acknowledged the existence of racial tensions and refused to blame African Americans. He also made a genuine effort, though an imperfect one, to support initiatives that offered the possibility of reducing racial tensions. Initiatives like the Racial Harmony Council or the larger Human Relations Council needed the support of commanders if they were to be effective. In most cases commanders were not supportive.

Conclusion

On August 29, 1968, the violence that erupted in the United States in the summer of 1967 and after King's assassination in April 1968 arrived in Vietnam. But the Long Binh Riot was not an isolated event. Between the last six months of 1968 and the end of 1971 thousands of incidents of racial violence were reported on or around military bases in every region of Vietnam. There was another war being fought, but this one was between servicemen wearing the uniforms of the U.S. military.

Domestic events contributed to the development of the other war, and tensions heightened considerably after King's assassination. Black servicemen reacted to King's death with sadness and anger, but some whites treated it as a cause for celebration. These differing reactions often led to violent confrontations. Still, King's assassination was simply the catalyst for already simmering tensions as African Americans had long complained of racial discrimination in the military. These complaints were legitimate, but military leaders largely ignored them. Their failure to address Black complaints helped create an environment of racial tension and distrust that often led to violence. Many African Americans concluded that racial discrimination was as pervasive in the military as in civilian life. They had physically left the United States, but they were unable to leave behind the racism and prejudice that regularly impacted their experiences at home.

Military officials were concerned about the detrimental effect violent racial incidents had on unity and morale. However, they focused their attention almost exclusively on African Americans. They ignored the role whites played and gave the impression that all African Americans, regardless of their thoughts and behavior, were responsible for the violence. In doing so, they failed to recognize or address the root cause behind much of the racial violence: the prevalence of racial discrimination in the military.

Some officials understood that racial discrimination and racial violence were linked. In July 1967 President Lyndon Johnson established the Kerner Commission to determine the causes of the recent Newark and Detroit Riots. The commission's report, released in February 1968, concluded, "Our nation is moving toward two societies, one Black, one white—separate and unequal. . . . Discrimination and segregation have long permeated much of American life; they now threaten the future of every American."[224] By August, the first major incidents of racial violence occurred in Vietnam. These eruptions and those that followed would similarly threaten to tear the military apart. Had an impartial commission been appointed to investigate racial tensions in the armed forces, it would have found that racial discrimination was linked to the rise in incidents of racial violence in Vietnam.

To be sure the primary goal of the armed forces was to win the war, but its failure to recognize discrimination and to deal effectively with the real causes of racial tension and violence weakened unity, reduced morale, and hampered the war effort.

CHAPTER 4

"I Thought of My Own People Back Home"

African American Servicemen and Vietnamese Civilians

On May 1, 1968, Akmed Lorence, a Black veteran, was interviewed about his experiences in Vietnam for a soon-to-be-released documentary entitled *No Vietnamese Ever Called Me Nigger*. He was asked about his experiences with and impressions of the Vietnamese. Lorence recalled an incident involving an elderly woman, accompanied by several children, who approached him asking for food. He initially refused but after she spent more than an hour begging, Lorence relented and gave her two boxes of C-Rations. He remembered, "I looked at her and I saw in this woman's face real, sincere begging. And I thought to myself, this woman could be my mother, this could be my grandmother, and that child she's holding could have been a relative of mine."[1]

Lorence's fellow servicemen were not happy with him as he had given away some of their food too, but he defended himself stating, "It was her land we had come to and destroyed, and she needed food for her child." The woman reciprocated by returning a few hours later to give him a bag of roasted peanuts. He recalled, "This really played a heavy part on me because it brought the Vietnamese people, through this lady, closer to me or closer to understanding them and their problems."[2]

The association Lorence made of Vietnamese poverty with African American poverty was not surprising. He grew up poor and Black in New York City and witnessed his mother's and grandmother's struggles with poverty and racism. Lorence even cited lyrics from a song he had written—"soon I'll be going back to the place where the rats and the roaches roam"—to express his feelings about returning to his apartment in Harlem.[3] Poverty and racism were well-known to him and his community.

Lorence's background was not unique. Most African American servicemen came from poor or working-class backgrounds.[4] They had experienced American racism. Knowing very little about Vietnam or its people, African Americans interpreted their experiences with the Vietnamese from a perspective shaped almost entirely by their own experiences with poverty and racial prejudice back home. This perspective largely explains why Lorence was willing to hand over part of his rations to an elderly woman he didn't know. Having lived in a "place where the rats and the roaches roam," he was empathetic to those living in poverty, whether in the United States or in Vietnam. He also identified with those experiencing racial discrimination. Lorence didn't compare her to just any woman; he compared her to Black women in his own family. He viewed her as a victim of more than just poverty.

Most African Americans shared Lorence's belief that Vietnamese civilians were victims of racial discrimination, and the continual use of racial slurs by white servicemen gave credence to this viewpoint. When African Americans heard these slurs, they understandably thought of those used against them. Black servicemen also believed that white servicemen were more likely to abuse or mistreat civilians. Dwyte A. Brown, who served with the navy in 1968–69, believed that many white servicemen viewed the Vietnamese from a position of "I am conqueror, I am supreme," and this led them to "treat Vietnamese, like dirt." To Brown and many other African Americans, the way some whites treated the Vietnamese was more than familiar; it was identical to the way whites treated them. Brown articulated this perception when he stated, "Me, myself, as a person, knowing from the experience that I had with whites back here in America, I could not go over there and degrade another human being. I see a little Vietnamese in trouble, I even bend over and help him out."[5]

As Brown saw it, while African Americans' experiences with racism and poverty led them to empathize with Vietnamese civilians, racist whites simply found a new target to oppress and mistreat. Black servicemen believed that white racism accompanied them to Vietnam where it found a new group to oppress in ways that were eerily familiar.

"Vietnamese Were Not Vietnamese"

Contemporary reports reveal that African Americans routinely expressed sympathy for Vietnamese people, frequently explaining their feelings in racial terms. Over a nine-week period in the spring of 1967, journalist Ethel L. Payne conducted hundreds of interviews with Black servicemen. She concluded that they overwhelmingly sympathized with the civilian population because they "equate the struggle of the Vietnamese people with the civil rights movement at home."[6]

A 1975 psychological study of American-Vietnamese relations based on a questionnaire administered anonymously to 126 Black and 359 white veterans revealed that African Americans were far less likely to express negative views of Vietnamese people than whites. Whites were much more likely to describe the Vietnamese collectively as "lazy, cowardly, and subhuman." In contrast, African Americans were "more likely to interact as social equals with the local populace than were whites." Black servicemen felt greater empathy for the Vietnamese "because both groups had been the target of extensive racial prejudice and had experienced the despair and frustration that are consequences of such treatment."[7]

The Veterans Administration's *Legacies of Vietnam* study is the most thorough examination of veterans' attitudes and experiences. When asked about their general feelings toward the Vietnamese, without distinguishing between civilian or combatant, 48 percent of Black veterans reported positive feelings while only 27 percent of white veterans reported the same. More striking, 32 percent of white veterans reported holding negative feelings but 9 percent of Blacks reported the same.[8]

These findings are more remarkable when considering that most servicemen—whatever their race—arrived in Vietnam with little knowledge of the country or its people. Many had never even traveled outside of the United States. Even those with more education had little opportunity to learn about Vietnam. Between 1954 and 1968 there were only two tenured professors at American universities who spoke Vietnamese. During the same period only 22 of 7,615 graduate dissertations in modern history, political science, or international relations dealt with Vietnam.[9]

Knowledge of and interest in Vietnam increased as the war progressed, but most servicemen had only a cursory knowledge of the country before entering the military. Albert French, who served with the 3rd Marine Division in 1965, remembered, "I didn't understand too much about Vietnam. I knew where it was, I had looked on a map. I didn't watch TV and really didn't know what was going on, other than that troops had been sent in and we were going to join them."[10] Anthony Martin read the newspaper every morning and absorbed information about the war, but his understanding was superficial at best. He remembered, "We weren't sophisticated enough. . . . All we knew is that communism was bad, and this was our time to go and fight communism."[11]

Bill C. Bryels, who served with the 101st Airborne Division in 1967–68, recalled that he "had no quarrel with the Vietnamese—never even heard of Vietnam until the war. It was not something we were taught in world history. We knew about China, but Vietnam was not something I knew about."[12] James Gillam learned about the war from watching the news, but his interest in the conflict expanded when his brother Edward was sent to Vietnam.[13]

Horace Coleman researched the conflict and Vietnam's history at the base library before being deployed. He was shocked to find that the United States was not the first country to try to impose its influence in Vietnam. When he read about the French Army's defeat at Dien Bien Phu, he began to question whether the war was a good idea.[14]

Generally, the earliest information servicemen received about Vietnamese people came during basic training. Each serviceman was given a small card listing the "Nine Rules of Conduct," which included instructions like "treat women with politeness and respect" and "always give the Vietnamese the right of way." They received a brochure with key Vietnamese phrases and a short description of the country. Any additional training was largely left to the discretion of commanders.[15]

In basic training, Anthony Martin was told to treat the Vietnamese with courtesy and kindness and to remember that as Americans they were guests in a foreign country.[16] Martin's experience appears to be the exception, however. In basic training, officers often collectively referred to the Vietnamese as "dinks," "slopes," "zipperheads," and "gooks."[17] Historian Peter S. Kindsvatter correctly notes that the enemy was dehumanized to stir up hatred and aggression against people whom the average trainee had little "animosity toward and hence no particular urge to kill."[18] However, these racist terms were often used to refer to everyone, including noncombatants. Trainees were told that civilians posed a threat and should not be trusted.[19]

Robert Louis Jr. was told by his drill instructor that all Vietnamese were "gooks" and that even those that appeared to be trustworthy would murder you in your sleep if given the opportunity.[20] Haywood T. Kirkland, who served with the 25th Infantry Division in 1967–68, remembered that almost immediately, "they told us not to call them Vietnamese. Call everybody gooks, dinks."[21] Arthur Barham recalled that instructors during NCO training used slurs "because they were trying to get us to hate these people" and reinforce the message of "don't trust anybody."[22]

In 1968 the MACV began to provide trainees with slightly more information about Vietnamese people and their customs. They instructed servicemen to avoid taking pictures of civilians without permission and that it was improper to "walk hand-in-hand with a Vietnamese woman."[23] Nonetheless, many instructors continued to express racist feelings toward the Vietnamese. Wayne Smith remembered that the Vietnamese were universally referred to as "gooks," "chinks," and "slopes" in basic training. As was the case with Barham, instructors told Smith never to trust any Vietnamese people.[24]

Lamont B. Steptoe remembered that in OCS instructors consistently referred to Vietnamese people as "gooks." They passed along demeaning and racist rumors including that the women had horizontal vaginas. He remembered, "They did everything in their power to convince us that the Vietnamese were nonhuman to justify our violent response to them."[25] James Gillam recalled that the trainers "othered" them, noting, "Vietnamese were not Vietnamese, they were referred to as gooks and dinks, and slopes and all those racist terms." Like Steptoe, Gillam believed the military did this to "reduce the other person to something less than human," which would allow servicemen to do whatever they wanted to the Vietnamese.[26] Freddie Edwards recalled that all they told him in training about the people was that they were "gooks."[27]

The racialization and dehumanization of the enemy was nothing new. Historian John W. Dower's *War without Mercy* notes that during World War II in the Pacific, military officials depicted the Japanese as universally immoral, animalistic, subhuman, and obsessed with killing Americans. This characterization had real repercussions as "race hate fed atrocities and atrocities in turn fanned the fires of race hate."[28] Yet, as Peter Kindsvatter points out, it wasn't until the Vietnam War that the dehumanization of the enemy "became integral to the training process."[29] The nature of the conflict made it difficult to determine who the enemy was. This likely explains why negative characterizations of the NLF and PAVN were extended to include civilians.

"We Didn't Have the Greatest House in the World but It Wasn't Cardboard"

Given what African Americans were taught in basic training, it would be understandable that they had negative views of the Vietnamese. However, in most cases they did not accept these negative images. Robert Louis Jr.

remembered, "When you got over there you found that, well, don't know who they were talking about because it's not the people I am looking at.... The people I am looking at are just poor."³⁰

Louis's description of the Vietnamese he encountered as poor is important. While the RVN did have wealthy landowners, an urban elite, and a middle class, servicemen were most likely to encounter tenant farmers who worked small plots of land or rice paddies for subsistence and made up three-fourths of the population in rural areas. They lived in thatched houses with dirt floors and without toilets, running water, refrigeration, or electricity.³¹

Refugees were another group servicemen encountered. The war caused the displacement of at least 5 million people, more than a fourth of the population. Most refugees lived in makeshift shantytowns or camps surrounding cities, towns, and even military bases. Their houses were often made from discarded American garbage.³² Sewage and sanitation services were almost nonexistent, and residents often "bathed, urinated, and washed their clothes in the same meager amount of water found in gutters, puddles, or drawn from wells." Disease was rampant. During the war, Saigon had the highest combined rate of smallpox, cholera, bubonic plague, and typhoid in the world.³³

Many servicemen, especially in cities or on military bases, interacted solely with Vietnamese civilians employed by the American military. It is estimated that the military employed roughly 100,000 civilians, but an even higher number likely worked unofficially. Young women known as "hooch maids" worked as cleaners, launderers, or maids for about five dollars a month. Even the lowest ranking private made between $150 and $200 a month, which meant he could afford the services of a "hooch maid" if he wanted one.³⁴

Many Black servicemen were shocked by the poverty they encountered in Vietnam. David Parks stated, "The villages we passed through were really poverty-stricken. People go to the bathroom in the streets, and the kids ran alongside the convoy begging for food."³⁵ As a child, Horace Coleman had been surprised by the poverty he had witnessed during a family visit to Mississippi but this was nothing compared to what he saw in Vietnam. Walking through the streets of Saigon, he was shocked to see numerous people with smallpox scars and uncorrected cleft palates. He recalled seeing a beautiful woman walking in the distance, only to realize she had smallpox scars all over her face once he drew closer. This shocked him as back home, "even the poorest kids would get free shots from the clinic."³⁶

James Daly, who served in the army in 1967–68, was surprised to find that "the people here are about a hundred years behind the Americans and I feel sorry for them." Daly related Vietnamese poverty to his own experiences growing up in a housing project in Bedford-Stuyvesant in Brooklyn.[37]

Daly was not the only one to see the similarities between poverty in Vietnam and in African American communities. Samuel Vance observed, "In Vietnam I often looked at the poor, deprived children and thought of my own people back home and how little they had. . . . I often prayed that other people could look at my people and other minority groups and feel this compassion."[38]

Robert Louis Jr. recalled, "I am from dirt deep down in poor, poor Louisiana and these people were worse off than I ever was or ever could have imagined." Louis was particularly stunned by "huts made out of straw and sticks, that's what they were living in, and this was their whole society, not just a few. The condition, if you will, of the entire society; that was a shock. Made that little four-room shack I was born in look good; didn't make me feel any better."[39] Louis experienced such a level of sympathy for the Vietnamese that he felt guilty he had grown up in better conditions. The fact that the people he encountered were living in houses made of straw and sticks made him feel neither proud nor superior but rather sad and reflective.

Growing up relatively poor in rural Virginia, George Hicks was surprised to find that many Vietnamese lacked the basic things that even he had as a boy. He remembered, "The one thing that I really couldn't wrap my arms around was that they didn't have any bathrooms." Equally shocking, many people built their houses out of anything they could find, including cardboard. He recalled, "A cardboard house? We didn't have the greatest house in the world but it wasn't cardboard."[40]

For Emmanuel J. Holloman, who served with the 25th Infantry Division in Cu Chi from 1966 to 1969 and again in Long Binh in 1971, poverty connected African Americans to the civilian population "because they knew the hardships the Vietnamese went through." Holloman described his own upbringing: "I had five brothers and three sisters. My mother worked, still works in an old folks home. An attendant changing beds and stuff. . . . I had to leave school after the eighth grade to work in North Carolina." But poverty was not the only thing that linked African Americans to Vietnamese civilians. Holloman implied that only Black people were truly able to relate to the Vietnamese because they had experienced both economic and social inequality. While there were poor whites, they had never experienced the social discrimination that a person of color faced.[41]

This isn't to say that whites were incapable of experiencing feelings of empathy. Speaking of his childhood in Rhode Island, white veteran Richard Marlotas recalled, "I had nothing. I used to wear the same clothes. We had no money to buy stuff—food or anything." He related to the poverty of the Vietnamese, recognizing that "those people don't have anything either."[42]

"You're Going to Call Them Gooks, You're Going to Call Me Nigger"

Many African Americans saw the common experience of poverty as linking them to Vietnamese civilians, while others highlighted that both were persons of color and victims of racial discrimination. For many African Americans the use of slurs like "gook" and "slope" reminded them of the way whites talked about them. Anthony Martin was eager to learn about Vietnamese culture, but he quickly realized that his curiosity was not shared by many white servicemen. Martin remembered that whites casually referred to the people as "slopeheads," which he reacted against "because I knew that's the way I was talked about." His attitude was, "You said that about them, I can only guess what you are saying about me behind my back." In contrast, Martin recalled, "I think most of the Black guys there . . . I think a lot of us felt the same way that I felt. These were people who were being discriminated against just as we were. . . . I don't recall any Blacks that I hung around with being vulgar toward these people."[43] He saw African Americans and the Vietnamese as victims of racial discrimination, a shared experience that led him to empathize with the Vietnamese and their struggles.

Arthur Barham thought that many whites viewed themselves as superior, and the way they talked about the Vietnamese reflected this belief. He recalled, "A lot of times you heard white soldiers talking about the Vietnamese and calling them gooks and yellow monkeys and slant eyes. . . . They always referred to them as objects, you know, things. Black soldiers didn't do that." Barham understood that the use of racial slurs was not unlike the use of slurs against African Americans.[44]

Others made similar observations. Robert Louis Jr. remembered thinking that soldiers who used terms like "gook" or "slope" would probably use the slur "nigger" in reference to African Americans if they thought they could get away with it.[45] Bernard McClusky, who served in 1967–68 with the 52nd Signal Battalion in Soc Trang, reached a similar conclusion. He asserted, "I never called the Vietnamese people 'gooks' or 'slant eyes,' because that was a nigger at home in America."[46] Brian Settles thought similarly. When he heard whites use slurs toward the Vietnamese, they "rang loud and too clear as synonyms for nigger, jigga-boo, jungle bunny, spear-chucker, terrapin, and Sambo." He further noted that to many whites, "there was no distinction drawn between North or South Vietnamese or Viet Cong; they were all gooks."[47]

Lamont B. Steptoe's decision to drop out of OCS two weeks before being commissioned was influenced by "the constant references to Vietnamese people as gooks. . . . I just didn't like what they were turning us into." The use of racial slurs dehumanized the Vietnamese, but they had the opposite effect on Steptoe, who immediately became more sympathetic because the slurs "resonated the word 'nigger'" to him.[48]

Horace Coleman believed that Vietnam was a "xenophobic, racist war," and the way civilians were talked about and treated reflected this reality. While riding on a bus from Tan San Nhut Air Base to Saigon he overheard two white soldiers talking about how dumb the Vietnamese were because "they don't even speak English." He believed the war provided whites with an opportunity to project racist feelings prevalent in American culture on to the Vietnamese. Vietnam gave "people who might have used their attitudes toward some other ethnicity that they encountered in the United States to make themselves feel better or justify whatever, they had somebody to displace their negative attitudes toward."[49]

Louis Perkins reached a similar conclusion. He felt the Vietnamese "were genuine good people" but that this was not an opinion shared by many whites. He remembered, "We [Blacks] could relate to them and the problems that they were having . . . because the white man has a tendency to degrade everybody, and I say that in respect that you gotta give them a nickname, 'the gooks,' or this, that, the other." He resented the use of racial slurs and saw them as identical to slurs used against African Americans, stating, "You're going to call them gooks, you're going to call me nigger."[50]

Wayne Smith "resisted ever calling the Vietnamese gooks or dinks or slopes or nips" because he had Asian friends back home but also because he understood that these terms were used to dehumanize and convince servicemen "we're not killing human beings, we're killing gooks." He understood "intellectually and emotionally . . . if we were fighting in the Congo everybody would be calling them niggers."[51]

Freddie Edwards observed, "I couldn't understand the hatred military people seemed to have for the Vietnamese." This hatred was particularly offensive to him as it conflicted with the values he had learned from his mother and from his Christian faith. He was taught that all people were equal and deserving of equal treatment, but other servicemen seemed to actively hate the Vietnamese. Dismayed, Edwards began telling "some of my military friends, I don't like that word, please don't use it around me," whenever he heard them using a racial slur.[52]

In January 1971 Brigadier General James J. Ursano, deputy chief of staff personnel and administration, sent investigators to interview prisoners at the Long Binh Stockade. These interviews revealed that Black prisoners strongly resented "white prejudice against the Vietnamese as personified by the use of the word 'Gook,'" seeing this as just "another example of the white man's prejudice against non-whites."[53] While one would expect prisoners to have many complaints, it is revealing that the use of derogatory epithets toward the Vietnamese was one of the more commonly heard objections from Black prisoners.

Incidentally, there is evidence that the armed forces recognized some whites were prejudiced against both groups. In June 1972 MACV circulated a leaflet with a cartoon drawing of a white soldier next to the caption, "I wish people would quit telling me to be nice to the Vietnamese—it's hard enough trying to get along with all the colored." In a letter explaining the significance and meaning of the leaflet, Major General A. J. Bowley, director for personnel, U.S. Air Force, stated that it was meant to illustrate the "commonality of Black/white bigotry and U.S/Vietnamese bigotry."[54]

"This Could Be My Mom, This Is What My Mom Would Do"

Many African Americans believed they shared common experiences with Vietnamese people. Sinclair Swan recalled that many Black servicemen related to the struggles of Vietnamese people because they were the "low man on the totem pole," a place normally held by African Americans.[55] Bernard McClusky explained that African Americans had a "better understanding" of the Vietnamese "because we were not considered a person in

America so how can I go to another country and not consider someone else a person?" He admitted that it was common for many whites to look down on the Vietnamese, but "it wasn't natural to me as a black man."[56] Ed Emanuel "acquired a secret admiration for the Vietnamese people" because they "endured the same harsh problems as the American black population. Both were victims of social and economic inequality."[57] Kent Garrett recalled that the African American servicemen he interviewed felt "a certain camaraderie" with the Vietnamese because they had "been screwed over in very much the same way as Blacks had been in the U.S." They related to the Vietnamese partly on racial grounds because, like African Americans, they were victims of racial oppression but also because both groups were "neglected" and forced to survive on the "lowest side of the economic spectrum."[58]

Many African Americans focused on the treatment of civilians employed by the armed forces. While the military thought they were providing much needed employment, many Blacks viewed the relationship as an example of white exploitation. Racist whites kept Blacks in a subservient position, and now they were doing the same thing to the Vietnamese. David Parks predicted in his diary that the southern whites he met in basic training would "probably treat the Vietnamese civilians like they treated the black people back where they came from."[59]

Others found Parks's predictions to be accurate. Bill C. Bryels immediately noticed that "they had Vietnamese people doing the kind of things I was accustomed to seeing African Americans do—laundry, sweeping, cleaning, garbage details, and those kinds of things." He confessed, "The thought occurred to me, which was later made very popular by Richard Pryor: They were the new 'niggers.'"[60]

Richard A. Guidry, who served with the 1st Battalion of the 4th Marines in 1967, questioned the use of civilian workers. He asked, "Isn't that just like Americans, always have to have someone cleaning up after them?" A white friend of his named Ciantar disagreed, countering, "Before you start branding anyone an ugly American . . . who do you think is going to wash the damn pots, a bunch of pot washers from Kansas? Besides, these guys probably make more money than they ever dreamed of." Guidry remained unconvinced by Ciantar's reasoning.[61]

Guidry's and Ciantar's opposing interpretations are revealing. Guidry argued that whites had placed the workers in a subservient position. In stating "isn't that just like Americans," he suggested that he saw himself as distanced from his fellow Americans. Ciantar believed that washing pots was appropriate and even beneficial—a paternalistic view.

Another time Guidry's platoon encountered an elderly woman who "emerged from the hut with a pot and several tin cups, wearing a smile that I had often seen southern blacks put on for white bosses."[62] Again Guidry created an image of the Vietnamese as the African Americans of Vietnam. They were forced to behave in a certain way, just like African Americans back home.

Others compared the status of Vietnamese civilians to that of African Americans. Ron Bradley believed that many servicemen, especially white ones, treated civilians as if they were their personal slaves.[63] When Wayne Smith's platoon walked into a small village, they were greeted by a woman who handed over soup and chicken that she had prepared for her own family. He remembered, "I could identify with the Vietnamese. . . . I thought this grandmotherly person who made dinner for us or gave us dinner from their dinner. This could be my mom, this is what my mom would do."[64]

While touched by this woman's gesture, especially as she reminded him of his mother, Smith, like Guidry and Bradley, found the relationship between the Vietnamese and the American military troubling. He claimed the Vietnamese were treated the "equivalent of like the southern states in the 1700s and 1800s with African American slaves. You know like they were always there but were semi-invisible."[65] Their poverty, their subordination, and the racial slurs directed at them led Bradley and Smith to connect the Vietnamese of the 1960s to Black slaves of the antebellum South.

"There Was This Thing toward the Vietnamese Like They Were a Lower Life Form"

Black servicemen believed that white mistreatment of the Vietnamese extended beyond insulting attitudes or racial slurs. Many agreed with Ron Copes's assertion that "there was this thing toward the Vietnamese like they were a lower life form."[66]

Historian Christian G. Appy noted that there was little consistency in the way serviceman treated civilians. Some behaved with compassion, others with hostility and contempt. Many servicemen were capable of both. Poor treatment "covered a huge spectrum, from taunts and insults to kicks and shoves to murder."[67] Many African Americans believed that whites were more likely to mistreat Vietnamese people. There is statistical evidence to suggest this was true. Dr. Jerome Kroll of the Rockland

Psychiatric Center examined the sentences handed down to 293 prisoners serving at Fort Leavenworth, concluding that whites were six times more likely to be imprisoned for crimes against Vietnamese people than Blacks.[68] Given that Blacks were more likely to be charged and convicted for crimes by military tribunals, this statistic is significant.

Many Black servicemen recalled incidents of whites mistreating Vietnamese civilians. Harold Bryant likely spoke for many when he concluded, "I learned that white people weren't the number one race. I found out that some of them were more animalistic than any black people I knew. I found out that some of them didn't have their shit together."[69] While walking through a hamlet in the Iron Triangle region, Robert Louis Jr. witnessed a white staff sergeant push a Vietnamese child into a dike unprovoked.[70]

Roosevelt Gore remembered that Black soldiers gave food and candy to children while whites routinely mistreated them. Gore recalled, "The biggest thing that bothers me has to do with some of our soldiers who would use their rifle butts to hit Vietnamese kids on the side of the head. The kids was begging the GIs for food, asking for a piece of C-ration candy or whatever, and the guys would just knock them out."[71]

Dwyte A. Brown witnessed white servicemen slapping civilians and even purposely running into them with their cars. In the mess hall one day, a white serviceman requested extra chicken from a server, but when she only gave him two pieces, "the guy grabbed her by the neck and stuck her head in the mashed potatoes."[72] Lamont B. Steptoe recalled that "guys would take C-Rations like canned soup or something, and as we rode by Vietnamese on their motorcycles, they would hit them in the head and cause them to crash."[73] Robert E. Holcomb witnessed a violent incident while serving with the 101st Airborne around Pleiku in 1970. Ordered to transport spoiled milk to a dump, he spotted whites from his company throwing the bottles of milk at civilians riding motorcycles. Holcomb was irate at their behavior and stopped them before they could hurt anyone else.[74]

David Parks reported that white soldiers made a game of abusing civilians. He remembered, "We're riding along and there's a group of hungry kids. Someone throws a piece of bread on the road. The kids go for it like a pack of wolves. Often one of them gets hit by a truck or several get hurt in the scramble." The white soldiers were amused, but Park maintained that you would "never see a soul doing anything like that."[75]

Emmanuel J. Holloman also distinguished between Black and white behavior. He remembered that "anything blacks got from the Vietnamese, they would pay for. You hardly didn't find a black cursing a Vietnamese. And a black would try to learn some of the words. And try to learn a few of their customs so they wouldn't hurt them." By contrast, most whites treated the Vietnamese like they were stupid and worthless. He noted numerous instances when whites abused civilians. Once while shopping in a village, a white soldier threw tear-gas grenades into a crowd of civilians causing many to pass out. During another incident a white soldier sat on a bridge shooting people with a slingshot. In a separate incident, Holloman saw an "MP who sat on that bridge all day and shot people going to work with his BB gun. I rode behind him once, and he shot at everybody for 5 miles."[76]

These accounts described whites purposely abusing Vietnamese civilians, but several African Americans remembered incidents that were even more violent, including rape and murder. Recent historiography on the subject suggests that these events may have been more common than previously thought. While the killing of hundreds of civilians at My Lai is well known, Michael Sallah and Mitch Weiss's *Tiger Force: A True Story of Men and War*, Deborah Nelson's *The War behind Me: Vietnam Veterans Confront the Truth about U.S. War Crimes*, and Nick Turse's *Kill Anything That Moves: The Real American War in Vietnam* have each documented numerous incidents of servicemen raping and killing civilians.[77]

There was almost no interest in prosecuting or even punishing servicemen who committed crimes against Vietnamese people. The LMDC did not defend servicemen accused of such crimes because prosecutions were so rare and convictions even rarer. David Addlestone recalled that the military's attitude was, "If the Vietnamese were the victim, the 'mere gook' rule would be used. If the victim was Vietnamese, they didn't give a shit."[78]

Anthony Martin believed that American forces often treated civilians like animals, which disgusted him. His dismay grew the day he overheard white marines bragging about raping women. He observed, "The amount of females, Vietnamese women, who are probably alive today who have been raped by Americans 'just because' was appalling to me." Martin was quick to differentiate between how white and Black marines acted, stating, "I don't recall any Blacks that I hung around with being vulgar toward these people or even considering the idea of you know 'let's take this chick and rape her.'"[79]

Martin was not the only African American to acknowledge women were raped in Vietnam. David Parks wrote in his diary that "some of the guys have indulged in some raping too. They even brag about it."[80] Dwyte A. Brown claimed that many white sailors thought they were entitled to sex with any Vietnamese woman, including those who worked on base. Brown raised a hypothetical situation in which a woman came on base to shine shoes. A Black sailor would give a dollar tip but a white guy would say, "You ain't do it good enough. Maybe smack her or throw her daughter down, pull her clothes up, try to have sex with her. She just thirteen or fourteen. She there tryin' to sweep the floor." Harold Bryant witnessed a white soldier raping a dead woman. Emmanuel J. Holloman claimed that many soldiers raped local women, and superior officers did little to stop the attacks; some even participated. Robert E. Holcomb found himself guarding a white sergeant accused of rape. The man told Holcomb that Vietnamese people "were animals and didn't deserve to be treated like people."[81]

Others witnessed the wanton murder of civilians. James Lewis described an incident in which soldiers drove their vehicle over a hut killing two small children and an old woman because they were too lazy to turn around. Just before Lewis left Vietnam, his driver told him that white soldiers would shoot at farmers as their trucks passed. Lewis was understandably disturbed by the incident but not surprised that Black soldiers were not involved. He recalled that "Black troops never did that. . . . Black troops did not go out of their way to harm them as far as I know. They spoke about them in much nicer terms." He theorized that while most white and Black servicemen got along, some whites projected their racist feelings onto the Vietnamese.[82]

As a "closet antiwar sympathizer," Brian Settles often felt conflicted about his role in the war, but he was glad that his job was to navigate a two-seater fighter plane as he didn't want to shoot anyone. During one mission, Settles escorted smaller RF-4 planes into the Democratic Republic of Vietnam (DRV) to film enemy truck and troop movements. It was a reconnaissance mission, and although pilots had permission to respond to enemy ground fire, they rarely did. Settles expected a boring mission, which it was until the other pilots, all white, decided to strafe fishing boats with machine-gun fire. He was outraged and confronted the pilot whose idea it was to shoot at the fishermen. Settles was unable to comprehend "how the United States could hold itself up to the world as some kind of moral authority if we could do some shit like firing on the water around those sampans."[83]

Emmanuel J. Holloman described a particularly gruesome murder. Three white soldiers came upon a young boy riding a water buffalo. Wanting to scare the boy they fired in his direction, but the bullet ricocheted, killing him almost instantly. Holloman observed that this sort of thing happened often. Harold Bryant saw a drunk white GI kill an elderly man, seemingly for no reason.[84] Robert Sanders witnessed an elderly man being killed by American soldiers.[85]

"Anybody with a Heart Wouldn't Turn People Down Like That"

In contrast, many African Americans recalled trying to help and befriend civilians. This often proved difficult as there were few opportunities to assist in any sort of systematic way. Donating food was often the easiest way. McArthur Moore gave food to civilians against the orders of his commanding officers, rationalizing that "anybody with a heart wouldn't turn people down like that." Moore's experience with these civilians and their living conditions had a profound effect on him. He remembered, "I saw those conditions and I saw the conditions that the people lived under, and I resolved that I was not going to be a complainer."[86] James Daly likewise gave food to civilians and in a letter home asked his family to send him candy to hand out to children.[87] Robert E. Holcomb gave away "big cans of beans, peaches, carrots, poncho liners, blankets, boots, socks, t-shirts" to the numerous Vietnamese he befriended.[88]

Some African Americans were able to provide more substantial help. As a medic, Wayne Smith had the opportunity to interact with civilians in a different way than the average infantryman. Smith asserted, "I am glad that my focus wasn't on killing the Vietnamese and really, truly, when they were wounded or injured or had diseases and if I had medications or if I could treat them, I did." Smith even helped deliver a baby, which he viewed as a redemptive moment in which he was able to bring a new life into the world in the midst of death and war.[89]

Luther C. Benton III, who served in 1967 and 1968, worked in hospital assistance in Hoi An, which made him responsible for providing medicines and drugs to small villages. He made sure the provincial hospital had the latest drugs, a working X-ray machine, and ambulances. He went far beyond his normal duties to provide whatever assistance village leaders requested including rice and livestock. When he wasn't working, he went into the city and bought shoes, food, and soap for local orphans.[90]

Emmanuel J. Holloman worked as an interpreter for four tours. One of his responsibilities was to file reports when a civilian was accidentally killed or their house was destroyed. His unit was "destroying quite a bit of stuff," and without Holloman's intervention "they would make payments only once in a while. But I would go out of my way to let the division hear about anything the Cav did. I would tell them we destroyed this or we killed that, so we must pay it." Holloman's actions earned him the ire of many white soldiers who believed that no damages were owed and that he was a traitor who cared more about the enemy than his fellow soldiers.[91]

Despite this response, he also collected food in the cafeteria, which he donated to orphanages or refugees. This angered his sergeant who told him, "Give them gooks everything. Make 'em fat. Raise 'em up so my kid will have to grow up and come over here to fight 'em too." The sergeant's superior overruled him and allowed Holloman to continue collecting food. Holloman believed his actions led him to become "real close to the people. I taught English to the orphans. If a house was destroyed someplace, me and my driver and some Vietnamese would rebuild the building. People got hurt, we'd go there and sit and eat and drink with them. If somebody got killed, it would be real tough. I would go to the wake or funeral, and they would all be looking at me. And they're sad. . . . I would try to make the payment as quickly as possible."[92]

Holloman was so committed to his charitable activities that he passed up promotion three times and extended his tour four times. His commitment to the local population led him to extend his tour again and again at great personal risk.[93]

Holloman was not the only Black serviceman to develop a close connection with the civilian population. Joshua Page, a naval cook from Columbus, Ohio, volunteered to work with a Village Assistance Team in Tam To, a small village outside of Da Nang. He oversaw the building and repairing of schools, houses, wells, sewage, and drainage ditches. He also took a personal interest in the health of the village children, educating them and their families on the dangers of smoking cigarettes.[94]

During the Tet Offensive in 1968 Page helped organize a self-defense force in Tam To, which was particularly welcome because most of the villagers were Catholic refugees from the DRV who feared being captured or killed. Page befriended a local Catholic priest who nicknamed him "Mr. Mountain" because of his height. He also became friends with an elderly woman whom he frequently helped with chores and advised on family and medical issues. After receiving a poor medical prognosis, she asked him if he would transport her in his jeep during her funeral procession. Page recalled it being "one of the most touching incidents of his life." Speaking of his friendship with yet another woman, Page proclaimed, "She's my second mother. Vietnamese are beautiful, beautiful people." Like Holloman, when Page's one-year tour of duty was up, he reenlisted so that he could stay in Tam To.[95]

Luther C. Benton III made a concentrated effort to avoid making friends with other servicemen because he feared forming attachments with people at high risk of being killed, but he befriended many civilians. He "spent a great deal of time discussing the problems of Vietnam with the Vietnamese people, what they felt, and what they thought about the Americans and their involvement." From these discussions he learned that many people were ambivalent about the survival of the RVN but were not enthusiastic supporters of the NLF or PAVN either.[96]

It was not uncommon for servicemen to develop friendships with orphans, who spent their days wandering around villages, cities, and military bases. While serving with the 25th Infantry Division in 1967–68, Richard J. Ford III became so close to an orphan that he and his fellow soldiers wanted to adopt him.[97] Richard A. Guidry befriended Mai and Mili, two little girls who lived at the Dong Ha city dump in Quang Tri Province. Lingering memories of their friendship remained with Guidry well past his tour of duty, and he recalled that "many years later, when I read of the Spring Offensive that rolled over Quang Tri Province in 1972, my thoughts were of Mai and Mili."[98]

Guidry also befriended a ten-year-old boy in Phong Dien village. Guidry recalled, "He sat with me and told me about his village and family, and I told him about big-city life in the USA, our conversation taking a humorous turn when I mentioned snow." When the topic of the war came up, Guidry expected the boy to be guarded in his discussions; instead, he openly affirmed his support for the NLF. Guidry believed the boy was upfront with his opinions because he was either too young to know any better or had correctly gauged that Guidry was sympathetic to him.[99] While they never discussed race, it is plausible that the boy thought he could be more open with a Black person.

While in Da Nang for a week, Anthony Martin spent time talking with civilians about their country. He recalled, "I wanted to know more about their culture. For me, even if I didn't realize it at the time, I was on more of an educational quest more than anything else. I was very inquisitive about the culture, the women and the men, and you know how they did things and why they did things." Martin developed a close friendship with a young boy. He remembered, "I got real close to him. And he would ask me a lot of questions about the United States and what it's like to be, you know, a Black man in the United States.... I just thought he was as curious about me as I was about him."[100]

"I Had Fallen in Love with a Vietnamese Woman"

Of course, not every relationship formed in Vietnam was about friendship. Others were more transactional. While little has been written on the topic, prostitution was common, widespread, and tolerated, if not outright sanctioned by the armed forces. In 1966 General Harry Kinnard reluctantly endorsed the building of a twenty-five-acre "plaza" in An Khe that included several brothels after it was revealed that nearly one-third of GIs with the 1st Cavalry Airmobile had venereal disease. Nicknamed "Disneyland" or "Sin City" it was surrounded by barbed wire and closely monitored by American MPs. Prostitutes were given ID cards that proved they were regularly tested for sexually transmitted diseases.[101] "Disneyland" also had establishments that catered to African Americans. Speaking of his experiences there, Harold Bryant recalled, "It had soul bars, a group of us would walk around to find a joint that would be playin' some soul music, some Temptations, Supremes, Sam and Dave."[102]

Smaller brothels were established near the marine base in Da Nang, outside of the 1st Infantry Division camp at Lai Khe and the 4th Infantry Division post in Pleiku. Much like at An Khe, the brothel at Lai Khe was protected by barbed-wire fencing and guarded by American MPs.[103] Servicemen didn't need to be stationed near a major military installation to have access to prostitutes. Wayne Smith remembered army-sanctioned "steam baths" in Tan Tru that were essentially "whorehouses."[104] Servicemen didn't necessarily even have to visit a brothel to participate in the sex trade. Lamont B. Steptoe claimed that unit commanders arranged for prostitutes to be brought into the area three or four times a week.[105] In January 1972 the army officially allowed prostitutes onto all military bases.[106]

Sometimes there was a racial component to prostitution. Harold Bryant noted that Black soldiers would actively seek out certain prostitutes in "Disneyland" because they were more friendly to Black clientele.[107] Others sought out the services of Cambodian and Senegalese-Asian women because their darker skin reminded them of Black women back home. These women worked in the Khan Alley area of Saigon, which was nicknamed "Soul Alley" because of its Black clientele.[108]

Not every Black serviceman approved of prostitution. Robert E. Holcomb's unit paid for a prostitute but he refused to participate because he felt sorry for her.[109] Wayne Smith felt disgusted by the prevalence of prostitution. He compared Vietnamese women, whom he saw as victimized, to his own family, stating, "Having five sisters, I remember thinking these could be my sisters."[110]

Black servicemen also formed relationships with Vietnamese women that were not sexual. While stationed at Da Nang Air Base, Brian Settles befriended two maids, Dao and Bong. He felt closer to them than many of the men he served with, whom he felt were bigoted. Speaking of their friendship, Settles recalled, "I treated them with genuine respect as people, beyond being Vietnamese and maids." Their friendship made him "feel better inside, somehow connected—less guilty for what I was doing to some of their people on missions at night while they slept dreaming of marriage, family, and perhaps peace." Not everyone was happy with this platonic friendship. Champ Henderson, a white pilot from Alabama, frequently teased Settles about sleeping with Dao and Bong. Henderson ended up sleeping with Bong, devastating Settles and Dao, who recognized that Henderson saw her as little more than "a gook, a dumb zip, or a slope head" to be used and abandoned.[111]

Lamont B. Steptoe also befriended a young "hooch maid." Unlike Settles, he wanted to be more than just her friend. He remembered, "I had fallen in love with a Vietnamese woman who was a hooch maid. . . . And I had asked her one time, you know, 'would you come back to America with me.'" The woman rejected his offer because her family had already arranged for her to marry an RVN soldier. When her new husband abused her, an enraged Steptoe tried to find the man to confront him.[112]

The military at best ignored and at worst encouraged prostitution, but it actively discouraged servicemen from dating and especially marrying Vietnamese women. African Americans did form serious romantic relationships with Vietnamese women. Robert E. Holcomb dated a woman who worked at the army base and they would eat together, talk about their lives, and listen to music. While it would be easy to be cynical about their relationship, Holcomb insisted that both were sincere, and neither sought to take advantage of the other. She came from an upper-middle-class background, spoke English fluently, and was not financially dependent on him.[113] Robert Sanders developed a genuinely close relationship with a woman who worked at the army cafeteria. He stayed at her house in Nha Trang, and she even hid him when the NLF came in the area. Sanders reflected that "she would take care of me. I hated to leave her, often I think back on her, wonder how she's doing."[114] Willie Thomas dated a woman whose family had fled North Vietnam after the country was partitioned in 1954. She even introduced him to her parents.[115] Scott Riley had a Cambodian girlfriend named Ba. While their relationship partly revolved around drug use, they clearly loved each other. On his flight home from Vietnam, Riley began crying because "I was fucked up about Ba and leaving her."[116]

It was official military policy to prohibit servicemen from marrying until ninety days before their tours of duty were due to end.[117] Servicemen also needed to obtain permission from their commanding officer and chaplain before marrying.[118] They were required to provide twenty documents "with the marriage application, including a security clearance which showed the family of the girl to be free from contact with the Vietcong." Considering some of the RVN's top officials had family members in the NLF, it would have been difficult to find anyone in the country without similar affiliations.[119] In spite of these policies, there were approximately six thousand marriages between Americans and Vietnamese women during the war.[120]

Emmanuel J. Holloman married Tran Thi Saly in a Vietnamese ceremony in 1968. When he tried to get the marriage certified at the American embassy so that he could bring Saly to the United States, officials discouraged him from doing so. When he insisted, they made the process as difficult as possible. He recalled, "They knew that if you were in a combat unit, you didn't have time to go to Saigon and wait in line from here to there forever. When the paperwork did get approved, it was too late. I was shipped home."[121]

It is estimated that fifteen to twenty thousand Amerasian children were born of relationships between Vietnamese women and servicemen during the war.[122] One must be careful not to generalize about these relationships, but one study conducted at the Philippine Refugee Processing Center found that 81 percent of the mothers of Amerasian children lived with their child's father at some point. This suggests that many of these children were not the results of casual relationships.[123]

During the war the Black press took an interest in Black Amerasian children. In December 1966 the *Philadelphia Tribune* reported, "Brown Babies Plentiful in Vietnam's War Zone."[124] The following year the *Tribune* alleged, "Many Vietnam Infants Fathered by Negro GI's Left Abandoned."[125] Neither article provided any statistics on the numbers of Black Amerasian children. In June 1973 the *New York Amsterdam News* noted that as many as half of the one thousand Amerasian children in local Saigon orphanages "obviously had black American fathers," but this was probably more a reflection of the taboo nature of Black-Vietnamese relationships.[126] In December 1972 when the American military effort was effectively over, *Ebony* discussed the difficulty in determining just how many Black Amerasians there actually were as reports claimed anywhere from five hundred to ten thousand.[127]

While some of these children were likely knowingly abandoned, it is unclear how many of these children's fathers were even aware they had children. Others were likely killed in action. Thu-Hien Lam was born in Saigon in 1970 but her father, "Ernie," an African American supervisor of the Bachelor Officers Quarters, "returned to the U.S. before her mother had a chance to tell him she was pregnant."[128] Others were in a situation like that of Emmanuel J. Holloman, who tried numerous times to bring his wife and child to the United States but was unsuccessful. He continued to send money, but when the RVN collapsed in 1975, communications were cut off entirely. He certainly did not willingly abandon his family and even years later remained hopeful that he would one day be able to bring Saly and their surviving son to the United States.[129]

In much the same way that the U.S. government discouraged GIs from marrying their Vietnamese girlfriends, officials did not show much interest in the welfare of Amerasian children. Children born of a French parent during the First Indochina War (1946–54) were granted French citizenship, but the U.S. government did not make similar allowances.[130] Complicating matters further, the RVN government viewed Amerasians as solely Vietnamese. In 1969 they heavily restricted foreign adoptions.[131] Children were still adopted, including Thu-Hien Lam, who was adopted by an American couple in 1973, but the U.S. government was not interested in any mass adoption of Amerasians. As the American military commitment decreased, African Americans in the United States showed an interest in adopting Black Amerasians, but these efforts were largely stymied by RVN policies.[132]

"Where's He Going to Go for Shelter with His Family"

Despite the empathy that many African Americans had for the Vietnamese, they were expected to follow orders. The contrast between the ways they felt about the Vietnamese and the ways they were ordered to treat them proved difficult to reconcile. Civilians were often injured or killed by American firepower, and these casualties led African Americans to empathize further. Robert Louis Jr. felt guilty when he was ordered to burn huts. He recognized that he was being ordered to burn an actual home and that he was placing already poor villagers in an even worse position. Speaking about a typical villager, he wondered, "What's this guy going to do, it's rainy season? It's going to start raining at two o'clock this afternoon and you just burned this little hooch down. Where's he going to go for shelter with his family?"[133]

Louis's concern for these villagers was remarkable. Burning the huts of villagers believed to be sympathetic to or supportive of the NLF was common military practice, and most servicemen likely did not question it, assuming the orders were justified. Louis questioned the morality behind these actions. He empathized with the villagers and wondered what sort of negative effect his own actions might have on them. He credited his "own upbringing and knowing how tough that it is" to be poor and a victim of racial discrimination for his empathy.[134] Louis carried his own experiences with racial discrimination and prejudice with him to Vietnam, and it influenced how he viewed and treated people.

On other occasions African Americans had to decide whether to kill civilians. Some refused outright. Reginald Edwards, who served with the 9th Marine Regiment in 1965–66, recalled an incident when a white sergeant ordered him to shoot an old man, but he purposely "missed this old man. Cause I really couldn't shoot him." Unfortunately, another soldier fired his grenade launcher, killing the old man and the children he was running to protect. Edwards came upon another civilian yelling "don't shoot." Unit policy was to shoot first and ask questions later, but he listened to the man who told him a nearby hut was filled with women and children. Edwards's refusal to follow orders saved them.[135]

Edwards's marine company was later involved in the killing of unarmed civilians in Cam Ne. On August 5, 1965, as they approached the village, he grew "afraid that there was going to be shooting people that day, so I just kind of dealt with the animals. You know, shoot the chickens. I mean I just couldn't shoot no people."[136] Terry Whitmore had a similar experience. After taking casualties, Whitmore's company commander ordered them to destroy a local village and kill everyone in it. Whitmore refused to kill anyone and kept busy shooting cattle.[137]

Options were limited for African Americans concerned about the mistreatment of civilians. They believed there was no higher authority to which they could appeal as there were few Black officers. Don L. Jernigan accurately described the situation: "There were guys that brutalized the women, slapped them, shot them—the kids, and the Blacks that were there sometimes had to witness it because we weren't always in command at the level that we, maybe needed."[138] Jernigan believed that Black officers would have provided different leadership and fewer civilians would have been hurt.

Blacks were rarely in positions of authority, but they did try to protect civilians. Wes Geary recalled an incident when he saw a Vietnamese girl, who regularly sold soft drinks, being chased by a white soldier. The girl was yelling "not one, not sale" as the soldier grabbed at her. Realizing the soldier was trying to rape her, Geary grabbed him and "shook him about four or five times and told him I would kick his butt" if he didn't leave her alone. The man backed off, but Geary remembered the event as an indication that some soldiers were willing to abuse nearly anyone, even a "little kid" selling soda.[139]

Dwyte A. Brown protected a woman and her daughter from the unwanted sexual advances of a white soldier. While showering on base, Brown noticed several maids cleaning one of the showers. He kept a towel around his waist out of respect for the women, but a white soldier removed his towel and grabbed the daughter of the maid and tried to sexually assault her. Brown rebuked the man and prevented him from going any further.[140]

Richard J. Ford III recalled an incident when a group of white soldiers discussed their intentions to shoot a Degar tribesman, called Montagnards by Americans. Davis, a Black soldier, told them to "get that thought out of your mind, cause I'll blow your brains out just for thinking it."[141] Ron Bradley recalled an incident in which a white sergeant began torturing a civilian. Outraged, Bradley threatened to shoot him if he didn't let the civilian go.[142]

Gerald Lynch was traveling through a crowded street when a white marine threw a carton of C-Rations at children begging for food in a clear attempt to injure them. Angered by the marine's callousness, Lynch hit him with his rifle. Believing his actions to be justified, Lynch was saddened when "everybody looked at me like I was the criminal." Understandably, Lynch believed the only one who had done anything criminal was the white marine.[143]

On February 14, 1970, a fight broke out in the 611th Transportation Company on Vinh Long Army airfield. A U.S. Army investigation concluded that the incident was "initiated when a white member of the company pinched a Vietnamese waitress while she was waiting on the table." The waitress informed a group of Black soldiers, who confronted the soldier and a fight broke out.[144]

Many African Americans believed that whites were more likely to regard the Vietnamese as inferior and mistreat them, but some African Americans were guilty of similar behavior. Black veteran Dwight Williams admitted, "We called the Vietnamese gooks too. Almost everybody took on some racist feelings, no question."[145] Nor were African Americans always kind. Horace Coleman admitted that there were Blacks who abused civilians because they thought, "this is my opportunity to be on top for once."[146] Harold Bryant knew some Black soldiers who gave trick cigarettes to civilians that were rigged to explode. While cruel, the intention of this act was to discourage civilians from asking for cigarettes, not to injure or kill them.[147]

Other African Americans were involved in more serious crimes, including rape and murder. While his squad was serving perimeter duty outside of a small village, Haywood T. Kirkland saw two Black soldiers from another squad raping a woman.[148] Terry Whitmore encountered a Black marine killing an unarmed Buddhist monk.[149] David Parks witnessed Jones, a Black soldier, kill an unarmed civilian in front of his own children because he didn't have proper identification.[150] Deborah Nelson's *The War behind Me*, which is based on recently declassified army documents regarding war crimes in Vietnam, describes an incident in which a Black soldier threw a grenade into a bunker, killing two children and a woman.[151] African Americans, most notably Varnado Simpson, were among those who participated in the My Lai massacre. Simpson admitted to killing as many as twenty-five unarmed civilians, most of them women and children.[152]

However, even in these cases, other African Americans condemned the behavior. Whenever Horace Coleman saw African Americans being racist toward or otherwise mistreating the Vietnamese, his immediate thought was, "You ought to know better than that."[153] Whitmore was disgusted by much of what he saw in Vietnam, but he was especially appalled by the actions of the Black marine who killed the monk, believing, like Coleman, that as an African American he should have known better.[154] Parks was horrified when Jones shot the civilian, partially blaming himself for not following proper protocol. Parks was supposed to tie the suspect up but didn't because he didn't want the man's family to "feel bad." He later recalled in his journal, "I can't stop thinking about those kids. They'll hate us for the rest of their lives. And who can blame them?"[155]

Most servicemen, regardless of race, were disgusted by the My Lai massacre. Anthony Martin was not surprised to learn about My Lai, "but it did surprise me that African Americans were involved in these atrocities."[156] While it is not known how many African Americans participated in the massacre, some did refuse to participate. Herbert Carter, a Black soldier, shot himself in the foot, possibly intentionally, to ensure that he didn't have to kill anyone, making him the only American casualty. In the early stages of the massacre, Carter refused to obey Lieutenant William Calley's orders to kill several children. Carter had previously been accused of assaulting a male suspect, but he drew the line at killing women and children. Speaking to investigators, Carter stated, "That day I tried my best to stay out of that whole mess. Some people might say that it was a cowardly act, but I just tried to stay out of it.... I don't know how those guys can sleep. I can hardly sleep now and I didn't even participate in any of this mess."[157]

Robert Maples, a Black soldier from Englishtown, New Jersey, had long disapproved of the way members of his company treated the Vietnamese. He was disgusted by soldiers who collected the ears of enemy soldiers, labeling it "gross" and "unwarranted." His disgust only grew when he realized soldiers were murdering civilians at My Lai. Reaching an open ditch filled with civilians, Calley ordered Maples to "load your machine gun and shoot these people." Maples shook his head and replied, "I'm not going to do that." In response Calley aimed his gun at him. Maples was surprised when other soldiers intervened and prevented Calley from shooting him.[158]

Harry Stanley, a Black soldier from Gulfport, Mississippi, also refused a direct order to shoot women and children. Raised by a single mother, Stanley was taught to "believe that everybody's equal," and he brought this perspective with him to Vietnam. In many ways, Stanley was the polar opposite of Calley and others like him. He was intrigued by the country, its people, and culture. Within three months of arriving, he "had taught himself to speak the language better than the company's GI interpreters," which earned him the derision of other soldiers who called him a "gook lover."[159]

Stanley was shocked when he came across dead civilians at My Lai and horrified when he realized that the goal was to kill everyone in the village. When ordered to kill women and children, he refused, later asserting that any order which required him to kill unarmed civilians was not an order worth obeying. He also saved several villagers. When he and Carter came across a small boy, he urged him to run away and hide. A survivor recalled that a Vietnamese-speaking Black soldier, almost certainly Stanley, accompanied him and six family members to the edge of the village, telling them to run away to another village. Another family of five provided a similar account. Of course, some white servicemen refused to kill civilians at My Lai and elsewhere too. At My Lai it was a helicopter gunship manned by three white servicemen that landed several times in the middle of the massacre and attempted to stop it.[160] Race was not the sole determinant of how individual serviceman treated the Vietnamese—personal values played an influential role.

The War behind Me discusses the experiences of George Lewis, an African American sergeant in the 9th Infantry Division from Columbus, Ohio, who served from June 1968 to June 1969 and earned a Purple Heart and other combat accommodation medals. After being discharged, Lewis sent letters to General William Westmoreland and other army leaders alleging that civilians were routinely being killed in Vietnam. Soldiers were ordered to shoot civilians who fled, snipers regularly shot unarmed farmers from four hundred yards away, and civilians were forced to walk through minefields. The military relied heavily on gunships and artillery strikes to ensure high body counts. He stated, "We were 'told' to kill many times more Vietnamese than at My Lay [My Lai], and very few per cents of them did we know were enemy."[161]

In a letter to Major General Orwin C. Talbott, commanding general at Fort Benning, Georgia, Lewis added, "The generals have got to do something about this pretty soon before anymore people get killed." His final letter threatened to contact two prominent Democratic politicians, California representative Ron Dellums and Massachusetts senator Ted Kennedy, stating, "All of you can explain why you got these letters and done nothing about the war crimes."[162]

While the pursuit of high body counts was apparently regarded as sound military practice, Lewis viewed it as immoral, and when it meant the intentional killing of civilians, a war crime. He did not argue that it was poor strategy, had a negative effect on the war effort, or lessened morale. Rather, his argument focused on the humanity of the Vietnamese and the immorality of killing innocent civilians.

Conclusion

The majority of Black servicemen shared Lewis's empathy for the Vietnamese. Most African Americans arrived in Vietnam knowing little about its people and what they learned in basic training portrayed the Vietnamese in a negative light. Black servicemen did know a lot about poverty and racial discrimination, however, and this influenced their view of Vietnamese civilians.

When African Americans witnessed poverty in Vietnam, they understandably connected it to economically disadvantaged Black communities back home. When Black servicemen heard whites using racist slurs, they heard echoes of the slurs regularly used against them. When white servicemen mistreated civilians, it reminded them of the treatment African Americans had experienced throughout America's history. As victims of poverty and racial discrimination themselves, African Americans empathized with Vietnamese civilians, who they believed faced similar conditions. When discussing Black views of the Vietnamese, Scott Riley explained, "I do think that most of us saw in them ourselves."[163]

African Americans typically portrayed whites as hostile, if not outright abusive, toward Vietnamese people. Whites had brought their own racist ideas about African Americans to Vietnam and continued to discriminate against them there. They also found a new object for their white supremacist ideology—the Vietnamese. The experiences of African Americans with domestic racism led many of them to empathize with the civilian population. In contrast, many whites who had discriminated against Blacks back home mistreated another vulnerable group without status or power.

African American servicemen developed strong opinions about the Vietnamese that were very different from most white servicemen. They also believed that the Vietnamese viewed them differently as well.

CHAPTER 5

"'You and Me—Same Same" and "They Called Me 'Monkey'"

Conflicting African American Views of Vietnamese Civilians

In *No Vietnamese Ever Called Me Nigger*, Dalton James, a Black Vietnam veteran, discussed his interactions with and perceptions of Vietnamese civilians. Like many others, he argued that African Americans overwhelmingly empathized with the Vietnamese as fellow victims of racial discrimination.[1] He took the discussion a step further by speculating about Vietnamese views of Black servicemen.

James insisted that the Vietnamese reciprocated Black feelings of empathy. He believed they favored African Americans over whites in part because of the way whites treated them. The Vietnamese understood that whites were more likely to use racial slurs while "a lot of colored guys wouldn't call a Vietnamese a gook or a slope . . . because it's a racial epithet." James also claimed that the Vietnamese believed they had a shared experience with African Americans. He argued, "The Vietnamese then saw what was happening back in the States was happening right there in their own country. There was racism right there in front of their eyes."[2]

On the surface, James's observations seem outlandish. Most civilians whom servicemen encountered were uneducated and poor.[3] They usually did not speak more than a few words of English, and most servicemen did not speak more than a few words of Vietnamese. It is unlikely that very many peasants, refugees, or civilian workers had even a cursory knowledge of American history or American race relations. Few civilians knew more about the United States than that it was a powerful country which had sent hundreds of thousands of troops to their country.[4]

These interactions occurred during an ongoing war. The Vietnamese likely had diverse opinions about American servicemen. Americans were an occupying military force, and this had a significant impact on their relations and the Vietnamese perceptions of these relations. Equally important, Vietnamese people had their own notions of race, which predated the Americans' arrival. Given these realities, James's conclusions about "progressive" Vietnamese views regarding race or African Americans should be viewed with skepticism.

Yet, James was not alone in his belief that Vietnamese civilians held positive views about African Americans and were sympathetic to the Black struggle against racial prejudice and discrimination. Influenced heavily by their own experiences with race in the United States and in Vietnam, many African Americans believed that the Vietnamese, who were not white and were victims of racial discrimination, would naturally be sympathetic toward them. These African Americans believed that skin color, race, and common experiences with discrimination bound them together.[5]

The reality is more complex. Vietnamese racial views were varied and often hard to pin down. There were racist civilians that discriminated against Black servicemen. However, when African Americans encountered Vietnamese racism, they blamed it on racist whites who had brought American racism to Vietnam and taught it to locals. The domestic racial situation remained the dominant influence on African Americans' interpretations of Vietnamese racial views. Friendly Vietnamese empathized with African Americans because they saw them as victims of racial discrimination. Unsympathetic Vietnamese were taught to dislike Blacks by white servicemen who had brought racist views from the United States.

"Me and You Same Same"

Several contemporary journalistic accounts recognized that Black servicemen believed Vietnamese people were sympathetic toward them. In January 1965 the *Cleveland Call and Post* quoted Felton McFarland, a Black air force staff sergeant, who described the Vietnamese as "most receptive, especially toward Negroes." He claimed that numerous Vietnamese "confided to him that colored people were warmhearted and friends, not cold and haughty like the French colonialists and some white Americans."[6]

In June 1966 Whitney M. Young Jr., executive director of the National Urban League, spent ten days traveling throughout Vietnam, concluding that with few exceptions relations between African Americans and civilians were quite positive. He noted that most African Americans believed the local population "feel special sympathy toward the Negro soldiers."[7]

In April 1967 Howard Jackson, a Black marine, told Ethel L. Payne that "the Vietnamese have no overt racial prejudice."[8] In 1969 Asa Martin of Chicago wrote in a letter to his mother that "the Vietnamese people treat 'brothers' like kings."[9]

More recent interviews with Black veterans support the sentiments expressed in contemporary reports. Anthony Martin recalled, "Everything that I received from Vietnamese people was a whole lot of curiosity and love." Martin believed they took an interest in the Black experience. He befriended a young boy who spoke some English and asked him, "What's it like to be, you know, a Black man in the United States."[10] Don L. Jernigan observed, "You certainly felt the kinship with the people of color.... In the villages and the hamlets, sometimes you felt that brotherhood in terms of reaching out and the warmth that you got from certain papasans and certain mamasans."[11] Louis Perkins believed that the Vietnamese liked African Americans better than whites because "the Vietnamese knew who were genuine and who were full of crap to be honest with you, and that's why they could relate to us Blacks a lot better than the whites."[12]

Others claimed that the Vietnamese favored them because they were persons of color and victims of discrimination. In November 1965 journalist Simeon Booker reported from Vietnam that Black servicemen were commonly welcomed into bars by women who "point to their skin as a sign of brotherhood in the worldwide order of darker people."[13] Emmanuel J. Holloman claimed that the Vietnamese would "warm right up to a black person even if they had never seen one," implying that they instinctively related to African Americans as persons of color.[14] James Lewis also concluded that the Vietnamese viewed African Americans in a positive light because they weren't white.[15] Harold Bryant believed that civilians favored Blacks because "Buddha was black. Take a good look at a Buddha. You'll see that he has thick lips and has a very broad nose and very kinky hair."[16] There is no evidence to support Bryant's claim, but his account illustrates that African Americans sought explanations for Vietnamese empathy.

Many African Americans claimed that Vietnamese civilians explicitly identified with them. Dalton James recalled several incidents in which civilians told him, "me and you same same," or "hey soul brother!" which he interpreted as an expression of empathy but also of shared struggle.[17] Dave Dubose observed that the Vietnamese were a "very open-minded people," and it was not uncommon for civilians to approach African Americans stating, "You and me—same same."[18] Thomas Brannon encountered Vietnamese people who told him, "You same same me."[19] Wayne Smith remembered, "There were some Vietnamese that said same same soul brother, same same soul sister. They wanted to identify with African Americans."[20]

Thomas Belton claimed that several civilians told him, "You GI you black you same same like me, have same problems." Some even questioned why he had come to Vietnam at all given that he faced a far more important "war at home" against prejudice and discrimination.[21] Belton's account demonstrates that some Vietnamese were aware of the status of African Americans in the United States.

Bernard McClusky believed that the relationship with the Vietnamese was symbiotic as both groups empathized with one another. He recalled, "As a Black man, I got invited to two Vietnamese houses of people that worked on the base with us. . . . I actually had the opportunity to be invited to people's homes and sit down with their daughters and their family and eat their buffalo stew."[22]

Ron Bradley claimed that the Vietnamese "preferred being with the Black soldiers and identifying with us and we got along better. They used to call the white soldiers devils with horns." He believed the Vietnamese felt an affinity for African Americans not only because Blacks treated the Vietnamese in a more humane manner than the average white soldier but also because they "identified with us because of what they heard . . . we were going through in America and how we were being treated as third-class people."[23] According to Bradley, the Vietnamese saw parallels in the way whites treated African Americans and the way they were often treated by whites.

Melvin Adams of Orangeburg, South Carolina, who served in 1966–67 and 1971–72, believed that the Vietnamese, especially those with some formal education, recognized that African Americans were victims of discrimination and prejudice in their own country and empathized with them. Accordingly, the Vietnamese "thought you had it worse off than they did because they're reading the paper 67, 68, Martin Luther King, the riots, and the police dogs and all that stuff." Adams believed that locals "wanted to identify with you from the standpoint that you're like them. The North Vietnamese are trying to run over you and the white people are trying to run over you."[24] Brian Settles also thought "there were a lot of Vietnamese women and men too who related to the brothers more than white dudes because of some understandings of how white-Black relationships were in the United States and relating more to the brothers as victims of oppression in America."[25]

Having positive relations with the local population could have very specific benefits. A December 1967 *Chicago Tribune* article, "Viet Cong Put Bounty on Yank but Villagers Snub Big Offer," discussed the efforts of Melvin Smith, a Black marine, to organize villagers into a militia in Tuy Loan. In response, the Viet Cong offered $1,700 to anyone who killed or captured him, an amount that was "exceptionally high." They distributed leaflets and broadcast the reward using bullhorns, but none of the villagers, who were poor, turned him in. Smith, known as Trung Si Mel, was so well liked by the villagers that instead of capturing or killing him they protected him.[26]

Robert E. Holcomb often gave food and other supplies to needy civilians. While his actions were motivated by a sincere concern for their welfare, he recognized that it earned him trust and respect in the community. He purchased eucalyptus oil from a local woman and she provided him with information about Viet Cong troop movements. Luther C. Benton III claimed that the friendships he formed with several orphans allowed him to drive through different villages unharmed.[27]

In Cam Ranh Bay in 1966–67 Eddie Wright developed a friendship with a maid. One night at around 4 a.m. she arrived at Wright's door, "grabbed my arm and said 'Papa San Dee Dee' and she risked her life to tell me that the Viet Cong would hit Cam Ranh Bay in two days and she didn't want me to be there."[28] This incident says much about their friendship as she came to his door well past curfew, risking death as it was military policy to shoot any Vietnamese person found on the base that late, to warn him about potential danger. Lee Ewing recalled a similar experience. Assisting in bridge construction over the Perfume River in 1967, he befriended a young woman who sold soft drinks. She warned Ewing and his fellow troops that if the NLF was planning an attack, she would not show up or leave early.[29]

"I'm Colored to Her, Same as I'm Colored to Anybody Else"

Many African Americans believed that their empathy for Vietnamese civilians was more than reciprocated, but others were skeptical. Clyde Jackson claimed that African Americans stationed in Phu Bai were regularly approached and told "soul-brother number one and you know white boy ten thousand."[30] He believed that some civilians were pretending to favor African Americans in hopes that they would buy whatever the Vietnamese were selling or otherwise help them. Some likely did have ulterior motives when they claimed "sameness" with African Americans.

A September 1965 *Jet* article discussed an anonymous Black airman's experiences with civilians. The man stated, "You go into a bar and the girl sits down next to you and points at her skin and then she points at mine. That's supposed to mean we're all the same." He did not believe these declarations of equality were genuine. He reasoned, "Hell, I know she's just trying to con me out of my money. I'm colored to her, same as I'm colored to anybody else."[31] To him the idea that Vietnamese civilians favored or empathized with African Americans was nothing more than a myth.

Some African Americans recognized that not every Vietnamese person identified with them. Lamont B. Steptoe had positive feelings toward the Vietnamese, but he also thought they were "racial purists" who did not believe it was acceptable to be anything but Vietnamese.[32] Steptoe believed that Vietnamese racial views were far different from what other African Americans perceived them to be.

Others understood that even if Vietnamese people liked African Americans, it wasn't necessarily an endorsement of their presence. Ron Bradley believed that while the Vietnamese favored African Americans over whites, most wanted all servicemen to leave the country as soon as possible. Their general attitude was, "We don't need you, we don't want you."[33] Ron Copes did not think they preferred African Americans or had any interest in or knowledge of American racial issues. Most just "wanted to be left alone.... We were all interrupters of their lifestyle.... They didn't want to deal with Americans, period."[34]

This more skeptical take on Vietnamese racial views is likely more realistic and accurate. There is evidence that many Vietnamese did not hold particularly "progressive" views on race. In April 1968 Thomas A. Johnson interviewed *Saigon Post* journalist Nguyen Lao, who admitted the "Vietnamese normally prefer a light skin over a dark skin. This is why you will not see Vietnamese girls sunbathing." Lao further explained why African Americans might have believed the Vietnamese preferred them over whites. He stated, "You will also find that Vietnamese will frequently approach a darker person before approaching a white person, feeling more comfortable and perhaps superior to the darker person."[35]

Other evidence suggests that some Vietnamese were uncomfortable with dark skin and viewed the presence of other races negatively. Historian Nu-Anh Tran described an incident involving James R. Kipp, a white serviceman, who wrote a letter in April 1966 to the English language *Saigon Daily News* criticizing Vietnamese society and culture. When it was reprinted in Vietnamese, readers angrily responded. Their responses underline "how the American presence generated acute anxiety among the South Vietnamese reading public concerning the maintenance of an authentic, autonomous identity." All the letters asserted that Americans and Vietnamese were different peoples. Some argued that the Vietnamese were far superior.[36]

Kipp's letter criticized Vietnamese women who, he alleged, were always ready to sleep with American servicemen. Several commentators focused on this allegation, claiming that any woman who slept with a foreigner was no longer Vietnamese but a race traitor. Respectable women were expected to be loyal to Vietnamese men and ignore Americans. These commentators were against Vietnamese women having sex with other "races" and believed that Vietnam needed to remain distinct and "pure."[37]

African American servicemen were not the first Black troops in Vietnam. France employed African soldiers throughout the First Indochina War. In 1946 thirty thousand African colonial troops, mostly from Senegal, Morocco, and Algeria, served in Vietnam. By 1950 the number had risen to fifty thousand. Little is known about how the Vietnamese viewed the African soldiers, but historian Shawn McHale has shown that the Viet Minh utilized racist propaganda, which portrayed African troops as animalistic cannibals bent on debasing Vietnamese society, to attract support during the war. This propaganda was designed to convince Vietnamese people that African soldiers were more likely to mistreat and kill civilians, a fear that increased after rumors spread that African troops had allegedly participated in the killing of six hundred civilians in the Mekong Delta. However, the Viet Minh may have focused on Africans simply "because Africans and Moroccans were more alien and unfamiliar than Frenchmen," making them "more convenient targets of hatred."[38] It is hard to know if the Viet Minh were stoking existing racial fears or if they were trying to spread the prejudice that Blacks should be feared and hated. Either way, McHale's article demonstrates that some Vietnamese had prejudiced opinions about Blacks before African Americans ever arrived.

"They Looked Like My Little Brothers"

Vietnam was not a racially homogenous society. Roughly 90 percent of the population was ethnically Vietnamese, known as Kinh, but the Republic of Vietnam included Chinese and Cambodian populations. There were also many smaller ethnic groups, most notably Montagnards, a collective term used to refer to dozens of Indigenous groups that resided in the Central Highlands region.[39]

A 1973 U.S. armed forces study on relations between the Montagnards and ethnic Vietnamese found that while Montagnards had a variety of different languages and cultural characteristics, they "have in common an ingrained hostility toward the Vietnamese." The RVN government was largely responsible for this hostility as "the Vietnamese had not only made no attempt to gain the support of the Montagnards and other minority groups but in the past had actually antagonized them." They generally viewed the Montagnards, who had darker skin, "as an inferior people, calling them 'moi,' or savages."[40]

Contemporary Black observers were aware of the treatment given to ethnic minorities. In May 1968 Donald Mosby suggested that if a person really wanted to know how the average Vietnamese person viewed African Americans, they just needed to look at the treatment of Montagnards. He accused the Vietnamese of "trying to exterminate the mountain tribesmen" because their "skin colors range in many instances from brown to deep black."[41] In an article the following month Mosby interviewed Black journalist Marion Williams, who had recently returned from Vietnam. She asserted, "Black soldiers have no business fighting and dying for these people, because the people hate them, just as they hate the Mountinards [sic], who are black people, too."[42]

Focusing on the plight of Montagnards, Mosby and Williams questioned how racially "progressive" the Kinh majority really were, but they also suggested that because they treated other "Black" people poorly, they would have no sympathy for African Americans. They asserted that the Vietnamese did not deserve the support of African Americans because of their history of discrimination.[43]

In August 1967 the *Christian Science Monitor* discussed the efforts of a Black lieutenant to organize Montagnards for an army project. His fellow officers warned him that the Montagnards would not be interested, but he successfully recruited a large group. When questioned about his recruiting tactics, he responded, "I told them I was the biggest Montagnard in the world and that they'd be hurting if they didn't help."[44]

Many African Americans agreed with the lieutenant's assertion that skin color linked African Americans to Montagnards. He used his own skin color to appeal to the Montagnards, but he also claimed that they responded to him because of his skin color. The Montagnards had previously been unwilling to help with the army project but changed their minds when a Black officer directed it.

Speaking of his interactions with Montagnards, Arthur Barham recalled, "When you would encounter them, they would come up to us, Black soldiers, and compare skin. They would hold their skin up to yours.... They embraced us as Black guys because our skin color was the same.... It made you smile because they could see the difference, they embraced the difference." In contrast, he remembered, "The Vietnamese soldiers showed them absolutely no respect.... They were treated differently."[45]

James Gillam's service in the Central Highlands led to numerous interactions with Montagnards. To Gillam, they were good people who looked like African Americans. He recalled, "They looked like my little brothers, how could you not like these guys?" On one memorable occasion, Gillam happened upon a Montagnard village where he was welcomed like a family member. He remembered, "It was definitely a visual and race thing for them.... I was a Montagnard homeboy until I opened my mouth."[46]

Gillam's reactions are striking. He compared the Montagnards he met to his own family, noting that the resemblance was so strong they could have been his brothers. Their darker skin immediately endeared them to him, and they responded to Gillam in much the same way. Their shared skin color united them and perhaps reflected a common experience.

Emmanuel J. Holloman recalled an incident when a thirteen-year-old Montagnard girl was shot and evacuated to a hospital in Long Binh. The girl's injuries included a broken jaw, which meant she could not communicate. Holloman recalled, "The first person she grabbed was me. She wouldn't let anybody feed her but me. I sat with her all night holding her hand.... I took care of her for four days."[47] Like Gillam, Holloman believed that his skin color endeared him to the young girl.

A 1972 Human Relations Council study revealed that many African Americans wore bracelets modeled after Montagnard bracelets normally reserved for honorary members. These actions suggest that African Americans saw themselves as honorary Montagnards or wanted others to see them that way.[48]

African Americans identified with Montagnards and knew about their mistreatment. James Gillam developed a level of antipathy for the Vietnamese majority because of the way they treated Montagnards.[49] He was not alone. Richard J. Ford III and his fellow Black soldiers considered Montagnards "brothers because they were dark." They also related to the Indigenous people because "the people in Vietnam didn't have anything to do with Montagnards. It was almost like white people in the States didn't have anything to do with blacks in the ghetto."[50] Ford was not the only one to see a parallel between the way Vietnamese treated Montagnards and the way whites treated Blacks. Oscar Roberts was in Pleiku as an advisor to the ARVN in 1968, and he reported that the "Montagnards are treated the way we used to be treated back home."[51]

Wayne Smith recalled that "some Vietnamese, you know they had some prejudices. . . . They were discriminating against the Montagnards, the mountain people of Vietnam, who were darker complexioned." Smith claimed that "the Montagnards would say to people like me 'me same same soul brother.'" The Cambodian workers that Smith encountered on military bases "were dark complexioned," and "the Vietnamese treated them like white people in the South treated African Americans."[52] Smith saw racism as the cause of the mistreatment meted out to the Montagnards and the Cambodians.

Scott Riley's girlfriend was Cambodian and because he was stationed in the Central Highlands, he also had interactions with various Montagnard groups. He explained that many Vietnamese felt that the "almost China tea-cup, white form of beauty" was "the beauty standard and those other peoples, Cambodians, and various other ethnic groups that interact with Vietnamese are always looked down upon" as a result.[53]

Horace Coleman understood that the "Vietnamese had some prejudices of their own. Vietnamese looked down on Cambodians. Vietnamese weren't that hot about ethnic Chinese, who had been living there for who knows how long."[54] A 1970 Army Counterintelligence investigation revealed that a large group of African Americans, most of whom had gone AWOL or deserted, were living in Saigon with Cambodians in the area surrounding Truong Minh Ky Street. Allegedly, they had "a mutual understanding of one another as 'oppressed minorities.'"[55]

The poor treatment afforded to Montagnards and other ethnic minorities reveals that Vietnamese society had its own problems with racial prejudice and discrimination. While it is difficult to determine if these groups faced discrimination solely because of their skin color, African Americans, operating from a perspective largely shaped by their own experiences back home, believed this was the case. They viewed Montagnards and Cambodians as fellow "Blacks" mistreated by an ethnic majority, a situation similar to, if not identical with, the situation they faced.

Interactions with Montagnards and other ethnic minorities revealed to African Americans that Vietnamese society was not free of racial prejudice, but it also gave them an opportunity to empathize with a group more oppressed than the Kinh majority. Many Blacks thought they had a bond with the Vietnamese, but others believed they had an even stronger bond with minorities like the Montagnards.

"By the Time I Got There They Were Calling Some Black Soldiers Niggers"

African Americans did not necessarily need to have any knowledge of discrimination against minorities to see evidence of Vietnamese racism. Some experienced it firsthand. In August 1968 the *Cleveland Call and Post* printed a letter written by Stanley Miller, a Black sergeant serving with the 3rd Battalion, 60th Infantry Regiment, which claimed, "The Vietnamese don't appreciate what we are doing for them. They steal from us; they try and cheat us out of our money. They call the Negro soldier names and treat him like dirt."[56]

Miller's depiction of Vietnamese attitudes contrasted sharply with African Americans who claimed the Vietnamese were sympathetic, but he was not alone in his observations. Others made similar claims that Vietnamese people used derogatory names in reference to African Americans. Wayne Smith recalled, "Despite what Muhammad Ali said, you know no Vietnamese ever called me nigger. By the time I got there [1969] they were calling some Black soldiers niggers."[57] While Joshua Page eventually befriended the people of Tam To, he was initially treated very poorly when he arrived in 1968. He recalled, "They called me 'monkey' and other names." Only after the local priest intervened did the townspeople begin to warm up to him.[58]

The Black press chronicled incidents of Vietnamese expressing racist views or mistreating African Americans. In March 1966 *Jet* discussed the contents of a letter allegedly written by a Vietnamese person who claimed the United States sent "Negro soldiers all over the world to pollute the races from Germany to Vietnam." The writer suggested, "Our signs should not be 'Yank go home' but 'Get your G D niggers out of our country.'"[59] The letter writer did not necessarily oppose the American war effort or the presence of hundreds of thousands of Americans. Rather, they only opposed the presence of African Americans.

Marion Williams spent seven months in Vietnam in 1967–68 and reported that most Vietnamese people disliked African Americans. She claimed that while African Americans wanted to help, this was a waste of time because the Vietnamese "hate them."[60]

During his 1968 visit to Vietnam Donald Mosby "encountered anti-Negro hate that rivaled attitudes in small Southern towns back in the States." After refusing to buy pornography, a salesman called him a "dirty black bastard." He asked a Black soldier why the salesman was rude to him, only to be told that "the Vietnamese are very prejudiced toward black people." The soldier, who worked in pacification in a local village, informed Mosby that old people routinely sent local children to insult Black servicemen. Mosby noted that Confederate flags, sold in Saigon, were among the most popular flags in the country.[61]

Mosby pointed to the taboo nature of Black-Vietnamese relationships as evidence that civilians were prejudiced. He observed that "while Vietnamese women walk freely with white servicemen, I never saw one with a black soldier." He claimed that any woman seen with a Black soldier in public would immediately be arrested under suspicion of prostitution.[62]

In a May 1968 article in the *Pittsburgh Courier* Mosby once again claimed that most Vietnamese he encountered were prejudiced against African Americans. Civilians regularly scowled at, laughed at, or insulted him. They "made it plain that they didn't want me in the country." Black servicemen fared no better as Mosby observed that "Vietnamese don't bother to hide their dislike of Negro GIs." Women were particularly contemptuous, and many prostitutes were unwilling to sleep with Blacks.[63]

Mosby's allegations should be taken with a grain of salt as the people he encountered were almost certainly speaking Vietnamese, which he did not speak. He only visited Saigon, limiting his ability to gauge accurately what people in other cities and towns were like. Additionally, it is unlikely Vietnamese vendors understood the connotations behind the Confederate flag, which was certainly being sold at the request of white servicemen and not the Vietnamese. Mosby's claim that women universally refused to date or be seen with Blacks on the street is exaggerated.

As previously noted, Vietnamese women dated and even married Black servicemen.

It is probably true, however, that some prostitutes refused to sleep with African Americans. In June 1966 the *Los Angeles Sentinel* noted that prostitutes were not as welcoming to Blacks as whites and that they refused to take Black customers.[64] Wayne Smith heard rumors that prostitutes refused to have sex with Blacks.[65] Lamont B. Steptoe agreed that there were prostitutes who refused to service African Americans, but others were uninterested in whites.[66] Arthur Barham supported Steptoe's claims.[67]

Mosby argued that the stigmatization of Black Amerasian children was proof of Vietnamese racism. He claimed that "white American babies are highly prized, while black babies are scorned." Families hired bodyguards to protect white Amerasian children from being stolen, but if the baby was Black Amerasian, the family would force the mother and baby to leave immediately.[68] Marion Williams made similar claims, alleging, "A Vietnamese girl thinks that the gods have smiled on her, if she has a white baby, but that the gods have cursed her, if she has a black baby."[69] In December 1967 the *Philadelphia Tribune* reported that "a bleak future is forecast for the thousands of new Negro Asian children because of the alleged color consciousness of the Vietnamese people."[70]

Other evidence supports the accuracy of these observations. In November 1972 the *Hartford Courant* estimated that about half of all Amerasian children in orphanages were Black. According to Wells Klein, general director of the American branch of International Social Service, a Black Amerasian faced "dim prospects because of his color. . . . Because there is no black community in Vietnam, he will grow up and live in relative social isolation. He will always be the oddball."[71] In late 1972 African American journalist Era Bell Thompson traveled to Vietnam for a story on Black Amerasians. She found that they were more likely to end up in orphanages and less likely to be adopted. She discovered that the "Vietnamese admit privately that their people are prejudiced against dark skin," and even those willing to adopt a Black Amerasian child are reluctant because "it is assumed that they will be rejected when older by the society into which they were born."[72]

These accounts suggest that Vietnamese attitudes toward skin color and race were more varied and complex than most African Americans believed them to be. While many Blacks believed Vietnamese people were free of prejudice, those who experienced racism directly challenged this notion.

The armed forces received numerous complaints from Black servicemen about Vietnamese discrimination. In December 1969 the Office of the Secretary of Defense released a report which revealed that some Vietnamese were discriminating against African Americans. Officials with the III Marine Amphibious Force in Da Nang reported "scattered instances of anti-Negro feeling by Vietnam nationals." Officials with the 12th Tactical Fighter Wing in Cam Ranh Bay noted that two waitresses had recently been dismissed for discriminatory treatment, but reports of staff members' racial discrimination continued.[73]

In 1970 the army received a complaint from the 525th Military Intelligence Group, eventually substantiated by investigators, that waitresses intentionally provided poor service to Black troops. Human relations officials informed the civilian workforce that they would be fired "if they were observed showing preferential treatment to club customers because of race." Reports of discrimination ended after this threat.[74] In April 1972 Michael Hayes filed a similar complaint against civilian workers, charging that "Vietnamese waitresses deliberately gave poor service to blacks."[75]

"You Had Vietnamese Whose Minds Had Been Turned against Black Soldiers"

There is evidence that some Vietnamese discriminated against African Americans. While some Blacks concluded that individual Vietnamese were racist, most looked for another explanation for what they regarded as aberrant behavior. Frequently, when African American servicemen encountered signs of Vietnamese racism, they held white servicemen responsible. Racist whites had brought their discriminatory views with them and taught them to Vietnamese civilians. It was bad enough that whites continued to discriminate against Black servicemen, but now they were attempting to convince civilians to do the same.

In November 1962, when there were relatively few Americans in Vietnam, Ronald Lewis, a Black airman, wrote a letter to *Ebony* charging that white servicemen were spreading racist information. Lewis claimed the Vietnamese had "been brain-washed to believe that our race is a violent, ignorant, and loud one." A shop owner told Lewis that information in *Ebony* contradicted everything whites had told him about African Americans, which was that "our race were the peasants of the United States and were inclined to cut you with a razor (which we all carry) almost any time." White servicemen had also told him that Blacks were only capable of working menial jobs and were not intelligent enough to attend school. Lewis believed that this man's views were not atypical and that many locals were taught by whites to have a negative image of African Americans.[76]

Other accounts support Lewis's observations. Ronald Manning, an African American from Elizabeth, New Jersey, served as an advisor to the ARVN in 1965. He noted that "the people show prejudice only when they have been 'indoctrinated' by whites."[77] In March 1969 Roman Metcalf wrote a letter to his mother claiming that racist whites "turn the Vietnamese against us."[78] Willie Thomas observed, "You had Vietnamese that loved Black soldiers and you had Vietnamese whose minds had been turned against Black soldiers." He believed that whites spread rumors that "Blacks were animals, you know we were monkeys, we really had tails."[79] Scott Riley agreed, "The civilian population and especially the young bar girls, the prostitutes, and this that and the other, were told by our white military counterparts that we had tails."[80]

When Lamont B. Steptoe first arrived in Vietnam in July 1969, a hooch maid pointed at him and said, "you same same monkey." Although shocked by her comments, Steptoe did not think that she came up with this offensive characterization on her own. He recalled, "I knew where she had gotten this attitude."[81] Arthur Barham was told by a prostitute in Tuy Hoa that white soldiers had warned her not to sleep with African Americans because they had tails.[82] During his R&R in Thailand several prostitutes told Ron Bradley that white soldiers had told them Blacks had tails.[83]

As a nurse at the 24th Evacuation Hospital in Long Binh, Constance Edwards rarely left the area immediately around the hospital, and she had limited experiences with the Vietnamese civilian population. However, during a trip to Bien Hoa, she too saw evidence of the negative influence white servicemen were having on the Vietnamese. Speaking of the small children who filled the streets, Edwards noted, "You could tell who the kids had been around, whether it was a white person or a Black person." Some of the kids would put their hands next to Edwards's hands and say, "mamasan, same same me . . . mamasan soul sister." In contrast, other children continually ran circles around Edwards's fellow nurse, who was also Black, while repeating "mamasan, no tail." Edwards concluded, "You could tell the white people had told them that black people had tails."[84]

The Vietnam War was not the first conflict in which white troops spread racist characterizations of Blacks to native populations. Willie Thomas was not shocked when he heard these stories as his father had told him whites spread similarly offensive characterizations of Blacks when he was in the military during World War II.[85] When George Brummell was stationed in Korea, local girls "would tell us the white guys always said that the Black guys had tails... that we were close to monkeys."[86]

In May 1968 the navy received numerous complaints from Chief Petty Officer Barry Wright, a Chicago native and Vietnam veteran. Wright claimed that white servicemen were openly "encouraging Vietnamese civilian employees to discriminate against Negro personnel."[87] That same month Willie McCarthy wrote to Democratic senator Abraham Ribicoff from Connecticut detailing his experiences with discrimination in Soc Trang. McCarthy claimed that whites told "Vietnamese people that colored people were number 10, (meaning no good) and that they were liars and thieves. This made the Vietnamese people scared to talk to Negroes for a long time until they found out different, but they still fear them some." He had heard similar reports in Can Tho and Vinh Long, and he feared these racist mischaracterizations had spread further.[88]

When *Black Journal* reporters traveled to Vietnam in 1969, they interviewed Black servicemen who experienced racism at the hands of the Vietnamese. In every case the African Americans held white servicemen responsible. Sylvester Bracey recalled an incident where a "Vietnamese girl, she called me a nigger. . . . I know it's not part of their language, can't nobody tell me it's part of their language." When asked who he thought was responsible, the man responded, "The beast, you know that?"[89]

Another marine added, "Now just like he said, these people, these oriental people don't know how, know where the word nigger came from or nothing. They have to learn how to speak it." White serviceman taught civilians offensive racial slurs and to discriminate against and fear African Americans. The marine recalled being thrown out of a club simply because he was Black: "They don't like us, they say we start trouble. Now who'd put this stuff in their mind? You know what I mean? The beasts came over here and brainwashed these people."[90]

Bobby Jenkins believed that whites did more than just teach their racist beliefs to the Vietnamese; they pressured them to discriminate against Blacks. He asserted, "There's some places you can't go up in Saigon. It's just like in Georgia. . . . You walk in there and you ain't welcome at all and they'll let you know it. But let a white man walk in there, he's welcome."[91] Kent Garrett confirmed that "there were definitely clubs in Saigon, for example, that you couldn't go into I mean, that you weren't welcome into, if you were black. And the same thing on the other side, if you were white there were places you couldn't go." He understood that this segregated environment "really mirrored a lot of the cultural stuff that was going on in the States." According to Garrett, segregated bars in Vietnam "were a result of the influence of Americans on the Vietnamese culture.... I don't think the Vietnamese, you know, had a culture of discrimination and distinguishing between black and white before the Americans showed up."[92]

Segregated bars were common in the United States, and the American military presence brought them to Vietnam. Many would have agreed with Ron Copes that some Vietnamese may have appeared to be racist but were just repeating what whites had taught them. According to Copes there were "establishments that catered to white soldiers" and "establishments that catered to Black soldiers." He remembered, "If you looked at it without seeing anything else, you would think that Vietnam, the Vietnamese people, were running a segregated situation, but it was the Americans that insisted upon it and they just complied." Copes believed that white soldiers pressured bar owners into admitting only whites into their clubs, and for financial reasons they obliged.[93] Similar complaints were made by Black servicemen in Germany, Japan, and the island of Okinawa during this same period.[94]

In a February 1971 article in the *New York Amsterdam News*, Reuben Davis, an African American veteran, recalled, "When I arrived in Vietnam I found that the Caucasians had taken their petty prejudices over there. The Vietnamese people referred to us as Mideim, which means black Devil." Davis maintained the Vietnamese had "been brainwashed by the white establishment" into thinking that African Americans were inferior and deserved mistreatment.[95]

Even Donald Mosby, who publicized Vietnamese discrimination against Blacks, Montagnards, and Amerasians, agreed that racist whites influenced Vietnamese views and behavior. Mosby claimed, "White servicemen in this country help promote the racism by infecting the local population with it, whenever they can." Nonetheless, he remained convinced that "the intensity of Vietnamese hatred of black people could not have been created in the short time that large numbers of white GIs have been in Vietnam."[96]

One should be careful not to hold white servicemen entirely responsible for the attitudes and actions of the Vietnamese. Blacks were part of an occupying military force, which was reason enough for some people to dislike them. As well, many African Americans felt and expressed empathy for the Vietnamese, and they wanted and likely expected reciprocation. Understandably, they were disappointed when they did not get it and sought an explanation. Whites discriminated against them back home, and it made sense they would bring their own beliefs to Vietnam, broadcast those ideas, and seek to instill them in others.

These complaints eventually came to the attention of armed forces officials. On December 4, 1969, L. Howard Bennett, deputy assistant secretary of defense for civil rights, sent a letter to Major General Jack Wagstaff, deputy commander, U.S. Military Assistance Command, Thailand, regarding his recent trip to Vietnam. Bennett warned that "the exportation of racial prejudice to Thai and Vietnamese nationals is a very serious problem and it demands close command attention." Two days later Bennett wrote to Admiral John S. McCain, commander in chief, Pacific command, warning him that the "exportation of American racism, prejudices, and discrimination" was a matter of serious concern. Bennett did not mince words as to who was responsible. He explained, "This was done by our white comrades-in arms. They will tell the Thai and the Vietnamese that the Blacks are really devils of a sort—that after 6 o'clock their tails come out or if you watch carefully there is a place in their head where horns might sprout."[97] Bennett's wording is almost identical to the allegations made by Willie Thomas, Lamont B. Steptoe, and others. Bennett's statement that white servicemen were telling the Vietnamese Blacks were devils with horns is identical to Reuben Davis's claim.

In April 1970 the Joint Office of the Secretary of Defense released a report, based almost entirely on Bennett's findings, which revealed that a primary source of conflict was that many African Americans blamed, often with justification, whites for exporting their racist views to the Vietnamese.[98]

During Bennett's December 1969 trip to Vietnam, investigators revealed several incidents of white servicemen encouraging discrimination. A white sergeant with the 12th Tactical Fighter Wing instructed workers to call Black airmen "boy," a practice that quickly spread. Race relations were particularly fractured in the 1st Aviation Brigade in Long Binh. Investigators discovered that the main cause of friction was a white sergeant who instructed "Vietnamese girls not to wait on Negroes."[99] Another report conducted by L. Howard Bennett's office revealed that "a mess sergeant had told the Vietnamese kitchen laborers not to obey a Negro Cook." Military officials intervened, but their solution to the problem left a lot to be desired: the mess sergeant was transferred to another unit but not punished.[100] Collectively, these incidents caused considerable racial tension leading investigators to determine that that the enlisted men's club was "ready to explode."[101]

Bennett's report appears to have had an impact. In September 1970 Brigadier General Jack MacFarlane sent a letter to Chief of Staff Major General Welborn G. Dolvin, MACV, warning that African Americans routinely complained they were "discriminated against by local girls at the instigation of white soldiers" and that this was causing significant tension. MacFarlane argued that the only way to prevent further racial problems was to address these and other allegations of racial discrimination directly.[102]

In November 1970 the Department of the Army organized a Race Relations Conference at Continental Army Command headquarters in Fort Monroe, Virginia. Recently returned from Vietnam, Lieutenant James Anderson reported that one of the most frequent complaints African Americans made was that "U.S whites encourage foreign nationals to discriminate against Black soldiers. Commanders do not require employers to comply with equal opportunity policies."[103]

Human Relations Council reports provide additional evidence that white servicemen were teaching Vietnamese people to discriminate against African Americans. On February 13, 1971, representatives from the Long Binh Post Human Relations Council discussed an accusation made by an unidentified Black soldier that a Vietnamese worker had told him Blacks were required to "drink milk and juice from one set of containers, and whites from another set" in the mess hall cafeteria. A chaplain named Barbinette verified the man's account and urged "the council that it is a matter for immediate command action." The "segregation" of containers replicated the policies of the segregationist South and was certainly disturbing. Even more troubling, the Council believed that it was possible that "someone in authority in the mess hall had instructed" the worker to do this.[104]

In February 1972 a Human Relations Council report provided further evidence of whites' pressuring Vietnamese workers to discriminate against African Americans. A Lieutenant Barksdale reported that a "majority of blacks" believed "the indigenous personnel has been threaten [sic] with dismissal if they are too friendly with the blacks on the compound." Similar accusations were repeated by four other servicemen present. A Human Relations Council officer named Mitchell assured them that it was official policy to inform every civilian worker that racial discrimination was prohibited. Mitchell's statement suggests this was not a new problem as a policy to address discrimination already existed. His statement was meant to reassure African Americans, but it also revealed that someone in a position of power was instructing workers to ignore established policy. As to the rumors that whites were threatening to dismiss workers if they were too friendly with African Americans, the report stated, "Considering the attitudes of some of the high ranking individuals who departed this compound, it is quite possible that there might be some truth to the rumor."[105]

The statement is telling because it suggests that the council was aware that high-ranking white officers held racist views and may have encouraged or even instructed Vietnamese workers to discriminate against Blacks, confirming the findings of the Long Binh Human Relations Council the previous year. This was contrary to official policy, but even when the workers' actions were exposed, they were not always fired because the same people who had put these ideas in their heads were responsible for hiring and firing.

Two Black servicemen discussed their experiences with one particular waitress who had a reputation for discriminating against Blacks. When an African American serviceman accidentally dropped money, the waitress shouted, "Black GI's are mother—ing number ten." She was supposed to be fired but the council noted, "A month later the waitress is still working in the club and apparently her attitude towards blacks has not changed. No one knows why she was not fired."[106] Her continued employment suggests that her supervisor was not particularly interested in punishing her or maintaining an environment free of discrimination. At worst it suggests that higher-ranking soldiers agreed with the waitress's views and may even have influenced them.

Conclusion

Vietnamese civilians likely assessed servicemen, including African Americans, from a variety of perspectives. Americans were defenders, customers, employers, and members of an occupying army. Vietnamese views likely changed over time in response to the war and Americans' actions in their country. Using traditional historical sources, it is difficult to know for certain how civilians viewed American troops.

Archival sources, contemporary journals and newspapers, and most importantly oral accounts and interviews provide considerable insight into how Black servicemen thought the Vietnamese viewed them. Many African Americans believed the Vietnamese favored them over whites and empathized with them as persons of color and victims of racial discrimination. They also claimed the Vietnamese were supportive of the Black struggle for full civil, political, and economic equality in the United States. These beliefs were in part influenced by the actions of Vietnamese civilians who commonly greeted Black servicemen with statements expressing familiarity and sameness: "You and me—same same."

Blacks had grown up in a world divided between Blacks and whites, and the most explicit sign of this division was skin color. As Blacks saw it, whites mistreated the Vietnamese in a similar manner to the way whites mistreated African Americans in the United States and Vietnam. It made sense to think that this shared status and experience would lead to a degree of empathy and unity.

The reality was Vietnam was not free of ethnic, color, or racial prejudice as evidenced by the historical mistreatment of Montagnards and other minority groups. African Americans, who were aware of this behavior, recognized the Vietnamese had their own problems with tolerance, acceptance, and equality. This realization led some African Americans to view the Vietnamese not solely as victims of racial discrimination but also perpetrators of racial discrimination against minorities in their own country.

Others experienced racism firsthand, further challenging the notion that Vietnamese people were free of racial animus or that there was a shared bond forged out of common experiences and skin color. The Vietnamese did not universally embrace the vision some Black servicemen propagated of a world in which skin color, race, and shared experiences with poverty and racism created close bonds among diverse peoples. African Americans made major assumptions when they assigned "progressive" racial attitudes to the Vietnamese.

Frequently, when African Americans encountered Vietnamese racism, they concluded that it must have been inspired or heavily influenced by whites who had brought their racist ideas to Vietnam and "taught" them to the people. In truth, their views were not all that different from African Americans who believed that Vietnamese civilians were sympathetic and supportive. Both groups believed that the Vietnamese were naturally free of racial prejudice and left to their own devices would embrace African Americans.

The American racial environment and particularly American racism once again loomed large, but this time it was influencing how the

Vietnamese viewed and treated African Americans. Vietnamese who empathized with African Americans allegedly did so in part because they supported the Black movement for equality in the United States. Vietnamese who discriminated against African Americans did so under the influence of racist whites who brought their racist attitudes and behavior from the United States and taught them to the Vietnamese.

Racist whites had indeed brought their American-born prejudices with them to Vietnam where they continued to discriminate against African Americans. It was plausible that these same people would try and teach these views to the Vietnamese. White influence does not adequately explain every incident of Vietnamese racism. Still, there is convincing evidence that whites did encourage civilians to discriminate against and otherwise mistreat Black servicemen. Official armed forces investigations reveal that the military was aware this was happening but did little to stop it or punish those responsible, further aggravating tensions.

As we will see in the following chapter, many African Americans alleged that it was not only civilians who favored them but also the NLF and PAVN they were tasked with fighting. These servicemen claimed communist forces were sympathetic to African Americans and supported the domestic Black struggle against racial prejudice and discrimination. Many African Americans believed that Vietnamese people, civilian or military, allies or enemies, empathized with African Americans and supported their domestic agenda.

CHAPTER 6

"We Won't Shoot You, but We'll Shoot the White Guy"

African American Views of Vietnamese Communist Forces

In 1966–67 Anthony Martin participated in numerous combat operations against communist forces in Con Thien Province. Reflecting on his experiences, Martin asserted, "Sometimes a statement like this gets me in trouble with many of my peers, but in my opinion the best soldier in the world was the Vietnamese soldier." Martin went even further, claiming the Vietnamese communists' "dedication to their freedom was no different than our dedication to freedom during our own Civil War."[1] Many Americans viewed the Vietnam War as a civil war. They also made comparisons between NLF forces and American soldiers in the Revolutionary War. Martin went a step further when he compared communist efforts to defeat the American-backed regime in Saigon with African American efforts to win their freedom during the Civil War. His perceptions of the enemy were heavily influenced by the Black historical experience.

In some respects, Martin's impressions were not surprising. African Americans viewed civilians through a similar lens. However, it is one thing to relate one's own experiences to a civilian population you are nominally responsible for protecting and quite another to do so with military forces you are tasked with fighting and killing and who are simultaneously trying to kill you. Martin went further than African American servicemen who identified with Vietnamese civilians. He was not alone.

Rumors spread among Black and even white servicemen that communist forces favored African Americans over whites. Martin recalled hearing "tales that the Viet Cong wouldn't raise their weapons against Black Americans."[2] He also heard that if servicemen were captured, they would kill the whites and let the African Americans go. Martin did not believe these rumors, but they nonetheless spread widely among Black servicemen. Collectively, these rumors claimed that the communist enemy did not want to kill African Americans, empathized with them, and supported the Black struggle. Their war was not with African Americans.

Communist officials helped spread these ideas. Wallace Terry recalled that Black servicemen routinely encountered "communist propaganda [which] urged you to go home instead of fighting another dark-skinned people."[3] Using leaflets and radio broadcasts, communist propaganda expressed sympathy for the civil rights movement, urged Black troops to stop fighting, and encouraged them to go home and fight for greater equality.

According to this propaganda the "real" war for African Americans was in the United States, a judgement most African Americans had difficulty ignoring or dismissing. This propaganda may not have convinced any Black servicemen to "go home," but it did help to create and nurture the perception that communist forces empathized with them and favored them over whites. It also placed the domestic racial environment front and center. African Americans viewed their experiences with racial issues through the lens of their own experiences in the United States, and the Vietnamese enemy strengthened this perspective by routinely reminding them of their status back home and in the military.

Black Internationalism

Black servicemen were not the first African Americans to believe that Asians or other groups involved in anticolonial conflict might be innately sympathetic to Blacks and their aspirations. Many twentieth-century Black intellectuals had earlier reached the same conclusion. Historian Marc Gallicchio's *The African American Encounter with Japan and China* highlights the efforts of African American leaders like W. E. B. Du Bois and Marcus Garvey to create an international alliance that linked the Black struggle for civil and political rights with global anticolonial movements. These "Black internationalists" believed that as victims of racism and imperialism, "darker" races had a common interest in overthrowing white supremacy and establishing an international order based on racial equality. In the years before World War II, these internationalists advocated the formation of an alliance first with Japan and then with China after the Pacific War began in 1941. They believed that as victims of imperialism and racism, the Japanese and Chinese would naturally sympathize with the African American struggle for greater civil and political rights.[4]

Historians Thomas Borstelmann, Mary L. Dudziak, Gerald Horne, and Michael Krenn have argued that African American efforts to link their struggle for equality to the struggles of people in Asia and Africa became all the more common and pronounced during the Cold War.[5] While this is valid, their conclusions are based on an examination of the views of a relatively small and exceptional group: Black intellectuals, academics, journalists, and leaders of civil rights organizations like the NAACP.

The views expressed by Anthony Martin and others demonstrate that Black servicemen, most of whom came from working-class or poor backgrounds, made similar observations.[6] There is no evidence that Black servicemen were influenced by or even aware of the opinions of Black intellectuals and leaders, but both groups began with the premise that people in Asia and Africa, as victims of racism, were innately sympathetic to African Americans and supportive of their struggles.

It was, of course, paradoxical that African Americans identified with their enemy and saw them as empathetic while simultaneously trying to fight and kill them. In this way, African American perceptions of Vietnamese communist forces were markedly different than that of Black intellectuals who tried to form alliances with Asian and African groups in countries that were allied with the United States or at least not at war with them.

"The Best Soldier in the World Was the Vietnamese Soldier": The NLF and PAVN

Few servicemen questioned the NLF's and PAVN's desire to fight. In 1966 General A. S. Collins, commander of the army's 4th Infantry Division, summed up the feelings of many servicemen when he stated, "I wish the southern members of the clan would display the fighting qualities of their northern brethren."[7] Most American servicemen, regardless of race, gave communist forces grudging respect. Yet, as the following accounts reveal, African Americans viewed the enemy differently than their white peers. Black accounts tended to concentrate on the enemy's underdog status and how they managed to survive and even succeed in the face of overwhelming American firepower. Survival in the face of adversity was something African Americans had experience with and admired.

In a 1986 *Frontline* PBS episode titled "The Bloods of 'Nam," Charles Strong discussed an incident in the Chu Lai region that accurately represents the way many Black troops saw enemy forces. Strong, along with thirty-five of his fellow soldiers, spent two hours trying to kill a lone PAVN soldier, eventually cornering him. Through an interpreter they offered him a chance to surrender, but when he refused, they dropped explosives in the hole, which failed to kill him. Strong recalled, "He would not give up and this is the day that I really will remember in my life that if a man have a belief, a real belief, he should be willing to die for it. Now I was proud of that North Vietnamese soldier because he gave me a living example of what a man's supposed to be."[8] While many whites respected the enemy's fighting abilities, it is unlikely that many were "proud" of PAVN or NLF resiliency.

African Americans often focused on the enemy's determination and commitment. Anthony Martin recalled, "We had tanks, we had ships, we had bombers, we had every known kind of weapon known to man . . . shooting down on them and they kept coming. And I often ask myself faced with the same firepower would I be just as dedicated?"[9] Sinclair Swan also pointed out that the NLF remained effective despite constant attacks from American ground forces, aircraft, and artillery.[10] Ron Copes described the NLF as "extremely determined with a strong belief in what they were doing."[11] Willie Thomas's impressions were that the enemy was "a dedicated force, they believed in what they were fighting for. . . . They wanted to unite their country and they were willing to sacrifice, fight, and die to unite their country."[12]

Agreeing with this characterization, Archie Biggers, who served near the demilitarized zone, stated that "the enemy would do anything to win. You had to respect that. They believed in a cause. They had the support of the people."[13] Robert M. Watters went even further, characterizing the NLF as almost invincible. He proclaimed that they "didn't care about dying. I mean, you would hit them with a 60 caliber right there in the fucking chest, and those sons of bitches keep coming. . . . I mean they were as strong mentally as they were strong physically. . . . You just kept shooting them, kept shooting them, and they kept coming."[14]

Watters's depiction of the enemy as almost superhuman was certainly an exaggeration, but many servicemen shared his belief that Vietnamese communist forces were strong, both physically and mentally. Not unrelated, African Americans frequently depicted the enemy as fiercely dedicated to a noble cause. Cephus Rhodes argued that the conflict was ultimately a civil war and that "we drew the line, they didn't draw the line" as to who was an authentic representative of Vietnam.[15] Speaking of communist forces, James Lewis asserted, "I don't know of any Vietnamese that come over here and slap my face or run over my yard.... I just didn't see any real basis for fighting the so-called North Vietnamese.... In hindsight I still don't see it."[16]

Lamont B. Steptoe respected the NLF for their willingness "to defend their country against foreign invaders." After he saw how some servicemen treated civilians and captured soldiers, Steptoe "began to identify more with the Viet Cong than the United States military." He resolved, "I told myself I am not going to feel any animosity toward them if I get wounded or if they take my life because I made the choice to come here.... When I left the military I left more as a guerilla than I did as an American soldier because I just felt so many parallels between what they were doing and what was happening to Black Americans."[17]

Rhodes, Lewis, and Steptoe depicted the American war effort as purposeless and misdirected, if not entirely immoral. They also presented the United States as the primary aggressor in the conflict. As each noted, Vietnamese communist forces were not threatening to invade the United States. In contrast, they argued that NLF and PAVN forces were justified in fighting American forces and trying to overthrow the American-backed regime. Only the Vietnamese had the right to form their own government. The United States had no business in Vietnam.

"It Got to the Point Where You Couldn't Rely on Them": The ARVN

Most American servicemen described the communist forces as capable and dedicated. In contrast, most viewed the ARVN as "ill-equipped, inadequately trained, and poorly led" but also cowardly. This perception became further magnified when ARVN troops fought and things went badly. As historian Peter S. Kindsvatter notes, it only "took one instance of ARVN cowardice to turn grunts against them."[18]

The depiction of the ARVN as universally incompetent or unwilling to fight is an exaggeration. Millions served in the ARVN, as well as with Regional and Popular Forces (RF/PF), and there were highly motivated

"We Won't Shoot You, but We'll Shoot the White Guy" 179

and effective servicemen among them. American strategy dictated that Vietnamese forces provide area security while American forces conducted field operations.[19] ARVN and NLF units occasionally signed localized cease-fires, which could explain some instances where they appeared hesitant to fight.[20] Roughly 250,000 ARVN soldiers were killed during the war, demonstrating that many were willing to fight and die in defense of their country.[21]

Nonetheless, most servicemen viewed the ARVN at best as ineffective or unreliable and at worst as an impediment to victory. This perception was not limited to any one group or race. Albert French described the ARVN as looking "like little toy soldiers with big guns," and he was not the only African American to question their professionalism and dedication to the war effort.[22] Willie Thomas stated that he was "never impressed with the Vietnamese desire to fight."[23] Robert Sanders recalled, "We never did see the regular South Vietnamese army in the field. They would be guarding the bridges or be hidden away in some compound somewhere.... We were fighting for them and they were scared to fight for themselves. They used to pick up and run."[24] Terry Whitmore claimed, "Patrol with ARVN was usually just diddley-bopping along through the jungle.... ARVN's were not too keen on combat.... If they thought that there would be some shooting, they'd be gone."[25]

Speaking of the ARVN, Ron Bradley recalled, "When we would have certain actions and they were supposed to cover our flanks or they were supposed to be there with us and things got heavy, they disappeared or they went home or they went to dinner.... It got to the point where you couldn't rely on them."[26] Melvin Adams recalled an incident in which an ARVN commander tried to call off a mission because he received a poor astrology report, which Adams assessed as a lack of interest in fighting.[27]

Sinclair Swan thought that the average ARVN soldier was poorly trained, poorly led, and lacked the necessary motivation and discipline to win the war. He believed that they purposely made noise during combat missions to scare off the enemy and prevent any sort of fight from occurring.[28] Lamont B. Steptoe complained that during a joint operation, ARVN forces allowed him and his dog to walk off aimlessly without following, which he saw as evidence that they were not really interested in finding the enemy.[29]

Samuel Vance portrayed ARVN soldiers as incompetent and unable or unwilling to fight, going so far as to claim that the war would only be won if they were all killed. He criticized the RVN government, believing that they were corrupt and uninterested in the welfare of their own people.[30] He was not the only one to connect government corruption with the seeming ineptitude of the ARVN. Horace Coleman met a bartender who, after being drafted into the ARVN, ceded his military pay to his commanding officer in exchange for not having to serve. Coleman believed this transaction symbolized much of what was wrong with the war effort.[31]

David Parks portrayed ARVN soldiers as good fighters but alienated from the population. They thought little of human life and didn't hesitate to kill civilians.[32] James Gillam agreed that the ARVN were often brutal in their treatment of civilians. When Gillam's squad found hundreds of AK-47 rounds hidden in an elderly woman's basket, they let her go "because we all knew she would never survive interrogation by the ARVN."[33] Gillam claimed this callousness extended to the local Montagnard population as when ARVN "were short a body count . . . the Vietnamese came through and killed them all."[34]

Some African Americans believed that the quality of ARVN soldiers varied. James Lewis acknowledged that some were terrible, but the scouts attached to his unit "were some of the best soldiers I have ever known."[35] Sinclair Swan thought little of the average soldier, but the elite ranger units were effective.[36] Ron Bradley claimed that the RVN military police and localized militia forces were dedicated and dependable.[37] Robert E. Holcomb became close friends with a scout assigned to his unit. In sharp contrast to the depictions that others made of ARVN soldiers, Holcomb's friend was dependable and fearless.[38]

During his second tour in 1969–70 Louis Perkins was an advisor to the ARVN. Speaking of his overall impressions, Perkins asserted, "Some of them were very professional, some of them were real great guys, and then there were those that were there to rip off anybody they could." Perkins believed that most of the men he worked with "were genuine good people," and he was especially "proud of the fact that my counterpart was a pretty straight guy. . . . He appeared to have his troops first in his mind, taking care of them."[39]

Ron Copes worked in MACV as an advisor to a district chief, a position that put him in daily contact with local RF/PF, during his second tour in 1969–70. He concluded that unlike the ARVN soldiers he had interacted with previously, they were efficient and reliable. He recollected, "I felt better about my two tours based on the second tour. If it had just been the first tour, I think I would have had a negative impression of the Vietnamese that was unjustified."[40]

Thomas Brannon described his interactions with ARVN soldiers in ways similar to how other African Americans portrayed their interactions with civilians. He recalled an incident in which his cavalry unit helped a stranded ARVN Ranger Battalion on Highway 13. He believed the rangers were impressed and even proud that an African American was commanding white troops. He recalled, "I could just look in their eyes . . . you know it was like a Black guy seeing a Black guy and you ain't seen him for a while, you can look each other in the eye and say, 'Man, I am glad to see you.'" Brannon believed the rangers viewed him as one of their own because he was Black. Whenever he worked with ARVN troops, he felt this same sense of kinship.[41]

Wayne Smith understood that it was "conventional thinking that they [the ARVN] cannot be relied on in battle; that they would abandon you or would simply not fight and if they did fight, they were not effective fighters." In retrospect, Smith believed the average soldier was misjudged, especially as hundreds of thousands of ARVN soldiers fought and died during the war.[42]

While Horace Coleman witnessed evidence of corruption, he also encountered soldiers who had lost nearly everything in the war. In his poem "War Stories" he memorialized "the ARVN who lost his arm to the PAVN, his wife to a free fire zone, and his kid to disease."[43] Coleman recognized that many ARVN soldiers made huge sacrifices during the war.

The ARVN's inability to defeat the communist insurgency had led American officials to send American forces to Vietnam. This no doubt impacted the assessments of American servicemen. Wes Geary recalled, "I really personally just didn't trust South Vietnamese. I developed a kind of . . . well I was angry with 'em because I didn't think that they was trying hard enough, you know."[44] James Gillam similarly theorized, "I didn't like the South Vietnamese because I figured they should have taken care of their own business."[45] The ARVN's inability to take "care of their own business" partly explains why Black servicemen tended to have a negative opinion of them.

Whatever sympathy or identification African Americans may have felt for the enemy and whatever disdain they may have felt for their allies, they were expected to fight NLF and PAVN forces alongside the ARVN. This placed them in the difficult position of fighting and killing people they respected and who they believed were fighting for their own freedom. Equally problematic, African Americans often served with white servicemen whose views of the enemy were different than their own.

The general dehumanizing of Vietnamese people contributed to the mistreatment of civilians, but it also impacted the way members of the U.S. military viewed and treated the enemy. Psychologist Jonathan Shay notes that Americans commonly referred to Vietnamese communist forces as "monkeys, insects, vermin," words also used to describe the Japanese during World War II. The average soldier was taught that the enemy was "deranged," "barbaric," "treacherous," and "bent on world conquest."[46] Anthony Martin recalled being indoctrinated to think that the PAVN were equal to the Nazis.[47]

This dehumanization extended to the way even dead NLF and PAVN soldiers were treated. Servicemen collected ears, teeth, and fingers of dead communist troops as trophies. It is impossible to assess the frequency of these actions, but they weren't rare.[48] Often African Americans expressed shock and disappointment at these practices. David Parks was disgusted when he witnessed a white sergeant cut off the finger of a dead NLF soldier.[49] David Tuck recalled that officers issued free beer "to American soldiers who return to camp with the largest number of dead enemies' ears."[50] Harold Bryant remembered that "white guys would sometimes take the dogtag chain and fill that up with ears. . . . They would nail 'em up on the walls to our hootch, you know, as a trophy." This was a point of contention between Black and white soldiers. Bryant thought it was "stupid and spiritually, I was lookin' at it as damaging a dead body. After a while, I told them, 'Hey, man, that's sick. Don't be around me with the ears hangin' on you.'"[51] Undoubtedly some African Americans kept similar "trophies," but Bryant made a clear racial distinction between whites who desecrated dead enemy soldiers and Blacks who refused to do so.

Wayne Smith believed the practice of removing ears or fingers from dead soldiers was "horrible" and "wrong," but it did happen. Smith labeled a white soldier nicknamed "Jungle Jordan" a "brutal son of a bitch" because he frequently cut the ears off dead soldiers and wore them as trophies.[52] A commander in Lamont B. Steptoe's unit encouraged "soldiers to became barbarians," promising three days off in Saigon to anyone who brought back a pair of ears. Steptoe was disgusted but he could do little to prevent these acts.[53]

Steptoe remembered another incident where two NLF soldiers were captured while hiding in a village. As they were dragged out of their huts, one of them grabbed the rafters. Rather than simply pull him out, Steptoe's sergeant cut his hands off with a machete. During another incident, Steptoe was asked to use his dog to torture a few prisoners to gain information. He refused the request, telling his fellow soldiers that he could not live with himself knowing that he had tortured a prisoner.[54]

"You Get to Live Another Day"

Black opinions of the NLF and PAVN went deeper than simply respecting their fighting abilities or acknowledging the worthiness of their cause. Many African Americans believed that NLF and PAVN soldiers favored them and would treat them differently from whites, even on the battlefield. In November 1965 Simeon Booker observed, "In Vietnam, a Negro GI can walk through downtown Saigon with virtual immunity, or he can go to the suburbs where Viet Cong assure him, 'There'll be no bombs or gunfights because you are our friends.'" Booker also claimed that "few grenades were thrown at dark skinned Americans" and "often times when attacking convoys, VC's shoot only at white soldiers." These incidents were sufficiently commonplace that officers suggested white soldiers blacken their faces with makeup to fool the NLF.[55] Booker's observations occurred within a few months of the arrival of the first American combat troops, and similar incidents would be reported for the duration of the war.

In 1968 African American cartoonist Morrie Turner spent twenty-seven days in Vietnam as a member of the National Cartoonist Society, drawing thousands of cartoons for injured servicemen and others in combat.[56] Two of these cartoons, which were later published, specifically addressed the Black perception that communist forces empathized with them and were supportive of the civil rights movement. One cartoon depicts an African American serviceman standing behind three NLF soldiers with their hands raised over their heads with the caption, "I just yelled 'Black power' and all three of 'em surrendered."[57] Turner's cartoon argues that the soldiers surrendered not out of fear or cowardice but because they didn't want to fight supporters of the Black power movement. The NLF did not view African Americans as the enemy and were not interested in fighting them.

The second cartoon depicts two camouflaged African Americans walking out of a jungle with one of the men remarking, "I could have sworn I heard Charlie singing 'we shall overcome.'"[58] Turner's depiction of NLF members singing the most well-known protest song of the civil rights movement suggests they not only empathized with the movement but viewed their own situation as analogous. While Turner's cartoons were meant to be humorous, he did not invent the scenarios or opinions expressed in them. They were based on conversations he had with servicemen. His cartoons reflected how many African Americans believed communist forces viewed them.

Morrie Turner was not the only one to depict the NLF as disinterested in fighting African Americans or as sympathetic toward the civil rights movement. In January 1971 the Army General Staff received a report from Army Counterintelligence noting that "a rumor still persists in the field units that the Viet Cong will not ambush Black soldiers, but only wish to kill whites." Army Counterintelligence interviewed several African Americans who claimed that "blacks in the field have been told that they will be warned by the Viet Cong of an impending ambush." Investigators highlighted an incident in which a Black warrant officer allegedly claimed in a speech to forty to fifty Black soldiers that he had "high-ranking contacts within the Viet Cong, and he had been guaranteed that the VC only wanted to kill the whites and not the blacks." While Army Counterintelligence was quick to point out there was no truth to these rumors, they admitted "the subject is being discussed by black troops throughout all of Vietnam."[59]

This report was troubling for several reasons. First, the rumors were sufficiently prevalent that they had gained the attention of army intelligence. The use of the phrase "a rumor still persists" suggests this rumor was ongoing. Investigators believed that the rumors were widespread, and that Black soldiers had been aware of them for some time.

Army Counterintelligence's assertion that these rumors were long-standing and widespread was accurate. Thomas Brannon, who served in 1966–67, recalled hearing that "often times the Viet Cong would let a Black point man go through. Not shoot him."[60] Wayne Smith, who served in 1968–69, heard a variation of this rumor—if Black soldiers didn't shoot at the NLF, they wouldn't shoot back.[61] James Gillam was in Vietnam from late 1969 until early 1970. He remembered, "It was talked about you know somebody would say, 'Well if you get in it tight and you're walking out by yourself on point and if you think the PAVN are out there, if you just take your rifle and sling it barrel down, you'll be okay.'"[62]

Lamont B. Steptoe, who served in 1969–70, "heard tales that you know the North Vietnamese would capture Black soldiers and give them political education and then release them because Ho Chi Minh, he liked Black people."[63] Supposedly, the PAVN wanted to educate African Americans but not kill them. In 1970 Eddie Greene heard that communist forces "wouldn't target them for sniper attacks as regularly as they would the whites." Greene was told the NLF were sympathetic toward African Americans. He recalled, "The scuttlebutt was that they knew the situation that African Americans were in in America. That we did not have true equal rights here in America. . . . We are not there on our own accord. We are there because really we are still slaves."⁶⁴

Some African Americans believed there was truth behind these rumors. Ron Bradley thought that if a squad was "predominantly Black they didn't shoot at us and they had hoped we didn't shoot at them."⁶⁵ Samuel Vance heard that "the Viet Cong wouldn't kill or harm a Negro unless a unit was ambushed or attacked and the Negro was a part of it." He believed that NLF soldiers would not kill African Americans unless they were left with no other option. Black servicemen were safe in the jungle and the city. Vance remarked, "There are places in Saigon where the Negroes can roam freely and stay out all of the night, and nothing ever happens to them. If a white man dared to travel anywhere alone, he'd be doomed."⁶⁶

In May 1968 *Newsday* interviewed an anonymous Black soldier who discussed an incident in which the NLF allegedly captured six white soldiers and one Black one. The soldier claimed, "They killed all six whites and they let this one blood (Negro) go." He added that intelligence supposedly interviewed the surviving Black soldier for days to ascertain why he hadn't been killed, "but this cat ain't telling them nothing."⁶⁷

Don F. Browne, who served in Saigon and Tuy Hoa in 1967–68, also argued that the "Viet Cong would shoot at a white guy, then let the Black guy behind go through, then shoot at the next white guy." Brown believed this rumor, but he argued that NLF soldiers deliberately differentiated Blacks from whites not out of racial solidarity or empathy but to increase tensions. Robert E. Holcomb maintained that it was not just African Americans who believed the rumor as "white guys would stay close to the black guys in the field because they thought the VC and PAVN didn't shoot at blacks as much as whites."⁶⁸

Rumors that the enemy wouldn't shoot African Americans were prevalent enough that even those in noncombat roles were exposed to them. Billy Jones, a psychiatrist, recalled, "I did hear of some situations in the field when the Vietcong would overrun a position. They would shoot the white folks and not the Blacks." While unsure if these rumors were true, he rationalized that if they were, then "Ho Chi Minh was really, you know, using some smarts" as this strategy could lead African Americans to second-guess their commitment to the war effort.⁶⁹

Some African Americans claimed they knew somebody who was spared or that they were themselves spared by communist forces. Melvin Adams had a Black friend who was responsible for delivering mail, but his vehicle was never fired on, even when he traveled to dangerous areas.

Adams's suspicions that the NLF weren't shooting at his friend because he was Black seemed to be confirmed when a white soldier traveled with him and the NLF "put two rounds through the windshield." Adams knew another African American whose special forces unit was overrun during the Battle of Dak Seang in April 1970. PAVN forces began to kill off the wounded soldiers but when a PAVN soldier approached, he simply "pointed his gun away and said, 'You get to live another day.'"[70]

Terry Whitmore claimed that he "ran right by Charlie. Right by him! And he just watched me. Didn't shoot, didn't move, nothing. He just watched me run by." During this same incident Whitmore managed to rescue an injured white marine. The NLF soldier shot the white marine but left Whitmore alone.[71]

Keith Freeman believed that communist forces made a concentrated effort to avoid killing Blacks. Freeman was discovered by a PAVN soldier while sneaking into a village, but instead of killing him the soldier said, "Come out soul brother. You're the same as me, I'm the same as you." When Thomas Belton was visiting a local brothel, an NLF soldier walked in. Belton was unarmed and feared he would be killed. Instead, the soldier sat down to eat with Belton, repeating the phrase, "you black you same same, like me, have same problems why you here, you got war at home."[72]

Richard Devore claimed that "the VC passed up brothers" and were only interested in killing whites. One day Devore was walking through a dark alley in Saigon when he encountered an armed NLF soldier. The soldier "pulled a hand grenade on me. I pulled out my 38 (revolver) but he told me 'this is not for you brother. It's for Charlie (whites).'"[73] Freeman, Belton, and Devore's accounts are revealing. In each case, enemy soldiers explicitly told them they were spared because they were Black. The Vietnamese also claimed that African Americans and communist forces were "brothers" who faced the same problems. These accounts suggest that some members of the NLF and PAVN did not wage war on African Americans.

Ron Bradley was out in the field one day when he encountered an NLF soldier pointing a rifle at him. The soldier could have easily killed him but he "didn't shoot"; Bradley killed him instead. He remembered, "That's one of the things I deal with and will have to deal with for the rest of my life. . . . I always wondered why to this day he didn't shoot." In a second incident, Bradley's squad became lost and mistakenly drove into a clearing filled with NLF soldiers. He assumed that he was about to be killed, but to his surprise and relief the NLF allowed them to turn around without incident. He believed they were allowed to leave because he was in the passenger seat next to a Black driver. He theorized that the NLF "were sympathetic to us because to them we were going through the same thing, the only difference was we were being used as tools against them."[74]

James Lewis recalled an incident in which the NLF shot a white soldier standing next to him when they could have easily shot him. This was mystifying because he was a captain and the white soldier was a private. He wondered about their reasoning: "Why would they have taken a private out? You know, a run-of-the-mill soldier, when they could have had the commander." Lewis also observed that Black soldiers in the Army Corps of Engineers were less likely to be hit by sniper fire than whites. These experiences led him to conclude there was some truth to the rumors.[75]

"I Am Not Going to Believe They're Not Going to Shoot Me"

Accounts of enemy empathy and forbearance are certainly intriguing, but the 5,570 African Americans killed during the war prove that NLF and PAVN forces were more than willing to kill African Americans.[76] Melvin Adams had a few friends who claimed they were spared by the NLF, but he thought this supposed commitment to spare Blacks was suspect. He felt they just "wanted to make the Black soldiers think different from the white soldiers . . . we won't shoot you, but we'll shoot the white guy." Years later, he pointed out that given the number of African Americans killed, one could just as easily have spread a rumor that the enemy was actively targeting Blacks.[77]

Adams was not the only African American to question the validity of these rumors. In November 1965 *Ebony* reported that many Black servicemen rejected the NLF's "claims of brotherhood" as a politically motivated attempt to demoralize and separate them from their white peers. An anonymous Black marine observed that anyone who expected "these cats to shoot the white guy next to you when he can kill you, you're crazy."[78]

Clyde Jackson recalled hearing that the enemy wouldn't shoot African Americans but he rejected this idea, theorizing, "I am not going to believe they're not going to shoot me especially because it's what they're out to do whether you're Black or white."[79] As Jackson noted, it made absolutely no sense from a military perspective for communist forces to spare African Americans.

Anthony Martin also questioned the plausibility of such a policy stating, "I don't know of any Viet Cong who was going to be so selective as to say, 'I'm gonna kill this white guy that's shooting at me, I am not gonna shoot the Black guy.'" From his own experiences he observed, "You really couldn't even see who you were shooting at" and thus couldn't determine the race of your enemy.[80] This is a valid point. Combat was often too chaotic for an enemy soldier to follow any sort of racially based intention had one even existed.

Martin pointed out that the rumor likely surfaced when servicemen tried to interpret what they saw and experienced in battle. A universal question in combat is why one individual is killed and another is not. He explained that "if a unit came under attack and one Black guy survived," the dominant narrative became that the enemy spared him.[81] Realistically, the survivor was probably just lucky. Many African Americans who claimed they were spared by the NLF or PAVN couldn't possibly have known the exact reason why they weren't injured or killed. There are numerous possible explanations: the enemy missed, ran out of ammunition, or never even saw the person.

Jim Houston recalled an incident when NLF soldiers walked by him while he was hiding on a pathway. Houston did not believe they refrained from shooting at him because he was Black but that "they just didn't see me." He was saved because he was a "dark skin black man" who was harder to see at night.[82]

Houston was not the only one to make this sort of connection. Robert Louis Jr. remembered that "it seemed like they weren't shooting at us, but they couldn't see us." The extreme heat caused everyone to take their shirts off, leaving only their flak jackets. Louis thought Blacks remained camouflaged by their darker skin while whites stuck out more, which resulted in them being shot in the chest. Once the commanders realized what was happening, they ordered everyone to wear their equipment. Speaking of the enemy, Louis concluded, "They did not differentiate, it was what they could see."[83]

A variation of the rumor that circulated among the Black soldiers James Gillam served with was that if African American servicemen did not raise their guns toward the enemy, the NLF would not kill them. He recalled thinking that anyone who seriously believed this rumor was both crazy and reckless. Speaking of a hypothetical encounter, Gillam reasoned, "What if this guy didn't get the word? You know, what if he can't see enough of me to see I am a Black man? He just sees a little bit of a Black rifle, a little bit of a green uniform, and I have my rifle on a sling barrel turned down. I am dead." Gillam maintained, "No Black man I ever saw in the field did that" as the risks far outweighed the benefits.[84]

Gillam's comments illustrate the potential risks in embracing these rumors as well as how difficult it would have been for enemy soldiers to carry out such a policy. The circumstances had to be almost ideal. African Americans had to be visible enough to be differentiated from their white peers. They would need to stand upright in an open, nonaggressive position, something few would have done considering the risks involved. African Americans would have to risk death to ensure the policy could be carried out.

Why did these rumors become so widespread? Herman Graham III argues that African Americans embraced these rumors because they provided "a sense of symbolic power because they forced white GIs—who believed that their white skin might have been making them targets of the enemies' weapons—to experience the anxiety of race."[85] There is an element of truth in this argument. A group whose skin color and race had denied them equality now enjoyed superiority. Yet, most likely the rumors proliferated because they were impossible to prove or disprove. Nobody knew what enemy soldiers thought or would do. It was natural to wonder why one person was killed and another survived. The rumors provided an explanation preferable to simple chance.

These rumors also fit into the general framework of African Americans' beliefs about the views of the Vietnamese. Many Black servicemen already thought civilians empathized with them as fellow victims of discrimination and prejudice. Adding the members of the NLF and PAVN to this group of empathetic Vietnamese was not as big a step as it might seem.

"Your Genuine Struggle Is on Your Native Land. GO HOME NOW AND ALIVE"

Equally significantly, these rumors flourished because communist officials did their best to convince African Americans that they empathized with and favored them over whites. Throughout the war they targeted Blacks with propaganda in the form of leaflets and radio broadcasts that declared what every African American already knew: African Americans did not enjoy equality at home. Therefore, why should they fight for a country that continued to discriminate against them? Communist propaganda provided a simple, easy answer. Blacks should leave Vietnam, go home, and fight the "real war" in America against the racist white establishment. There is no evidence these propaganda efforts convinced anyone to desert, but by focusing on Black inequality they convinced some African Americans that the Vietnamese enemy empathized with them and wanted to advance Black equality.

A few of these leaflets have survived. One begins by evoking the mistreatment of Black people in Alabama stating, "I wish I were an Alabama trooper. That is what I would truly like to be. I wish I were an Alabama trooper Cause then I could kill niggers legally."[86] This leaflet referenced police brutality in Alabama, which was linked to the harshest discrimination and violence against African Americans. Communist officials clearly had some knowledge of the domestic racial environment as they understood that referencing Alabama would gain the attention of African Americans in a way that mentioning a northern or midwestern state would not.

This leaflet noted that "the racists in the States are the very same as those who want Negroes to die in Vietnam," evoking the rumor that the government was purposely sending African Americans to their deaths. However, Black servicemen had options, and they should "demand to be sent home now and alive." These instructions suggested that the enemy did not want Blacks to die in Vietnam, a position supported by the rumors which spread among Black servicemen that enemy forces did not want to kill them. African Americans needed to leave their country and fight "the Negroes real struggle" in the United States.[87]

Some leaflets emphasized that African Americans were only in Vietnam because of discriminatory practices. One NLF leaflet claimed that while Blacks made up 11 percent of the domestic population, they represented 30 percent of servicemen and 40 percent of combat deaths. The only way to "stay out of the 40 percent column" was to "Go home!"[88] This phrasing was deliberate and telling given that Blacks were initially overrepresented in combat units, which led to disproportionate numbers being killed. While African Americans never represented 30 percent of servicemen in Vietnam nor 40 percent of combat deaths, the NLF was obviously aware of the controversies surrounding Black military service and seeking to exploit them. Additionally, the leaflet's wording suggested that the enemy cared more about the lives of African Americans than the "white" American government.

Another leaflet reminded African Americans that they were mistreated in the United States and Vietnam. It proclaimed, "In the States, you are called niggers. . . . Your enemies are those who are carrying out harsh exploitation and extremely barbarous racial discrimination against American blacks." Things were no better in Vietnam, where Blacks were forced to "go first," "withdraw last," "stay in the outer ring," and "do the hardest and most dangerous jobs." These statements touched a sensitive nerve as African Americans often complained that they were given the hardest and most dangerous jobs. The leaflet explained that the impact of these assignments was "casualty rates of black GIs are much higher than whites!" In response, African Americans should "refuse to obey all combat orders! Sit on the Fence! Refuse to interfere in the internal affairs of your Vietnamese brothers! Refuse to perpetuate crimes against them!" Instead, Blacks ought to "lay down your weapons, let yourselves be captured: you will be taken alive and will eventually be allowed to return home."[89]

While communist propaganda occasionally noted the mistreatment of African Americans in Vietnam, most focused on the racism and discrimination faced by Blacks back home. One leaflet included a picture of a white police officer arresting an African American man with the caption, "Your real enemies are those who call you 'Niggers'. Your genuine struggle is on your native land. GO HOME NOW AND ALIVE." Another leaflet began with the reminder that 20 million African Americans were "ABUSED, OPPRESSED, EXPLOITED, MANHANDLED, MURDERED BY RACIST AUTHORITIES." African Americans and their "Vietnamese brothers" shared the same enemy in the form of "racist authorities Johnson, Dean Rusk, Mac Namara, Westmoreland." African Americans could fight back against their oppressors by refusing "any order of patrolling, shelling, bombing, launching moping-up operations or terrorist raids against the Vietnamese people."[90]

In March 1967 the *Chicago Tribune* reported that servicemen routinely found NLF pamphlets which stated, "Twenty million fellow countrymen of yours in the U.S are being abused, oppressed, exploited, manhandled, murdered by racist authorities."[91] In January 1968 *Newsday* reported that leaflets were found near the base camp of the 1st Battalion of the 7th Marine Regiment southwest of Da Nang Air Base, which stated in almost identical language, "Colored American servicemen twenty million fellow countrymen of yours in the U.S.A. are being abused, oppressed, exploited, manhandled, murdered by racist authorities. You don't forgot (sic) the bloody Alabama cases, don't you."[92] The reference to the "bloody Alabama cases" again illustrates that the leaflet authors had some knowledge of the most notorious incidents of racial violence of the 1950s and 1960s.

Like others, this leaflet claimed that the same people responsible for mistreating African Americans back home were forcing them against their will "to slaughter the South Vietnamese people who are struggling for peace, independence, freedom, democracy, national reunification, for equality, and friendship between the peoples all over the world." African Americans and the Vietnamese had common goals, faced similar problems, and shared an enemy. As such, African Americans should refuse combat duty or "let yourselves be captured by the Liberation armed forces: Don't resist. Throw your weapons far away and lie still; Hand your weapons over to the Liberation combatants, quickly follow them out to safer areas; Through the front's lenient policy, you will be well-treated and the South Vietnamese National Liberation Front will arrange your repatriation."[93]

Allegedly, whites were using Blacks to fight a war against the Vietnamese, who wanted their political freedom just as African Americans wanted to be free from discrimination and oppression. As victims of white racism and discrimination, African Americans and the NLF had a common interest in working together to end racial discrimination. Like others, this leaflet claimed that the NLF had no interest in imprisoning or killing African Americans. Blacks who surrendered would be repatriated, an offer not made to whites. Oddly, Claude McClure, a Black soldier captured by the NLF on November 23, 1963, was mentioned as an example of what servicemen who surrendered could expect, even though he was not repatriated until November 27, 1965, more than two years after he was captured.[94]

After raiding an NLF base camp in 1966–67, Wes Geary's regiment found flyers that stated, "Colored infantryman lay down your arms, don't fight for this racist LBJ."[95] Louis McQueen, a Black marine who served in 1966–67, recalled seeing similar leaflets that questioned, "Why are you over here killing us and they (white Americans) are killing you at home?"[96] In May 1968 *Newsday* revealed that servicemen had found leaflets asking, "Black man, why are you fighting here? We don't want to fight you. Your war is against the white man back home."[97]

Ron Bradley, who served in 1967–68, found leaflets stating that both Vietnamese people and Blacks were victims of white mistreatment. They warned African Americans not to treat Vietnamese people the same way whites treated Blacks in the United States.[98] During the same period, Bernard McClusky saw leaflets which read, "Go home black man, this is not your war. You have a war in America," a message he believed there was "some truth to."⁹⁹ In 1968–69 Robert Sanders also found leaflets that reminded African Americans that racism in the United States was endemic and that racist whites treated the Vietnamese in a similar fashion to Blacks. One leaflet stated, "They call us Gooks here and they call you niggers over there. You're the same as us. Get out, it's not your fight."¹⁰⁰ That same year Wayne Smith found leaflets on base and in the bush that stated, "Soul Brother, No Vietnamese ever called you nigger."¹⁰¹ In 1969–70 Willie Thomas found leaflets at a firebase that noted, "We are closer to you as people than whites," referencing the alleged relationship Vietnamese people had formed with Blacks. The flyer also reminded African Americans of their inferior status at home, questioning why Blacks were willing to fight for a country where they "can't even walk down the street."¹⁰² Collectively, these leaflets spoke to African Americans in a language they understood and evoked a perspective they agreed with. The real war was in the United States, not in Vietnam.

"You Can Hear the Appeal from the Negroes in Your Native Land"

The most common channel of communication other than leaflets was the radio. Radio Hanoi could be heard in most areas of the country, and many servicemen listened to its English-language shows because they played American music banned by Armed Forces Radio. Particularly entertaining were the daily "news" reports delivered by a soft-spoken Vietnamese woman known as Hanoi Hannah, especially as she frequently singled out African Americans for attention.¹⁰³

As early as November 1965 *Ebony* discussed Radio Hanoi and its efforts to appeal to Black servicemen. Radio Hanoi praised the civil rights movement but also questioned why African Americans were fighting in Vietnam and not in the United States. It urged them to return home and "win the real battle."¹⁰⁴ Its strategy was clear. Radio Hanoi wanted to convey sympathy, but its announcers also sought to remind Black servicemen of the more important struggle for American racial equality. Radio Hanoi asked African Americans a very simple question: wouldn't the civil rights movement be better served if Black servicemen were back home fighting for civil rights and political equality?

Radio Hanoi occasionally broadcast stories that focused on the mistreatment of Black servicemen in Vietnam. During one broadcast Hanoi

Hannah discussed the trial of Billy Smith, an African American soldier charged with killing his white superior officer with a fragmentation grenade on the Bien Hoa Army Base on March 15, 1971. Hannah claimed Smith was arrested not because any evidence tied him to the crime but because he was "black, poor and against the war and the army and refusing to be a victim of racism."[105]

While this story focused on the alleged mistreatment of a Black soldier in Vietnam, most of Radio Hanoi's reporting focused on the mistreatment of African Americans in the United States. Stories charged that racism was widespread and the government's attempts to combat prejudice and discrimination were woefully inadequate or more likely intentionally a failure. Because Blacks had few, if any, rights, they should not fight in Vietnam but instead should fight for equality back home.

The messages Radio Hanoi directed at African Americans were occasionally pointed and graphic. Richard J. Ford III remembered a particular broadcast by Hanoi Hannah that stated, "Soul brothers, go home. Whitey raping your mothers and your daughters, burning down your homes. What you over here for? This is not your war." The claim that whites were raping Black women struck a sensitive nerve. Radio Hanoi typically emphasized the discrimination and even violence African Americans experienced, but this broadcast hit them at a visceral level.[106]

Radio Hanoi occasionally provided African Americans with new information. Black veteran Mike Roberts first heard about the rioting in his hometown of Detroit on Armed Forces Radio, but newsreaders failed to address the possible motivations behind the riots. By contrast, Hanoi Hannah provided a detailed discussion. She even knew what national guard units had been sent to quell the riots. This report taught Roberts that Armed Forces Radio "knew more than they broadcasted" as it seemed unlikely that Hannah would have information the military did not. Hannah expressed sympathy for African Americans while also questioning, "Why are you fighting? You have your own battle to fight in America."[107] Arthur Barham remembered that Hannah provided far more detailed information about Martin Luther King Jr.'s assassination than that given on Armed Forces Radio. He was understandably shocked that an enemy radio station was more concerned with providing information about King's murder than a military station.[108] Barham concluded that Radio Hanoi was sympathetic and supportive of the aspirations of African Americans.

Radio Hanoi did more than report on the mistreatment of African Americans. It "employed" African Americans to convince Black servicemen to stop fighting. In June 1966 African American Korean War defector Clarence C. Adams appeared on an episode. Adams was not the best choice to encourage Blacks to return to the United States and fight against racism and prejudice, given that rather than returning home he fled to China.[109] Nonetheless, Adams argued, "You are supposedly fighting for the freedom of the Vietnamese, but what kind of freedom do you have at home, sitting in the back of the bus, being barred from restaurants, stores and certain neighborhoods, and being denied the right to vote.... Go home and fight for equality in America."[110]

In August 1967 the *Washington Post* reported, "North Vietnam has been beaming almost daily broadcasts in English to Negro GIs in South Vietnam urging them to stop fighting." The broadcasts featured what the *Washington Post* described as distorted or inaccurate reports of racial violence but also antiwar messages from Black activists like Stokely Carmichael and H. Rap Brown. Their statements provided Radio Hanoi with a level of legitimacy as they were able honestly to claim, "You can hear the appeal from the Negroes in your native land—Come home." The *Post* article noted that Radio Hanoi allegedly employed a Black announcer named Jackson Turner.[111] Turner was likely a creation of Radio Hanoi and not a real person, but his presence was meant to lend legitimacy to the idea the Vietnamese supported African Americans and that if they deserted, they would be welcomed into a united Vietnam.

The *Baltimore Sun* in August 1969 wrote that Radio Hanoi was broadcasting messages which described "the Communist fight in South Vietnam as another front of the American Negro's struggle against white oppression." These broadcasts included the words of James A. Johnson, a Black antiwar advocate and member of the Fort Hood Three, who refused to go to Vietnam in 1969. Johnson was a real person, but the newspaper was skeptical as to whether it was really him on the radio. Nonetheless, he described the war in racial terms, alleging that Black participation served the interests "of a few greedy white racists" at the expense of African Americans who "are already dying at a disproportionately high rate to whites in Vietnam." He added that "the only battlefield for black people is America, from Harlem to Watts."[112]

The attention Radio Hanoi gave to Black antiwar activists was shrewd. African American servicemen were more likely to listen to them than to unknown Vietnamese broadcasters. African American antiwar activists expressed opinions that were almost identical to those made by Radio Hanoi. In November 1970, after returning from a two-week trip to the

DRV, Reverend Phillip Lawson, appearing on an American radio station, instructed Blacks, "Do not kill your Vietnamese brothers." He insisted that the DRV was supportive of the African American civil rights movement, and while "some criticize me for combining the black American and Vietnamese struggles, but I see the oppression of black people on the American scene as logically extending itself on the international scene."[113]

Lawson was not the only prominent African American to refer to the North Vietnamese as brothers or challenge Black participation in the war. Muhammad Ali famously declared that African Americans should not fight their "Asian brothers" because "they never lynched you, never called you nigger, never put dogs on you, never shot your leaders," a message that reminded Blacks of their mistreatment while further asserting the real fight was at home.[114]

There is no evidence that Black domestic antiwar activists or Radio Hanoi were influenced by one another or coordinated their efforts. For example, BPP statements about Black participation in the war were far more extreme than Radio Hanoi. In a March 22, 1970, *Black Panther* article, Eldridge Cleaver ordered Blacks to "kill General Abrams and his staff, all his officers. Sabotage supplies and equipment or turn them over to the Vietnamese people and tell them you want to join the Black Panther Party to fight for the freedom and liberation of your own people."[115]

Cleaver was not the only one to argue that Black servicemen should kill white officers in Vietnam. In September 1967 the *Norfolk Journal and Guide* noted that the People's Republic of China had begun distributing pamphlets through the U.S. Postal Service urging "negro soldiers to kill their white colleagues in Vietnam." These pamphlets provided "pointers on how to sabotage urban facilities, sewer lines, electric power stations, and highways." By following these instructions, Blacks would ensure that "these racists will not be able to return home and intensify the brutalization and extermination of black people."[116]

Communist officials, the Black Panthers, and China all appealed to African Americans, but their messages were distinctive and did not necessarily complement one another.[117] Vietnamese propaganda asked Blacks to stop fighting, but they never asked them to join the NLF, kill fellow soldiers, or sabotage the American war effort. It asked them to disengage in a foreign conflict and reengage in a domestic cause, not to commit acts of subversion and violence. The Vietnamese argued that African Americans could serve their own interests by leaving the country altogether, whereas

Eldridge Cleaver and the Chinese urged them to stay, switch sides, and kill white enlisted men and officers.

Some Black servicemen deserted the military with most fleeing to the relatively safe confines of Saigon. In many cases they ended up at "Soul Alley," a two-hundred-yard back street located one mile from the U.S. military headquarters in Saigon. In December 1970 *Time* claimed that on average, "between 300 and 500 Black AWOLS and deserters" resided in Soul Alley.[118] Yet there is no evidence that communist propaganda led them to desert. Additionally, they were deserters, not defectors.

There were some reports of Black servicemen defecting to the NLF. Ron Bradley heard rumors about three Black soldiers who had supposedly defected.[119] The *Boston Globe* claimed that the military's Defense Intelligence Agency compiled a report on a Black soldier, known by the code name "Pepper," who had allegedly deserted to the PAVN.[120] There were persistent rumors that McKinley Nolan, a Black soldier who went AWOL in 1967, had joined the NLF.[121] Even if all these men defected to the enemy—and there is not sufficient evidence that any had—four or five servicemen would not constitute a large number.

Communist propaganda efforts failed to convince large numbers of Black servicemen to desert or surrender, but they may have adversely affected their morale. Their messages reminded African Americans of the prejudice, discrimination, and even violence they faced in the United States. These propaganda efforts helped bolster the idea that the enemy identified with Blacks and were concerned about their welfare. The propaganda did not provide any new, significant revelations, but it did reinforce what Black servicemen already knew—racial discrimination remained pervasive in the United States. Many agreed with an anonymous Black serviceman who after reading an NLF leaflet which argued that Blacks should be fighting in the United States and not Vietnam responded, "Man, you're right."[122]

Black Prisoners of War, Amerasians, and the Montagnards

Some Vietnamese communist leaders may have believed that African Americans and the Vietnamese had common experiences and aspirations. Most available evidence suggests these appeals were little more than propaganda and not a genuine expression of sympathy and identification. Communist officials produced leaflets and radio broadcasts that criticized American racism, but they used racial and color prejudice for their own benefit. Shawn McHale has noted that the Viet Minh, a precursor to the NLF and PAVN, used racist fearmongering to try to unite the people against French colonial forces from Africa during the First Indochina War. In December 1951 they circulated a tract claiming the French were "turning Vietnamese soldiers into black soldiers. The French are bringing one hundred youths to the Cape, to the electric ovens, transforming them into blacks." Another tract from January 1952 stated that the French were "seizing people and cooking them black, distending their lips and twisting their hair—it's truly savage."[123] Viet Minh officials were quite willing to appeal to offensive racial characterizations if they thought it would translate into greater support for the war effort.

Cole Whaley, a Black infantryman, claimed these tactics were used during the Vietnam War too. In 1965 he found leaflets in an abandoned NLF base that stated, "Negro troops are inferior, won't fight, and have no sustaining power," suggesting the NLF may have denigrated African American servicemen to bolster morale and support among the Vietnamese population.[124]

The treatment afforded to Black prisoners of war further indicates that communist appeals to Black troops were not a reflection of any deep sympathy. James E. Jackson Jr., a Green Beret medic from Talcott, West Virginia, spent eighteen months in an NLF prison. Jackson was initially told he would receive special privileges because he was Black, but when he "saw the miserable shape the other Negro prisoners were in" and his captors pressured him to denounce the war, he realized they were only interested in using Black prisoners for propaganda purposes. He recalled, "One thing that was constantly slapped in my face was the race situation in the United States. . . . They told me that Negroes were getting machine gunned in the streets of America and that Newark and all those places had blown up." Jackson's race made him a target for harassment as there was an expectation he would speak out publicly against the United States. When he refused, it confused and angered his captors.[125]

Norman Alexander McDaniel of Fayetteville, North Carolina, was a prisoner of war from 1966 to 1973, mostly in the notorious "Hanoi Hilton." He was repeatedly tortured and when he complained, citing the Geneva Convention, his torturers laughed in his face and said, "You're not qualified to be treated as a prisoner of war. You're a criminal, black American criminal." Guards routinely taunted McDaniel and other Black prisoners, calling them "the blackest of the black criminals."[126]

Fred V. Cherry of Suffolk, Virginia, was also a prisoner at the Hanoi Hilton from 1965 to 1973, and his race appears to have brought him extra harassment. He was injured when his plane crashed, but camp officials refused to provide him with bandages. When he became sick enough to need an operation, they refused to give him anesthetic.[127] Cherry's captors obsessed about his skin color, giving him the nickname Xu, the Vietnamese word for a copper coin. They placed him in a cell with a white southerner hoping the two would fight. They tried to "educate" Cherry about the Black experience in America in hopes that he would denounce the United States. When he refused, they tortured him viciously. A guard once walked into Cherry's cell with a picture of Wilt Chamberlain, exclaiming, "He looks just like a monkey. Where does he ever find a woman who can satisfy him?"[128] Jackson's, McDaniel's, and Cherry's experiences as prisoners demonstrate that Vietnamese communists were not as sympathetic to African Americans as their propaganda claimed.[129]

Amerasians and Montagnards likewise remained victims of racial or skin color prejudice long after reunification. Psychiatrist Robert S. McKelvey's research on Amerasians reveals that even decades after the war, Black Amerasians experienced greater prejudice, harassment, and discrimination than white Amerasians. While whites experienced discrimination, "their fair skin bestowed certain advantages on them in Vietnam, where it is considered attractive." By contrast, Black Amerasians were routinely taunted about their skin color.[130]

Ethnic minorities fared no better after reunification. In 2002 Human Rights Watch reported that the communist government discriminated against Montagnards in "all aspects of their lives—not only access to land, but education, medical care, government services, and even allocation of trading stalls in the market."[131] Lap Siu, a Jarai Montagnard, recalled that authorities frequently justified their mistreatment of his people in racial terms. He noted that authorities referred to the Jarai as savages and that they "would call us dirty people, dark skinned people ... look like mud."[132]

Conclusion

African Americans overwhelmingly viewed the communist forces they were tasked with fighting not only as capable fighters but also as men and women fiercely dedicated to the communist cause. Black servicemen recognized the enemy's underdog status and respected their refusal to give up even in the face of overwhelming American fire power.

Since the formation of the United States, slavery, segregation, political disenfranchisement, and other forms of discrimination had ensured that African Americans were the perennial underdog. They faced barriers when they attempted to overcome these problems. Black servicemen linked their own experiences with racism to the struggles faced by Vietnamese combatants. In making these comparisons and connections, African Americans placed the Black experience with race at the center of their analysis. They correctly viewed themselves as victims of white American racism, and this led them to conclude that the Vietnamese were also victims of racism and exploitation at the hands of the American government.

African Americans viewed enemy combatants through a lens similar to the one through which they viewed civilians—one of empathy and respect. Paradoxically, while many African Americans respected the enemy and even believed their reasons for fighting were justified, most had a far less charitable view of ARVN forces, whose dedication and fighting abilities they routinely questioned.

Many African Americans believed that the empathy and respect they had for their Vietnamese opponents was more than reciprocated. Rumors circulated claiming that communist forces did not want to kill Black servicemen because they identified with them as victims of discrimination and prejudice. Essentially, the argument went, the NLF and PAVN were trying to protect African Americans and ensure that they could continue to fight for their civil and political rights at home. The rumors expressed support for African Americans but also hostility toward whites, whom the Vietnamese held responsible for the mistreatment of Blacks in the United States. The domestic racial environment impacted the way African Americans viewed communist forces, but it also allegedly influenced the way Vietnamese communists viewed African Americans.

Vietnamese communists promoted these ideas with leaflets and radio broadcasts directly addressed to Black servicemen. The Black experience with racism and prejudice was at the center of these appeals. Vietnamese propaganda expressed empathy for African Americans and the civil rights movement but also asserted that Black servicemen should be fighting for their civil and political rights at home, especially given that the war only benefited white racists. Vietnamese propaganda was written in a language Black servicemen understood. African Americans viewed racial issues in

Vietnam through a lens heavily influenced by their own experiences with racial issues, and Vietnamese propaganda embraced a similar perspective. The war could not be separated from the American home front.

The reality was Vietnamese communists were not as free from prejudice or as committed to racial equality as their appeals to African Americans claimed. Leaflets and radio broadcasts were political tools meant to dampen the morale of Black troops and possibly persuade them to stop fighting and desert. Yet, whatever their aim, the propaganda efforts were highly successful in nurturing and reaffirming the perception of many Black servicemen that African Americans and the Vietnamese, civilians or combatants, had similar aspirations to escape prejudice and discrimination.

CHAPTER 7

"I Had Left One War and Come Back to Another"

African Americans Return Home

When Black servicemen came home from Vietnam, they returned to a changed but familiar environment. Sometimes it was too familiar. Eugene L. Brice saw significant combat duty during the Tet Offensive. During a particularly fierce battle in which twenty-three soldiers were killed and dozens, including Brice, were injured, he prayed, "Lord, if you let me go home alive, I promise I'll work for veterans." When he returned home in 1969 he made good on his promise. However, Brice's service in Vietnam and his commitment to veterans did not protect him from racism in his own country.[1]

One October day Brice pulled his van into a disabled parking spot at an East Longmeadow, Massachusetts, grocery store. He was prevented from lowering the ramp he used to transport his buggy by a car parked "halfway over the lines." Brice politely asked the white female driver to move her car, but after initially appearing cooperative, she screamed, "N——, just keep moving." Angry and shaken, Brice entered the store to complain, only to overhear another white customer comment that the incident wouldn't have happened if he "had not come to East Longmeadow to shop." Brice was living in a place where "duty, honor and service are not shields from racism." His "day in hell" did not take place in a far-off, long-past time in history. The incident speaks as much to our present as to our past, especially because it occurred on October 30, 2021.[2]

Racism accompanied African Americans to Vietnam, and when they returned as veterans, it continued to impact significantly their experiences. Prejudice and discrimination continued to permeate American society, and their status as veterans gave them little, if any, protection from this reality.

"Thought I'd Left All My Problems Behind"

In 2015 Sylvester Bracey, whom *Black Journal* featured prominently in its coverage of the Vietnam War, wrote in his journal, "The oppressor will deceive the oppressed, seek to misinform them, lie to them . . . all while not realize'n that all men are created equal."[3] African Americans were sometimes confronted with the oppression and racism Bracey described almost immediately upon landing back home. On September 13, 1967, David Parks flew home to New York via San Francisco. At the airport a white clerk gave him a dirty look and "pitched my ticket at me like I was dirt." Park recalled, "I'm a Negro and I'm back home where color makes a difference. . . . I was feeling good on that plane from Namsville. Thought I'd left all my problems behind."[4]

The realization that they were returning to a country whose racial customs had not really changed was a hard pill to swallow. Carl Witherspoon spoke for many Black veterans when he observed, "Sometimes I feel it was all for nothing. . . . You know, we go over there and tell them their house is dirty, before our own house is clean."[5]

On March 24, 1968, Floyd McKissick, national director of the Congress of Racial Equality, was at Kennedy International Airport in New York City when he noticed a group of Black servicemen, recently returned from Vietnam, trying to hail a taxi. They could not find a way home because "one white cab driver after another refused service." McKissick understood that "black veterans of Vietnam are frequently subjected to the same racist insults when in the uniform of their country, as at any other time."[6]

In June 1970 James Gillam was flying home to Cleveland when he went out drinking during a stopover in Chicago. He ended up paying a prostitute to hail him a cab to the airport because "they wouldn't stop for a Black man, even in uniform. I was pissed."[7] Gillam had risked his life in Vietnam but he could not get a cab in his own country. Speaking of his return to Pittsburgh in 1970, Lamont B. Steptoe recalled, "I was standing on a streetcar stop waiting for a streetcar to take me to my mother's house and a carload of white men called me a nigger and I hadn't been home thirty seconds."[8]

African Americans hoped for change but it didn't take long to realize that racial prejudice and discrimination remained strong. As Rudolph Bridges of Muskogee, Oklahoma, observed, "Lots of black guys went to the Nam and came back thinking somehow it was gonna be different here in the States. Then they found nothing had changed."[9]

Black veterans wanted to construct or reconstruct a "normal" life when they returned home. Chief among their concerns was finding a place to live. However, they were no more welcome in white neighborhoods than they had been before. White resistance to residential integration remained strong. In April 1967 Jesse Woodbridge, a Black Vietnam veteran, purchased a home in an all-white neighborhood in southwest Philadelphia. Three days after moving in with his wife and four children, angry whites threw bricks through the window and yelled, "You niggers, go back home." Two days later more bricks were thrown.[10]

In August 1968 Charles Bolton, another veteran recently returned from Vietnam, bought a house in a predominantly white neighborhood in Chicago. A few days later someone drew "a Nazi swastika smeared in red paint" on the living room window and wrote "obscenities, such as 'You die! You Black'" on the back wall and garage.[11]

In May 1967 William Hines accused twelve trailer parks in Santa Ana, California, of refusing to rent to his family because they were African American. Hines's wife, Evelyn, recalled, "We were told by one court that they had never rented to Negroes and they were afraid we'd create problems. Another place said they'd let us in, but we'd have to pay for each lot that was vacated if white tenants moved out."[12]

Despite passage of the Civil Rights Act of 1964, white-owned businesses continued to deny service to African Americans. In 1968 Lee Ewing returned home to Jeffersonville, Indiana, where he spent more than five months in the hospital. After his release Ewing was denied service at a local restaurant, which taught him, "You can go and kill for this country and damn near die for this country, but you can't sit down and eat a sandwich? And I will never forget it."[13]

Things were even worse in the South. In October 1972 Edgar A. Huff, recently retired from the Marine Corps, was sitting on his front porch in Hubert, North Carolina, when four white marines threw phosphorus grenades at his house. Once caught, the marines were transferred or discharged. Feeling these punishments were too lenient, Huff confronted their commanding officer, who told him the men admitted to attacking his house because "they didn't understand how a nigger could be living this way, sitting out there eating on a nice lawn, under the American Flag I fly every day."[14]

On his way to visit a friend at Fort Bragg, North Carolina, Louis Callendar was told by a waitress at a roadside café, "We don't serve niggers." He recalled, "I was wearing my uniform decorated with combat medals all during this time. That incident really shook me and also woke me up."[15] When his flight landed in Dallas, Rudolph Bridges went to a restaurant wearing his uniform and medals but the waitress refused to serve him. He remembered, "It really hurt me. Tears came into my eyes. I had been looking for something that wasn't there."[16] Bridges was looking for acceptance and even appreciation for his service, but all he found was the same old racism.

In February 1968 Roosevelt Gore returned to Mullins, South Carolina. He was disappointed to find that "not much had changed for blacks . . . during the two years I was gone, and so far as I could see, it didn't show much inclination to change." A few years later Gore went to a local bar with two fellow veterans, one Black and one white, but the owner tried to block them from entering. When they pushed their way inside, the owner took all the pool balls off the table, stating, "Niggers ain't allowed to stay here." The friends were eventually arrested but not before the police chief told Doug Lewis, Gore's white friend, that they wouldn't arrest him if he blamed his Black friends. Lewis refused, and all were charged with inciting a riot.[17]

As Gore's account suggests, some white veterans remained committed to the Black friends they made in Vietnam. Racism continued to infect American society, but friendships like the one Gore formed with Lewis meant that some African Americans were not as isolated as previous generations when confronting racial prejudice.

However, prevailing racial customs could take a toll on these friendships. Whites were not always willing to violate established modes of behavior. George Brummell and Jim Houston befriended Hinkel, a white soldier from Ohio, while stationed together in Hawaii. After their service in Vietnam, Brummell and Houston ended up in the Cleveland area, and they decided to contact Hinkel. Brummell recalled, "He said that 'we put the military stuff behind us, the friendship in the military. . . . Now I am married, I got a wife, and I want nothing to do with you niggers.'"[18] Brummell and Houston were shocked and disappointed. Houston remembered, "We spent a whole year together, got to be good friends like hometown buddies. . . . But when I called him after I got back to the States it was really a totally different story."[19]

Returning Black veterans did not need to challenge longstanding racial customs to become victims of white racial violence. Sometimes their very existence was enough to elicit hostility. On February 19, 1966, Mickey Garron, a twenty-two-year-old Black sailor on leave from Vietnam, was shot and killed by three white men "who had a grudge against Negroes" while he was visiting his fiancée in the Watts area of Los Angeles. Garron was in uniform when he was murdered, and his killers knew he was in the military.[20] His status as a serviceman did not protect him. If anything, it made him a target—evoking painful memories of past wars in which returning Black veterans were targeted by racist whites.

"This May Be the Last Barrier of Discrimination"

African Americans did not even need to return home alive to experience discrimination. On May 7, 1966, Jimmy Williams, a Black Green Beret from Metumpka, Alabama, was killed in Vietnam. When his body was shipped home, his family was unable to "find a satisfactory final resting place in his hometown." The local cemetery was segregated, and the Black section was full. While his parents filed a complaint with the Justice Department, they eventually decided to bury their son in Andersonville National Cemetery.[21] Williams's mother explained, "My son died on the front for all of us. He didn't die a segregated death and he'll not be buried in a segregated cemetery."[22]

Before leaving for Vietnam, Bill Terry Jr. of Birmingham, Alabama, told his sister Phyllis "that if he didn't come back home, make it back safely, that he would like to be buried at Elmwood," an all-white cemetery near his home. He repeated his wish in subsequent letters to his family, but when he was killed in March 1969, the cemetery refused to sell them a plot. Jimmie Lee Terry, Bill's mother, and Margaret Faye Terry, his fiancée, with the aid of the NAACP Legal Defense and Educational Fund, sued Elmwood for discrimination in federal court. The U.S. District Court ruled in their favor, declaring that Elmwood was legally obligated to sell burial plots "without regard to race or color."[23]

On January 3, 1970, Terry's body was exhumed from the all-Black Shadow Lawn Cemetery, and a thousand marchers accompanied his body for reburial at Elmwood. Before the march Father Eugene Ferrell, the priest at the family church, declared, "It is not a time for mourning, but rejoicing. We rejoice that we on Earth have been able to respond to his last will." Ferrell recognized the larger significance of the moment. He observed, "I hope this burial is a symbol of a new age. This may be the last barrier of discrimination."[24]

Unfortunately, segregated cemeteries did not disappear. On August 8, 1970, Pondextuer Eugene Williams of Fort Pierce, Florida, was killed in Vietnam. Mary Campbell, Williams's mother, contacted Hillcrest Memorial Gardens because it offered free plots for fallen servicemen. Her request was denied because of the cemetery's policy "that no bodies except those of the white or Caucasian race be interred in said lots." Hillcrest offered to buy her son a plot in an all-Black cemetery, but Campbell "tearfully refused" because she wanted him buried at Hillcrest.[25] Campbell sued Hillcrest, and Williams's body remained in the morgue awaiting the outcome of the case. Willie Edwards, Williams's friend, perceptively noted that he was a "man without a country . . . because he doesn't have six feet of U.S. ground."[26] On August 27 the U.S. District Court ruled in Campbell's favor, and her son was buried at Hillcrest two days later. Minister Richard Barry noted that the entire ordeal demonstrated that "black soldiers are not going to Vietnam to fight and come back to this kind of injustice."[27]

Racial discrimination remained, but the activism of women like Jimmy Williams's mother, Margaret Faye Terry, Jimmie Lee Terry, and Mary Campbell ensured that at the very least African Americans who made the ultimate sacrifice in Vietnam would be buried in the cemetery of their choice. Segregated cemeteries were no longer legal.

"I Had Just Left People Who Were Fighting and Dying"

All veterans faced potential issues readjusting to civilian life. Still, as Ron Bradley noted, if "the average Vietnam veteran was catching hell, the average African American veteran was catching more hell."[28] A 1990 Veterans Administration (VA) study on trauma among Vietnam veterans revealed that Black veterans experienced more severe readjustment problems than white veterans.[29]

Little effort was made by military officials to reintegrate veterans back into society. In roughly forty hours Anthony Martin went from fighting in Vietnam to sitting in his mother's living room. This experience led him to question, "How many times was it repeated? A combat veteran has gone from combat to citizen in less than a week and got no treatment. . . . How many drug addicts? How many people who are now in prison, would not have been there had they gotten the proper care?"[30]

James Gillam explained that the "adjustment period when I got back was really strange. I had less than forty-eight hours, maybe seventy-two hours between the last time somebody tried to kill me and moving into an all-girls dorm at Ohio U."[31] He remembered, "My friends weren't dying in combat anymore, but friendships I had before I was drafted, or new ones I tried to make when I came home were dying because of the war and my clumsy attempts to make the transition from hunting and killing people to pretending to be a normal college student."[32]

When he visited his home, his mother insisted they attend church. Parishioners "started talking to my family like I wasn't there. They were saying things like 'he looks good considering.'" When somebody asked his father if I had learned anything in Vietnam, Gillam exploded, "Yes, I did. I learned that you don't have to fuckin' die to go to Hell."[33]

When Wayne Smith returned home, he felt completely alienated from his friends who only cared about "going to the beach or who was dating who, I had just left people who were fighting and dying." He now considered Rhode Island "another fucking planet, like an episode out of *The Twilight Zone*." Smith "hated our materialistic superficiality and our indifference" to such an extent that he wished he was back in Vietnam.[34] He recalled, "My mom wanted me to go to church again in my uniform, and we had a big blowout about that, I refused." While his friends and family tried to be supportive, Smith "wasn't able to play soldier any longer. I wasn't able to be the dutiful son or brother or friend."[35]

Improved medical technology, new drugs, and speedy evacuations meant far fewer fatalities, but it also meant that many servicemen who would have died in previous wars returned home seriously wounded. During the Korean War 22 percent of all wounded soldiers died while only 13 percent did in the Vietnam War.[36] Servicemen like Reuben "Sugar Bear" Johnson, who lost his legs in a mine explosion, and Robert L. Mountain, who lost part of one leg from a mortar, faced challenges largely unknown to servicemen from past conflicts.[37]

After surviving a landmine explosion, George Brummell woke up at Brooks Medical Center in San Antonio to the voices of doctors discussing a patient's condition. One stated, "The poor fellow's blind," while another replied, "He's got burns over sixty percent of his body." A third added, "That left hand looks as though it might have to be amputated." Brummell felt sorry for this badly injured soldier. When one doctor realized Brummell was awake, he told him, "We are trying to decide which ward would be the best for you." Brummell was the soldier the doctors were discussing. He told the doctor that he "could see if you'd just take these bandages off." The doctor replied, "You don't have any bandages on." Brummell would never see again, and he discusses his "journey through Vietnam, blindness, and back" in his excellent autobiography *Shades of Darkness*.[38]

It is difficult to estimate how many injured African Americans sought treatment in VA hospitals. In 1990 the National Vietnam Veterans Readjustment Study found that African Americans were more likely to use VA inpatient (24 percent) and outpatient (43 percent) services than others.[39] Many VA hospitals were overwhelmed by the sheer number of returning veterans, which sometimes led to impersonal and inefficient service.[40] Thomas Belton alleged that "the Veterans Administration belittles you, makes you look small, makes it seem like what you're asking for you're not entitled to."[41] Robert M. Watters claimed that a VA hospital lost his medical records and initially denied him treatment during an emergency, incorrectly claiming he was not a veteran.[42] For years Jim Houston did not receive full disability payments because a VA doctor insisted "there's nothing wrong with your legs." Houston had been medevacked out of Vietnam after being shot in the legs. He believed strongly that the doctor was unsympathetic because he was Black.[43]

"Once You've Fought in Vietnam You Can't Stop Thinking about It"

Not all injuries were physical. In 1980 the American Psychiatric Association identified a new war-related anxiety disorder, post-traumatic stress disorder (PTSD), earlier called shellshock or battle fatigue. PTSD was defined as "severe personality changes brought on by the fear and rage experienced by men in combat." Common symptoms include intense feelings of grief, guilt, depression, anxiety, and estrangement from family and friends. Those afflicted can experience delusions, nightmares, flashbacks, and even erratic outbursts of violence.[44] Hundreds of thousands of veterans likely experienced some form of the disorder.[45]

Veterans of all backgrounds were diagnosed with PTSD, but there is some evidence that African Americans were more likely to experience the disorder. A 2008 study published in the *Journal of Traumatic Stress* reveals that Black veterans were almost twice as likely to have PTSD as whites. They were also more likely to have PTSD for prolonged periods of time.[46] Another study found that 11 percent of Black Vietnam veterans sought help from VA mental health services compared to 7 percent of whites.[47]

Many cases went untreated and undocumented. Eddie Greene believed that "there was so many that came back with PTSD and never got any type of treatment."[48] Treatment did not always bring immediate or complete recovery. Reginald Edwards recalled thinking, "I wasn't affected by Vietnam, but I been livin' with Vietnam ever since I left. You just can't get rid of it. It's like that painting of what Dali did of melting clocks. It's a persistent memory."[49] Similarly, Thomas Belton noted, "The war leaves some permanent scars on you around values and norms."[50]

PTSD manifests itself differently for each veteran. Eddie Greene experienced severe night sweats and occasional bouts of anger. He noted, "I guess that's where PTSD comes into effect. I have to be by myself sometimes. It's like I tell people sometimes I can't stand myself so I know others can't."[51] Horace Coleman recalled, "I think I had a case of quote 'frozen emotions,' that I wasn't as demonstrative or as open with, say, people I was close to as I had been in the past." He also admitted to feeling a degree of survivor's guilt.[52]

Thomas Brannon exhibited similar symptoms. He struggled to reconcile "the overwhelming feeling you're so happy to be alive but you feel so guilty about it." He speculated, "Once you've fought in Vietnam you can't stop thinking about it. . . . Once you've been in combat, once you've heard guys screaming for their momma, guys pissing on themselves, you can never get it out of your life." Brannon recalled a recent family Thanksgiving when, even as he was enjoying his children's and grandchildren's company, his mind wandered toward the war and how the event would never have been possible if he had died in Vietnam.[53]

Eugene L. Brice experienced severe guilt because he survived and his friend Fred Williams did not. He saw himself as "just a young wild single guy, I didn't have no responsibilities, no family, but he had just gotten married and had a little girl." Brice's guilt became so severe that he struggled to function. When he managed to fall asleep, he experienced vivid nightmares that he was back in Vietnam.[54]

Robert E. Holcomb repeatedly dreamed that he was back in Vietnam and had "run out of ammunition and we were getting overrun. And this VC is coming at me with a machine gun. I jump him and I'm killing him."[55] When he awoke, he would find his arms and hands bruised and scarred from punching the walls next to his bed. More than once, Eddie Wright awoke to find that he had kicked out his windows while having a vivid nightmare. One night, he dreamed he was killing an enemy soldier and was awakened by his screaming girlfriend, whom he was about to punch in the face.[56]

During a fight at the Cambodian border, James Gillam ran out of ammunition and was forced to fight an enemy soldier with only a knife. After Gillam stabbed him, he soldier "started making a sound I had never heard a human being make before." He heard the dying man's screams in nightmares well into the 1980s.[57]

Robert M. Watters's nightmares were so intense "my first wife never slept with me, never. Because that's when I would have my nightmares, when I would close my eyes I would see the war, see combat." He had flashbacks whenever he became tense or upset. Fearing what he might do, Watters removed all weapons from his home. He recalled, "I used to keep 15–20 guns, because I felt safe. I felt safe, but I realized in the same anger, you know, you got a gun, going to use it, and I don't want to do that."[58]

Jim Houston experienced nightmares, intense anxiety, and delusions. He recalled, "It don't really ever go away, it just goes on and on, you know, and sometimes now, like, I don't know whether it's war related, but it seems like I see things.... At times when I wake up it seems like lint or something is coming down in my face."[59]

Lamont B. Steptoe struggled to fall asleep, and when he did he had nightmares. He recalled, "Nobody told us that later on in life we would have, we would suffer from PTSD and experience uncontrollable rage and depression and survivor's guilt and all the other things that come with that." His struggles with PTSD were obvious enough that his three-year-old daughter told him, "Daddy you have a serious problem."[60]

While the stereotyped image of the violent, out-of-control veteran has been exaggerated, some veterans with PTSD did struggle with thoughts of hurting others. Steptoe fantasized about shooting people because he wanted others to feel the daily terror he felt. He recalled, "The only thing that stopped me was the thought came to me—what will your mother feel the day after?" He also came to believe, after reading a book by famed photographer Gordon Parks, that he could affect more positive change by writing poetry about his experiences.[61]

Anthony Martin remembered, "I was full of anger and when I thought about killing a person, it didn't mean nothing. Anger at Vietnam, anger at the military, anger at people."[62] Rueben "Sugar Bear" Johnson admitted that if the Marine Corps had not taken his weapons, he likely would have gone on "the streets and shot some people."[63]

After an argument with his wife, Charles Strong "put on my fatigues, and put this ice pick by my side. When I couldn't find her, I just totally demolished my house." He was later hospitalized. Richard J. Ford III shot at a group of men who laughed at him when he jumped at the sound of firecrackers. He later shot at a car after it cut him off. He remembered, "I forgot all about my mother and wife in the car. I took off after them. . . . I just forgot where—and Vietnam does that to you—you forget where you are."[64]

Thankfully, many of the veterans discussed above sought professional help that allowed them to process their anger. Some veterans turned to alcohol or drugs to deal with psychological problems. Emmanuel J. Holloman became an alcoholic in Vietnam, eventually overcoming his addiction through counseling.[65] Eugene L. Brice's drug addiction landed him in the hospital and jail before he managed to get clean.[66] Lee Ewing was jailed three times for drug possession and eventually ended up in a psychiatric hospital. On two occasions he sat at "the edge of my bed with a pistol in my hand and put it up to my head. . . . I thank Vietnam for some things 'cause I didn't want my family to come in and see me splattered all over the wall, because I know what a bullet can do to a human body." Ewing served in Vietnam in 1965, but he did not become sober until 1991.[67]

In Vietnam Scott Riley became a heroin addict. When he left Vietnam, his girlfriend, Ba, sensing that he no longer belonged in his old life, told him he "could never go back to America." Her warning proved prescient. Riley noted, "When I came home, I realized there was no home for me here." As the heroin epidemic raged in Harlem, Riley fell further and further into addiction. He recalled, "It would take me thirty years, thirty years of active drug addiction, and you name it, jail times, and all kinds of other bullshit to finally get clean."[68]

Wayne Smith became addicted to heroin in Vietnam, and he too brought his addiction home. Within three weeks of being discharged he accidentally shot and killed a friend in a dispute over drugs in his hometown of Providence, Rhode Island. He was convicted of manslaughter and sentenced to ten years in prison. While he was awaiting trial, his dead friend's mother visited him in jail and "told me she forgave me, that she would pray for me." Smith used this moment of forgiveness as a source of motivation to get clean and earn a college degree. When he was released from prison, he began working in drug rehabilitation and mental health counseling.[69]

While Holloman, Brice, Ewing, Riley, and Smith developed their addictions in Vietnam, others started abusing drugs and alcohol once they returned to the United States. Surprisingly, drug use in Vietnam did not necessarily continue when servicemen returned. The most thorough study of heroin use by veterans revealed that as few as 5 percent of veterans who were addicted to heroin in Vietnam continued their addiction on returning to the United States.[70]

Alcohol and drugs did not help veterans dealing with psychological problems. However, even veterans whose problems weren't aggravated by drugs or alcohol sometimes met a tragic end. Dwight Johnson was awarded the Congressional Medal of Honor, but his transition from soldier to civilian was not an easy one. Johnson's neighborhood in Detroit where "thousands of poor black youngsters . . . struggled against the grinding life of the ghetto" had limited opportunities. His cousin Tom Tillman recalled, "For two months, we (he and Johnson) went around to place after place (looking for a job) and got doors slammed in our face."[71]

Johnson struggled with his mental health. He was jittery, acted strangely in job interviews, and had vivid nightmares in which a PAVN soldier he had killed "stood in front of him, the barrel of his AK-47 as big as a railroad tunnel, his finger on the trigger, slowly pushing it."[72]

The army hired Johnson as a spokesperson and recruiter, but when he stopped showing up to work they placed him in treatment. On April 29, 1971, Johnson, on a six-day leave from the hospital, attempted to rob a store and was shot dead by its owner. Johnson received more attention from the army than other Black veterans, but it wasn't enough. An anonymous army employee who worked with Johnson observed, "I think a lot of promises were made to the guy that couldn't be kept. You got to remember that getting this guy back in the Army was a feather in the cap of a lot of people."[73]

Henry Brown Jr., who served with the 24th Infantry Division in 1968–69, returned home a changed but troubled man. Having been raised in a "neighborhood devoid of racial antagonism," he was unprepared for the "prejudice, the intense racial animosity and bitter confrontations" he witnessed in Vietnam. Living in the Washington, DC, suburbs, Brown married and had three children, but a sense of peace eluded him. He struggled to sleep, believing some unseen force was after his family. He fantasized about organizing veterans and "enacting change through violence." In 1977

Brown checked into Springfield State Hospital for thirty-two days. Despite his obvious troubles, the VA denied his claim of having paranoid schizophrenia, even though it had been diagnosed by doctors, and awarded him 20 percent disability, eighty-eight dollars a month.[74]

On May 14, 1977, Brown's wife, Bettye, drove him to the hospital, but he refused to go inside, claiming "no one can help me." Fearful of what her husband might do, she took their children to her mother's house that same night. Brown wandered outside and when a police officer, also a Vietnam veteran, arrived, he tackled and stabbed him in the arm. The officer shot and killed Brown. Speaking of her husband's death, Bettye noted, "At last, the war is over for him."[75]

James Gillam visited his brother Edward in the hospital after his return from Vietnam but was shocked when "I didn't recognize him. We shared a room together and I didn't recognize my own brother. He was like 111 pounds." Edward recovered physically but not psychologically. Gillam remembered, "He was an alcoholic. He was basically homeless. He had been through three marriages. He just didn't have a damn life when he got done."[76] Gillam dedicated his book to his brother: "He too lost his life in Vietnam, and he died in Ohio in January of 2005."[77]

"When I Get Back to the World, to the States, I'm Not Going to Have a Job"

For many Black veterans the transition to civilian life was further complicated by the difficulty they had finding jobs. Kent Garrett interviewed several Black servicemen in Vietnam who complained, "I am over here fighting for the country and when I get back, I'm not going to, when I get back to the world, to the states, I'm not going to have a job. I'm not going to be able to find work or get paid."[78]

Their fears were accurate. Willie Thomas noted, "It gave you a feeling like you didn't have a country . . . because you know you came back to very few job opportunities, along with the hatred, it didn't give you a lot to look forward to."[79] Anthony Martin agreed that "most African Americans who came home could not find jobs, there were no resources for us."[80]

African Americans who stayed in the military remained employed. Ron Copes, Wes Geary, and James Lewis reenlisted because they wanted the job security they might not have otherwise.[81] Most had no enthusiasm for a military career, which was not surprising since a majority of

Black servicemen were draftees or draft-motivated volunteers. Sometimes their experiences in the military post-Vietnam demonstrated they were not wanted. After serving in Vietnam, Thomas Brannon was stationed in Fort Knox, Kentucky, where a white soldier from Mississippi disparaged his Bronze Star, sneering, "Did you earn that Bronze Star or they just give it to you?" Brannon asserted, "He felt he had license to do that . . . just the fact that he's white and I am Black."[82]

In 1967 Anthony Martin was sent to Yorktown Naval Weapons Station in Virginia. He was told he would be promoted to sergeant but upon arriving a white captain told him bluntly that "'the South was not ready to have niggers telling white men what to do' . . . and he tore my warrant up in front of my face." Equally humiliating, Martin, a corporal, found himself taking orders from a white private first class. He recalled, "I myself was a victim of something that still burns in my soul today, and I will never ever forgive the persons that did it."[83]

Civilian employers did not exactly rush to hire Black veterans. Dwyte A. Brown remembered "pounding the pavement for about a year looking for work. I could not get a job. . . . Being ex-serviceman Vietnam meant nothin'. . . . I done sacrificed for my country in Vietnam and what do I get. I just become a street urchin."[84] Ron Bradley's previous employer, Bonwit Teller, promised to hold his job for him, but when he returned from Vietnam, they did not rehire him. He struggled to find another job because of "being Black and having to deal with racism in the workplace."[85] Eddie Greene had a similar experience. He remembered, "When I was drafted, I was working at AAA [American Automobile Association] in data processing. When I got out, they refused to give me my job back. We have replaced you."[86]

A hearing organized by the Senate Veterans Affairs Committee in 1971 revealed that the unemployment rate for Black veterans was 21 percent, "a figure comparable to Depression years."[87] The 1981 *Legacies of Vietnam* study determined that Black Vietnam veterans were more than five times as likely to be unemployed than white veterans. The Black unemployment rate was 22 percent, compared to 4 percent for whites. Black veterans twenty-nine years of age or younger had an unemployment of nearly 30 percent while it was 4 percent for whites in that age group.[88]

Black veterans disproportionately received dishonorable discharges, which contributed to their difficulties finding civilian jobs. In 1971 Illinois state senator Richard Newhouse acknowledged that Black veterans with less-than-honorable discharges "face a bleak future in a hostile environment."[89] A 1972 Southern Illinois University–Edwardsville study revealed that the "largest single problem for black veterans" in terms of employment "is the growing number of 'bad paper' discharges. . . . Most 'bad paper' discharges are a lifetime stigma. . . . Few employers make distinctions among the four types of such discharges." The study acknowledged that Black servicemen routinely accepted discharges to get out of military prisons and/or avoid further punishment. They believed these discharges could easily be upgraded in the future, a perspective their mostly white officers promoted. This rarely happened. Of the twenty-thousand bad-paper discharges for which Blacks sought reconsideration, the military reversed fewer than a dozen.[90]

Unemployment remained a significant issue of concern. After working in a Kroger warehouse from 1968 to 1984, Jim Houston found himself unemployed for two years and at risk of losing his house. He remembered, "I was almost giving up. You know I was just stressed that I didn't have no job, I was forty years old." Unemployment had a terrible impact on his mental health. He lamented, "I had got to the end of the road, I just didn't know what to do, and I was about to almost, about to go off the deep end. I was struggling so bad because I just didn't have anything left."[91]

Houston eventually found a job at the post office, but his experiences over the years demonstrate that unemployment was not a temporary problem for Black veterans.[92] A 2007 study in *Monthly Labor Review* compared unemployment rates for veterans over a fifteen-year period. In 1989, 16.5 percent of Black Vietnam veterans were unemployed compared to 7.8 percent of white veterans. By 1999, 23.3 percent of Black veterans were unemployed compared to 12.3 percent of whites. By 2003, Black unemployment had risen to 27.5 percent while it was 13.7 percent for whites.[93]

Even more surprising and troubling, while the *Legacies* study showed the unemployment rate for Black Vietnam veterans was 22 percent, it was only 15 percent for nonveterans. Black Vietnam veterans were more likely to be unemployed than Blacks without military service. The exact opposite was true for whites, where the unemployment rate was higher for nonveterans.[94] A 1990 *Monthly Labor Review* study found that Black Vietnam-era veterans and Black nonveterans had equal rates of unemployment.[95]

These statistics are more disturbing when one remembers that military service was historically viewed by African Americans as an avenue for economic mobility. Most did not willingly join the armed forces to fight in the Vietnam War, but even many draftees believed they would gain the training and experience needed to secure civilian employment. This proved not to be the case.

Even African Americans who found work experienced discrimination. A 1971 *Newsday* report found that starting salaries for Black Vietnam veterans were on average fifteen dollars a week less than for white veterans.[96] White employers and coworkers did not exactly roll out the red carpet for Black veterans. Robert Vonner, a Vietnam-era veteran, recalled working at the phone company with racist whites who "tell me they was bigoted. They will tell you they are bigoted. . . . I worked with folks that were part of [the] KKK."[97]

Anthony Martin's first job after military service was as a camera operator with an NBC affiliate, but on his first day he was told he would be sweeping floors. Purina later hired him to drive a truck, but he ended up loading them. In the early 1970s he was hired by the Illinois State Police, but the other officers were less than welcoming. He recalled, "I mean, here you are, three years earlier you had served your country in Vietnam, and now you are fighting just to keep a job. You're fighting to get recognized as equal among peers doing the same type of work." One white captain threatened Martin, "We're gonna get rid of you niggers."[98]

"There Is No Way a Vet Can Go to College on the G.I. Bill"

Some African American veterans hoped to get government financial support for additional education, but government funding proved insufficient. G.I. bills were passed in 1966, 1972, and 1974, but they were not nearly as generous as those given to veterans of World War II and the Korean War. The 1966 bill provided $100 a month for tuition and living expenses. In comparison, the World War II G.I. Bill covered full tuition and provided at least $50 a month to live on. By 1972 married veterans without children received $205 a month, $60 under the federal poverty level. The 1972 and 1974 bills increased the amount to $220 and then to $320, but most Black veterans still could not afford higher education.[99]

In 1972 Frank V. Votto, director of the New York Division of Veterans Affairs, admitted, "There is no way a vet can go to college on the G.I. Bill today, unless he's got some money of his own."[100] Black veterans rarely had the supplementary funds to attend college or benefit from the limited education initiatives the federal government offered them. By 1973 only 25 percent of Black Vietnam veterans had used their education benefits compared to 46 percent of whites. A 1980 VA survey revealed that only 36.4 percent of African Americans who used the Vietnam-era G.I. bills for college had completed their degrees, in comparison to 60.2 percent of whites.[101]

Nor was a degree a guarantee of employment. Robert L. Daniels earned a degree under the G.I. bill from Northwestern Business College in Illinois. After graduation, he applied for forty jobs in a two-year period but never found one. He recalled, "Nobody never really wanted to give me a break. I was black. A amputee. And it was an unpopular war." Eventually he stopped looking and lived off disability and Social Security.[102]

Civil rights organizations tried to support veterans. The National Urban League operated a "housing, job, school, and welfare service," but its ability to help veterans was "limited by size and support." By November 1970 its services were available in only nine cities.[103] The organization did not have the resources needed to help veterans.

Traditional avenues of support for veterans like the Veterans of Foreign Wars and American Legion were often unavailable. Many Black veterans felt these groups were racist or unwilling and unable to address their problems. Horace Coleman noted that "traditional veteran's organizations, say like VFW or American Legion, were too conservative and weren't doing really anything about PTSD or Agent Orange."[104] In 1971 Earl B. Dickerson, a Black World War I veteran and one of the founders of the legion, accused the organization of being "one of the most reactionary and racially prejudiced groups in the country. They stand for everything that I am against." In 1972 there was no African American in a leadership position in the American Legion.[105] In the early 1970s Allen Thomas Jr. was rejected for membership at his local American Legion. In 1986 a group of Black Vietnam veterans was asked to leave a legion post because of their race.[106]

African Americans faced significant obstacles when they returned home. Many agreed with Reginald Edwards's observation that he "had left one war and come back to another."[107] Their status as veterans did not protect them from continued racial discrimination, which remained a dominating force.

Conclusion: "Our War Is Here"

The story of Black Vietnam veterans is not solely one of hardship. It is also a story of survival, resilience, and resistance. The world that they returned to did not differ significantly from the world they left, but in many respects they had changed. Black veterans came home newly emboldened to continue the fight against prejudice and discrimination. They believed their service to their country gave them the right to demand better treatment.

On July 24, 1967, the *Washington Post* interviewed an unnamed Black veteran while he was "standing in the midst of broken glass that hung over Twelfth and Blaine Streets" on the second day of the Detroit Riots. The veteran observed, "I just got back from Vietnam a few months ago . . . but you know I think the war is here."[108] Many Black veterans agreed that the real war was in the United States, and this was a war they intended to win.

Roderick T. Jerrett, a Black Vietnam veteran, observed, "When a Black soldier gets out of the army, he's not likely to be complacent about racism and discrimination. He'll make demands and be very emphatic about it."[109] The Black servicemen Kent Garrett met in Vietnam expressed similar views. They "were angry about what they felt they would be facing when they went into the world," but their experiences in Vietnam "sort of made them stronger in the sense that they were not going to be pushed around when they got back to the world." They were adamant that they were not going to "go back to the same situation they had before."[110]

Service in Vietnam taught Larry Smith, a disabled veteran from New York, that "Blacks shouldn't fight anybody else's war. . . . Our war is here." Jay Jones, a Black veteran who drove a tank in Vietnam, recalled, "I voluntarily signed up at age 16 to fight for my country's honor and freedom. But now I see that the real enemy is right here in this country."[111] When Jessie Woodbridge's family home was vandalized by racists, he remained resolute: "I'm prepared to stay: we are ready to fight and all those people who don't like it can go back to Mississippi."[112] Woodbridge was not alone.

When existing veterans' organizations proved unwelcoming, African Americans joined others like Veterans for Peace (VFP) and Vietnam Veterans Against the War (VVAW). Horace Coleman joined the latter because "their hearts were in the right place" and they directly addressed issues like PTSD and Agent Orange.[113] In 1978 Vietnam Veterans of America (VVA) was formed, and it welcomed Black veterans. Wayne Smith helped found its Rhode Island branch and served the national organization in a variety of capacities for decades.[114] Others joined organizations that weren't exclusively for Vietnam veterans but included many among their members. George Brummell, for instance, joined the Blinded Veterans Association, eventually becoming its national field service director.[115]

African Americans formed their own organizations as well. In June 1968 Barry Wright formed Concerned Veterans from Vietnam. Membership was open to all Vietnam veterans but most members were Black, and they directed their attention toward issues disproportionately affecting Black veterans like drug addiction, unemployment, and the reversal of less-than-honorable discharges. By November 1970 there were chapters throughout the United States.[116]

In 1969 seven Vietnam combat veterans in Milwaukee formed Interested Veterans of Central City, which become the National Association for Black Veterans (NABVETS) in 1973. It was created to help Black Vietnam veterans file benefit claims and upgrade discharges. In 1998 they were officially certified by the VA to represent veterans filing benefit claims. They currently have one hundred chapters in the United States and Puerto Rico. The group's impact has been significant. From 1969 until the present, they have assisted more than 65,000 veterans file claims equaling over $69 million.[117]

On April 18, 1978, a group of African Americans in Brooklyn formed Black Veterans for Social Justice. The group was created to combat "racism and racist policies," which frequently condemned African Americans to second-class citizenship within the veteran community. They continue to provide significant support for veterans of all eras dealing with issues like mental health, housing, food insecurity, and unemployment.[118]

Many of these organizations have extended support and mentorship to veterans who served after Vietnam. Bernard McClusky, a longtime member of the Springfield, Massachusetts, chapter of NABVETS, remembered coming home and "the only person glad to see me was my mommy."[119] He was committed to ensuring that veterans of future conflicts had greater support. McClusky was not alone. Horace Coleman remained a member of VVAW and VFP in large part out of a desire to help veterans returning from Afghanistan and Iraq.[120] Wayne Smith's commitment to veterans was such that he served on the board of directors for Iraq and Afghanistan Veterans of America.[121]

When African Americans returned home, they faced another war, a war against prejudice and discrimination. It would clearly not be an easy fight, but many were committed to waging it. As a longtime member of the Springfield NABVETS, Eugene L. Brice helped thousands of veterans over the years. Bernard McClusky noted, "Eugene and people like him have made it better for veterans coming back from Iraq and Afghanistan" as well. After Brice's encounter with the racist woman at the supermarket, he struggled to control his PTSD and "a related speech impediment." However, he remained resolute that "more than 50 years of service to the country should not be ruined by one hellish moment in a grocery store."[122] On December 22, 2021, he attended a food drive organized by the Mental Health Association in his honor where he reasserted his commitment to the fight for veterans. Brice insisted, "We're veterans and we do matter and our mission never quits. We swore to protect our country and now we swore to protect our community."[123] Racism was strong, but Black veterans were stronger.

CONCLUSION

When Black servicemen were sent to Vietnam, they physically left their country behind. However, in some respects they never left. The domestic racial environment proved to be powerful and resilient, and it followed African Americans to Vietnam.

Black servicemen were hardly strangers to racial prejudice, discrimination, and tension, but when they encountered these problems in Vietnam, they understandably compared these experiences to the historical and contemporary racial environments in which they had grown up. Sometimes, what they encountered differed from previous experiences; other times it seemed as though nothing had changed.

Blacks found both harmony and division in Vietnam. In combat, they often experienced a degree of racial equality and friendship with whites. These relationships formed because combat forced Blacks and whites to become dependent on one another for survival. At least temporarily, they escaped from the toxic racial environment in the United States. These experiences contrasted sharply with the tense and even violent relations in the United States during the Vietnam War era.

The friendships Blacks and whites formed in Vietnam continued to have significance long after their military service was over. Reminiscing on his friendship with a white soldier killed in Vietnam, Charles Strong recalled, "I've carried this with me from that day until now. I will never ever forget Joe. Although Joe's family might forget him, his wife and his child might forget him, but I will never ever forget Joe."[1]

A 1992 *Social Science Quarterly* study revealed that "there is at least some survey evidence that interracial contact within the military reduces support for racial separatism."[2] Black veterans would continue to experience prejudice and discrimination, but many believed they had new allies. Anthony Martin recalled the situation in 1966–67: "It was the white guys that stood next to us in war, that bonded in friendship in a time of war, that eventually went on to become senators, and alderman, and commissioners and politicians who remembered those relationships in war. . . . It was that war that brought us together and those people are now the leaders today."[3] Speaking of Vietnam veterans, Ron Bradley stated, "We don't see color, we see brotherhood. So that to me would be the strongest contribution. That Blacks and whites through unity, through working together, have become more unified and more respected as a people."[4]

These positive relations were only a part of the Black experience. American racism accompanied American servicemen to Vietnam, and African Americans quickly and routinely complained of discrimination. They protested that they were disproportionately assigned menial tasks and denied promotions. As in the civilian world, African Americans were intended to occupy the lower rungs of the ladder in the armed services without opportunity for advancement. Sadly, their complaints were often justified.

Others criticized the military justice system for disproportionately and systematically targeting African Americans for punishment. These complaints suggested that new roles had been established for African Americans in the military—as criminals or prisoners. These accusations were more than justified as African Americans were disproportionately punished, using both judicial and nonjudicial punishments. Military stockades were disproportionately filled with Black prisoners. Most had not been convicted of anything and were being held pretrial for relatively minor, nonviolent crimes.

The impact of the wartime criminal justice system on Black servicemen resembled the impact of the civilian criminal justice system on them back home. Khalil Gibran Muhammad's *The Condemnation of Blackness: Race, Crime, and the Making of Modern Urban America* highlights American society's propensity to define criminality in starkly racial terms. Muhammad has observed that the American justice system operates under the principle that "whites commit crimes, but black males are Criminals."[5] This thesis also applied to the military justice system in Vietnam.

The military justice system in the Vietnam War became the model for the domestic justice system. In reaction to a 1971 congressional report which claimed that between 10 and 15 percent of servicemen in Vietnam were addicted to heroin, the Nixon administration launched the "War on Drugs."[6] Thus began the mass incarceration of African Americans, which Michelle Alexander's *The New Jim Crow* has described as a result of this war on drugs. The incarceration of African Americans *en masse* for minor drug-related crimes first occurred in the armed forces during the Vietnam War. Alexander scrutinizes the widespread use of plea deals whereby defendants, some of whom are innocent and others who are likely to be judged not guilty, are encouraged by prosecutors and even their own public defense lawyers to plead guilty to get out of jail or to avoid the possibility of more severe sentences. She notes, "Prosecutors admit that they routinely charge people with crimes for which they technically have probable cause but which they seriously doubt they could ever win in court" to pressure them into accepting plea bargains. Alexander credits the Anti-Drug Abuse Act of 1986, which established mandatory minimum prison sentences for low-level drug dealers and crack cocaine possession, for helping to create a justice system where plea deals are the norm.[7]

These changes in pleas and sentencing had already been put in place for military defendants during the Vietnam War. Black servicemen were encouraged by their commanding officers and even by their own lawyers to plead guilty to charges of which they were innocent or which could not have been successfully prosecuted. Others were pressured to accept less-than-honorable discharges. Black servicemen pled guilty to avoid additional or more severe punishment, to get out of the stockades, or to escape the military altogether. They later found these decisions would haunt their lives as veterans.

In addition to their complaints about the military judicial system, African Americans complained that they were disproportionately given dangerous duties or jobs, which suggested the military viewed them as expendable. In the early years of the war African Americans were disproportionately drafted, placed in combat units, and killed. While Black death rates decreased significantly by 1967, the perception that Black lives were expendable remained, so much so that rumors proliferated that authorities were using the war and high Black fatality rates to remove African Americans from the United States. While these rumors were false, when one remembers government-sponsored programs like the Tuskegee Experiment, one can understand why some Blacks believed them.[8] African Americans knew that their lives were not valued equally to those of whites in the United States, and it was not unreasonable for them to reach the same conclusion in Vietnam.

The racial violence that gripped the United States nearly every summer from 1965 to 1968 also spread to Vietnam. After Martin Luther King Jr.'s assassination in April 1968, the first major incidents of racial violence appeared. Soon they would become commonplace. During the next three-and-a-half years thousands of incidents of racial violence involving American servicemen were reported throughout Vietnam. The "other war" had arrived.

One might conclude that the absence of racial incidents early in the war or even the positive relationships many Black and white servicemen formed indicated an environment of unity, good feelings, and high morale, Black complaints of discrimination prove this was not the case. The armed forces' failure to address sufficiently these complaints alienated African Americans, increased tensions, and over time contributed to outbreaks of violence. The origins of the "other war" in Vietnam lay in American racism and racial discrimination. Military officials compounded the problem by blaming African Americans collectively for the violence and ignoring the role racist whites played.

The domestic racial environment impacted Black interactions with and perceptions of the Vietnamese. Most African Americans viewed Vietnamese civilians from a perspective heavily influenced by their own experiences with racial discrimination in the United States. Having themselves experienced racism and in many cases poverty, African Americans felt empathy toward the Vietnamese population who faced similar challenges. African Americans contrasted their behavior with the mistreatment whites directed at Vietnamese civilians. When Black servicemen heard whites hurl slurs at the Vietnamese, they were reminded of racial epithets whites directed at Blacks back home and in Vietnam. When they witnessed whites mistreat the Vietnamese, they were reminded of the abuse the Black community had experienced throughout its history in America. The Black experience with racism in the United States was always *the* reference point.

In turn, many African Americans believed the Vietnamese empathized with them as fellow persons of color and as victims of white racism. The Vietnamese were, they thought, well-aware of the domestic racial situation and supportive of Black civil rights. This perception was strengthened by the large number of Vietnamese people who approached African Americans and insisted that they were the "same."

The reality was more complex. Some Vietnamese discriminated against African Americans. The historical mistreatment of minorities and

Indigenous groups demonstrated that Vietnam was not free of ethnic and racial prejudice. However, when African Americans encountered Vietnamese racism, they often blamed white servicemen, accusing them of bringing their racist attitudes and behaviors to Vietnam and teaching them to the locals. American racism threatened to redefine, damage, and destroy the positive relations African Americans believed they had with Vietnamese civilians. These accusations were valid. Some whites did teach the Vietnamese to hate Blacks. American racism, once again, easily traveled to Vietnam.

Black-Vietnamese relations complicated Black-white relations, especially when whites discriminated against or mistreated civilians. In some cases, white mistreatment of the Vietnamese was the catalyst for violent outbreaks between Blacks and whites. The belief that Black Americans had an important bond with the Vietnamese was also troubling because it suggested that a foreign people, with whom African Americans had no prior interactions, were more sympathetic to Black aspirations than their own countrymen. Blacks viewed the Vietnamese as empathetic and supportive of the civil rights movement, while the military hierarchy and individual whites routinely discriminated against them.

African Americans also developed strong opinions about the NLF and PAVN forces they were tasked with fighting. They recognized the communist enemy as capable fighters and respected their refusal to surrender even when faced with overwhelming American firepower. African Americans understood what it was like to face white American power, and they frequently compared the Black historical fight against racism with the Vietnamese fight against American war power.

Black servicemen likewise believed that the Vietnamese communist forces were empathetic toward African Americans and the civil rights movement. This belief was supported by rumors circulating among Black and even white servicemen that communist soldiers wouldn't shoot African Americans unless forced to. It was one thing for African Americans to believe Vietnamese civilians favored them but quite another to believe that communist forces, who killed thousands of African Americans during the conflict, were sympathetic.

These rumors reveal just how negatively many African Americans had come to view American military leaders and the war effort. The prevalence of racial discrimination and concerns about the number of African Americans being drafted, placed in combat, and dying in Vietnam convinced many that the military did not value their lives or appreciate their sacrifices. Rumors that communist forces would try to avoid killing African Americans suggested that the enemy was more concerned about the lives of African Americans than the American military.

African Americans did not come up with these ideas entirely on their own. Vietnamese communist propaganda in leaflets and radio broadcasts directly appealed to African Americans by recalling their historical and contemporary mistreatment. This propaganda urged them to return home to fight for their civil and political rights. It also reinforced the idea that the enemy was empathetic toward African Americans and supportive of the civil rights movement. These appeals were effective, not because communist officials were really empathetic or supportive but because they spoke factually, at least in a general sense, about the status of African Americans back home. African Americans did not enjoy equality at home. If they had, Vietnamese communist appeals would have had no impact.

The emphasis on American racism in communist propaganda pointed out a potential Achilles heel for the American military. Why should African Americans serve a government and country that didn't value their rights or lives? It was a valid question. By focusing attention on American history and contemporary developments, communist officials argued that the war should not and could not be separated from domestic events. The Vietnam War and the domestic racial situation, including the civil rights movement, were bound together—at least for African American servicemen.

The domestic racial situation of the 1960s and 1970s was inextricably linked to Black servicemen's experiences in Vietnam—they could not be separated. The racial prejudice, tension, and even violence that African Americans experienced in Vietnam had their origins in the United States, and that racism traveled easily from the United States to Vietnam. Blacks could leave American territory for military service in a foreign country, but they could not escape the racism and discrimination that was part of the American cultural and political landscape.

Notes

INTRODUCTION

1. "The Black GI," *Black Journal*, episode 22, directed by Stan Lathan, produced by William Greaves, aired March 30, 1970, National Education Television, http://americanarchive.org. While the exact dates of the interviews the *Black Journal* conducted in Vietnam and Okinawa are unknown, production began in October 1969 and it appears as though most, if not all, of the interviews were completed before the new year.
2. Sherie Merson and Steven Schlossman, *Foxholes and Color Lines: Desegregating the U.S. Armed Forces* (Washington, DC: Johns Hopkins University Press, 1998).
3. George C. Herring, *America's Longest War: The United States and Vietnam, 1950–1975* (New York: McGraw-Hill, 2002), 155–56.
4. The Vietnam Veterans Memorial: The Wall–USA, s.v., "Raymond Leon Horn," http://thewall-usa.com.
5. James E. Westheider, *The African American Experience in Vietnam: Brothers in Arms* (Lanham, MD: Rowman and Littlefield, 2007), xix, 49. Black women also served in Vietnam. Heather Stur, *Beyond Combat: Women and Gender in the Vietnam Era* (New York: Cambridge University Press, 2011), provides an excellent discussion on the contributions of Black nurses, Women's Army Corps members, and so-called donut dollies.
6. U.S. Census Bureau, "Summary of General Characteristics," 1970, table 48, https://www2.census.gov/. According to the 1960 census African Americans were 10.5 percent of the population. By 1970, they accounted for 11.1 percent of the American population.
7. On July 28, 1967, President Lyndon Johnson established the National Advisory Commission on Civil Disorders to investigate the causes of racial rioting in Newark and Detroit. Known more commonly as the Kerner Commission, after its chair, Ohio governor Otto Kerner, the commission later released its findings in a 426-page report on February 29, 1968.
8. Tommy Lee Lott, "Documenting Social Issues: *Black Journal*, 1968–70," in *Struggles for Representation: African American Documentary Film and Video*, ed. Phyllis Rauch Klotman and Janet Cutler (Bloomington: Indiana University Press, 1999), 71–73.

9. "The Black GI."
10. Ibid.
11. Ibid.
12. Ibid.
13. Wallace Terry, "Black Power in Vietnam," *Time*, September 19, 1969, https://content.time.com.
14. "The Black GI."
15. Lamont B. Steptoe, *Uncle's South Sea China Blue Nightmare* (Philadelphia: Plan B Press, 1995), 42.
16. Thomas Brannon, interview by author, December 6, 2011.
17. "The Black GI."
18. Westheider, *The African American Experience in Vietnam*; James E. Westheider, *Fighting on Two Fronts: African Americans and the Vietnam War* (New York: New York University Press, 1997).
19. Herman Graham III, *The Brothers' Vietnam War: Black Power, Manhood, and the Military Experience* (Gainesville: University Press of Florida, 2003).
20. Lawrence Allen Eldridge, *Chronicles of a Two-Front War: Civil Rights and Vietnam in the African American Press* (Columbia: University of Missouri Press, 2011).
21. Jeremy Maxwell, *Brotherhood in Combat: How African Americans Found Equality in Korea and Vietnam* (Norman: University of Oklahoma Press, 2018).
22. Kyle Longley, *Grunts: The American Combat Soldier in Vietnam* (Armonk, NY: M. E. Sharpe, 2008).
23. Christian G. Appy, *Working Class War: American Combat Soldiers and Vietnam* (Chapel Hill: University of North Carolina Press, 1993); Richard Moser, *The New Winter Soldiers: GI and Veteran Dissent during the Vietnam Era* (New Brunswick, NJ: Rutgers University Press, 1996); David Cortright, *Soldiers in Revolt: GI Resistance during the Vietnam War* (Chicago: Haymarket Books, 2005).
24. Isaac Hampton II, *The Black Officer Corps: A History of Black Military Advancement from Integration through Vietnam* (New York: Routledge, 2013).
25. George Lepre, *Fragging: Why U.S. Soldiers Assaulted Their Officers in Vietnam* (Lubbock: Texas Tech Press, 2011).
26. Kimberly L. Phillips, *War! What Is It Good For? Black Freedom Struggles and the U.S. Military from World War II to Iraq* (Chapel Hill: University of North Carolina Press, 2012).
27. Gary D. Solis, *Marines and Military Law in Vietnam: Trial by Fire* (Washington, DC: History and Museums Division, 1989); William Thomas Allison, *Military Justice in Vietnam: The Rule of Law in an American War* (Lawrence: University Press of Kansas, 2007).
28. Norman A. McDaniel, *Yet Another Voice* (New York: Hawthorne Books, 1975); Samuel Vance, *The Courageous and Proud* (New York: Norton, 1979); Stanley Goff and Robert Sanders with Clark Smith, *Brothers: Black Soldiers in the Nam* (Novato, CA: Presidio Press, 1982); David Parks, *GI Diary* (Washington, DC: Howard University Press, 1984); Albert French, *Patches of Fire: A Story of War and Redemption* (New York: Doubleday, 1997); Richard A. Guidry, *The War in I Corps* (Raleigh, NC: Ivy Books, 1997); Terry Whitmore, *Memphis, Nam, Sweden: The Story of a Black Deserter* (Jackson: University of Mississippi Press, 1997); Ed Emanuel, *Soul Patrol* (New York: Random House, 2003); George E. Brummell, *Shades of Darkness: A Black Soldier's Journey through Vietnam, Blindness, and Back* (Silver Spring, MD: Pie, 2006); Brian H. Settles, *No Reason for Dying: A*

Reluctant Combat Pilot's Confession of Hypocrisy, Infidelity and War (Charleston, SC: Booksurge, 2009); James Gillam, *Life and Death in the Central Highlands: An American Sergeant in the Vietnam War, 1968–1970* (Denton: University of North Texas Press, 2010).

29. Wallace Terry, *Bloods: An Oral History of the Vietnam War by Black Veterans* (New York: Random House, 1984). *Bloods* includes interviews with veterans who served during different periods of the conflict, in different areas of Vietnam, and in different branches of the armed forces. It includes testimonies from draftees, enlistees, and members of the officer corps.

30. Eddie Wright, *Thoughts about the Vietnam War: Based on My Personal Experience, Books I Have Read and Conversations with Other Veterans* (New York: Carlton Press, 1986). Testimonials from African American Vietnam veterans are also found in James R. Wilson, *Landing Zones: Combat Vets from America's Proud, Fighting South Remember Vietnam* (Durham, NC: Duke University Press, 1990); Christian G. Appy, *Patriots: The Vietnam War Remembered from All Sides* (New York: Penguin, 2000); and Benjamin Fleury-Steiner, *Disposable Heroes: The Betrayal of African American Veterans* (Lanham, MD: Rowman and Littlefield, 2012).

31. *Same Mud, Same Blood* (video), December 1, 1967, http://archives.museum.tv; *No Vietnamese Ever Called Me Nigger* (video), 1968, https://www.youtube.com; "The Bloods of 'Nam" *Frontline*, produced, directed, and photographed by Wayne Ewing, PBS, 1986, https://www.youtube.com.

32. Lamont B. Steptoe, *Mad Minute* (Camden, NJ: Whirlwind Press, 1993); Steptoe, *Dusty Road: A Vietnam Suite* (Camden, NJ: Whirlwind Press, 1995); Steptoe, *Uncle's South China Sea Blue Nightmare*; Horace Coleman, *In the Grass* (Woodbridge, CT: Vietnam Generation and Burning Cities Press, 1995).

CHAPTER 1: "WE WAS JUST US"

1. *Same Mud, Same Blood* (video), December 1, 1967, http://archives.museum.tv.
2. Sherie Mershon and Steven Schlossman, *Foxholes and Color Lines: Desegregating the U.S. Armed Forces* (Washington, DC: Johns Hopkins University Press, 1998).
3. *Same Mud, Same Blood.*
4. Ibid.
5. Ibid.
6. Ibid.
7. Ibid.
8. Stanley Goff and Robert Sanders with Clark Smith, *Brothers: Black Soldiers in the Nam* (Novato, CA: Presidio Press, 1982), 147–48.
9. Vietnam was not the first conflict in which Blacks and whites interacted in these ways, but because the Vietnam War was the first conflict in which the U.S. military was desegregated for the duration of the conflict, these relationships were more common than in previous conflicts.
10. Ethel L. Payne, "GIs Tell How They Stand on the Viet War," *Chicago Daily Defender*, April 11, 1967.
11. Thomas A. Johnson, "The U.S. Negro in Vietnam," *New York Times*, April 29, 1968.
12. *Same Mud, Same Blood.*

13. Simeon Booker, "An American Is an American," *Jet*, June 30, 1966, 22.
14. Leon Daniel, "Negro Finding Home in Armed Forces," *Boston Globe*, April 9, 1967.
15. "Armed Forces: Democracy in the Foxhole," *Time*, May 26, 1967, http://content.time.com.
16. George W. Ashworth, "GI Integration Meets Battle Test: Race Held Unimportant," *Christian Science Monitor*, August 23, 1967.
17. Donald Mosby, "Our Man Mosby Finds No Prejudice in Viet Conflict," *Chicago Daily Defender*, May 23, 1968.
18. Johnson, "The U.S. Negro in Vietnam," 16.
19. "Black GI Wants New Answers," *New Pittsburgh Courier*, May 18, 1968.
20. Thomas A. Johnson, "Negroes in 'The Nam,'" *Ebony*, August 1968, 37–38.
21. Johnson, "The U.S. Negro in Vietnam," 16.
22. Jim Houston, interview by author, December 1, 2011.
23. Goff and Sanders, *Brothers*, 67.
24. Eddie Wright, *Thoughts about the Vietnam War: Based on My Personal Experience, Books I Have Read and Conversations with Other Veterans* (New York: Carlton Press, 1986), 93.
25. Wayne Smith, interview by author, October 25, 2011.
26. Robert M. Watters, interview by George C. Herring and Terry L. Birdwhistell, May 16, 1985, 25, University of Kentucky Libraries Vietnam Veterans in Kentucky Oral History Project, King Library, Lexington.
27. Bob Steck, interview by author, November 30, 2011.
28. David Parks, *GI Diary* (Washington, DC: Howard University Press, 1984), 24, 137.
29. Anthony Martin, interview by author, September 12, 2011.
30. Goff and Sanders, *Brothers*, 67.
31. Wright, *Thoughts about the Vietnam War*, 107.
32. George Brummell, interview by author, October 21, 2011.
33. Daniel Burress, interview by Ashley McKinney, April 18, 2002, 8–9, Veterans History Project, Library of Congress, Washington, DC.
34. Dave Dubose, "Combat Knows No Color," *Vietnam*, December 1990, 25.
35. Lee Sleemons Ewing, interview by Pat McClain, 11, Veterans History Project, Library of Congress.
36. Goff and Sanders, *Brothers*, 136–38.
37. Scott Riley, interview by author, May 7, 2022.
38. Bernard McClusky, interview by author, May 18, 2022.
39. Smith interview.
40. Horace Coleman, interview by author, June 12, 2012.
41. Ron Bradley, interview by author, October 23, 2011.
42. James Gillam, interview by author, March 14, 2008.
43. Lamont B. Steptoe, interview by author, June 25, 2012.
44. Wallace Terry, *Bloods: An Oral History of the Vietnam War by Black Veterans* (New York: Random House, 1984), 119.
45. Sinclair Swan, interview by author, August 11, 2011.
46. Nate Mondy, interview by author, September 19, 2012.
47. Clyde Jackson, interview by author, January 8, 2012.
48. Brummell interview.
49. Martin interview.
50. Brian Settles, interview by author, October 1, 2012.

51. Terry, *Bloods*, 4–5.
52. James R. Wilson, *Landing Zones: Southern Veterans Remember Vietnam* (Durham, NC: Duke University Press, 1990), 101.
53. Robert Louis Jr., interview by author, November 30, 2011.
54. James Lewis, interview by author, March 20, 2012.
55. Eddie Greene, interview by author, March 12, 2012.
56. Wes Geary, interview by author, August 7, 2009.
57. Swan interview.
58. McClusky interview.
59. Coleman interview.
60. Arthur Barham, interview by author, February 19, 2013.
61. Thomas Brannon, interview by author, December 6, 2011.
62. Bradley interview.
63. Ed Emanuel, *Soul Patrol* (New York: Random House, 2003), 128.
64. Terry, *Bloods*, 57.
65. Ibid., 119.
66. Ibid.
67. Ibid.
68. Ibid.
69. Steptoe interview.
70. Terry, *Bloods*, 111–13.
71. Naomi Zack, *Race and Mixed Race* (Philadelphia: Temple University Press, 1993), 118, 77. These laws were never meant to criminalize relations between white men and Black women; rather, they were meant to prevent sexual relations between Black men and white women.
72. Terry, *Bloods*, 113.
73. Smith interview.
74. Terry, *Bloods*, 23.
75. Riley interview.
76. Terry Whitmore, *Memphis, Nam, Sweden: The Story of a Black Deserter* (Jackson: University of Mississippi Press, 1997), 79.
77. Anne Keegan, "Vietnam Hero Gets Lost in a City Jungle," *Chicago Tribune*, August 12, 1988.
78. Terry, *Bloods*, 151–52.
79. Gillam interview.
80. James Goodrich, "Nation Honors Negro GI Who Gave Life for Mates," *Los Angeles Sentinel*, April 28, 1966.
81. Booker, "An American Is an American," 20.
82. *Same Mud, Same Blood*.
83. Paul Hathaway, "Negro in Viet: Not That Far from the Ghetto," *Newsday* (New York), May 15, 1968.
84. Wright, *Thoughts about the Vietnam War*, 93.
85. Wilson, *Landing Zones*, 82.
86. Terry, *Bloods*, 57.
87. Anne Keegan, "Letters from the Front: One American Family's Private History of Vietnam," *Chicago Tribune*, January 27, 1983.
88. Ibid.
89. Ibid.

90. *Same Mud, Same Blood.*
91. Ibid.
92. Johnson, "The U.S. Negro in Vietnam," 16.
93. Lewis Downey, interview by author, June 11, 2012.
94. Theodore Belcher, interview by author, December 6, 2011.
95. Ibid.
96. Thomas Rogan, interview by author, December 14, 2012.
97. Jack Whitted, interview by author, July 11, 2012.
98. Ibid.
99. Robert Whitaker, *On the Laps of Gods: The Red Summer of 1919 and the Struggle for Justice That Remade a Nation* (New York: Broadway Books, 2009).
100. *My Vietnam, Your Iraq*, directed by Ron Osgood, aired 2011, PBS.
101. Jim Magee, "Death of Negro GI in Vietnam Triggers Letter: Dying Negro Soldier," *Philadelphia Tribune*, December 25, 1965.
102. Hathaway, "Negro in Viet," 37.
103. Herman Graham III, *The Brothers' Vietnam War: Black Power, Manhood, and the Military Experience* (Gainesville: University Press of Florida, 2003), 47.
104. Emanuel, *Soul Patrol*, 128.
105. Wilson, *Landing Zones*, 79.
106. Rogan interview.
107. Brummell interview.
108. Whitted interview.
109. Dubose, "Combat Knows No Color," 25.
110. Coleman interview.
111. *No Vietnamese Ever Called Me Nigger* (video), 1968, https://www.youtube.com.
112. Brannon interview.
113. Goff and Sanders, *Brothers*, 148.
114. Swan interview.
115. Emanuel, *Soul Patrol*, 124.
116. Parks, *GI Diary*, 137.
117. Cephus "Dusty" Rhodes, interview by author, January 19, 2012.
118. Goff and Sanders, *Brothers*, 139.
119. Similar depictions of Black-white friendships can be found in Bill C. Bryels's account in Robert E. Vadas, *Cultures in Conflict: The Vietnam War* (Westport, CT: Greenwood Press, 2002), 124; Wilson, *Landing Zones*, 104; Robert M. Watters, interview by George C. Herring and Terry L. Birdwhistell; and Daniel Burress, interview by Ashley McKinney.
120. Samuel Stouffer, *The American Soldier: Combat and Its Aftermath* (Princeton, NJ: Princeton University Press, 1949), 97, 137.
121. Goff and Sanders, *Brothers*, 67.
122. Christian G. Appy, *Working Class War: American Combat Soldiers and Vietnam* (Chapel Hill: University of North Carolina Press, 1993), 163. Appy cites studies which claim that NLF and PAVN forces initiated anywhere from 75–88 percent of all combat incidents.
123. Byron F. Fiman, Jonathan F. Borus, and M. Duncan Stanton, "Black-White and American-Vietnamese Relations among Soldiers in Vietnam," *Journal of Social Issues* 31, no. 4 (Fall 1975): 41, 46.

124. Bavarskis, "Vietnam Veteran Decides to Join the Black Struggle," *Norfolk [VA] Journal and Guide*, May 26, 1973.
125. Riley interview.
126. Lewis interview.
127. Greene interview.
128. Willie Thomas, interview by author, September 3, 2011.
129. Hathaway, "Negro in Viet," 37.
130. Freddie Edwards, interview by author, December 2, 2011.
131. Martin interview.
132. Smith interview.
133. Jackson interview.
134. Appy, *Working Class War*, 232.
135. *Same Mud, Same Blood.*
136. Jonathan Shay, *Achilles in Vietnam: Combat Trauma and the Undoing of Character* (New York: Scribner, 1994), 19.
137. George Hicks, interview by author, April 28, 2012.
138. Rhodes interview.
139. Houston interview.
140. Bradley interview.
141. Coleman interview.
142. Ron Copes, interview by author, November 17, 2011.
143. Clay Risen, *A Nation on Fire: America in the Wake of the King Assassination* (Hoboken, NJ: Wiley, 2009), 7.
144. Errol Wayne Stevens, *Radical L.A.: From Coxey's Army to the Watts Riots, 1894–1965* (Norman: University of Oklahoma Press, 2009), 306–7.
145. Kevin Mumford, "Harvesting the Crisis: The Newark Uprising, the Kerner Commission, and Writings on Riots," in *African American Urban History since World War*, ed. Kenneth L. Kusmer and Joe W. Trotter (Chicago: University of Chicago Press, 2009), 2:203.
146. Thomas J. Sugrue, *Race and Inequality in Postwar Detroit* (Princeton, NJ: Princeton University Press, 1996), 259.
147. Risen, *A Nation on Fire*, 232.
148. Goff and Sanders, *Brothers*, 26.
149. Ibid.
150. *Same Mud, Same Blood.*
151. Lewis interview.
152. Copes interview.
153. Karl Marlantes, interview by author, September 24, 2012. In *Matterhorn* much of the racial tension is portrayed as occurring in combat, but in reality these tensions occurred outside of combat.
154. Edwards interview.
155. Smith interview.
156. Zalin Grant, "Whites against Blacks in Vietnam," *New Republic*, January 8, 1969, 15.
157. Fiman, Borus, and Stanton, "Black-White and American-Vietnamese Relations," 39.
158. *Same Mud, Same Blood.*

159. "'Safer in Vietnam or U.S.?' Marine Wonders," *Jet*, September 1, 1966, 23.
160. "Rather Stay in Vietnam Than Return to Georgia," *Jet*, December 8, 1966, 8.
161. Smith interview.
162. Lamont B. Steptoe, *Uncle's South Sea China Blue Nightmare* (Alexandria, VA: Plan B Press, 2003), 40.
163. Bradley interview.
164. Jackson interview.
165. Emanuel, *Soul Patrol*, 128.
166. Samuel Vance, *The Courageous and Proud* (New York: Norton, 1979), 44.
167. Parks, *GI Diary*, 123.
168. "Editorials: Military Racism," *Pittsburgh Courier*, September 6, 1969.
169. Earle Wheeler to Robert D. Murphy, December 19, 1969, box 22, folder 5, Deputy Chief of Staff for Personnel, Policy Files on Discrimination in the Army, U.S. Army Heritage and Education Center, Carlisle Barracks, PA.
170. James J. Ursano, report, January 7, 1971, Reference Paper Files, Stockade Project, box 2, U.S. Forces in Southeast Asia, 1950–75, U.S. National Archives, College Park, MD.
171. Wallace Terry, "Black Power in Vietnam," *Time*, September 19, 1969, https://content.time.com.
172. Maria Wilhelm, "An Angry Vietnam War Correspondent Charges That Black Combat Soldiers Are Platoon's M.I.A.'s," *People*, April 20, 1987.
173. Johnson, "The U.S. Negro in Vietnam," 16.

CHAPTER 2: "BROTHERS AS MANY BROTHERS AS THEY CAN FIND"

1. "The Bloods of 'Nam," *Frontline*, produced, directed, and photographed by Wayne Ewing, 1986, PBS.
2. C. V. Glines, "Black VS White: Confrontation in the Ranks Is Calling for Improved Human Relations—Or Else," *Armed Forces Management*, June 1970, 21.
3. *No Vietnamese Ever Called Me Nigger* (video), 1968, https://www.youtube.com.
4. William Chapman, "Qualified Negro Is Found to Receive Inequitable Treatment under Draft," *Washington Post*, March 5, 1967.
5. Herman Graham III, *The Brothers' Vietnam War: Black Power, Manhood, and the Military Experience* (Gainesville: University Press of Florida, 2003), 1.
6. Thomas A. Johnson, "Blacks Don't Feel They Get a Fair Shake," *New York Times*, November 29, 1970.
7. Fred Bonaparte, "Bias Hurts GI's Morale Says Georgie after Tour of Vietnam," *Philadelphia Tribune*, February 19, 1966.
8. "Black Senator to Visit Vietnam to Probe Bias," *Jet*, December 19, 1968, 4.
9. Glines, "Black VS White," 27.
10. "Black GIs Caught in Vise," *Jet*, December 2, 1971, 14–15.
11. Colonel Richard A. Edwards Jr. to Brigadier General Edward Bautz Jr., April 30, 1968, box 16, folder 2, Deputy Chief of Staff for Personnel, Policy Files on Discrimination in the Army, U.S. Army Heritage and Education Center, Carlisle Barracks, PA (hereafter DCSPER/USAHEC). This letter reveals that Parks served in Company B, 5th Battalion, 60th Infantry Regiment, of the 9th Infantry Division.

12. David Parks, *GI Diary* (Washington, DC: Howard University Press, 1984), 54, 77, 108. Several white soldiers confronted Paulson's superior about his behavior and demanded that he make changes.
13. Anthony Martin, interview by author, September 12, 2011.
14. Clyde Jackson, interview by author, January 8, 2012.
15. Willie L. Hamilton, "The Black Vietnam Veteran and His Problems: Fifth in a Series," *New York Amsterdam News*, February 20, 1971.
16. James Gillam, interview by author, March 14, 2008.
17. David F. Addlestone and Susan Sherer, "Battleground: Race in Vietnam," *Civil Liberties*, February 1973, 1.
18. David Addlestone, interview by author, May 3, 2018.
19. Glines, "Black VS White," 24.
20. Dennis M. Kowal to Deputy Chief of Staff Personnel and Administration, report, September 19, 1971, Staff Visits, Reference Paper Files, box 2, U.S. Forces in Southeast Asia, 1950–75, U.S. National Archives, College Park, MD (hereafter USFSEA/NACP).
21. Glines, "Black VS White," 22.
22. Ibid., 27, 21.
23. Christian G. Appy, *Working Class War: American Combat Soldiers and Vietnam* (Chapel Hill: University of North Carolina Press, 1993), 22.
24. Bonaparte, "Bias Hurts GI's," 4.
25. "Armed Forces: Democracy in the Foxhole," *Time*, May 26, 1967, https://content.time.com.
26. Alex Poinsett, "The Negro Officer: Limited Numbers Spotlight Tokenism in the Military," *Ebony*, August 1968, 137–39.
27. "Black GIs Caught in Vise," 13.
28. Sinclair Swan, interview by author, August 11, 2011. Swan was originally slated to serve with the 101st Airborne Division in Vietnam.
29. Louis Perkins, interview by author, December 17, 2011.
30. Isaac Hampton, *The Black Officer Corps: A History of Black Military Advancement from Integration through Vietnam* (New York: Routledge, 2013).
31. Ron Copes, interview by author, November 17, 2011.
32. Willie Thomas, interview by author, September 3, 2011.
33. James E. Westheider, *Fighting on Two Fronts: African Americans and the Vietnam War* (New York: New York University Press, 1997), 123–24.
34. Robert Louis Jr., interview by author, November 30, 2011.
35. Faith C. Christmas, "Mother of GI Seeks Vietnam Bias Probe," *Chicago Daily Defender*, February 26, 1969.
36. Willie L. Hamilton, "The Black Vietnam Veteran and His Problems: Fourth in a Series," *New York Amsterdam News*, February 13, 1971.
37. "The Black GI," *Black Journal*, episode 22, directed by Stan Lathan, produced by William Greaves, aired March 30, 1970, National Education Television, http://americanarchive.org.
38. Ibid.
39. Kent Garrett, interview by author, March 22, 2022.
40. Glines, "Black VS White," 26.
41. Thomas Anderson to L. Howard Bennett, briefing, November 28, 1969, Visit of Mr. Howard Bennett, Equal Opportunity Reporting File-Survey, box 1, USFSEA/NACP.

42. David I. Cooper Jr. to L. Howard Bennett, report, December 1969, Racial Literature, Race Relations Briefing for the Secretary of the Army, Fragging, box 4, USFSEA/NACP. Similar complaints were made by African American members of the 3rd Marine Expeditionary Force in Da Nang.
43. Ibid.
44. L. Howard Bennett to John S. McCain, briefing, December 6, 1969, Racial Literature, Race Relations Briefing for the Secretary of the Army, Fragging, box 4, USFSEA/NACP.
45. Jack MacFarlane to Welborn G. Dolvin, briefing, September 1970, Equal Opportunity and Racial Unrest, Equal Opportunity Reporting File-Survey, box 1, USFSEA/NACP.
46. James R. Anderson, report, December 29, 1970, Staff Visits, Reference Paper Files, box 2, USFSEA/NACP.
47. Benjamin E. Smith to Human Relations Branch, report, September 3, 1971, Staff Visits, Reference Paper Files, box 2, USFSEA/NACP.
48. "Armed Forces: Black Powerlessness," *Time*, November 29, 1971, https://content.time.com. The article states that the hearing was organized by the Democratic Black Caucus, but by this point they were known as the CBC.
49. "Black GIs Caught in Vise," 15.
50. Report, 1972, Subordinate Unit Publications, Equal Opportunity Reporting Files–MACV Publications, box 5, USFSEA/NACP.
51. Lorenzo Clark, interview by author, April 25, 2012.
52. David I. Cooper Jr. to L. Howard Bennett, report, December 1969.
53. Copes interview.
54. Wayne Smith, interview by author, October 25, 2011.
55. Hamilton, "The Black Vietnam Veteran and His Problems: Fifth in a Series."
56. David I. Cooper Jr. to L. Howard Bennett, report, December 1969.
57. Ibid.
58. James R. Anderson, report, December 29, 1970.
59. Benjamin E. Smith to Human Relations Branch, report, September 2, 1971.
60. Report, 1972, Subordinate Unit Publications.
61. "GI Justice in Vietnam: An Interview with the Lawyers Military Defense Committee," *Yale Review of Law and Social Action* 2 (1972): 34.
62. Addlestone interview.
63. "GI Justice in Vietnam," 31.
64. Ibid.
65. David I. Cooper Jr. to L. Howard Bennett, report, December 1969.
66. Jack MacFarlane to Welborn G. Dolvin, briefing, September 1970.
67. James R. Anderson, report, December 29, 1970.
68. "Black GIs Caught in Vise," 14.
69. Herald F. Stout Jr. to Roland Day, report, April 18, 1972, Racial Incidents, Equal Opportunity Reporting Files–MACV Publications, box 5, USFSEA/NACP.
70. Addlestone and Sherer, "Battleground: Race in Viet Nam," 3.
71. David Cortright, *Soldiers in Revolt: GI Resistance during the Vietnam War* (Chicago: Haymarket Books, 2005), 207.
72. "Area Army Camp Hit with Race Bias Charge," *New Pittsburgh Courier*, September 13, 1969.

73. Glines, "Black VS White," 26.
74. Jack MacFarlane to Welborn G. Dolvin, briefing, September 1970.
75. "Black Senator to Visit Vietnam to Probe Bias."
76. Cortright, *Soldiers in Revolt*, 207.
77. "Black GIs Caught in Vise," 14.
78. Mark Boulton, "How the G.I. Bill Failed African American Vietnam War Veterans," *Journal of Blacks in Higher Education*, no. 58 (Winter 2007–8): 60.
79. Cortright, *Soldiers in Revolt*, 208.
80. "Attack Raw Deal Black Veterans Get after Discharge from Army," *Jet*, October 28, 1971, 27.
81. Addlestone and Sherer, "Battleground: Race in Viet Nam," 1.
82. Addlestone interview.
83. James E. Westheider, *The African-American Experience in Vietnam: Brothers in Arms* (Lanham, MD: Rowman and Littlefield, 2008), 60–61.
84. "The Black GI."
85. David I. Cooper Jr. to L. Howard Bennett, report, December 1969.
86. Addlestone and Sherer, "Battleground: Race in Vietnam," 1.
87. Westheider, *The African-American Experience in Vietnam*, 120.
88. Ibid.
89. Addlestone interview.
90. Ibid.
91. Addlestone and Sherer, "Battleground: Race in Vietnam," 4.
92. Ibid.
93. Addlestone interview.
94. "Area Army Camp Hit with Race Bias Charge."
95. Thomas A. Johnson, "GI's in Germany: Black Is Bitter," *New York Times*, November 23, 1970.
96. Cortright, *Soldiers in Revolt*, 208.
97. "Black GIs Caught in Vise," 14.
98. Long Binh Stockade Riot, August 29–30, 1968, Vietnam Reference Files, Record Group 472, CID Report of Investigations, Records of the USARV, National Archives and Records Administration, Washington, DC.
99. David I. Cooper Jr. to L. Howard Bennett, report, December 1969.
100. Richard Moser, *The New Winter Soldier: GI And Veteran Dissent during the Vietnam Era* (New Brunswick, NJ: Rutgers University Press, 1996), 52.
101. David I. Cooper Jr. to L. Howard Bennett, report, December 1969.
102. Addlestone and Sherer, "Battleground: Race in Vietnam," 1.
103. "Black GIs Caught in Vise," 14.
104. Addlestone and Sherer, "Battleground: Race in Viet Nam," 1.
105. Long Binh Stockade Riot, August 29–30, 1968.
106. Ibid.
107. Ibid.
108. Addlestone and Sherer, "Battleground: Race in Viet Nam," 1.
109. Long Binh Stockade Riot, August 29–30, 1968. It is unclear why they were not all released.
110. Ibid.
111. Ibid.

112. Ibid.
113. Billy Jones, interview by author, May 22, 2018.
114. Appy, *Working Class War*, 283–85.
115. Addlestone interview.
116. Addlestone heard the men refer to the vial as "coke," but given the description it might have been heroin.
117. Ibid.
118. Susan Osnos, interview by author, May 21, 2018.
119. Morgan Murphy and Robert Steele, "The World Heroin Problem" (Washington, DC: U.S. Government Printing Office, 1971), 1, https://www.cia.gov.
120. Cortright, *Soldiers in Revolt*, 29–31.
121. Jeremy Kuzmarov, *The Myth of the Addicted Army: Vietnam and the Modern War on Drugs* (Amherst: University of Massachusetts, 2009).
122. Jonathan Strum, "How Long Does Heroin Stay in Your System?" The Recovery Village, https://www.therecoveryvillage.com.
123. Lee N. Robins, Darlene H. Davis, and David N. Nurco, "How Permanent Was Vietnam Drug Addiction?" *American Journal of Public Health* 64 (December 1974): 39. Heroin was the most commonly used narcotic in Vietnam. Of respondents who admitted to using narcotics, 79 percent admitted to using heroin.
124. "GI Justice in Vietnam," 40, 34.
125. Westheider, *The African American Experience in Vietnam*, 57.
126. Cortright, *Soldiers in Revolt*, 207–8.
127. Jones interview.
128. Ibid.
129. Addlestone interview.
130. Addlestone and Sherer, "Battleground: Race in Vietnam," 1.
131. "GI Justice in Vietnam," 28.
132. "High Vietnam Negro GI Death Rate Is Charged to 'Valor,'" *Philadelphia Tribune*, March 26, 1966.
133. "Negro Deaths Exceed Whites' in Viet Nam," *Pittsburgh Courier*, May 28, 1966.
134. Faith C. Christmas, "Mother of GI Seeks Probe of Bias in Viet," *Chicago Daily Defender*, February 12, 1969.
135. Report, November 18, 1970, box 2, folder 37, DCSPER/USAHEC.
136. James R. Anderson, report, December 29, 1970. This document does not say how this information was used.
137. "Armed Forces: Black Powerlessness."
138. Parks, *GI Diary*, 76–79.
139. Lamont B. Steptoe, interview by author, June 25, 2012.
140. Copes interview.
141. James R. Wilson, *Landing Zones: Southern Veterans Remember Vietnam* (Durham, NC: Duke University Press, 1990), 104.
142. Arthur Barham, interview by author, February 19, 2013.
143. George W. Ashworth, "Background Factors Send Negroes into Combat," *Christian Science Monitor*, August 31, 1967.
144. Paul Hathaway, "Negro in Viet: Not That Far from the Ghetto," *Newsday* (New York), May 15, 1968.
145. Louis interview.
146. Brian Settles, interview by author, October 1, 2012.

147. "Armed Forces: Black Powerlessness."
148. Garrett interview.
149. Westheider, *The African American Experience in Vietnam*, 46.
150. Stanley Goff and Robert Sanders with Clark Smith, *Brothers: Black Soldiers in the Nam* (Novato, CA: Presidio Press, 1982), 75–76.
151. Gillam interview. Edward Gillam was the brother of James Gillam.
152. Westheider, *The African American Experience in Vietnam*, 23.
153. Deckie McLean, "The Black Man and the Draft," *Ebony*, August 1968, 61.
154. Joshua D. Angrist, *The Draft Lottery and Voluntary Enlistment in the Vietnam Era* (Cambridge, MA: National Bureau of Economic Research, 1990), 31.
155. Westheider, *The African American Experience in Vietnam*, 23.
156. McLean, "The Black Man and the Draft," 62.
157. Graham, *The Brothers' Vietnam War*, 17.
158. Freddie Edwards, interview by author, December 2, 2011.
159. Westheider, *The African American Experience in Vietnam*, 26.
160. Lawrence M. Baskir and William A. Strauss, *Chance and Circumstance: The Draft, the War, and the Vietnam Generation* (New York: Knopf, 1978), 47.
161. Osnos interview.
162. McLean, "The Black Man and the Draft," 64.
163. Chapman, "Qualified Negro Is Found to Receive Inequitable Treatment under Draft."
164. Baskir and Strauss, *Chance and Circumstance*, 99.
165. Westheider, *The African American Experience in Vietnam*, 29.
166. Marilyn Young, *The Vietnam Wars, 1945–1990* (New York: Harper Collins, 1991), 321.
167. Lawrence Allen Eldridge, *Chronicles of a Two-Front War: Civil Rights and Vietnam in the African American Press* (Columbia: University of Missouri Press, 2011), 50.
168. Geoffrey W. Jensen, "A Parable of Persisting Failure: Project 100,000," in *Beyond the Quagmire: New Interpretations of the Vietnam War*, ed. Geoffrey W. Jensen and Matthew M. Stith (Denton: University of North Texas Press, 2019), 146–48.
169. Ibid., 145.
170. Ibid., 162.
171. Edward J. Drea, *McNamara, Clifford, and the Burdens of Vietnam, 1965–1969* (Washington, DC: Department of Defense, 2011), 269.
172. Eldridge, *Chronicles of a Two-Front War*, 50.
173. Westheider, *The African American Experience in Vietnam*, 48–49.
174. "Armed Forces: Democracy in the Foxhole."
175. Thomas A. Johnson, "The U.S. Negro in Vietnam," *New York Times*, April 29, 1968.
176. McLean, "The Black Man and the Draft," 62.
177. George W. Ashworth, "Ratio of U.S. Negro Troops Declines," *Christian Science Monitor*, May 18, 1968.
178. "Tuck Brothers Speak out against the Vietnam War," *Cleveland Call and Post*, December 2, 1967.
179. Ron Bradley, interview by author, October 23, 2011.
180. Louis interview.
181. Scott Riley, interview by author, May 7, 2022.

182. Johnson, "The U.S. Negro in Vietnam."
183. "The Black GI."
184. Appy, *Working Class War*, 22.
185. Ashworth, "Background Factors Send Negroes into Combat."
186. Chapman, "Qualified Negro Is Found to Receive Inequitable Treatment under Draft."
187. Cephus "Dusty" Rhodes, interview by author, January 19, 2012.
188. David I. Cooper Jr. to L. Howard Bennett, report, December 1969.
189. Appy, *Working Class War*, 22.
190. "Black GI Death Rate in Vietnam Cut in Half," *Jet*, September 7, 1972, 46.
191. Peter B. Levy, "Blacks and the Vietnam War," in *Legacy: Vietnam in the American Imagination*, ed. D. Michael Shaffer (Boston: Beacon Press, 1990), 212.
192. Ashworth, "Background Factors Send Negroes into Combat."
193. Hathaway, "Negro in Viet."
194. David Lorens, "Why Negroes Re-Enlist: High Re-Enlistment Is Rooted in Economics and Psychodynamics," *Ebony*, August 1968, 87–88.
195. Steptoe interview.
196. Martin interview.
197. Rhodes interview.
198. Louis interview.
199. James Lewis, interview by author, March 20, 2012.
200. Horace Coleman, interview by author, June 12, 2012.
201. Copes interview.
202. Appy, *Working Class War*, 22.
203. Johnson, "The U.S. Negro in Vietnam."
204. Lorens, "Why Negroes Re-Enlist," 88.
205. William E. Alt and Betty L. Alt, *Black Soldiers, White Wars: Black Warriors from Antiquity to the Present* (Westport, CT: Praeger, 2003), 111.
206. Eldridge, *Chronicles of a Two-Front War*, 63.
207. F. W. Norris to Chairman of the Joint Chiefs of Staff, February 18, 1967, box 2, folder 2, DCSPER/USAHEC.
208. "Negroes Dying Faster Than Whites in Vietnam," *New York Amsterdam News*, March 19, 1966.
209. "High Vietnam Negro GI Death Rate Is Charged to 'Valor.'"
210. "Negro Deaths Exceed Whites' in Viet Nam."
211. "High Vietnam Negro Death Rate Revealed," *Los Angeles Sentinel*, March 2, 1967.
212. "Negro Deaths Exceed Whites' in Viet Nam."
213. Johnson, "The U.S. Negro in Vietnam."
214. "Black GI Death Rate in Vietnam Cut in Half," 46.
215. Westheider, *The African American Experience in Vietnam*, 49.
216. Mrs. Lorenzo C. Maulden to Lyndon B. Johnson, August 25, 1966, box 8, folder 7, DCSPER/USAHEC.
217. Ibid.
218. The Vietnam Veterans Memorial: The Wall-USA, s.v., "Lorenzo Columbus Maulden," http://thewall-usa.com. According to the Vietnam Veterans Memorial Wall, Lorenzo Maulden was killed on July 26, 1966.
219. Hathaway, "Negro in Viet."

220. Gillam interview.
221. Jackson interview.
222. Perkins interview.
223. Patrick McLaughlin, interview by author, July 25, 2009.
224. Eldridge, *Chronicles of a Two-Front War*, 54.
225. Thomas A. Johnson, "State's N.A.A.C.P Opposes the War and New Charter," *New York Times*, October 23, 1967. Debate over this issue was intense with the final vote 102–72 in favor of the resolution. The national NAACP took no position on the war and generally defended Lyndon Johnson's administration.
226. Joseph L. Turner, "Do Black GI's Get Justice in the Army," *Chicago Daily Defender*, November 30, 1968.
227. "Black GI Death Rate in Vietnam Cut in Half," 46.
228. Addlestone and Sherer, "Battleground: Race in Viet Nam," 2.
229. Hathaway, "Negro in Viet."
230. Hamilton, "The Black Vietnam Veteran and His Problems: Fourth in a Series."
231. Steptoe interview. Other accounts of these rumors can be found in Goff and Sanders, *Brothers*, 12; Ed Emanuel, *Soul Patrol* (New York: Random House, 2003), 58; Eddie Wright, *Thoughts about the Vietnam War: Based on My Personal Experience, Books I Have Read and Conversations with Other Veterans* (New York: Carlton Press, 1986), 111; and Hamilton, "The Black Vietnam Veteran and His Problems: Fourth in a Series."
232. George Brummell, interview by author, October 21, 2012.
233. Rhodes interview.
234. Thomas interview.
235. Nate Mondy, interview by author, September 19, 2012.
236. Bradley interview.

CHAPTER 3: "TEARING THE SERVICES APART"

1. Long Binh Stockade Riot, August 29–30, 1968, Vietnam Reference Files, Record Group 472, CID Report of Investigations, Records of the USARV, National Archives and Records Administration, Washington, DC.
2. Ibid.
3. Ronald H. Spector, *After Tet: The Bloodiest Year in Vietnam* (New York: Free Press, 1993), 242–59. Spector is one of the few historians to discuss racial violence in any detail. This chapter provides an account of the Long Binh Riot and other incidents of racial violence.
4. Long Binh Stockade Riot, August 29–30, 1968.
5. Ibid.
6. John Darrell Sherwood, *Black Sailor, White Navy: Racial Unrest in the Fleet during the Vietnam War* (New York: New York University Press, 2007), 27.
7. Robert D. Heinl Jr., "The Collapse of the Armed Forces," *Armed Forces Journal*, June 7, 1971, 332. Heinl was a twenty-seven-year veteran of the Marine Corps who after retiring from the military in 1964 served as a military analyst for several newspapers and journals.
8. Lieutenant General Perkins to Deputy Chief of Staff, Personnel and

Administration, report, October 1971, Race Relations Briefing for the Secretary of the Army, Fragging, box 4, U.S. Forces in Southeast Asia, 1950–75, U.S. National Archives, College Park, MD (hereafter USFSEA/NACP).
9. "'Nigger' Slur Causes Racial Brawl in Vietnam," *Jet*, September 22, 1966, 27.
10. "Negro Marine Says He Fights Two Enemies in Vietnam," *Philadelphia Tribune*, September 5, 1967.
11. Edith Payne, "Vietnam Troop Integration Image Marred by Near Riots," *Philadelphia Tribune*, March 25, 1967.
12. Simeon Booker, "An American Is an American," *Jet*, June 30, 1966, 22; Ethel L. Payne, "GIs Tell How They Stand on the Viet War," *Chicago Daily Defender*, April 11, 1967.
13. Donald Mosby, "Black GIs in Viet Won't Wait for Their Freedom," *Chicago Daily Defender*, May 29, 1968.
14. Lawrence Allen Eldridge, *Chronicles of a Two-Front War: Civil Rights and Vietnam in the African American Press* (Columbia: University of Missouri Press, 2011), 89–94.
15. Wallace Terry, *Bloods: An Oral History of the Vietnam War by Black Veterans* (New York: Random House, 1984), 167.
16. James E. Westheider, *The African American Experience in Vietnam: Brothers in Arms* (Lanham, MD: Rowman and Littlefield, 2008), 133.
17. Mosby, "Black GIs in Viet Won't Wait for Their Freedom."
18. Joshua Bloom and Waldo E. Martin Jr., *Black against Empire: The History and Politics of the Black Panther Party* (Oakland: University of California Press, 2016), 32, 124, 2.
19. Wallace Terry, "Black Power in Vietnam," *Time*, September 19, 1969, https://content.time.com.
20. Kent Garrett, interview by author, March 22, 2022.
21. Wallace Terry, "Bringing the War Home," *Black Scholar* 2, no. 3 (November 1970): 17, 13. Terry did note the presence of a few members of the BPP and Ron Karenga's US movement in Vietnam, but he did not provide any evidence of a large-scale movement.
22. Bloom and Martin, *Black against Empire*, 41.
23. Ibid., 270–71, 273, 275.
24. Eldridge Cleaver, "To My Black Brothers in Vietnam," *Black Panther*, March 21, 1970, 4, 20.
25. Bloom and Martin, *Black against Empire*, 147.
26. Terry, "Black Power in Vietnam." While Terry did not elaborate, the Blackstone Rangers were a well-known Chicago street gang.
27. Richard Moser, *The New Winter Soldiers* (New Brunswick, NJ: Rutgers University Press, 1996), 58–62; David Cortright, *Soldiers in Revolt: GI Resistance during the Vietnam War* (Chicago: Haymarket Books, 2005), 42; "Black Militance Joins the Army," *Soul City Times* (Milwaukee), March 19, 1970.
28. Moser, *The New Winter Soldiers*, 59.
29. Spector, *After Tet*, 249.
30. Zalin Grant, "Whites against Blacks in Vietnam," *New Republic*, January 8, 1969, 15.
31. "Negro Soldiers Scuffle with Whites in Japan," *Jet*, April 25, 1968, 45.
32. Grant, "Whites against Blacks," 16.

33. Eugene Boyd to Clark M. Clifford, April 16, 1968, box 10, folder 11, Deputy Chief of Staff for Personnel, Policy Files on Discrimination in the Army, U.S. Army Heritage and Education Center, Carlisle Barracks, PA (hereafter DCSPER/USAHEC).
34. Eldridge, *Chronicles of a Two-Front War*, 195. Brackets in original.
35. Eddie Wright, *Thoughts about the Vietnam War: Based on My Personal Experience, Books I Have Read and Conversations with Other Veterans* (New York: Carlton Press, 1986), 95–96.
36. Spector, *After Tet*, 250–51.
37. Grant, "Whites against Blacks," 16.
38. Terry, "Black Power in Vietnam."
39. Brian H. Settles, *No Reason for Dying: A Reluctant Combat Pilot's Confession of Hypocrisy, Infidelity and War* (Charleston, SC: Booksurge, 2009), 183.
40. Bavarskis, "Vietnam Veterans Decides to Join the Black Struggle," *Norfolk [VA] Journal and Guide*, May 26, 1973.
41. Terry, *Bloods*, 167.
42. Gary Skogen, interview by author, October 6, 2012.
43. James Woods, "In Vietnam after King's Murder," *Chicago Daily News*, April 17, 1968.
44. John H. Maddox to Lieutenant Colonel Howard, May 31, 1968, box 10, folder 7, DCSPER/USAHEC.
45. Bobby L. Harris to Secretary of the Army Stanley Resor, April 15, 1968, box 10, folder 2, DCSPER/USAHEC.
46. Spector, *After Tet*, 252–53.
47. Cecil Burr Currey, *Long Binh Jail: An Oral History of Vietnam's Notorious U.S. Military Prison* (Dulles, VA: Brassey's, 1999), x.
48. Ibid., 104.
49. Billy Jones, interview by author, May 22, 2018.
50. Long Binh Stockade Riot, August 29–30, 1968.
51. Ibid.
52. Ibid.
53. Ibid.
54. Ibid.
55. Ibid.
56. Ibid.
57. Spector, *After Tet*, 254.
58. "The Forgotten History of a Prison Uprising in Vietnam," *All Things Considered*, produced by Sarah Kate Kramer and Radio Diaries, aired on August 29, 2018, NPR.
59. Scott Riley, interview by author, May 7, 2022.
60. Currey, *Long Binh Jail*, 104.
61. Long Binh Stockade Riot, August 29–30, 1968.
62. Ibid.
63. Ibid.
64. Ibid. "Hole" was another word used for the box.
65. Ibid.
66. Ibid.

67. Ibid. It is difficult to read the guard's name on the document.
68. Riley interview.
69. Ibid.
70. Ibid. The names are redacted in this document.
71. Ibid.
72. Ibid.
73. Ibid.
74. Ibid.
75. Ibid.
76. Thaddeus J. Bara to DCSPER, report, February 16, 1969, box 5, folder 35, DCSPER-USAHEC.
77. "Navy Admits Racial Flareups in Vietnam," *Pittsburgh Courier*, November 2, 1968.
78. "Black and White Soldiers Fighting Each Other 'Harder' Than Vietcong," *Philadelphia Tribune*, November 23, 1968.
79. Grant, "Whites against Blacks," 15. The guard may have been accidentally killed by another Black serviceman.
80. Report, September 19, 1969, Blue Bell Report Regarding Incidents in Vietnam, Korea, Okinawa, Hawaii, Japan and Thailand from January 1 to September 18, 1969, box 2, DCSPER/USAHEC. Other racial incidents occurred on May 26 at Camp Hochmuth, July 19 at Long Binh, and July 31 in Qui Nhon.
81. Terry, "Black Power in Vietnam."
82. Walter T. Kerwin to Vice Chief of Staff of the Army, October 22, 1970, box 22, folder 25, DCSPER/USAHEC.
83. Report, April 1971, Provost Marshal Report on Serious Incident Reports with Racial Overtones, MACV Publications, box 3, USFSEA/NACP.
84. George S. Bowman Jr. to Military Assistance Command, Vietnam, report, January 18, 1970, Equal Opportunity Reporting File: Council Meetings, box 1, USFSEA/NACP. An unrelated incident, in which six African Americans attacked two white soldiers, occurred on December 11.
85. Sherwood, *Black Sailor, White Navy*, 28.
86. David Addlestone, interview by author, May 3, 2018.
87. Report, April 16, 1971, Provost Marshal Report on Serious Incident Reports with Racial Overtones, MACV Publications, box 3, USFSEA/NACP; Report, 1971, Race Relations Briefing for the Secretary of the Army, Fragging, box 4, USFSEA/NACP.
88. "'Black Power' Activity Described in Vietnam," *Norfolk Journal and Guide*, January 23, 1971.
89. Report, 1971.
90. Lieutenant General Perkins to Deputy Chief of Staff, Personnel and Administration, report, October 1971.
91. Report, April 16, 1971. Harger was stabbed on January 2 and 9, 1971.
92. David F. Addlestone and Susan Sherer, "Battleground: Race in Vietnam," *Civil Liberties*, February 1973, 4.
93. Report, April 16, 1971.
94. Report, 1971.
95. "Riot among Americans in Vietnam Shuts Clubs," *Norfolk Journal and Guide*, January 16, 1971.
96. Report, April 16, 1971.

97. Report, 1971.
98. Report, April 16, 1971.
99. Report, September 22, 1970, box 2, folder 21, DCSPER/USAHEC.
100. Addlestone and Sherer, "Battleground: Race in Vietnam," 4. The LMDC defended the shooter, James Moyler, in court.
101. Report, April 16, 1971. Other less serious assaults were reported at An Khe on October 4 and November 6, 1970.
102. Report, 1971; Report, April 16, 1971.
103. Report, April 16, 1971. This was not the first racial incident at Tuy Hoa as there were other reports of violence on November 27, 1970, and January 29, 1971.
104. Report, 1971.
105. Harold Phillips to Commanding General, report, September 11, 1971, Reference Paper Files, box 2, USFSEA/NACP. The assault on February 20 was just one of many assaults that occurred between February 14 and February 20.
106. Report, April 16, 1971. Some or all of these incidents likely involved the same people.
107. Ibid.
108. Report, October 1970, box 2, folder 28, DCSPER/USAHEC.
109. Report, December 1970, Race Relations Briefing for the Secretary of the Army, Fragging, box 4, USFSEA/NACP.
110. Report, April 16, 1971. There were other incidents of racial violence at Long Binh on January 19, February 16, and March 18, 1971.
111. "GIs Jailed on Mutiny Charges in Vietnam Wanted to Attend Memorial," *Jet*, November 4, 1971, 31; Moser, *The New Winter Soldiers*, 61–62. Charges were later dropped.
112. Dale E. Patrick to Commander in Chief, United States Army Pacific, April 16, 1970, Racial Literature, Race Relations Briefing for the Secretary of the Army, box 4, USFSEA/NACP.
113. Larry Delorne to Hugh Scott, February 18, 1970, Racial Literature, Race Relations Briefing for the Secretary of the Army, box 4, USFSEA/NACP.
114. Ibid.
115. Report, April 13, 1970, box 2, folder 18, DCSPER/USAHEC; Report, April 16, 1971; Report, 1971.
116. George Lepre, *Fragging: Why U.S. Soldiers Assaulted Their Officers in Vietnam* (Lubbock: Texas Tech Press, 2011), 102.
117. Dennis M. Kowal to Provost Marshal, report, March 1971, Provost Marshal Report on Serious Incident Reports with Racial Overtones, MACV Publications, box 3, USFSEA/NACP.
118. Colin Powell, *My American Journey* (New York: Random House, 1995), 133.
119. Bruce Crawford, interview by author, December 4, 2011.
120. Cortright, *Soldiers in Revolt*, 47.
121. "South Viet Nam: The War within the War," *Time*, January 25, 1971, https://content.time.com.
122. Ben Cloud, interview by author, September 16, 2017.
123. Nate Mondy, interview by author, September 19, 2012.
124. Ibid.; George C. Wilson, "Navy Mobilizing for Racial Reforms," *Washington Post*, November 5, 1972.

125. "Kitty Hawk Crew Describes Racial Battle Aboard Ship," *Washington Post*, November 24, 1972.
126. Cloud interview.
127. Mondy interview.
128. Wilson, "Navy Mobilizing for Racial Reforms."
129. Cloud interview.
130. David Almond, *A Sailor's Story: In Black and White Battle for Kitty Hawk* (Maitland, FL: Xulon Press, 2013).
131. "Kitty Hawk Crew Describes Racial Battle Aboard Ship."
132. Cloud interview.
133. Wilson, "Navy Mobilizing for Racial Reforms."
134. Henry P. Liefermann, "A Sort of Mutiny: The Constellation Incident," *New York Times*, February 18, 1973.
135. Dalinda Johnson to Bob Mathias, December 26, 1969, box 11, folder 3, DCSPER/USAHEC.
136. Anthony Zinni, interview by author, June 22, 2011. Zinni would later become a four-star general in the Marine Corps and the commander in chief of U.S. Central Command.
137. Michael Hagee, interview by author, June 16, 2011. Hagee would later become a four-star general and the commandant of the U.S. Marine Corps.
138. Mr. and Mrs. Rannie Bowen to President Lyndon Johnson, July 16, 1968, box 17, folder 3, DCSPER/USAHEC.
139. Report, August 1970, box 2, folder 19, DCSPER/USAHEC.
140. Thomas A. Johnson, "GI's in Germany: Black Is Bitter," *New York Times*, November 23, 1970.
141. Thomas A. Johnson, "'I'll Bleed for Myself,' Says Black U.S. Soldier in Europe," *New York Times*, October 11, 1970.
142. Bob Steck, interview by author, November 30, 2011.
143. Royal Brightball, "Society Blamed in Race Friction on Marine Base," *Chicago Daily Defender*, August 19, 1969.
144. "Marine Race Clash Coming?" *Chicago Daily Defender*, September 23, 1969.
145. Report, April 1971.
146. Liefermann, "A Sort of Mutiny."
147. Cloud interview.
148. Ibid.
149. Mondy interview.
150. "Navy Admits Racial Flareups in Vietnam."
151. F. W. Oseth to Deputy Chief of Staff for Personnel, report, 1970, box 29, folder 1, DCSPER/USAHEC.
152. Report, August 29, 1969, box 28, folder 4, DCSPER/USAHEC.
153. Johnson, "GI's in Germany: Black Is Bitter."
154. Thomas A. Johnson, "Blacks Don't Feel They Get a Fair Shake," *New York Times*, November 29, 1970.
155. Jones interview.
156. Ray Morrissette to "Mother," January 14, 1968, box 9, folder 27, DCSPER/USAHEC.
157. Edward Bautz Jr. to J. L. LeFlore, January 1968, box 9, folder 27, DCSPER/USAHEC.

158. "In the Wake of Fatal Melee: Say Marines Knew of Race Ills," *Chicago Daily Defender*, August 12, 1969.
159. "Text of Camp Lejeune Committee's Report to Commanding General," *New York Times*, August 10, 1969.
160. "Black Marines Get Ok for Afros, 'New Salute,'" *Chicago Daily Defender*, September 4, 1969.
161. James J. Ursano, report, January 7, 1971, Reference Paper Files, Stockade Project, box 2, USFSEA/NACP.
162. David I. Cooper Jr. to L. Howard Bennett, report, December 1969, Racial Literature, Race Relations Briefing for the Secretary of the Army, Fragging, box 4, USFSEA/NACP.
163. Ibid.
164. Westheider, *The African American Experience in Vietnam*, 101. One can assume that the DOD made these changes because they felt pressured to do so or because they came to believe that complaints concerning military justice issues had merit.
165. "Black GIs Caught in Vise," *Jet*, December 2, 1971, 15–16.
166. Morris J. MacGregor Jr., *Integration of the Armed Forces, 1940–1965* (Washington, DC: Center of Military History, 1981), 559.
167. Karl Marlantes, interview by author, September 24, 2012.
168. Steck interview.
169. Constance Edwards, interview by author, June 27, 2022.
170. J. L Richardson to Hy Silverman, April 29, 1965, box 6, folder 30, DCSPER/USAHEC.
171. Curtis Daniell, "Germany Trouble Spot for Black GI's," *Ebony*, August 1968, 126.
172. Jerry Boyd to Louis Stokes, September 10, 1970, box 11, folder 11, DCSPER/USAHEC.
173. Robert A. Little to Chief of Staff, memorandum, October 6, 1969, box 29, folder 19, DCSPER/USAHEC.
174. Zinni interview.
175. Ibid.
176. Westheider, *The African American Experience in Vietnam*, 56, 83.
177. "GIs in Vietnam Ask Jet for Help against Bigotry," *Jet*, December 12, 1968, 54.
178. "Black Marines Get Ok for Afros." Chapman never actually used the word "dapping" or a Black power salute but it is clear that was what he was referencing.
179. Addlestone interview.
180. Paul J. Bailey, report, November 27, 1972, Equal Opportunity Reporting Files, Staff Visits, box 5, USFSEA/NACP.
181. "The Black GI," *Black Journal*, episode 22, directed by Stan Lathan, produced by William Greaves, aired March 30, 1970, National Education Television, http://americanarchive.org.
182. Ibid.
183. Ibid. It was not uncommon for African Americans to refer to whites as "the beast." Sylvester Bracey claimed they were called this "because they act savage and barbarous like animals." *Black Journal* did not identify Bracey by name. However, his family identified him after viewing the episode. Isoke Samuel, "Old Footage of Vietnam Vet Surprises His Family When It Goes Viral," NBC News, August 14, 2020, www.nbcnews.com.

184. Ibid.
185. Ibid.
186. Ibid.
187. Garrett interview.
188. "The Black GI."
189. Ibid.
190. Ibid.
191. Robert Vonner, interview by author, March 15, 2008.
192. Richard F. Ward, report, December 1971, Reference Paper Files, Stockade Project, box 2, USFSEA/NACP.
193. Major Pace, report, November 20, 1970, Alcohol and Drug Abuse Prevention and Control Plan, Racial Unrest, box 2, USFSEA/NACP.
194. Ibid.
195. Leonard H. Carter to Robert S. McNamara, January 31, 1968, box 31, folder 3, DCSPER/USAHEC.
196. Winant Sidle to Deputy Chief of Staff for Personnel, July 30, 1970, box 31, folder 11, DCSPER/USAHEC.
197. Ibid.
198. Jack MacFarlane to Welborn G. Dolvin, briefing, September 1970, Equal Opportunity and Racial Unrest, Equal Opportunity Reporting File-Survey, box 1, USFSEA/NACP.
199. Major Pace, report, January 6, 1971, Alcohol and Drug Abuse Prevention and Control Plan, Racial Unrest, box 2, USFSEA/NACP.
200. Report, April 16, 1971.
201. Moser, *The New Winter Soldiers*, 59–60.
202. James J. Ursano to Richard F. Ward, report, June 15, 1971, Alcohol and Drug Abuse Prevention and Control Plan, Stockade Project, box 2, USFSEA/NACP.
203. Major Pace, report, January 6, 1971. Between November 1970 and January 1971 large groups of African Americans met in Long Binh eleven different times.
204. Report, 1971.
205. Major Pace, report, January 6, 1971.
206. Ibid.
207. Jones interview.
208. "The Black GI."
209. Garrett interview.
210. "The Black GI."
211. Ibid.
212. Thomas A. Johnson, "Pentagon and Racism: Directive Stems from Tensions That Have Plagued Services for 3 Years," *New York Times*, March 6, 1971.
213. Richard F. Ward, report, December 1971.
214. Johnson, "Pentagon and Racism."
215. Liefermann, "A Sort of Mutiny."
216. Wilson, "Navy Mobilizing for Racial Reforms."
217. Liefermann, "A Sort of Mutiny."
218. Ibid.
219. Paul J. Bailey, report, November 27, 1972.

220. "Fort Carson's Racial Harmony Council: Ethnic Groups at Army Post Are 'Keeping It Together.'" *Commanders Digest*, May 18, 1972, 6–7.
221. Wes Geary, interview by author, August 7, 2009.
222. "Fort Carson's Racial Harmony Council," 6.
223. Geary interview.
224. *Kerner Commission: The National Advisory Commission on Civil Disorders* (Princeton, NJ: Princeton University Press, 2016), 1.

CHAPTER 4: "I THOUGHT OF MY OWN PEOPLE BACK HOME"

1. *No Vietnamese Ever Called Me Nigger* (video), 1968, https://www.youtube.com.
2. Ibid.
3. Ibid.
4. Christian G. Appy, *Working Class War: American Combat Soldiers and Vietnam* (Chapel Hill: University of North Carolina Press, 1993), 22.
5. Wallace Terry, *Bloods: An Oral History of the Vietnam War by Black Veterans* (New York: Random House, 1984), 264–65.
6. Ethel L. Payne, "GIs Tell How They Stand on the Viet War," *Chicago Daily Defender*, April 11, 1967.
7. Byron F. Fiman, Jonathan F. Borus, and M. Duncan Stanton, "Black-White and American-Vietnamese Relations among Soldiers in Vietnam," *Journal of Social Issues* 31, no. 4 (Fall 1975): 42, 47.
8. Arthur Egendorf et al., *Legacies of Vietnam: Comparative of Vietnam Veterans and Their Peers* (Washington, DC: U.S. Government Printing Office, 1981), 392.
9. Gerard J. Degroot, *A Noble Cause? America and the Vietnam War* (New York: Pearson Education, 2000), 83.
10. Albert French, *Patches of Fire: A Story of War and Redemption* (New York: Doubleday, 1997), 18.
11. Anthony Martin, interview by author, September 12, 2011.
12. Robert E. Vadas, *Cultures in Conflict: The Vietnam War* (Westport, CT: Greenwood Press, 2002), 99.
13. James Gillam, interview by author, March 14, 2008.
14. Horace Coleman, interview by author, June 12, 2012.
15. Edward Doyle et al., *A Collision of Cultures: The Americans in Vietnam, 1954–1973* (Boston: Boston Publishing, 1984), 27, 29.
16. Martin interview.
17. Appy, *Working Class War*, 106–7.
18. Peter S. Kindsvatter, *American Soldiers: Ground Combat in the World Wars, Korea and Vietnam* (Lawrence: University Press of Kansas, 2003), 194.
19. Appy, *Working Class War*, 106.
20. Robert Louis Jr., interview by author, November 30, 2011.
21. Terry, *Bloods*, 90.
22. Arthur Barham, interview by author, February 19, 2013.
23. Doyle et al., *A Collision of Cultures*, 29.
24. Wayne Smith, interview by author, October 25, 2011.
25. Lamont B. Steptoe, interview by author, June 25, 2012.

26. Gillam interview.
27. Freddie Edwards, interview by author, December 2, 2011.
28. John W. Dower, *War without Mercy: Race and Power in the Pacific War* (New York: Pantheon Books, 1986), 11.
29. Kindsvatter, *American Soldiers*, 193.
30. Louis interview.
31. Appy, *Working Class War*, 288.
32. Ibid., 289.
33. Doyle et al., *A Collision of Cultures*, 77–78.
34. Appy, *Working Class War*, 289.
35. David Parks, *GI Diary* (Washington, DC: Howard University Press, 1984), 49.
36. Coleman interview.
37. James Daly, *Black Prisoner of War: A Conscientious Objector's Vietnam Memoir* (Lawrence: University Press of Kansas, 2000), 52, 70–71. This is not the same James Daly that appeared in *No Vietnamese Ever Called Me Nigger*.
38. Samuel Vance, *The Courageous and Proud* (New York: Norton, 1979), 159.
39. Louis interview.
40. George Hicks, interview by author, April 28, 2012.
41. Terry, *Bloods*, 83–84.
42. Appy, *Working Class War*, 291.
43. Martin interview.
44. Barham interview.
45. Louis interview.
46. Bernard McClusky, interview by author, May 18, 2022.
47. Brian H. Settles, *No Reason for Dying: A Reluctant Combat Pilot's Confession of Hypocrisy, Infidelity and War* (Charleston, SC: Booksurge, 2009), 286, 176.
48. Steptoe interview.
49. Coleman interview
50. Louis Perkins, interview by author, December 17, 2011.
51. Smith interview.
52. Edwards interview.
53. James J. Ursano to Richard F. Ward, report, March 29, 1971, Reference Paper Files, Stockade Project, box 2, U.S. Forces in Southeast Asia, 1950–75, U.S. National Archives, College Park, MD (hereafter USFSEA/NACP).
54. A. J. Bowley to Lieutenant Colonel Randall, June 6, 1972, Equal Opportunity Reporting Files, MACV Publications, box 5, USFSEA/NACP.
55. Sinclair Swan, interview by author, August 11, 2011.
56. McClusky interview.
57. Ed Emanuel, *Soul Patrol* (New York: Random House, 2003), 130.
58. Kent Garrett, interview by author, March 22, 2022.
59. Parks, *GI Diary*, 31.
60. Vadas, *Cultures in Combat*, 99.
61. Richard A. Guidry, *The War in I Corps* (Raleigh, NC: Ivy Books, 1997), 21.
62. Ibid., 37.
63. Ron Bradley, interview by author, October 23, 2011.
64. Smith interview.
65. Ibid.

66. Ron Copes, interview by author, November 17, 2011.
67. Appy, *Working Class War*, 290–94.
68. William Thomas Allison, *Military Justice in Vietnam: The Rule of Law in an American War* (Lawrence: University Press of Kansas, 2007), 85–86.
69. Terry, *Bloods*, 23.
70. Louis interview.
71. James R. Wilson, *Landing Zones: Southern Veterans Remember Vietnam* (Durham, NC: Duke University Press, 1990), 106.
72. Terry, *Bloods*, 265.
73. Steptoe interview.
74. Terry, *Bloods*, 207.
75. Parks, *GI Diary*, 71. African Americans were called souls by fellow Black servicemen and even the Vietnamese.
76. Terry, *Bloods*, 81–83.
77. Michael Sallah and Mitch Weiss, *Tiger Force: A True Story of Men and War* (New York: Little, Brown, 2006); Deborah Nelson, *The War behind Me: Vietnam Veterans Confront the Truth about U.S. War Crimes* (New York: Basic Books, 2008); Nick Turse, *Kill Everything That Moves: The Real American War in Vietnam* (London: Picador, 2013).
78. David Addlestone, interview by author, May 3, 2018.
79. Martin interview.
80. Parks, *GI Diary*, 110. Parks did not outright say that the accused rapists were white, but he always identified Black soldiers as such, suggesting strongly they were.
81. Terry, *Bloods*, 265, 27, 82, 206.
82. James Lewis, interview by author, March 20, 2012.
83. Settles, *No Reason for Dying*, 179, 181–82.
84. Terry, *Bloods*, 82–83, 26.
85. Stanley Goff and Robert Sanders with Clark Smith, *Brothers: Black Soldiers in the Nam* (Novato, CA: Presidio Press, 1982), 157. Although Sanders believed that the soldiers were wrong in killing the elderly man, he did not report the incident to authorities.
86. McArthur Moore, interview by Terry L. Birdwhistell, June 25, 1985, 21–22, University of Kentucky Libraries Vietnam Veterans in Kentucky Oral History Project, King Library, Lexington.
87. Daly, *Black Prisoner of War*, 52.
88. Terry, *Bloods*, 209.
89. Smith interview.
90. Terry, *Bloods*, 65–68.
91. Ibid., 80.
92. Ibid., 80–81.
93. Ibid.
94. Tom Chance, "'Mr. Mountain': U.S. Navyman Fights His Own Very Special War," *Ebony*, January 1969, 61.
95. Ibid., 59–61. It is not entirely clear if Page relied on an interpreter or if he spoke Vietnamese to the villagers.
96. Terry, *Bloods*, 67. It is unclear if these conversations occurred in English or Vietnamese. The young men in Hoi An whom Benton knew were middle-class and educated. They may have spoken English.

97. Ibid., 43.
98. Guidry, *The War in I Corps*, 98.
99. Ibid., 98–100.
100. Martin interview.
101. "Disneyland East," *Time*, Friday, May 6, 1966, https://content.time.com.
102. Terry, *Bloods*, 25.
103. Heather Marie Stur, *Beyond Combat: Women and Gender in the Vietnam Era* (New York: Cambridge University Press, 2012), 163,
104. Smith interview
105. Steptoe interview.
106. Stur, *Beyond Combat*, 167.
107. Terry, *Bloods*, 25.
108. James E. Westheider, *The African American Experience in Vietnam: Brothers in Arms* (Lanham, MD: Rowman and Littlefield, 2007), 77.
109. Terry, *Bloods*, 210.
110. Smith interview.
111. Settles, *No Reason for Dying*, 279, 284, 286. Both Dao and Bong spoke English.
112. Steptoe interview.
113. Terry, *Bloods*, 211.
114. Goff and Sanders, *Brothers*, 203.
115. Willie Thomas, interview by author, September 3, 2011.
116. Scott Riley, interview by author, May 7, 2022.
117. Doyle et al., *A Collision of Cultures*, 38.
118. Judy Klemesrud, "Vietnamese War Brides: Happiness Mixed with Pain," *New York Times*, September 13, 1971.
119. Lance Woodruff, "Many Vietnam Infants Fathered by Negro GI's Left Abandoned," *Philadelphia Tribune*, December 26, 1967.
120. Doyle et al., *A Collision of Cultures*, 38. It is unknown how many of these marriages involved African Americans.
121. Terry, *Bloods*, 84.
122. Anne Keegan, "Children of Vietnam Find Few Fathers at U.S. Doors," *Chicago Tribune*, May 13, 1987.
123. Robert S. McKelvey, *The Dust of Life: America's Children Abandoned in Vietnam* (Seattle: University of Washington Press, 1999), 45.
124. "Brown Babies Plentiful in Vietnam's War Zone," *Philadelphia Tribune*, December 31, 1966.
125. Lance Woodfruff, "Many Vietnam Infants Fathered by Negro GI's Left Abandoned," *Philadelphia Tribune*, December 26, 1967.
126. George Todd, "What about These Black Babies Left in Vietnam?" *New York Amsterdam News*, June 2, 1973.
127. Era Bell Thompson, "The Plight of Black Babies in South Vietnam," *Ebony*, December 1972, 107.
128. "Adopted by Family in U.S., Vietnamese Beauty Now Searches for Her Father, a Black Vietnam War GI," *Jet*, October 11, 1999, 36.
129. Terry, *Bloods*, 85. Holloman's first child died in infancy. He later remarried but remained committed to getting Saly and his son out of Vietnam.

130. "And Now a Domestic Baby Lift," *Ebony*, June 1975, 134.
131. "Many Illegitimate Children Stay in Vietnam as GI Fathers Leave," *Hartford Courant*, November 9, 1972.
132. Ibid. More information on these matters can be found in Thompson, "The Plight of Black Babies," and "Orphans of the Storm," *Chicago Daily Defender*, June 25, 1973.
133. Louis interview.
134. Ibid.
135. Terry, *Bloods*, 2–3.
136. Ibid., 14. It is unclear how many civilians were actually killed at Cam Ne.
137. Terry Whitmore, *Memphis, Nam, Sweden: The Story of a Black Deserter* (Jackson: University of Mississippi Press, 1997), 62.
138. Eddie Wright, *Thoughts about the Vietnam War: Based on My Personal Experience, Books I Have Read and Conversations with Other Veterans* (New York: Carlton Press, 1986), 94.
139. Wes Geary, interview by author, August 7, 2009.
140. Terry, *Bloods*, 265.
141. Ibid., 40.
142. Bradley interview.
143. Bavarskis, "Vietnam Veteran Decides to Join the Black Struggle," *Norfolk [VA] Journal and Guide*, May 26, 1973.
144. Dale E. Patrick to Commander in Chief, United States Army Pacific, April 16, 1970, Racial Literature, Race Relations Briefing for the Secretary of the Army, box 4, USFSEA/NACP.
145. Appy, *Working Class War*, 225.
146. Coleman interview.
147. Terry, *Bloods*, 26.
148. Ibid., 93.
149. Whitmore, *Memphis, Nam, Sweden*, 62.
150. Parks, *GI Diary*, 110–11.
151. Nelson, *The War behind Me*, 126.
152. Michael Bilton and Kevin Sim, *Four Hours in My Lai* (New York: Penguin Books, 1993), 3, 7. The My Lai Massacre took place on March 16, 1968, when members of the 11th Light Infantry Brigade of the 23rd Infantry Division entered an undefended village on the coast of central Vietnam. Over a roughly four-hour period, they murdered upwards of five hundred old men, women, and children.
153. Coleman interview.
154. Whitmore, *Memphis, Nam, Sweden*, 62.
155. Parks, *GI Diary*, 111. Parks fell asleep while waiting for local police to come and identify the man. He was jarred awake by the sound of Jones shooting the man.
156. Martin interview.
157. Bilton and Sim, *Four Hours*, 134, 122, 79, 299.
158. Ibid., 111, 123.
159. Ibid., 49, 62.
160. Ibid., 112, 19, 117, 161. Helicopter pilot Hugh Thompson immediately reported the massacre to officials.

161. Nelson, *The War behind Me*, 82, 75–78.
162. Ibid., 80–81.
163. Riley interview.

CHAPTER 5: "YOU AND ME—SAME SAME" AND "THEY CALL ME 'MONKEY'"

1. *No Vietnamese Ever Called Me Nigger* (video), 1968, https://www.youtube.com.
2. Ibid.
3. Christian G. Appy, *Working Class War: American Combat Soldiers and Vietnam* (Chapel Hill: University of North Carolina Press, 1993), 288–89. Civilians are defined as noncombatant civilians of no confirmed political affiliation. African Americans interacted with civilian supporters of the NLF, better known as the Viet Cong, but unless otherwise noted, political opinions were unknown and assumptions cannot be made about their views on American intervention.
4. Members of the middle class, academics, politicians, and higher-ranking military officials were more likely to know something about American race relations, but most servicemen had little, if any, interactions with these groups.
5. Skin color and race are not necessarily the same thing, but African Americans viewed their skin color and racial background as intrinsically linked. They carried this viewpoint with them to Vietnam.
6. Dan Day, "Call-Post Correspondent Reports from War-Torn Vietnam: Negro GI's 'Not Angry; Just Confused,'" *Cleveland Call and Post*, January 2, 1965.
7. John Randolph, "Integration Needs Viet Approach, Negro Says: Leader Impressed by Teamwork Found among U.S. Troops on Visit to Saigon," *Los Angeles Times*, July 24, 1966.
8. Ethel L. Payne, "GIs Tell How They Stand on the Viet War," *Chicago Daily Defender*, April 11, 1967.
9. "Mother Seeks More Info on Son Slain in Vietnam," *Jet*, April 3, 1969, 25.
10. Anthony Martin, interview by author, September 12, 2011.
11. Eddie Wright, *Thoughts about the Vietnam War: Based on My Personal Experience, Books I Have Read and Conversations with Other Veterans* (New York: Carlton Press, 1986), 94. "Mamasan" and "Papasan" were colloquial terms used by servicemen when referring to older women and men.
12. Louis Perkins, interview by author, December 17, 2011.
13. Simeon Booker, "Negroes in Vietnam: 'We Too, Are Americans,'" *Ebony*, November 1965, 89.
14. Wallace Terry, *Bloods: An Oral History of the Vietnam War by Black Veterans* (New York: Random House, 1984), 84.
15. James Lewis, interview by author, March 20, 2012.
16. Terry, *Bloods*, 25.
17. *No Vietnamese Ever Called Me Nigger*.
18. Dave Dubose, "Combat Knows No Color," *Vietnam*, December 1990, 20, 22.
19. Thomas Brannon, interview by author, December 6, 2011.
20. Wayne Smith, interview by author, October 25, 2011.
21. Wright, *Thoughts about the Vietnam War*, 68.
22. Bernard McClusky, interview by author, May 18, 2022.

23. Ron Bradley, interview by author, October 23, 2011.
24. Melvin Adams, interview by author, March 14, 2012.
25. Brian Settles, interview by author, October 1, 2012.
26. "Viet Cong Put Bounty on Yank but Villagers Snub Big Offer," *Chicago Tribune*, December 16, 1967.
27. Terry, *Bloods*, 208, 68.
28. Wright, *Thoughts about the Vietnam War*, 120.
29. Lee Ewing, interview by Pat McClain, n.d., 5, Veterans History Project, Library of Congress, Washington, DC. Civilians certainly helped or provided information to white servicemen as well.
30. Clyde Jackson, interview by author, January 8, 2012.
31. "GI's in Vietnam Have Their Say on L.A. Riot," *Jet*, September 2, 1965, 60.
32. Lamont B. Steptoe, interview by author, June 25, 2012.
33. Bradley interview.
34. Ron Copes, interview by author, November 17, 2011.
35. Thomas A. Johnson, "The Negro in Vietnam: An Opportunity to Win the Career Man's Reward," *Globe and Mail* (Toronto), April 30, 1968.
36. Nu-Anh Tran, "South Vietnamese Identity, American Intervention, and the Newspaper Chinh Luan, 1965–1969," *Journal of Vietnamese Studies* 1, nos. 1–2 (2006): 170.
37. Ibid., 186–94.
38. Shawn McHale, "Understanding the Fanatic Mind? The Viet Minh and Race Hatred in the First Indochina War (1945–1954)," *Journal of Vietnamese Studies* 4, no. 3 (Fall 2009): 122, 98–100.
39. David L. Anderson, *The Vietnam War* (New York: Palgrave Macmillan, 2005), 2.
40. Verne Bowers and Francis J. Kelly, *Vietnam Studies: U.S. Army Special Forces, 1961–1971* (Washington, DC: Department of the Army, 1973), 30–31.
41. Donald Mosby, "Young and Old Vietnamese Wish Black GIs Would Leave Country," *Chicago Daily Defender*, May 21, 1968.
42. Donald Mosby, "Woman Reporter Tells of Race Hate in Viet: Mrs. Williams Irked by Bias in War Area," *Chicago Daily Defender*, June 5, 1968.
43. Ibid.
44. George Ashworth, "GI Integration Meets Battle Test: Race Held Unimportant," *Christian Science Monitor*, August 23, 1967.
45. Arthur Barham, interview by author, February 19, 2013.
46. James Gillam, interview by author, March 14, 2008.
47. Terry, *Bloods*, 84.
48. Report, 1972, Subordinate Unit Publications, Equal Opportunity Reporting Files–MACV Publications, box 5, U.S. Forces in Southeast Asia, 1950–75, U.S. National Archives, College Park, MD (hereafter USFSEA/NACP).
49. Gillam interview.
50. Terry, *Bloods*, 40.
51. Thomas A. Johnson, "The U.S. Negro in Vietnam," *New York Times*, April 29, 1968.
52. Smith interview.
53. Scott Riley, interview by author, May 7, 2022.
54. Horace Coleman, interview by author, June 12, 2012.
55. Major Pace, report, January 6, 1971, Alcohol and Drug Abuse Prevention and Control Plan, Racial Unrest, box 2, USFSEA/NACP.

56. "Black Soldier Tells of Treatment in Vietnam," *Cleveland Call and Post*, August 10, 1968.
57. Smith interview.
58. Tom Chance, "'Mr. Mountain': U.S. Navyman Fights His Own Very Special War," *Ebony*, January 1969, 61.
59. "A Racist South Vietnamese Wants Negroes Out," *Jet*, March 3, 1966, 5.
60. Mosby, "Woman Reporter Tells of Race Hate in Viet," 10.
61. Mosby, "Young and Old Vietnamese," 5.
62. Ibid.
63. Donald Mosby, "Mosby Meets Anti-Negro Hate: What's This? Jim Crow Found in Saigon Brothels," *Pittsburgh Courier*, May 18, 1968.
64. Bob Lucas, "'Jim Crow at Home': Added Foe for GI's," *Los Angeles Sentinel*, June 30, 1966.
65. Smith interview.
66. Steptoe interview.
67. Barham interview.
68. Mosby, "Young and Old Vietnamese," 5.
69. Mosby, "Woman Reporter Tells of Race Hate in Viet," 10.
70. Lance Woodruff, "Many Vietnam Infants Fathered by Negro GI's Left Abandoned," *Philadelphia Tribune*, December 26, 1967.
71. "Many Illegitimate Children Stay in Vietnam as GI Fathers Leave," *Hartford Courant*, November 9, 1972.
72. Era Bell Thompson, "The Plight of Black Babies in South Vietnam," *Ebony*, December 1972, 108.
73. David I. Cooper Jr. to L. Howard Bennett, report, December 1969, Racial Literature, Race Relations Briefing for the Secretary of the Army, Fragging, box 4, USFSEA/NACP.
74. E. L. Barnard to Commanding General, report, April 12, 1971, Race Relations Survey, Provost Marshal Report on Serious Incident Reports with Racial Overtones, box 3, USFSEA/NACP. This is one of the few documents that provides information on how officials responded to these sorts of accusations.
75. Herald F. Stout Jr. to Roland Day, report, April 18, 1972, Racial Incidents, Equal Opportunity Reporting Files–MACV Publications, box 5, USFSEA/NACP. These documents do not contain a response from the Office of the Secretary of Defense.
76. "Ebony Helps Abroad," *Ebony*, November 1962, 22.
77. Dan Day, "Dan Day Interviews Negro GI's in Viet Nam," *Cleveland Call and Post*, January 9, 1965.
78. Faith C. Christmas, "Sons Fighting in Vietnam: Mothers Ask GI Bias Probe," *Chicago Daily Defender*, April 12, 1969.
79. Willie Thomas, interview by author, September 3, 2011.
80. Riley interview.
81. Steptoe interview.
82. Barham interview.
83. Bradley interview.
84. Constance Edwards, interview by author, June 27, 2022.
85. Thomas interview.
86. George Brummell, interview by author, October 21, 2011.

87. Ethel L. Payne, "Navy Plays Down Racial Bias in Vietnam," *New Pittsburgh Courier*, May 25, 1968.
88. Willie McCarthy to Abraham Ribicoff, May 25, 1968, Complaint Regarding Alleged Racial Discrimination in Vietnam, Submitted by Senator Abe Ribicoff on Behalf of Willie McCarthy, box 5, folder 5, Deputy Chief of Staff for Personnel, Policy Files on Discrimination in the Army, U.S. Army Heritage and Education Center, Carlisle Barracks, PA (hereafter DCSPER/USAHEC). Many Vietnamese interpreted the American colloquial phrase "You are number one" to mean that calling a person anything less than one must be an insult, hence the phrase "you are number ten."
89. "The Black GI," *Black Journal*, episode 22, directed by Stan Lathan, produced by William Greaves, aired March 30, 1970, National Education Television, http://americanarchive.org.
90. Ibid.
91. Ibid.
92. Kent Garrett, interview by author, March 22, 2022.
93. Copes interview.
94. Maria Hohn, *GIs and Frauleins: The German-American Encounter in 1950s West Germany* (Chapel Hill: University of North Carolina Press, 2002), 208–11; Brummell interview; Robert Louis Jr., interview by author, November 30, 2011; James Johnson to Unknown, September 19, 1966, box 8, folder 10, DCSPER/USAHEC.
95. Willie L. Hamilton, "The Black Vietnam Veteran and His Problems: Fifth in a Series," *New York Amsterdam News*, February 20, 1971.
96. Mosby, "Young and Old Vietnamese," 5.
97. L. Howard Bennett to Jack Wagstaff, briefing, December 4, 1969, Racial Literature, Race Relations Briefing for the Secretary of the Army, Fragging, box 4, USFSEA/NACP. Admiral John S. McCain was the father of the now deceased senator John McCain of Arizona. There is no evidence that Bennett received a reply from Wagstaff or McCain.
98. Ibid.
99. Cooper to Bennett, report, December 1969.
100. Thomas Anderson to L. Howard Bennett, briefing, November 18, 1969, Visit of Mr. Howard Bennett, Equal Opportunity Reporting File-Survey, box 1, USFSEA/NACP.
101. Cooper to Bennett, report, December 1969.
102. Jack MacFarlane to Welborn G. Dolvin, briefing, September 1970, Equal Opportunity and Racial Unrest, Equal Opportunity Reporting File-Survey, box 1, USFSEA/NACP. MacFarlane's first name is illegible on the file, but given the other details, it is Jack MacFarlane.
103. James R. Anderson, report, December 29, 1970, Staff Visits, Reference Paper Files, box 2, USFSEA/NACP. Anderson did not state what policies Blacks were referring to, but the comments suggest that the armed forces had policies in place which forbade workers from engaging in racial discrimination.
104. Richard F. Ward to Human Relations Branch, report, February 14, 1971, Staff Visits, Reference Paper Files, box 2, USFSEA/NACP.
105. Report to the Department of the Army, February 13, 1972, Racial Incidents, Equal

Opportunity Reporting Files–MACV Publications, box 5, USFSEA/NACP. The report does not state where in Vietnam the meeting took place.
106. Ibid.

CHAPTER 6: "WE WON'T SHOOT YOU, BUT WE'LL SHOOT THE WHITE GUY"

1. Anthony Martin, interview by author, September 12, 2011.
2. Ibid.
3. "The Bloods of 'Nam," *Frontline*, produced, directed, and photographed by Wayne Ewing, 1986, PBS.
4. Marc Gallicchio, *The African American Encounter with Japan and China* (Chapel Hill: University of North Carolina Press, 2000).
5. Thomas Borstelman, *Cold War and the Color Line: American Race Relations in the Global Arena* (Boston: Harvard University Press, 2003); Mary L. Dudziak, *Cold War Civil Rights: Race and the Image of American Democracy* (Princeton, NJ: Princeton University Press, 2011); Gerald Horne, *Ends of Empire: African Americans and India* (Philadelphia: Temple University Press, 2009); Michael Krenn, *Black Diplomacy: African Americans and the State Department, 1959–1969* (Armonk, NY: M. E. Sharpe, 1999).
6. Christian G. Appy, *Working Class War: American Combat Soldiers and Vietnam* (Chapel Hill: University of North Carolina Press, 1993), 22.
7. George C. Herring, *America's Longest War: The United States and Vietnam, 1950–1975* (New York: McGraw-Hill, 2002), 199–200.
8. "The Bloods of 'Nam."
9. Martin interview.
10. Sinclair Swan, interview by author, August 11, 2011.
11. Ron Copes, interview by author, November 17, 2011.
12. Willie Thomas, interview by author, September 3, 2011.
13. Wallace Terry, *Bloods: An Oral History of the Vietnam War by Black Veterans* (New York: Random House, 1984), 109.
14. Robert M. Watters, interview by George C. Herring and Terry L. Birdwhistell, May 16, 1985, 11, University of Kentucky Libraries Vietnam Veterans in Kentucky Oral History Project, King Library, Lexington.
15. Cephus "Dusty" Rhodes, interview by author, January 19, 2012.
16. James Lewis, interview by author, March 20, 2012.
17. Lamont B. Steptoe, interview by author, June 25, 2012.
18. Peter S. Kindsvatter, *American Soldiers: Ground Combat in the World Wars, Korea and Vietnam* (Lawrence: University Press of Kansas, 2003), 145.
19. Ibid.
20. Marilyn Young, *The Vietnam Wars, 1945–1990* (New York: HarperCollins, 1991), 148.
21. Appy, *Working Class War*, 16.
22. Albert French, *Patches of Fire: A Story of War and Redemption* (New York: Doubleday, 1997), 113.
23. Thomas interview.

24. Stanley Goff and Robert Sanders with Clark Smith, *Brothers: Black Soldiers in the Nam* (Novato, CA: Presidio Press, 1982), 150.
25. Terry Whitmore, *Memphis, Nam, Sweden: The Story of a Black Deserter* (Jackson: University of Mississippi Press, 1997), 55.
26. Ron Bradley, interview by author, October 23, 2011.
27. Melvin Adams, interview by author, March 14, 2012.
28. Swan interview.
29. Steptoe interview.
30. Samuel Vance, *The Courageous and Proud* (New York: Norton, 1979), 73, 70.
31. Horace Coleman, interview by author, June 12, 2012; Herring, *America's Longest War*, 287. Soldiers like the one Coleman interacted with were known as "ghost soldiers." Herring estimates that in some units the rate of ghost soldiers was as high as 20 percent.
32. David Parks, *GI Diary* (Washington, DC: Howard University Press, 1984), 83.
33. James Gillam, *Life and Death in the Central Highlands: An American Sergeant in the Vietnam War, 1968–1970* (Denton: University of North Texas Press), 83.
34. James Gillam, interview by author, March 14, 2008.
35. Lewis interview.
36. Swan interview.
37. Bradley interview.
38. Terry, *Bloods*, 208.
39. Louis Perkins, interview by author, December 17, 2011.
40. Copes interview.
41. Thomas Brannon, interview by author, December 6, 2011.
42. Wayne Smith, interview by author, October 25, 2011.
43. Horace Coleman, *In the Grass* (Woodbridge, CT: Viet Nam Generation and Burning Cities Press, 1995), 30.
44. Wes Geary, interview by author, August 7, 2009.
45. Gillam interview.
46. Jonathan Shay, *Achilles in Vietnam: Combat Trauma and the Undoing of Character* (New York: Scribner, 1994), 105.
47. Martin interview.
48. Nick Turse, *Kill Anything That Moves: The Real American War in Vietnam* (New York: Metropolitan Books, 2013).
49. Parks, *GI Diary*, 85.
50. "Tuck Brothers Speak Out against the Vietnam War," *Cleveland Call and Post*, December 2, 1967.
51. Terry, *Bloods*, 24.
52. Smith interview.
53. Steptoe interview.
54. Ibid.
55. Simeon Booker, "Negroes in Vietnam: 'We Too, Are Americans,'" *Ebony*, November 1965, 89, 92.
56. V. I. Hudson, "Legendary 'Wee Pals' Cartoonist Morrie Turner, 90, Passes Away," *Oakland [CA] Post*, January 27, 2014.
57. Morrie Turner, "G.I. Humor," *Ebony*, August 1968, 108.
58. Ibid.

59. Major Pace, report, November 20, 1970, Alcohol and Drug Abuse Prevention and Control Plan, Racial Unrest, box 2, U.S. Forces in Southeast Asia, 1950–75, U.S. National Archives, College Park, MD.
60. Brannon interview.
61. Smith interview.
62. Gillam interview.
63. Steptoe interview.
64. Eddie Greene, interview by author, March 12, 2012. Greene's account is all the more remarkable considering he was only in Vietnam for a few weeks before being medivacked out.
65. Bradley interview.
66. Vance, *The Courageous and Proud*, 132–33.
67. Paul Hathaway, "Negro in Viet: Not That Far from the Ghetto," *Newsday* (New York), May 15, 1968.
68. Terry, *Bloods*, 167, 212.
69. Billy Jones, interview by author, May 22, 2018.
70. Adams interview.
71. Whitmore, *Memphis, Nam, Sweden*, 71.
72. Eddie Wright, *Thoughts about the Vietnam War: Based on My Personal Experience, Books I Have Read and Conversations with Other Veterans* (New York: Carlton Press, 1986), 104, 67–68.
73. Willie L. Hamilton, "The Black Vietnam Veteran and His Problems: Fourth in a Series," *New York Amsterdam News*, February 13, 1971.
74. Bradley interview.
75. Lewis interview.
76. William E. Alt and Betty L. Alt, *Black Soldiers, White Wars: Black Warriors from Antiquity to the Present* (Westport, CT: Praeger, 2003), 110.
77. Adams interview.
78. Booker, "Negroes in Vietnam," 89, 96.
79. Clyde Jackson, interview by author, January 8, 2012.
80. Martin interview.
81. Ibid.
82. Jim Houston, interview by author, December 1, 2011.
83. Robert Louis Jr., interview by author, November 30, 2011.
84. Gillam interview.
85. Herman Graham III, *The Brothers' Vietnam War: Black Power, Manhood, and the Military Experience* (Gainesville: University Press of Florida, 2003), 118.
86. Herbert Freidman, "National Liberation Front (NLF) Anti-American Leaflets of the Vietnam War," Psywarrior, http://www.psywarrior.com. This is an interesting website that provides numerous primary documents concerning psychological warfare. The leaflets are not dated, making it difficult to interpret changes over time. Contemporary journals, newspaper stories, and oral histories suggest they are representative.
87. Ibid.
88. Ibid.
89. Ibid.
90. Ibid.

91. "Viet Nam War Also Waged with Words," *Chicago Tribune*, March 5, 1967.
92. "Cong Ask Negroes to Desert," *Newsday*, January 6, 1968.
93. Ibid.
94. Ibid.
95. Geary interview.
96. "Consensus: Vietnam a Large Waste of Black Lives and Time," *Jet*, May 22, 1975, 53.
97. Hathaway, "Negro in Viet."
98. Bradley interview.
99. Bernard McClusky, interview by author, May 18, 2022.
100. Goff and Sanders, *Brothers*, 148–49.
101. Smith interview.
102. Thomas interview.
103. Don North, "The Search for Hanoi Hannah," Psywarrior, http://www.psywarrior.com.
104. Booker, "Negroes in Vietnam," 89. Unfortunately, few of Hanoi Hannah's broadcasts are available today.
105. North, "The Search for Hanoi Hannah." While North claims that this broadcast took place on March 30, 1968, considering the incident referenced didn't happen until March 1971, it must have occurred much later.
106. Terry, *Bloods*, 39. It is always possible that Ford's account was an exaggerated version of what was actually broadcast. It is hard to know for certain as what little we know about Radio Hanoi comes from contemporary newspaper articles and oral history accounts.
107. North, "The Search for Hanoi Hannah."
108. Arthur Barham, interview by author, February 19, 2013.
109. "Korean Encourages Negroes to 'Stop Fighting,'" *Los Angeles Sentinel*, June 13, 1966.
110. Michael Lollar, "The Long Road Home: Memphian Turned Back on Racist America after Korean POW Camp, Found Freedom in Red China," *Commercial Appeal* (Memphis), September 16, 2007.
111. "Hanoi Propaganda Tuned to Negro GIs," *Washington Post*, August 31, 1967. I found no other record of Jackson Turner.
112. "Radio Hanoi Has Message Especially for Negro GI's," *Baltimore Sun*, August 16, 1969.
113. "Minister Sees Link in Black, Vietcong Struggles," *Jet*, November 12, 1970, 12.
114. Graham, *The Brothers' Vietnam War*, 73.
115. Major Pace, report, November 20, 1970. Cleaver also appeared on Radio Hanoi where he read a less incendiary version of these statements.
116. "Racial Violence Aim: Post Office Distributes Peking 'Hate' Pamphlet," *Norfolk [VA] Journal and Guide*, September 2, 1967.
117. Paul Ward, "Soviet Radio Urges Negro to Desert: English Broadcast Is Aimed at U.S. Forces in Vietnam War," *Baltimore Sun*, September 3, 1967. The Soviet Union also broadcast appeals to African Americans, but there is no evidence that they influenced Vietnamese appeals. This article claims that the Soviet Union was following Hanoi's lead.
118. "South Viet Nam: Soul Alley," *Time*, Monday, December 14, 1970, https://content

.time.com. In most cases, they did not intend to stay for long but trying to leave would have exposed them to arrest, court-martial, and other punishments. Instead, they created a temporary community for Black deserters in Soul Alley.
119. Bradley interview.
120. Joseph Volz, "Did Two GIs Aid Hanoi?" *Boston Globe*, February 6, 1979.
121. *The Disappearance of McKinley Nolan*, directed by Henry Corra, Corra Films, 2010.
122. Hathaway, "Negro in Viet."
123. Shawn McHale, "Understanding the Fanatic Mind? The Viet Minh and Race Hatred in the First Indochina War (1945–1954)," *Journal of Vietnamese Studies* 4, no. 3 (Fall 2009): 98–99. It is unclear what cape they are referring to.
124. Booker, "Negroes in Vietnam," 92.
125. James E. Jackson Jr., "As a Viet Cong Prisoner: Ordeal at Hands of Guerrillas," *Ebony*, August 1968, 116.
126. Terry, *Bloods*, 134.
127. Ibid., 281. Cherry was the first African American captured in the DRV.
128. James S. Hirsch, *Two Souls Indivisible* (New York: Houghton Mifflin, 2004), 75, 169–72.
129. James A. Daly, *Black Prisoner of War: A Conscientious Objector's Vietnam Memoir* (Lawrence: University Press of Kansas, 2000) Daly was also a prisoner in the Hanoi Hilton, and he believed that he was treated better by his captors because he was Black. However, Daly's treatment was likely more a reflection of his willingness to sign numerous documents critical of the American government.
130. Robert S. McKelvey, *The Dust of Life: America's Children Abandoned in Vietnam* (Seattle: University of Washington Press, 1999), 47.
131. Human Rights Watch, *Repression of Montagnards: Conflicts over Land and Religion in Vietnam's Central Highlands* (New York: Human Rights Watch, 2002).
132. Lap Siu, interview by author, March 15, 2008.

CHAPTER 7: "I HAD LEFT ONE WAR AND COME BACK TO ANOTHER"

1. Ron Chimelis, "Disabled Vietnam Veteran Eugene Brice Finds Service to Country Doesn't Shield Him from Racism," *Republican* (Springfield, MA), November 21, 2021.
2. Ibid.
3. Sylvester Bracey's journal printed with permission of Sylvester Bracey Jr. and family.
4. David Parks, *GI Diary* (Washington, DC: Howard University Press, 1984), 123.
5. "Vietnam Vets Faced with Hostility, Says Time Report," *Philadelphia Tribune*, January 13, 1968.
6. Floyd McKissick, "Black Vets and White Racism," *New York Amsterdam News*, April 27, 1968.
7. James Gillam, interview by author, March 14, 2008.
8. Lamont B. Steptoe, interview by author, June 25, 2012.
9. Stanley W. Beesley, *Vietnam: The Heartland Remembers* (Norman: University of Oklahoma Press, 1987), 15.

10. Les Fuller and Chet Coleman, "Whites Harass Vet and Family; Home Attacked," *Philadelphia Tribune*, April 25, 1967.
11. "Vietnam Vet Faces Racism after Moving in New Home," *Jet*, August 22, 1968, 24.
12. "Vietnam Vet Sues 'Biased' Trailer Pks. for $500,000," *Los Angeles Sentinel*, May 11, 1967.
13. Lee Ewing, interview by Pat McClain, n.d., 13, Veterans History Project, Library of Congress, Washington, DC.
14. Wallace Terry, *Bloods: An Oral History of the Vietnam War by Black Veterans* (New York: Random House, 1984), 152–53.
15. Ponchita Pierce and Peter Bailey, "The Returning Vet: Despite Re-Adjustment Programs, Black Ex-GIs Face Rough Road Back Home," *Ebony*, August 1968, 147.
16. Beesley, *Vietnam*, 15.
17. James R. Wilson, *Landing Zones: Southern Veterans Remember Vietnam* (Durham, NC: Duke University Press, 1990), 107–9.
18. George Brummell, interview by author, October 21, 2011.
19. Jim Houston, interview by author, December 1, 2011.
20. "Slayer of Sailor 'Had Racial Grudge,'" *Los Angeles Sentinel*, May 5, 1966.
21. "Alabama Family Say Town Refuses to Bury Viet Hero," *Jet*, June 9, 1966, 4.
22. Lawrence Allen Eldridge, *Chronicles of a Two-Front War: Civil Rights and Vietnam in the African American Press* (Columbia: University of Missouri Press, 2011), 70.
23. Soloman Crenshaw Jr. "Killed in War, Bill Terry Jr. Was First Black Buried in Birmingham's Elmwood Cemetery," *Birmingham [AL] Times*, February 26, 2002.
24. "Soldier Killed in Vietnam Is Reburied in All-White Cemetery after Legal Bout." *Philadelphia Tribune*, January 6, 1970.
25. Robert A. Taylor, "In the Interests of Justice: The Burial of Pondextuer Eugene Williams," *Florida Historical Quarterly* 82, no. 3 (2004): 275.
26. "Cemetery with JFK Monument," *Jet*, September 10, 1970, 5.
27. Taylor, "In the Interests of Justice," 286.
28. Ron Bradley, interview by author, October 23, 2011.
29. Richard Kulka et al., *Trauma and the Vietnam War Generation: Report of Findings from the National Vietnam Veterans Readjustment Study* (New York: Brunner/Mazel, 1990), 140.
30. Anthony Martin, interview by author, September 12, 2011.
31. Gillam interview.
32. James T. Gillam, *War in the Central Highlands of Vietnam, 1968–1970* (Lewiston, NY: Edwin Mellon Press, 2006), vi.
33. Ibid., 318.
34. Christian G. Appy, *Patriots: The Vietnam War Remembered from All Sides* (New York: Penguin Group, 2003), 366.
35. Wayne Smith, interview by author, October 25, 2011.
36. Kyle Longley, *Grunts: The American Combat Soldier in Vietnam* (Armonk, NY: M. E. Sharpe, 2008), 166.
37. Reuben "Sugar Bear" Johnson, interview by author, March 15, 2008; Terry, *Bloods*, 181.
38. George E. Brummell, *Shades of Darkness: A Black Soldier's Journey through Vietnam, Blindness, and Back* (Silver Spring, MD: Pie, 2006), 207–8.

39. Kulka et al., *Trauma and the Vietnam War Generation*, 213.
40. Longley, *Grunts*, 168.
41. Eddie Wright, *Thoughts about the Vietnam War: Based on My Personal Experience, Books I Have Read and Conversations with Other Veterans* (New York: Carlton Press, 1986), 69.
42. Robert M. Watters, interview by George C. Herring and Terry L. Birdwhistell, May 16, 1985, 42, University of Kentucky Libraries Vietnam Veterans in Kentucky Oral History Project, King Library, Lexington.
43. Houston interview.
44. David L. Anderson, *The Vietnam War* (New York: Palgrave Macmillan, 2005), 122.
45. Longley, *Grunts*, 176.
46. Bruce Dohrenwend et al., "War-Related Posttraumatic Stress Disorder in Black, Hispanic, and Majority White Vietnam Veterans: The Roles of Exposure and Vulnerability," *Journal of Traumatic Stress* 21, no. 2 (April 2008): 133–41.
47. Kulka et al., *Trauma and the Vietnam War Generation*, 225.
48. Eddie Greene, interview by author, March 12, 2012.
49. Terry, *Bloods*, 14.
50. Wright, *Thoughts about the Vietnam War*, 69.
51. Greene interview.
52. Horace Coleman, interview by author, June 12, 2012.
53. Thomas Brannon, interview by author, December 6, 2011.
54. Wright, *Thoughts about the Vietnam War*, 119.
55. Terry, *Bloods*, 213.
56. Wright, *Thoughts about the Vietnam War*, 118.
57. Gillam, *War in the Central Highlands*, 291.
58. Watters interview, 31, 39.
59. Houston interview.
60. Steptoe interview.
61. Ibid.
62. Martin interview.
63. Johnson interview.
64. Terry, *Bloods*, 60, 32.
65. Ibid., 87.
66. Wright, *Thoughts about the Vietnam War*, 116.
67. Ewing interview, 20.
68. Scott Riley, interview by author, May 7, 2022. Riley details his experiences with addiction and recovery in his family memoir, coauthored with his twin daughters. Scott Riley, Hasha Riley, and Libra Riley, *Grace in the Wilderness: A Family's Story of Love, Loss and Redemption* (Self-Published, 2013).
69. Smith interview.
70. Lee Robins et al., "Vietnam Veterans Three Years after Vietnam: How Our Study Changed Our View of Heroin," *American Academy of Addiction Psychiatry* 19, no. 3 (April 15, 2010): 203–11.
71. Jim Nordheimer, "From Vietnam to Detroit: Death of a Troubled Hero," *New Pittsburgh Courier*, June 1971; "Got Doors Slammed in Face, GI Hero Killed in Hold-Up," *Jet*, May 20, 1971, 17.
72. Nordheimer, "From Vietnam to Detroit."
73. Ibid.

74. Art Harris, "Belated Victim of a Haunting War," *Washington Post*, June 21, 1980.
75. Ibid.
76. Gillam interview.
77. Gillam, *War in the Central Highlands*, dedication.
78. Kent Garrett, interview by author, March 22, 2022.
79. Willie Thomas, interview by author, September 3, 2011.
80. Martin interview.
81. Ron Copes, interview by author, November 17, 2011; Wes Geary, interview by author, August 7, 2009; James Lewis, interview by author, March 20, 2012.
82. Brannon interview
83. Martin interview.
84. Terry, *Bloods*, 264.
85. Bradley interview.
86. Greene interview.
87. "Attack Raw Deal Black Veterans Get after Discharge from Army," *Jet*, October 28, 1971, 27.
88. Arthur Egendorf et al., *Legacies of Vietnam: Comparative Adjustment of Vietnam Veterans and Their Peers* (Washington, DC: U.S. Government Printing Office, 1981), 200.
89. "Attack Raw Deal."
90. "Study Shows Black GIs in Vietnam Treated Unequal, Slighted by Employers Back Home," *New Pittsburgh Courier*, April 29, 1972.
91. Houston interview.
92. Ibid.
93. Greg A. Greenberg and Robert A. Rosenheck, "Are Male Veterans at Greater Risk for Nonemployment Than Nonveterans," *Monthly Labor Review* 130, no. 12 (December 2007): 27.
94. Egendorf et al., *Legacies of Vietnam*, 199–200.
95. Sharon R. Cohany, "Employment and Unemployment among Vietnam-Era Veterans," *Monthly Labor Review* 113, no. 4 (April 1990): 25.
96. Patrick Brasley and Sidney Schaer, "The Forgotten Warriors: A Special Report on Vietnam Veterans," *Newsday* (New York), November 20, 1971.
97. Robert Vonner, interview by author, March 15, 2008.
98. Martin interview.
99. Mark Boulton, "How the G.I. Bill Failed African American Vietnam War Veterans," *Journal of Blacks in Higher Education*, no. 58 (Winter 2007–8): 58; Iver Peterson, "Most Veterans of Vietnam Fail to Seek Aid under the G.I. Bill," *New York Times*, April 9, 1972.
100. Peterson, "Most Veterans of Vietnam Fail to Seek Aid under the G.I. Bill," 2.
101. Boulton, "How the G.I. Bill Failed African American Vietnam War Veterans," 57.
102. Terry, *Bloods*, 234.
103. Wallace Terry, "Bringing the War Home," *Black Scholar* 2, no. 3 (November 1970): 16.
104. Coleman interview.
105. "Blacks Seek New Role in American Legion; a Black Founder Scoffs," *Jet*, September 7, 1972, 47.
106. James E. Westheider, *The African American Experience in Vietnam: Brothers in Arms* (Lanham, MD: Rowman and Littlefield, 2007), 109.

107. Terry, *Bloods*, 12.
108. Jesse W. Lewis, "'I Think the War Is Here...': Viet Vet Views a 'War' in Detroit," *Washington Post*, July 25, 1967.
109. Mary Merrifield, "Viet Nam Veterans: Back on Campus and Ready for Change," *Chicago Tribune*, March 24, 1968.
110. Garrett interview.
111. Angela Jones, "For Black Vets Vietnam Still On," *New York Amsterdam News*, December 25, 1982.
112. Fuller and Coleman, "Whites Harass Vet and Family."
113. Coleman interview.
114. Smith interview; Mary K. Talbot, "Veterans Voice: Former Vietnam War Medic Has Spent a Lifetime Advocating for Others," *Providence [RI] Journal*, July 19, 2021.
115. Brummell, *Shades of Darkness*, 339.
116. "Racism Led to New Group for Viet Vets," *Jet*, November 5, 1970, 25.
117. "Our Impact," National Association for Black Veterans, https://www.nabvets.org.
118. "Our History," Black Veterans for Social Justice, https://bvsj.org/.
119. Ron Chimelis, "Springfield Black Veterans Group Welcomes $100K State Support," *Republican*, August 21, 2020.
120. Coleman interview.
121. "People," Iraq and Afghanistan Veterans of America, https://iava.org.
122. Chimelis, "Disabled Vietnam Veteran."
123. "MHA Hosts Food Drive to Support Black Veterans Group in Springfield," WWLP, December 22, 2021, https://www.wwlp.com.

CONCLUSION

1. "The Bloods of 'Nam," *Frontline*, produced, directed, and photographed by Wayne Ewing, 1986, PBS.
2. Christopher G. Ellison, "Military Background, Racial Orientations, and Political Participation among Black Adult Males," *Social Science Quarterly* 73, no. 2 (June 1992): 363.
3. Anthony Martin, interview by author, September 12, 2011.
4. Ron Bradley, interview by author, October 23, 2011.
5. Khalil Gibran Muhammad, *The Condemnation of Blackness: Race, Crime, and the Making of Modern Urban America* (Cambridge, MA: Harvard University Press, 2010).
6. Morgan Murphy and Robert Steele, "The World Heroin Problem" (Washington, DC: U.S. Government Printing Office, 1971), 1, https://www.cia.gov.
7. Michelle Alexander, *The New Jim Crow: Mass Incarceration in the Age of Color Blindness* (New York: New Press, 2014), 87–88.
8. Susan M. Reverby, *Examining Tuskegee: The Infamous Syphilis Study and Its Legacy* (Chapel Hill: University of North Carolina Press, 2013).

Index

III Marine Amphibious Force, 97, 165
III Marine Amphibious Force Brig, 60, 89

absent without leave (AWOL), 15, 61, 64, 161, 197
Adams, Clarence C., 195
Adams, Jack, 93
Adams, Melvin, 155, 179, 185–87
Addlestone, David, 47, 63, 65, 98–99, 112, 137. *See also* Lawyers Military Defense Committee
Ali, Muhammad, 162, 196
Amerasians, 144–45, 164, 168, 199
American Legion, 218
Anderson, James, 170
Anderson, Joseph, 66
Armed Forces Radio, 193–94
Army Corps of Engineers, 187
Army Counterintelligence, 56, 115, 117–18, 161, 184
Army of the Republic of Vietnam (ARVN), 161, 166
    corruption in, 179–80
    criticism of, 178–81, 200
    cruelty of, 180
    identification with, 181
    respect for, 180–81
    sacrifices of, 179–81
AWOL. *See* absent without leave

Baldwin, James, 102
Baile, Sergeant, 122
Barham, Arthur, 20, 67, 127–28, 131, 160, 164, 166, 194
Barnes, James, 67
Barnes, John, 59
Barry, Richard, 207
BBU. *See* Black Brothers United
Belcher, Theodore, 28, 30
Belton, Thomas, 155, 186, 209–10
Bennett, John C., 121–22
Bennett, L. Howard, 1, 42, 113, 108–9, 169–70. *See also* Human Relations Councils; military justice system: article 15s; racial discrimination: assignments; racial discrimination: promotions
Benton, Luther C., III, 139, 141, 156
Biggers, Archie, 22–23, 177
Black Brothers United (BBU), 87, 117–18
Black Journal, 1–6, 50–51, 73, 113–14, 167. *See also* Garrett, Kent
Black Panther Party (BPP), 84–86, 196
Black power movement, 65, 84–87, 115, 183
    Afros, 65, 112, 114
    dapping, 85, 112, 114, 121
    salute, 103, 105, 112, 114
    slave bracelets, 65, 85, 112, 114, 121
Black Veterans for Social Justice, 220

Blinded Veterans Association, 219
The Bloods of 'Nam, 44, 177
Bond, Julian, 70, 121
Booker, Simeon, 154, 183
Booth, William, 71
Borus, Jonathan F., 33
Bowley, A. J., 133
Boyd, Jerry, 111
Bracey, Sylvester, 113–15, 167, 203
Bradley, Ron, 18
    ARVN and RVN military forces, 179–80
    communist forces, 185–87, 192, 197
    race relations in Vietnam, 20–21, 35, 41
    racial discrimination, 72, 80, 167
    veteran experiences, 207, 215, 223
    Vietnamese civilians, 135, 147, 155, 157
Brannon, Thomas
    ARVN forces, 181
    communist forces, 184
    race relations in Vietnam, 20, 29–32
    racial discrimination, 215
    veteran experiences, 29–32, 210, 215
    Vietnamese civilians, 6, 154–55
Brice, Eugene L., 202, 210, 212–13, 220–21
Bridges, Rudolph, 203–5
Brown, Dwyte A., 125, 136, 138, 147, 215
Brown, Henry, Jr., 213–14
Brown, H. Rap, 195
Browne, Don F., 84, 88, 185
Brummell, George, 18
    race relations in Vietnam, 16, 28, 30–31
    racial discrimination, 79, 167, 205
    veteran experiences, 30–31, 205, 208–9, 219
Bryant, Harold, 23–24, 136, 138–39, 142, 148, 154, 182
Bryels, Bill C., 127, 134
Bullard, Joseph, 94–95
Bullock, John, 94–95
Burress, Daniel, 16
Burton, Ted A., 30

Calley, William, 149
Camp Baxter, 53, 55, 98
Campbell, Mary, 207
Camp Brooks Marine Base, 98
Camp Carter, 117
Camp Eagle, 58–59
Camp Hochmuth, 97
Camp Horn, 97–98
Camp Lejeune, 48, 104, 107–8
Camp McCarly, 83
Camp McDermott, 52, 56–57, 117
Camp Radcliff, 99
Camp Tien Sha, 39, 87, 96
Carmichael, Stokely, 84–85, 195
Carter, Herbert, 149
Chapman, Leonard F., Jr., 42, 108, 112
Cherry, Fred V., 199
Chew, Charles, 46, 57
Chisolm, Shirley, 60
civil rights movement, 2, 11–12, 22, 36, 78, 116
    alleged communist support for, 175–76, 183–87, 189–97, 200, 226–27
    fracturing of movement, 83–84
    servicemen participation in, 115–19
    support for veterans, 218
    Vietnamese civilians view of, 152–55, 225–26
    Vietnamese fight for independence compared to, 126, 174
    war's influence on, 70, 78, 80
Clark, Lorenzo, 53
Clayborne, Willie, 99
Cleaver, Eldridge, 84, 86, 196–97
Coleman, Horace, 18, 20, 75
    ARVN, 180–81
    opinion on the war, 127, 132
    race relations in Vietnam, 31, 36
    veteran experiences, 210, 218–20
    Vietnamese civilians, 129, 132, 148, 161
combat troops, 72
    Armed Forces Qualification Tests, 73–74
    disproportionate assignments, 72–74
    financial motivations, 74
    See also race relations in military

Concerned Veterans from Vietnam, 220
Congressional House Armed Services Committee, 121
Congress of Racial Equality, 203
Copes, Ron, 75, 180
   communist forces, 177
   race relations in Vietnam, 36, 38
   racial discrimination, 50, 54, 67, 75
   RF/PF, 180
   veteran experiences, 214
   Vietnamese civilians, 135, 157, 168
Coppage, David E., 91–93, 95
Crawford, Bruce, 102
Crawford, Jeanette, 70
Curry, Robert, 59–60

Daly, James A., 130, 139
Daniel, Leon, 13
Dave (interviewed by *Black Journal*), 50–51
Davidson, John, 40
Davidson, William James, 93–95
Davis, Reuben, 168–69
Davison, Frederick E., 1, 107, 119
death rates, 76–78, 224
Dellums, Ron, 150
Delorne, Larry, 100–101
De Mau Mau, 87, 102–3, 112
Department of Defense (DOD), 50, 57, 63–64, 70, 76, 84, 88, 120
Devore, Richard, 50, 78, 186
Dickerson, Earl B., 218
Dolvin, Welborn G., 170
Donald, Charles, 74
Donovan, Dede, 64. *See also* Lawyers Military Defense Committee
Downey, Lewis, 28
draft
   boards, 70
   deferments: academic, 69; conscientious objector (CO), 70; medical, 69–70
   inequalities in, 45, 69–70, 80, 215
   opposition to, 78–79, 85–86
   percentage of draftees, 69
   See also Project 100,000

drug use, 62
   heroin, 55, 63–64, 212–13, 224
   marijuana, 55, 59, 63, 91–92
   "War on Drugs," 63–64, 224
Dubose, Dave, 16, 31, 154
Dyson, Hosea, 26, 30, 34

Edwards, Constance, 110, 166
Edwards, Freddie, 34, 39, 69, 128, 133
Edwards, Reginald, 19, 146, 210, 218
Edwards, Willie, 207
Ellison, Willie, 26–27
Emanuel, Ed, 21, 30, 32, 41, 134
Ewing, Lee, 16–17, 156, 204, 212–13
Executive Order 9981, 1

Ferrell, Eugene, 206–7
First Indochina War, 127, 145, 158, 198
FO. *See* forward observer
Ford, Richard J., III, 141, 147, 161, 194, 212
Fort Benning, Georgia, 150
Fort Bragg, North Carolina, 53, 74, 116, 205
Fort Carson, Colorado, 121
Fort Hood Three, 195
Fort Jackson, South Carolina, 20
Fort Knox, Kentucky, 215
Fort Leavenworth, Kansas, 136
Fort Leonard Wood, Missouri, 116
Fort Lewis, Washington, 15
Fort Monroe, Virginia, 52, 66, 170
Fort Pierce, Florida, 207
Fort Rucker, Alabama, 116
forward observer (FO), 66
Freeman, Keith, 16, 186
French, Albert, 126, 179
Frost, Alphonso, 96

Garnett, Harry, 25
Garrett, Kent, 2–4, 68, 85, 114, 119–20, 134, 168, 214, 219. See also *Black Journal*
Garrett, Thaddeus, 60–61
Garron, Mickey, 206
Gaxiola, Rockland, 103

Geary, Wes, 19, 29, 31, 121–22, 147, 181, 192, 214
Gibel, Antonio Aguinaldo, 93
G.I. Bill, 217–18
Gibson, Craig, 112
Gillam, Edward, 68, 127, 214
Gillam, James, 18, 127
    ARVN, 180–81
    communist forces, 184, 188–89
    Montagnards, 160–61, 180
    race relations in Vietnam, 25
    racial discrimination, 47, 77
    veteran experiences, 203, 208, 211, 214
    Vietnamese civilians 128, 161
Goff, Stanley, 17, 32, 37–38, 68
Goodman, Harry, 25
Gore, Roosevelt, 19, 30, 67, 136, 205
Greaves, William, 1–4
Green, Herbert, 90, 92
Greene, Eddie, 19, 34, 184–85, 210, 215
Gregory, Dick, 121
Griswold, Charles W., 82, 93, 95–96
Guidry, Richard A., 134–35, 141

Hagee, Michael, 104
Hall, Victor, 74
Hanoi Hannah, 193–94
Harkless, Lawrence, 74
Hawkins (interviewed in *Same Mud, Same Blood*), 27, 39
Hayes (interviewed by *Black Journal*), 5, 73
Hayes, Michael, 56, 165
Henderson, Robert, 94
Hicks, George, 35, 130
Hines, William, 204
Ho Chi Minh, 184–85
Holcomb, Robert E., 136, 138–39, 143, 156, 180, 185, 210
Hollier, Louis S., 108
Holloman, Emmanuel J., 130, 136–41, 144–45, 154, 160, 212–13
"hooch maid," 129, 143, 166
Horn, Raymond Leon, 1–2
Houston, Jim, 14, 35, 188, 205, 209, 211, 216

Howard, Stephen A., 18, 21–22
Huff, Edgar A., 25, 204
Human Relations Councils, 48, 53, 55–56, 115, 119–22, 160, 165, 170. *See also* Bennett, L. Howard
Hutchinson, James, 93

Iraq and Afghanistan Veterans of America, 220
Iraq War, 220

Jackson, Clyde, 18, 34, 41, 47, 77, 156–57, 187
Jackson, Howard, 154
Jackson, James E., Jr., 198–99
Jackson, Robert L., 39–40
JAG. *See* Judge Advocate General
James, Dalton, 45, 152–54
James, Daniel "Chappie," Jr., 107
James, Robert, 70
Jefferson, Bob "Pee Wee," 24
Jenkins, Bobby, 6, 58, 113, 167
Jernigan, Don L., 15, 26, 88, 147, 154
Johnson, Dalinda, 103
Johnson, Dwight, 213
Johnson, Lyndon, 71–72, 77, 87, 123, 191
Johnson, Reuben "Sugar Bear," 208, 211
Johnson, Thomas A., 9, 14, 43, 60, 72–73, 157, 195
Johnson, Vernon D., 81, 91, 93–96
Jones, Billy, 62, 64–65, 90, 107, 119, 185
Jones, Jay, 219
Jones, Jim, 27
Judge Advocate General (JAG), 54–55, 58–59, 90, 92

Kastenmeier, Robert, 69
Kelley, Roger T., 109
Kennedy, Robert F., 72
Kennedy, Ted, 150
Kenney, Thomas, 93
Kerner Commission, 2, 123
King, Freddie, 26–27
King, Martin Luther, Jr., 43
    reaction to assassination in Japan, 87
    reaction to assassination in United States, 2, 4, 37, 81–85

reaction to assassination in
	Vietnam, 4, 81–85, 87–89, 106,
	122–23, 225
  Vietnamese reaction to assassination, 155, 194
Kinnard, Harry, 142
Kirkland, Haywood T., 127, 148
Kitty Hawk Riot, 102–3, 105–6, 120–21
Korean War, 46, 195, 208, 217
Ku Klux Klan (KKK), 17, 20, 24, 104,
	110, 116–17, 217

Larry, Lewis B., 11–12, 39
Lawson, Phillip, 195–96
Lawyers Military Defense Committee
	(LMDC) 55–60, 65, 78. *See also*
	Addlestone, David; Donovan,
	Dede; Osnos, Susan
Legacies of Vietnam, 126, 215–16
Lee, Billy, 118
Lewis, Doug, 205
Lewis, George, 150
Lewis, James, 19, 75, 214
  ARVN, 180
  communist forces, 178, 187
  race relations in Vietnam, 34, 38
  Vietnamese civilians, 138, 154
Lewis, Jesse M., 72
Lewis, Ronald, 165–66
LMDC. *See* Lawyers Military Defense
	Committee
Long Binh Jail
  conditions of, 60–62, 91–94
  prisoners in, 61–62, 90–91
  riot, 81–82, 90–96, 122
Lorence, Akmed, 31, 124–25
Louis, Robert, Jr., 19, 75
  communist forces, 188
  racial discrimination, 50, 67, 72
  Vietnamese civilians, 127–32, 136, 146
Love, Andrew, 117
Loving v. Virginia, 23
Lynch, Gerald, 34, 88, 147

MacFarlane, Jack, 170
MACV. *See* Military Assistance
	Command Vietnam

Majette, Mildred, 117
Malcolm X, 4
Manning, Ronald, 166
Maples, Robert, 149
Marlantes, Karl, 38, 110
Marlotas, Richard, 131
Martin, Anthony, 18, 75
  communist forces, 174–77, 182, 188
  race relations in Vietnam, 15, 34
  racial discrimination, 47, 75, 215
  veteran experiences, 207–8, 211,
	214–15, 217, 223
  Vietnamese civilians, 127, 131, 137,
	141, 148–49, 154
  view of the war, 126–27
Martin, Asa, 154
Mathias, Bob, 103
Mavroudis, Anthony, 12, 27, 38
McCain, John S., 52, 169
McCarthy, Willie, 167
McClure, Claude, 192
McClusky, Bernard, 17–18, 20, 132–34,
	155, 192–93, 220
McDaniel, Norman Alexander, 198–99
McFarland, Felton, 153
McGee, Frank, 11–13, 35, 39, 42
McKissick, Floyd, 203
McLemore, Gerald, 59, 98
McNamara, Robert, 88, 116, 191
McQueen, Louis, 192
Meerbot, Colonel, 118–19
Metcalf, Roman, 50, 66, 166
Military Assistance Command
	Vietnam (MACV), 36, 52, 55, 128,
	133, 170, 180
military justice system, 4, 44, 54–65,
	223
  article 15s, 44, 55–57, 108–9
  court-martial, 44, 55–61, 109, 113, 117
  less-than-honorable discharges,
	57–58, 60, 71, 120, 215–16, 220,
	224
  pretrial confinement, 57, 61–65, 90,
	92–93, 118–20, 223
  prison population, 60–62, 89–96
  regulation 633-1 and regulation
	27-1, 61–62

Miller, Stanley, 162
Mondy, Nate, 18, 79, 102
Montagnards (Degar), 147, 159–62, 172, 199
Moore, McArthur, 139
Morrissette, Ray, 107
Mosby, Donald, 9, 14, 84, 159, 163–64, 168
Mountain, Robert L., 208
Murdock, Eugene, 93–94
Murphy, Morgan F., 63
My Lai massacre, 137, 148–50

National Association for Black Veterans (NABVETS), 220
National Association for the Advancement of Colored People (NAACP), 60, 78, 88, 116, 176, 206
National Liberation Front (NLF), 5–6, 25, 146, 156, 174, 179, 182
  alleged sympathy for African Americans, 173, 183–89, 200, 226
  appeals to Black troops, 6–7, 189–98, 201, 227
  civilian view of, 141
  dehumanization of, 181–82
  fighting capabilities of, 176–78, 187, 226
  racism against African Americans, 198
  strategy, 17, 24, 33
  See also People's Army of Vietnam; rumors: enemy empathy
National Urban League, 153, 218
Newhouse, Richard, 215
New York City Human Rights Commission, 71
NLF. *See* National Liberation Front
Nolan, McKinley, 197

Oakdale Army Camp, 59
Officer Candidate School (OCS), 67, 128, 132
Okinawa, 1–2, 51, 103–4, 111, 114–15, 168
Olive, Milton Lee, 25

Olivier (interviewed by *Black Journal*), 120
Osnos, Peter, 63
Osnos, Susan, 63, 69–70

Pace, Bobbie Lee, 111
Page, Joshua, 140–41, 162
Parks, David
  ARVN, 180
  communist forces, 182
  race relations in Vietnam, 15, 32
  racial discrimination, 46–47, 66
  veteran experiences, 41, 203
  Vietnamese civilians, 129, 134, 136–37, 148
Parks, Gordon, 211
PAVN. *See* People's Army of Vietnam
Payne, Edith, 83
Payne, Ethel L., 9, 126, 154
Pentagon, 51, 60, 76, 78, 107, 109
People's Army of Vietnam (PAVN), 5–6, 141, 181, 213
  alleged sympathy for African Americans, 173, 183–89, 200, 226
  appeals to Black troops, 6–7, 189–98, 201, 227
  dehumanization of, 181–82
  fighting capabilities of, 176–78, 187, 226
  strategy, 17, 24, 33
  See also National Liberation Front; rumors: enemy empathy
People's Republic of China, 196
Perkins, Louis, 50, 77, 132, 154, 180
Planter, Charles C., 91, 93–95
Powell, Adam Clayton, 71
Powell, Colin, 101
Project 100,000, 70–72, 102
propaganda
  leaflets, 6–7, 175, 189–93, 196–98, 200–201, 227
  radio broadcasts, 6–7, 175, 189, 193–98, 200–201, 227
prostitution, 142–43, 163–64, 166–67
protest, 56–57, 66, 82, 86–89, 102–3, 105, 115–19, 122

race relations in military
  basic training, 15–16, 20
  combat, 12–17, 20–35, 42
  rear line, 36–43
  Vietnam compared to United States, 17–20, 36–39
  See also racial violence; Vietnamese civilians
racial discrimination, 44
  accusations of genocide, 78–79
  assignments: dangerous jobs, 45, 65–69, 72–76, 106, 223; menial work, 4, 44, 46–49, 79–80, 106
  death rates, 76–78
  draft disparities, 45, 69–72
  evaluation scores, 50
  military response, 47–48, 82, 89, 106–11, 119–23, 225
  promotions, 4, 45, 49–53, 223
  scarcity of Black officers, 44, 49–52, 146–47
  See also Human Relations Councils; military justice system
racial violence
  Asia, 102–5, 111
  Europe, 104
  military response to, 47–48, 105–6, 109–18, 225
  United States (military bases), 47, 104–5, 108
  Vietnam, 4–5, 42, 59, 80–83, 87–102, 113, 122–23, 225
  See also Long Binh Jail: riot; riots
Radio Hanoi, 193–96
reenlistment, 75–76
Regional and Popular Forces (RF/PF), 178–79
Remcho, T. Joseph, 65
Render, Frank W., II, 46, 53, 56–57, 109
Republic of Vietnam (RVN)
  American mission, 5
  civilian view of, 141
  demographics of, 129, 159
  government policies toward Amerasians, 145
  poverty in, 129–31, 134–35, 146, 150–52, 156, 172

  treatment of ethnic minorities, 159–62, 172, 225–26
  See also Montagnards
Rhodes, Cephus "Dusty," 32, 35, 73, 75, 79, 178
Ribicoff, Abraham, 167
Riley, Scott, 17
  race relations in Vietnam, 24, 34
  racial discrimination, 72–73, 92, 94
  veteran experiences, 212–13
  Vietnamese civilians, 144, 151, 161, 166
riots, 2, 12, 29, 36–37, 39, 80, 115, 123
  Detroit, 2, 4, 12, 36–37, 81, 86, 123, 194, 219
  Elaine Race Riot, 29
  after King's assassination, 4, 37, 81, 155
  Los Angeles (Watts), 4, 36–37
  Newark, 2, 4, 12, 36–37, 81, 86, 123
  See also Kerner Commission; *Kitty Hawk* riot; Long Binh Jail
Roberts, Mike, 194
Roberts, Oscar, 161
Rogan, Thomas, 29–30
rumors
  Black defection, 197
  discriminatory, 166–67, 169
  enemy empathy, 174–75, 183–90, 200, 226–27
  racial genocide, 45, 65, 77–79, 224
Rusk, Dean, 191
RVN. *See* Republic of Vietnam
Ryan, Michael P., 48

Same Mud, Same Blood, 11–13, 25, 27, 38–39
Sanders, Robert, 12–16, 32–33, 139, 143–44, 179, 193
Sands, Milton, 30
Sawyer, Ron, 47, 54
Scott, Eddie, 116
Scott, Hugh, 100–101
Sellers, Cleveland, 78
Settles, Brian, 18–19, 67, 88, 132, 138, 143, 155
Sidle, Winant, 116–17
Simpson, David, 30

Simpson, Varnado, 148
Siu, Lap, 199
Smith, Billy, 193–94
Smith, Larry, 219
Smith, Melvin, 156
Smith, Wayne, 18
    ARVN, 181
    communist forces, 182, 184, 193
    Montagnards, 161
    race relations in Vietnam, 15, 23, 34, 39–40
    racial discrimination, 54
    veteran experiences, 208, 212–13, 219–20
    Vietnamese civilians, 128, 132–33, 135, 139, 142–43, 155, 161–62, 164
"Soul Alley," 142, 161, 197
soul music, 112–14, 142
Stanley, Harry, 149–50
Steck, Bob, 15, 104, 110
Steele, Robert H., 63
Steptoe, Lamont B., 5, 18, 40
    ARVN, 179
    communist forces, 178, 182, 184
    race relations in Vietnam, 22, 40
    racial discrimination, 67, 74, 78–79
    veteran experiences, 203, 211
    Vietnamese civilians, 128, 132, 136, 142–43, 157, 164, 166, 169
Stokes, Louis, 111
Stouffer, Samuel, 33
Strong, Charles, 21, 26, 177, 212, 222
Swan, Sinclair, 18
    ARVN, 179–80
    communist forces, 177
    race relations in Vietnam, 29, 32
    racial discrimination, 20, 49–50
    Vietnamese civilians, 133

Talbott, Orwin C., 47, 51, 57, 150
Talps, Ernest, 94–95
Terry, Bill, Jr., 206–7
Terry, Jimmie Lee, 206–7
Terry, Margaret Faye, 206–7
Terry, Phyllis. 206
Terry, Wallace, 4, 8–9, 42–44, 67–68, 85–88, 97, 175

Tet Offensive, 87, 140, 202
Thailand, 29, 53, 63, 167, 169
Thomas, Allen, Jr., 84, 218
Thomas, Willie
    ARVN, 179
    communist forces, 177, 193
    race relations in Vietnam, 34
    racial discrimination, 50, 79
    veteran experiences, 214
    Vietnamese civilians, 144, 166–67, 169
Titus, Thomas, 29
Townsend, Marland, Jr., 103, 106
Traegerman, Richard, 28
Tuck, David, 72, 182
Tucker, Bennie, 70
Turner, Herbert, 89
Turner, Jackson, 195
Turner, Morrie, 183–84

United Service Organizations (USO), 63, 117
Ursano, James J., 42, 108, 133
U.S. Army Republic of Vietnam (USARV), 32, 52, 55, 61–62, 93, 115
USS *Constellation*, 103, 105, 121
USS *Hassayampa*, 103
USS *Ogden*, 47

Vance, Samuel, 41, 130, 179–80, 185
Veterans for Peace (VFP), 219, 220
veterans issues
    alcohol and drug abuse, 212–13
    housing discrimination, 204
    impact of the less-than-honorable discharges, 215–16
    medical treatment, 208–9
    post-traumatic stress disorder (PTSD), 207–14
    racism against, 202–7, 217–21
    unemployment, 214–17
    veterans organizations, 219–21
    Vietnam G.I. Bills, 217–18
    wage disparities, 217
Veterans of Foreign Wars, 218
Viet Minh, 158, 198

Vietnamese civilians
    abuse of, 135–39, 147
    anti-Black racism of, 162–65
    Black empathy for, 6, 124–26,
        133–37, 139–40, 145–48, 150–51,
        225–26
    Black friendships with, 139–43
    crimes against, 137–39, 148–50
    dehumanization of, 127–28
    empathy for African Americans,
        152–56, 171–73
    poverty of, 6, 129–31, 134–35, 146,
        150–52, 156, 172
    racial views of, 157–58
    racism against: in basic training
        127–28, 150; in Vietnam, 131–33,
        135, 152, 225–26
    romantic relationships with, 143–45
    treatment of racial minorities, 159–
        62, 172
    white influence on, 6, 165–73,
        225–26
Vietnam Veterans Against the War
    (VVAW), 219–20
Vietnam Veterans of America (VVA), 219
Vonner, Robert, 115, 217
Voting Rights Act of 1965, 2, 11, 36

Wagstaff, Jack, 169
Ward, John, 103, 105
Ward, Richard F., 115, 120
War on Poverty, 71
Watters, Robert M., 15, 177, 209, 211
Westmoreland, William, 150, 191
Whaley, Cole, 198
Whitmore, Terry, 24, 146, 148, 179, 186
Whitted, Jack, 29, 31
Wilkins, Harold, 20, 30
Williams, Dwight, 148
Williams, Jimmy, 206–7
Williams, Marion, 159, 163–64
Williams, Pondextuer Eugene, 207
Witherspoon, Carl, 203
Woods, Georgie, 46, 49
Woods, James, 89
World War II, 128, 166–67, 175–76, 182, 217
Wright, Barry, 167, 220
Wright, Eddie, 156, 211
Wright, Ulysses, 100–101

Young, Whitney M., Jr., 153

Zinni, Anthony, 103–4, 111–12
Zumwalt, Elmo, 120–21

GERALD F. GOODWIN is adjunct professor of history at Le Moyne College and adjunct professor of political science at Onondaga Community College–SUNY.